I0042343

The Political Economy of Decentralization in Sub-Saharan Africa

The Political Economy of Decentralization in Sub-Saharan Africa

A New Implementation Model in
Burkina Faso, Ghana, Kenya, and Senegal

Bernard Dafflon and Thierry Madiès, Editors

A copublication of the Agence Française de Développement and the World Bank

© 2013 International Bank for Reconstruction and Development / The World Bank
1818 H Street NW, Washington DC 20433
Telephone: 202-473-1000; Internet: www.worldbank.org

Some rights reserved
1 2 3 4 15 14 13 12

This work is a product of the staff of The World Bank with external contributions. Note that The World Bank and the Agence Française de Développement do not necessarily own each component of the content included in the work. The World Bank and the Agence Française de Développement therefore do not warrant that the use of the content contained in the work will not infringe on the rights of third parties. The risk of claims resulting from such infringement rests solely with you.

The findings, interpretations, and conclusions expressed in this work do not necessarily reflect the views of The World Bank, its Board of Executive Directors, or the governments they represent, or the Agence Française de Développement. The World Bank does not guarantee the accuracy of the data included in this work. The boundaries, colors, denominations, and other information shown on any map in this work do not imply any judgment on the part of The World Bank concerning the legal status of any territory or the endorsement or acceptance of such boundaries.

Nothing herein shall constitute or be considered to be a limitation upon or waiver of the privileges and immunities of The World Bank, all of which are specifically reserved.

Rights and Permissions

This work is available under the Creative Commons Attribution 3.0 Unported license (CC BY 3.0) http://creativecommons.org/licenses/by/3.0. Under the Creative Commons Attribution license, you are free to copy, distribute, transmit, and adapt this work, including for commercial purposes, under the following conditions:

Attribution—Please cite the work as follows: Dafflon, Bernard, and Thierry Madiès. 2013. *The Political Economy of Decentralization in Sub-Saharan Africa: A New Implementation Model in Burkina Faso, Ghana, Kenya, and Senegal.* Africa Development Forum series. Washington, DC: World Bank. DOI 10.1596/978-0-8213-9613-1. License: Creative Commons Attribution CC BY 3.0

Translations—If you create a translation of this work, please add the following disclaimer along with the attribution: *This translation was not created by The World Bank and should not be considered an official World Bank translation. The World Bank shall not be liable for any content or error in this translation.*

All queries on rights and licenses should be addressed to the Office of the Publisher, The World Bank, 1818 H Street NW, Washington, DC 20433, USA; fax: 202-522-2625; e-mail: pubrights@worldbank.org.

ISBN (paper): 978-0-8213-9613-1
ISBN (electronic): 978-0-8213-9614-8
DOI: 10.1596/978-0-8213-9613-1

Cover image: Anonymous, D.R. Congo, 21st century
Embroidered Cloth, Southern Savannah style, raffia
World Bank Art Collection PN 206709a–d

Cover design: Debra Naylor, Naylor Design, Inc.

Translation: Gill Gladstone

Library of Congress Cataloging-in-Publication Data
Dafflon, Bernard.
  The political economy of decentralization in Sub-Saharan Africa : a new implementation model in Burkina Faso, Ghana, Kenya, and Senegal / Bernard Dafflon and Thierry Madiès.
    p. cm.
  Includes bibliographical references and index.
  ISBN 978-0-8213-9613-1— ISBN 978-0-8213-9614-8 (electronic)
  1. Local finance—Africa, Sub-Saharan. 2. Decentralization in government—Economic aspects—Africa, Sub-Saharan. 3. Fiscal policy—Africa, Sub-Saharan. 4. Finance, Public—Africa, Sub-Saharan. 5. Intergovernmental fiscal relations—Africa, Sub-Saharan. I. Madiès, Thierry. II. Title.
  HJ9610.D34 2012
  336.01467—dc23

                                                      2012029831

Africa Development Forum Series

The **Africa Development Forum Series** was created in 2009 to focus on issues of significant relevance to Sub-Saharan Africa's social and economic development. Its aim is both to record the state of the art on a specific topic and to contribute to ongoing local, regional, and global policy debates. It is designed specifically to provide practitioners, scholars, and students with the most up-to-date research results while highlighting the promise, challenges, and opportunities that exist on the continent.

The series is sponsored by the Agence Française de Développement and the World Bank. The manuscripts chosen for publication represent the highest quality in each institution and have been selected for their relevance to the development agenda. Working together with a shared sense of mission and interdisciplinary purpose, the two institutions are committed to a common search for new insights and new ways of analyzing the development realities of the Sub-Saharan Africa region.

Advisory Committee Members

Agence Française de Développement
Rémi Genevey, Director of Strategy
Robert Peccoud, Director of Research

World Bank
Shantayanan Devarajan, Chief Economist, Africa Region
Célestin Monga, Senior Adviser, Development Economics and Africa Region
Santiago Pombo-Bejarano, Editor-in-Chief, Office of the Publisher

Sub-Saharan Africa with featured countries

CAPE VERDE

MAURITANIA

MALI

NIGER

CHAD

SUDAN

ERITREA

THE GAMBIA

SENEGAL

GUINEA-BISSAU

GUINEA

BURKINA FASO

BENIN

NIGERIA

ETHIOPIA

SIERRA LEONE

CÔTE D'IVOIRE

GHANA

CENTRAL AFRICAN REPUBLIC

SOUTH SUDAN

SOMALIA

LIBERIA

TOGO

CAMEROON

EQUATORIAL GUINEA

UGANDA

KENYA

SÃO TOMÉ AND PRÍNCIPE

GABON

CONGO

DEMOCRATIC REPUBLIC OF CONGO

RWANDA

BURUNDI

TANZANIA

SEYCHELLES

COMOROS

ANGOLA

MALAWI

Mayotte (Fr.)

ZAMBIA

ZIMBABWE

MOZAMBIQUE

MADAGASCAR

MAURITIUS

Réunion (Fr.)

NAMIBIA

BOTSWANA

SWAZILAND

SOUTH AFRICA

LESOTHO

IBRD
39497
October 2012

Titles in the Africa Development Forum Series

Africa's Infrastructure: A Time for Transformation (2010) edited by Vivien Foster and Cecilia Briceño-Garmendia

Gender Disparities in Africa's Labor Market (2010) edited by Jorge Saba Arbache, Alexandre Kolev, and Ewa Filipiak

Challenges for African Agriculture (2010) edited by Jean-Claude Deveze

Contemporary Migration to South Africa: A Regional Development Issue (2011) edited by Aurelia Segatti and Loren Landau

Light Manufacturing in Africa: Targeted Policies to Enhance Private Investment and Create Jobs (2012) by Hinh T. Dinh, Vincent Palmade, Vandana Chandra, and Frances Cossar

The Informal Sector in Francophone Africa: Firm Size, Productivity, and Institutions (2012) by Nancy Benjamin and Ahmadou Aly Mbaye

Financing Africa's Cities: The Imperative of Local Investment (2012) by Thierry Paulais

Structural Transformation and Rural Change Revisited: Challenges for Late Developing Countries in a Globalizing World (2012) by Bruno Losch, Sandrine Fréguin-Gresh, and Eric Thomas White

Empowering Women: Legal Rights and Economic Opportunities in Africa (2013) by Mary Hallward-Driemeier and Tazeen Hasan

Contents

Boxes

Figures

Tables

Acknowledgments

This book would not have seen the light of day without help from the many people we met in the field who greatly facilitated our task. In the hope that we have left no name out, we wish to express our gratitude here to all those who participated. Réjane Hugounenq, from the Agence Française de Développement (AFD) Research Department, was the mainstay of this project. She was unflagging in her efforts and vitality in initiating and copiloting this study. Thanks also to Gill Gladstone, translator, and Janice Tuten, production editor; both did a tremendous job so that the present book is more than the translation of the French original.

In Burkina Faso, the following people helped us with our fieldwork and shared with us their vision of decentralization in situ: Toussaint Abel Coulibaly, deputy minister in charge of local government, Ministry of Territorial Administration and Decentralization (MATD); Evariste Millogo, director of the *Appui aux collectivités territoriales* under the General Directorate for Budget; Bénéfou Traore, *inspecteur du trésor DAF* (*directeur de l'administration des finances*) under the Ministry of Basic Education and Literacy; Blaise Bado, director-general of the *Fonds permanent pour le développement des collectivités territoriales*; Patrice Nikiema, president of the Regional Council of the Centre Region; Charles Niodogo, secretary-general of the Centre Region; Somwaya Patrice Syan, second vice president of the Regional Council of the Centre-Nord Region, *Association des régions du Burkina Faso*; Hélène Bouda, mayor of Bakata for the *Association des maires du Burkina Faso* (AMBF); Passoalègba Benjamin Kagambega, mayor of Laye (AMBF); Nabié Nimaye, mayor of Koti (AMBF); El Hadj Dramane Compore, second deputy mayor; Sébastien Kima, secretary-general; Mrs. Ouaba, *directrice des affaires financières*, Commune of Ouagadougou; Julien Nonguierma, mayor of the rural commune of Komsilga; Mrs. Tiendrebeogo, secretary-general, rural commune of Komsilga; Raogo Antoine Sawadogo, former minister of MATD; Peter Hochet, *Labo Citoyenneté*; Patrice Tranchant, director of the AFD in Burkina Faso; Christophe Barat, AFD project manager for macroeconomics, water, and sanitation; Olivia Dabbous and David Willecome, AFD, Paris; Jean-Michel Bretel, AMBF technical adviser; Jean-Marc Lecoq, technical adviser, General Directorate of Taxation; Frédéric Raynouard, City of Lyon adviser for Ouagadougou; Bertrand Riffiod, MATD technical advisor; and Pierre Hassan Sanon, attaché for local governance cooperation.

In Ghana, we were able to count on the support of Hon. Joseph Yieleh Chireh, minister of the Ministry of Local Government and Regional Development and Environment (MLGRDE); D.A. Nyankamawu, chief director of the MLGRDE; Johnson M. Alifo, Local Government Inspectorate of the MLGRDE; Kwamena Ahwoi, advisor to the president and lecturer at the Ghana Institute of Management and Public Administration; Eva Esselba Mends, head of the Budget Development Unit at the Ministry of Finance; Yaw Okyere-Nyako, director, External Resource Mobilization (ERM)-Bilateral at the Ministry of Finance and Economic Planning; Emma Lilian Bruce-Lyle, Ministry of Chieftaincy and Culture; Alhaji Ibrahim Mohammed Sherif, president of the National Association of Local Authorities of Ghana; Hon. Samuel Ofosu-Ampofo, minister of the East Region; Hon. Baba Jamal, deputy regional minister of the East Region; Hon. John Kwao Sackey, Ga East Municipal Assembly; Kollan K. Seidu, Ga East Municipal Assembly; Mawuli V. Hewlett, Ga East Municipal Assembly; Hon. Inush Abdulai B. Fuseini, chairman of constitutional, legal, and parliamentary affairs for the Tamale Central Constituency; Lydia Esther Naa Adjeley Sackey, budget director for the Metropolitan Assembly of Accra; Joshua Magnus Nicol, District Assembly Common Fund administrator; Dr. Isaac F. Mensa-Bonsu, director of planning and coordination for the National Development Planning Commission; Swanzy George Winful, Ghana Audit Service; Volker Monikes, German Agency for Technical Cooperations; Peter Wefers, German development bank KfW (Kreditanstalt für Wiederaufbau); Martin Knoll, KfW; Lars Moller Larsen, Royal Danish Embassy; Barbara Murray, Canadian International Development Agency; Francis Hurtut, ambassador of France; Christian Joly, cooperation attaché with the French Embassy; Bruno Deprince, AFD, Accra; and Anne Chapa Chapalain, AFD, Paris. The authors extend their thanks to Augustine Atiah for his difficult search for statistical documents and figures as well as to Samuel Lefèvre (AFD project manager for Ghana) for his comments, which enabled us to enrich the original text of chapter 3 on Ghana.

In Kenya, the research team was able to count on assistance and inputs from Bernard Calas, *Institut Française de Recherches en Afrique* (IFRA); Joséphine Kanyi, Ministry of Finance, Department of Economic Affairs; Leah Rotitch, Ministry of Education; Ruth Kiiru and David Tambo, Ministry of Local Government; Angeline Hongo and Simon Lapper, Ministry of Local Government, Kenya Local Government Reform Program; Murimi Murage, Local Authority Transfer Fund Advisory Committee; Agnès Odhiambo,

Constituency Development Fund Board; John Mue, Nairobi City Council; John Kitilit, Pamelah Osano, and Milicent Yugi, Municipal Council of Nakuru; Jimmy Waititu, County Council of Kiambu; Hamisi Mboga, Association of Local Government Authorities of Kenya; and Emilie Coindet, Olivier Delefosse, Anthea Manasseh, and Jean-Pierre Marcelli from the AFD in Nairobi.

Our interlocutors in Senegal were Amadou Moctar Gaye, director of the Financial Department of the Directorate of Local Government; Mbaye Toure, administrative and financial director for the Town of Dakar; Ibrahima Ndiagne, technical director of the *Communauté des agglomérations de Dakar* (CADAK); Ibrahima Sokho, prefect of the Department of Dakar; El Hadji Malick Gakou, president of the Dakar Regional Council; Alain N'Door, Mamadou Ndione, and Moctar Thiam, World Bank; Cheif Macky Salle, mayor of Guediawaye; Mamadou Moustapha Diop, secretary-general of the Commune of Guediawaye; Mamadou Oumar Bocoum, municipal tax collector for Dakar; Khalifa Ababacar Sall, mayor of Dakar; Rahmatouca Sow, *directrice de cabinet adjointe de la mairie de Dakar*; Joseph Ndour, Boubacar Traore, and Ahmadou Lamina Kebe, Court of Accounts magistrates; Babakar Fall and Mamadou Alhousseynou, *Agence de la statistique*; Alione Ndoye, mayor of Plateau Arrondissement; Kébir Sow, Cheifh T. Sene, and Pierre Coly, *Agence de développement municipal*; Abdou Diao and Ariama Cisse, Ministry of Education, Directorate of Basic Education; Papa Oumar Diallo, General Directorate of Taxes; Gorgui Cisse, president of the rural community of Yenn; Denis Castaing, director of the AFD in Senegal; Mathieu Vasseur, Alexandra Diaby, and Géraldine Barbe, AFD project managers; and François R. Gil, AFD, Paris.

The people whom we interviewed provided answers, possible solutions, and suggestions for improvements as well as offering their points of view. This cooperation enabled us to identify various points to be pondered. As a result, we were able to complete, refine, and clarify our own notes and analyses while writing the chapters that follow. We are deeply grateful to them. The analyses and conclusions in this book, of course, remain the full responsibility of the authors and, as is customary, do not necessarily represent the official point of view of the AFD, its partner institutions, or those we visited. We dare to hope that these chapters will contribute to a better understanding of decentralization processes in the developing countries we visited in Africa as well as of this splendid initiative that aims to develop even further the budgetary autonomy of local governments, participatory democracy, and good local governance.

About the Authors

Bernard Dafflon (PhD, 1971, University of Fribourg, Switzerland, and DPhil, 1976, University of York, U.K.) has been professor of public finance at the University of Fribourg since 1987. Previously he was chief economist at the Department of Institutions and Decentralization of the canton Fribourg (1977–90). He also has served as external consultant for the Council of Europe (1994–2006); the World Bank (since 1999); the Agence Française de Développement (AFD), Paris (since 2008); the Swiss Development and Cooperation Agency, Bern (since 2008); the Forum of Federation (since 2010); and several Swiss cantons and local authorities. He has published extensively on fiscal federalism and decentralization, local public finance, equalization, deficit and debt limit, and on the amalgamation of local government; taxation; and the user-pays principle in drinkable water, wastewater, and solid waste recycling and treatment.

Guy Gilbert (PhD, 1979, University of Paris) has been professor of public finance and public economics at *Ecole Normale Supérieure de Cachan* (ENS), Paris, since 2000 and previously at the Universities of Rennes, Paris (1985–89). He has also been an invited professor at the Universities of Geneva and Moscow as well as a visiting scholar at the University of Montreal. He has consulted for French (*Conseil des Impôts*, AFD, and the Ministries of Finances, Social Affairs, and Interior), foreign (Fiscal and Financial Commission of the Republic of South Africa), and international organizations (European Bank for Reconstruction and Development, World Bank Institute). He has published extensively on fiscal federalism, decentralization, taxation, and local public finance.

Réjane Hugounenq (PhD, 1996, public economics, *Ecole des Hautes Etudes en Sciences Sociales*) joined the AFD Research Department in 2007, where she is an economist, working on topics related to governance, decentralization, and taxation in developing countries. Previously she spent three years at the issuing institutes for the French overseas departments and territories (*Instituts d'Emission d'Outre-Mer*) and seven years at the French Observatory of Economic Conditions (*L'Observatoire français des conjonctures économiques*) of the National Foundation of Political Science, where she worked on a variety of topics including taxation in Europe and wage inequality between men and women.

Abraham Ky (PhD, political economy, 2010, University of Fribourg, Switzerland) works in financial administration at the Ministry of Economy and Finance, Burkina Faso, and is a lecturer at the Burkinabé National School of Administration and Magistracy (*Ecole Nationale d'Administration et de Magistrature*), from which he graduated in 2001. He served as a financial auditor in various ministries and public institutions in Burkina Faso before starting his doctoral research on federalism and decentralization in Burkina Faso. He also serves as a consultant on decentralization, local governance, and financial and institutional auditing. Ky is now at the Ministry of Finance, Burkina Faso, *Directeur général du contrôle des marchés publics et des engagements financiers.*

Thierry Madiès (PhD, economics, 1997, University of Paris I Panthéon Sorbonne) has been a professor of international and regional economics at the University of Fribourg (Switzerland) since 2003 and a senior lecturer in public finance at the *Institut d'Etudes Politiques de Paris*. He has long taught at the University of Paris I Panthéon Sorbonne and at the ENS Cachan, Paris. He also served as an economic adviser to the Council of Economic Analysis to the French Prime Minister (2006–10). He has been a scientific adviser to the AFD since 2008 and an external consultant to the World Bank since 2010. He has published extensively on public economics and public policies, taxation, and decentralization.

Yvon Rocaboy has been a professor of economics at the University of Rennes 1, France, since 1998 and director of the Center for Research in Economics and Management. He has published widely in French and international journals and books. The main focus of his work is local public economics (tax competition, location choice, optimal jurisdiction size, and fiscal federalism) and public choice (yardstick political competition, and political fragmentation), with a particular focus on French local government.

Emmanuelle Taugourdeau (PhD, economics, 2000, University of Paris I) has been a research fellow at the National French Institute for Scientific Research (*Centre national de la recherche scientifique*; CNRS), Paris, since 2003. She is a member of the *Centre d'Economie de la Sorbonne* (University of Paris I) and joined the Paris School of Economics in 2012. She is also a member of the Institute of Public Economics in Marseille. She has published articles in the areas of fiscal federalism, taxation, and social insurance in high-quality academic journals.

François Vaillancourt (PhD, Queen's University, Kingston, Ontario, Canada), Member of the Royal Society of Canada (MRSC), is a fellow at Centre interuniversitaire de recherche analyse des organisations (CIRANO) in Montreal and professor emeritus of economics, University of Montreal. He has published extensively in the areas of fiscal federalism, language policy, and taxation. He has been a visiting scholar at the University of Toronto (1991); the Federalism Research Centre (1991); FUCaM (2006); ENS Cachan, Paris (2006 and 2008); and the Andrew Young School of Policy Studies, Georgia State University, Atlanta (2007 and 2009). He was also the Shastri Institute lecturer (India, 1993) and a Fulbright Scholar (Kennesaw State University, Georgia, 2007). He has consulted for both Canadian (Auditor General Canada, Canadian International Development Agency, Council of Federation, Finance Canada and Finance Québec, House of Commons, Law Reform Commission) and foreign organizations (AFD, Organisation for Economic Co-operation and Development, United Nations Development Programme, and the World Bank).

Contributors to Chapter 7, "Comments and Concrete Ways Forward":
Frédéric Audras (*Institut d'Etudes Politiques de Bordeaux* and Bordeaux School of Management) has been head of the AFD for the French Polynesia region since 2011. He began his professional curriculum as a consultant in local public finances, becoming head of fiscal and financial strategy of the Urban Community of Marseilles–Provence Métropole in 2001. In 2004, he joined the government of New Caledonia as economic adviser for finances and project evaluation. In 2007, he joined the AFD Paris as project manager, Local Governments and Urban Development Division.

Gérard Chambas (PhD in economics) is a researcher at the CNRS and research director, Centre for Studies and Research on International Development (CERDI) at the University of Auvergne Clermont-Ferrand 1. He joined the CERDI in 1994 as a team leader in academic research at the University of Clermont-Ferrand specializing in economic development. He has authored numerous publications and project evaluations concerning taxation and public finance in developing countries.

Abbreviations

ADM	Agency for Municipal Development (*Agence de développement municipal*; Senegal)
AFD	Agence Française de Développement
AGETIP	Public Works Executing Agency (*Agence d'exécution des travaux d'intérêt public*; Senegal)
CA	arrondissement commune (Senegal)
CADAK	Communauté des agglomérations de Dakar (Senegal)
CAR	Communauté des agglomérations de Rufisque (Senegal)
CCL	Code of Local Government (*Code des collectivités locales*; Senegal)
CDF	Constituency Development Fund (Kenya)
CEO	chief executive officer
CFO	chief financial officer
CGCT	General Code of Territorial Collectivities (*Code général des collectivités territoriales*; Burkina Faso)
CGI	General Tax Code (*Code général des impôts*; Senegal)
CGU	combined business tax (*Contribution Générale Unique*; Senegal)
CNDCL	National Council on Local Development (*Conseil national de développement des collectivités locales*; Senegal)
COE	Committee of Experts on Constitutional Review (Kenya)
CR	rural community (Senegal)
CT	territorial collectivity (*collectivité territorial*; Burkina Faso, Senegal)
CU	urban community (Senegal)

CVD	village development council (*Conseil villageois de développement*; Burkina Faso)
DA	district assembly (Ghana)
DACF	District Assembly Common Fund (Ghana)
DC	district council (Ghana)
DCE	district chief executive (Ghana)
DCL	Directorate of Territorial Collectivities (*Direction des collectivités locales*; Senegal)
DDF	District Development Facility (Ghana)
DGE	Block grants for investment expenditures (*Dotation générale d'équipement*; Burkina Faso)
DGF	Grant for recurrent expenditures (*Dotation globale de fonctionnement*; Burkina Faso)
DGI	General Directorate of Taxation (*Direction générale des impôts*; Burkina Faso)
DGID	General Directorate of Taxation and Property (*Direction générale des impôts et des domains*; Senegal)
FDD	Decentralization Allocation Fund (*Fonds de dotation de la décentralisation*; Senegal)
FECL	Fund for Local Government Infrastructures (*Fonds d'équipement des collectivités locales*; Senegal)
FPDCT	Permanent Development Fund for Territorial Collectivities (*Fonds permanent pour le développement des CT*; Burkina Faso)
GPT	graduated personal tax (Kenya)
HIPC	Heavily Indebted Poor Countries (program)
IGF	internally generated funds (Ghana)
K Sh	Kenyan shilling
LA	local authority
LATF	Local Authority Transfer Fund (Kenya)
LASDAP	Local Authority Service Delivery Action Plan (Kenya)
LGA	Local Government Act (Kenya)
LI	legislative instrument (Ghana)
LPG	local public good
MA	Ministry of Agriculture (Burkina Faso)
MATD	Ministry of Territorial Administration and Decentralization (Burkina Faso)
MDAs	ministries, departments, agencies

MEBA	Ministry of Basic Education and Literacy (Burkina Faso)
MEF	Ministry of Economy and Finance (Burkina Faso)
MLGRDE	Ministry of Local Government and Regional Development and Environment (Ghana)
MMDAs	metropolitan, municipal, and district assemblies (Ghana)
MP	member of parliament
NDPC	National Development Planning Commission (Ghana)
NGO	nongovernmental organization
PAC	Support Program to Communes (*Programme d'appui aux communes*; Senegal)
PC	provincial commissioner (Kenya)
PEFA	Public Expenditure and Financial Accountability (report)
PNDC	Provisional National Defense Council (Ghana)
PTPP	proceeds of the petroleum products tax (*Produit de la taxe sur les produits pétroliers*; Burkina Faso)
PRECOL	Program to Strengthen Local Government Investment (*Programme de renforcement et d'équipement des collectivités locales*; Senegal)
RCC	regional coordinating council (Ghana)
SAEDH	Zoning Plan for Housing (*Schéma d'aménagement de l'espace d'habitation*; Burkina Faso)
SDAU	Urban Planning Master Plan (*Schéma directeur d'aménagement urbain*; Burkina Faso)
SRA	Regional Development Plan (*Schéma régional d'aménagement*; Burkina Faso)
TFPB	tax on developed property (*Taxe foncière sur les Propriétés Bâties*; Senegal)
TRIMF	*Taxe Représentative de l'Impôt du Minimum Fiscal*
UC	unit committee (Ghana)
VAT	value added tax
UEMOA	West African Economic and Monetary Union (*Union Economique et Monétaire Ouest Africaine*)

Introduction

Bernard Dafflon, Réjane Hugounenq, and Thierry Madiès

For two decades now—in fact, ever since the splintering of the former Communist Bloc—experiments in decentralization and federalization have been developing in a large number of countries, not only in the formerly communist states of Eastern Europe but also in Asia and Africa, each time raising the same questions: What real responsibilities should be assigned to the decentralized tiers of government? What concomitant own resources, what transfers, and what equalization mechanisms should be maintained or introduced?

The decentralization policies implemented in developing countries over the past 20 years or so are parts of this process. They have changed—and are still changing—the institutional landscapes in these countries. Many of the powers previously in the hands of the central government or its deconcentrated structures have been transferred to decentralized levels of government. Additionally, in a recent but increasingly widespread trend, local governments are gradually emerging as development actors and are now being assigned responsibilities for territorial development.

Whatever the reasons governing a decentralization process, the transfer of new functions to the local government layer can be substantive, at least in intent. This raises a second set of questions: What are the origins and causes of these moves toward greater decentralization? Does actual decentralization on the ground coincide with the decentralization intended—as written in constitution or law? How can gaps between intended and actual decentralization be explained? Does the existing institutional design hinder decentralization, or can it be rethought and reformed to encourage even deeper decentralization?

A Focus on Sub-Saharan Africa

In Africa, the current phase of decentralization began in the 1990s with the drafting of legislation indicating the political will to decentralize. The effort aimed to redefine the necessary institutional frameworks.[1] However, by the late 1990s, the implementation phase had turned out to be problematic. This is still the case today in many countries (Martinez-Vazquez and Vaillancourt 2011). Most of them are experiencing a gap between the institutional structure of decentralization and the ongoing centralized management of public affairs, including at the deconcentrated level. In practice, these countries find themselves up against the fiscal and financial mechanisms of decentralization, discovering all the particularities and requirements involved, often without being able to rely on a "guiding hand." The effective discharge of responsibilities is hampered by the lack of precision regarding the decentralized tasks to be performed and the hazy lines delimiting the responsibilities of the different tiers of government. Most often, added to this is poor allocation of financial resources or even the complete lack of these resources.

It is against this backdrop that the Agence Française de Développement (AFD) currently operates in the developing countries of Sub-Saharan Africa. Its direct interventions with local governments take the form of local budget support and project finance. Its indirect interventions support central governments through lines of credit (or by fueling municipal development funds or specialized financial institutions) whose funds are ultimately intended for financing local governments, the final beneficiaries. In this case, central governments are responsible for allocating the transfers to local governments.

To reframe its actions within the institutional settings of the countries concerned—and, by so doing, gain insight into the effectiveness of their interventions—the AFD launched a four-country study to examine the overall design of local government financing systems. This study was launched by the AFD's Research Department in conjunction with its Local Government and Urban Development Department on the initiative of Samuel Lefèvre, who also selected the benchmark countries: two French-speaking countries in West Africa (Burkina Faso and Senegal) and two English-speaking countries (Ghana [West Africa] and Kenya [East Africa]). These countries were not chosen as being particularly representative of developing countries in Sub-Saharan Africa but rather on account of the AFD's activities there, with the objective of validating the relevance of the analytical guide as a suitable methodological approach.

The Department of Political Economy at the University of Fribourg (Switzerland) was tasked with carrying out the study under the responsibility of Professors Bernard Dafflon (who piloted the study) and Thierry Madiès as well as Réjane Hugounenq, a member of the AFD Research Department. The research team comprised Professors Dafflon and Madiès (University of Fribourg), Guy Gilbert (Ecole Nationale Supérieure de Cachan), Yvon Rocaboy (University of Rennes I), François Vaillancourt (University of Montreal), and Emmanuelle Taugourdeau (research fellow, Centre National de la Recherche Scientifique, Paris).

Analytical Approach

This book gathers the research results of this teamwork. The analytical approach was divided into four stages:

1. Development of an analytical guide and compilation of the legislation of decentralization in the four countries selected
2. An institutional economy study of the countries' decentralization design
3. A political economy field study of the mechanisms for funding decentralized territorial collectivities
4. On-the-ground verification.

At a more detailed level, each stage was organized along the lines described below.

Stage 1: Analytical Guide
The first stage involved constructing an analytical guide to decentralization, the purpose being to produce a comparative table enabling cross-country analysis, for the four countries selected, of the themes recognized as relevant to all decentralization policies (chapter 1 presents this guide). At the same time, once this guide has been validated in the field, it should serve as a benchmark for the other countries in which the AFD is active—and not only in Africa.

The analytical guide offers a coherent and organized way to gather the information on the organization of decentralized government units, the assignment of functions and resources, the budgeting and accounting systems (the selected issues) from the constitution, and the organic laws or other official documents of the country under investigation. This provides the material for the second stage.

Stage 2: Institutional Economy Study
The so-called deskwork stage involved a study of the institutional framework for decentralization in each of the four countries. The institutional economy analysis[2] of the legislation on local government organization, devolved responsibilities, sources of funding, and transfer formulas gives a picture of the ideal decentralization targeted—not in the optimal sense of the term but according to the preferences and choices expressed by each country's sovereign authorities (executive power) and legislature.

Stage 3: Political Economy Field Study
The third stage consisted of fieldwork by two-person teams to see how institutional design measured up to reality. Interviews were organized with representatives of the ministries affected by decentralization and with local government associations. These interviews were followed by visits to local authorities and

interviews with local individuals who were particularly aware of the history and practices of decentralization.

Chapters 2 to 5 present, for the four developing countries, the findings of our comparisons between each country's targeted ideal and the realities on the ground as we understood them. To improve the comparative quality of the chapters on the individual countries, each country chapter was written by the visiting team and then submitted to another team for critical and careful reading.

Stage 4: On-the-Ground Verification

The final stage, which is reported in chapter 6, draws general conclusions from the analytical method: What common points, strengths, and weaknesses can be identified in the decentralization experiences of the four countries analyzed? Can lessons be drawn from these national contexts, and can proposals be formulated to consolidate, or even strengthen, decentralization processes? What institutional—or financial—risks are run by the external, national, international, and nongovernmental organizations participating in a top-down approach to the decentralization process? How can this process be contextualized in a way that gives local actors full ownership of this approach?

Methodology

From a methodological standpoint, the approach to decentralization unfolds in three key phases:

- The first, upstream phase identifies what kind of decentralization a developing country wishes or chooses to undertake. At this point, the approach and method used must be clear: it is not a matter of defining a theoretical norm for decentralization and forcing the country under study into the straight-jacket of this norm. The question here concerns the developing country's decentralization, analyzed according to its own expectations. The analysis, in fact, answers this question: How do you define *your* decentralization and how it materializes on an institutional level? We will study whether the actions implemented on the ground to promote decentralization are consistent with this stated political will.

- The second phase unfolds downstream and relates to performance. Decentralization purports to fulfill manifold objectives: strengthen local governance, better serve local residents in line with their democratically expressed preferences, reduce local pockets of poverty, and stimulate and drive local development. The challenge is to target those objectives that have been set, not always explicitly, and to identify the explanatory variables that make it possible to quantify and assess the ground already covered. It is impossible to judge progress in the areas of democracy, the fight against poverty, and local development without first establishing the causal relationship between decentralized functions, explanatory variables, and outcomes.

- The third phase is funding. To complete the decentralization process, it is not enough to distribute funds or budget grants. The allocated resources must be firmly grounded within a budgetary system that will ensure the long-term sustainability of local government funding and create conditions conducive to the financial accountability of local elected officials. From this perspective, it is imperative to set up the operational logistics for a budgetary, fiscal, accounting, and administrative system, not only for technical reasons but also for the sake of economic analysis, which makes it possible to measure and assess the progress, performance, and effects of decentralization.

Contributions of This Volume

The approach developed in this book is, for the first time, clearly restated in writing[3] and systematically applied in parallel to four countries. This treatment is new in that it is clearly "policy-implementation-oriented" and, in that time, allows not only for the study of individual countries but also for comparison between countries on similar issues based on the same blueprint. The purpose of the analysis is not to assess whether the chosen model of decentralization is the right one—in fact, there is no "decentralization model" that would serve as a benchmark, as the causes are many (Bird and Ebel 2007). Its aim is to take stock of what decentralization initiatives have achieved so far, in specific national settings, and to compare those achievements with the institutional design announced. The divergences revealed through observation and analysis thus enable a country to decide on appropriate reforms.

The method, described in detail in chapter 1, clearly states this point: there is no transposition of a "Western" or "European"[4] analysis to an African state. The approach is clearly contextualized to each country. The interpretive reference framework offers an analytical approach that integrates not only economic or budgetary arguments but also sociopolitical ones. It sets out a series of questions designed to bring out a necessary coherence in responses and thus also in the approach to decentralization. The analytical guide gives no answers or models. It is up to the stakeholders involved in decentralization negotiations to make this interpretative framework their own and to use it within the specific contexts and characteristics of their own decentralization processes.

Notes

1. This aim, of course, does not imply that the political environment preceding recent legislation on decentralization had not played an important role. But as our study is not a historical approach, we have not gone back in time. The reader can consult, for example, Bayart (2009), which also provides a well-furnished bibliography on this theme. Likewise, following the logic of the analytical guide developed in chapter 1, our interest lies in the gap existing between the institutional design of decentralization and the achievements on the ground in the states studied. But we have not examined which individuals or authorities initiated or strongly influenced the constitutional and legal design upstream. This is also the case for national sociopolitical factors as much as for external factors, particularly the role of the World Bank, the International Monetary Fund, foreign national agencies contributing financial development aid, and nongovernmental organizations. Such historical analysis is beyond the scope of this book.

2. In the present book, institutional economics analyzes, from the point of view of political economy, the organization of the state and the interrelation between state institutions that are involved in the process of decentralization. We are not reading constitutional and organic law from a legal point of view but as economists (who controls what, how does it function, and what are the consequence?).

3. The theories of Fiscal Federalism Second Generation (Oates 2005; Weingast 2006) are innovative in the sense that, in addition to pure economic arguments for (de)centralization that characterize first-generation theories (Oates 1972; King 1984), they add other noneconomic, sociodemographic, historical, and political variables. But there is no serious attempt to develop the consequences in terms of implementation. Wiseman (1989; 1990) and Dafflon (1977) were the first to develop a logical construct capable of embracing the complexity of objectives endemic to federal countries in the real world. The method has been further developed over the last 30 years and applied to many issues, first at the local, cantonal, and federal levels in Switzerland. It has also been experimented with in several country cases where Dafflon has been active: for the Council of Europe in the Balkan area and particularly Albania (Dafflon 2011), in the Baltic countries; for the Swiss Cooperation and Development Agency in several Indian states, including Sikkim (Dafflon 2009) and Nepal; and for the World Bank in Senegal, the Democratic Republic of Congo (Champagne et al. 2001), and Cameroon (World Bank 2011). The method is oriented toward the practical and implementation-related problems of decentralization, backed by the experience gained by this author during the period (1977–90) in which he acted as chief economist at the Department of Local Government in the Ministry of Institution, Forestry and Agriculture of the canton of Fribourg, Switzerland.

4. "European" here refers to the way that the European Charter of Local Self-Government has been transposed to Sub-Saharan Africa (Council of Europe 1986).

References

Bayart, J.-F. 2009. "La démocratie à l'épreuve de la tradition en Afrique subsaharienne." *Pouvoirs* 2009/2 (129): 27–44.

Bird, R.-M., and R.-D. Ebel, eds. 2007. *Fiscal Fragmentation in Decentralized Countries: Subsidiarity, Solidarity and Asymmetry*. Cheltenham, U.K.: Edward Elgar Publishing; Washington, DC: World Bank.

Champagne, E. et al. 2001. *Relations intergouvernementales et gouvernance locale en Afrique*. Mimeo, World Bank, Dakar, Senegal. October 8–12, 2001.

Council of Europe. (1986) 1996. *European Charter of Local Self-Government* and its *Explanatory Report*. Strasbourg: Council of Europe.

Dafflon B. 1977. *Federal Finance in Theory and Practice, with Special Reference to Switzerland*. [Schriftenreihe Finanzwirtschaft und Finanzrecht, vol. 21.] Bern: Haut Verlag.

———. 2009. "The Political Economy of Decentralisation in Sikkim: Strengthening Gram Panchayat Planning and Budgeting." Government of Sikkim, ISMS Gangtok and Rural Management and Development Department (RMDD), SDC Swiss Embassy, New Delhi; also working paper 424, Faculté SES, Université de Fribourg. http://doc.rero.ch/collection/UNIFR_WORKING_PAPERS_SES.

———. 2011. "Conceptual Problems in the Assignment of Functions in SEE: The Case of Albania." In *Decentralization in Developing Countries: Global Perspectives on the Obstacle to Fiscal Devolution*, ed. J. Martinez-Vazquez and F. Vaillancourt, 23–82. Cheltenham, U.K.: Edward Elgar.

King, D. 1984. *Fiscal Tiers: The Economics of Multi-Level Government*. London: George Allen and Unwin.

Martinez-Vazquez, J., and F. Vaillancourt, eds. 2011. *Decentralization in Developing Countries: Global Perspectives on the Obstacles to Fiscal Devolution*. Cheltenham, U.K.: Edward Elgar.

Oates, W. 1972. *Fiscal Federalism*. Harbrace Series in Business and Economics. New York: Harcourt Brace Jovanovich.

———. 2005. "Toward a Second-Generation Theory of Fiscal Federalism." *International Tax and Public Finance* 12: 349–74.

Weingast, B. R. 2006. "Second Generation Fiscal Federalism: Implications for Decentralized Democratic Governance and Economic Development." Working paper, Hoover Institution on War, Revolution, and Peace, Stanford University, Stanford, CA. http://ssrn.com/abstract=1153440 or http://dx.doi.org/10.2139/ssrn.1153440.

Wiseman J. 1989. "The Political Economy of Federalism: a Critical Appraisal." In *Cost, Choice and Political Economy*, ed. J. Wiseman, 71–111. Aldershot, U.K.: Edward Elgar.

———. 1990. "Principles of Political Economy: An Outline Proposal Illustrated by an Application to Fiscal Federalism." In *Constitutional Political Economy*, vol. 1/1.

World Bank. 2011. "Cameroon: The Path to Fiscal Decentralization, Opportunities, and Challenges," Report 63369-CM, Poverty Reduction and Economic Management, Africa Region, World Bank, Washington, DC.

Chapter 1

Institutional and Fiscal Decentralization: Blueprint for an Analytical Guide

Bernard Dafflon

The approach proposed in this chapter is to apply an analytical method derived from institutional political economy and grounded in many years of decentralization practice (Dafflon 2009, 2010a). The method breaks down into two steps: an institutional study and a field study.

First, we examine the objectives of decentralization and the means used to implement it, as set out in national legislation. This allows us to analyze the degree of consistency between the decentralization mechanisms proposed and the stated goals. At this stage, we can already gauge whether the decentralization policy goes no further than lip service or whether there is a will, particularly from politicians and central administrations, to push through genuine devolution of responsibilities and financial resources.

Second, we compare the institutional design with what is actually happening on the ground. Analyzing this from an institutional political economy perspective enables us to measure—or at least to assess—the road traveled. It also highlights the achievements of decentralization (which may need to be consolidated); the shortcomings to be corrected; and the deficits still to be overcome.

This method offers at least two advantages:

- *It does not refer to a theoretical norm but calls on a positive approach.* The benchmark is not an optimal state of what decentralization should be according to the theories of fiscal federalism—or even second-generation fiscal federalism (Dafflon and Madiès 2008)—but instead according to the institutional "design" of the country studied. In other words, the benchmark does not constitute a model but rather what a specific country has set as its own objectives—with the proviso that an initial coherence exists and is checked between objectives and mechanisms in the design stage.

- *It sidelines quantitative data and can thus be applied even when reliable quantitative data on decentralized expenditure and revenue are not available.* The method integrates the lack or incompleteness of statistics as being indicative of serious weakness, but such deficits are not methodological stumbling blocks: the researcher is not left high and dry if a decentralization ratio cannot be computed.

The method also takes into account the specific contexts of individual countries. Each of the four country chapters can be read independently of the others. For example, in chapter 2, which presents the analysis of Burkina Faso's decentralization, the country's declared intentions are compared with what is implemented on the ground. There is no need to consult the three other case studies to understand what is at stake in the Burkinabé decentralization process. Moreover, nothing prevents this approach from being contextualized to countries other than the four selected for this volume by Agence Française de Développement (AFD).

At the same time, that these four case studies follow the same approach opens up new cross-cutting avenues of investigation. It thus becomes possible to compare decentralization processes and to capitalize on the learning-by-doing principle. AFD selected these countries to afford a cross-cutting view in Sub-Saharan Africa. Chapters 6 and 7 summarize this cross comparison.

The four chapters on the decentralization of public finances in Burkina Faso, Ghana, Kenya, and Senegal are aligned along the same analytical blueprint, following this sequence:

- A concise history of the country's decentralization
- A description of the institutional design of decentralized subnational governments
- A review of the decentralized budget
- The assignment of functions and responsibilities among the different tiers of government in terms of deconcentration, delegation, and devolution
- A review of revenue structures and systems, including own versus delegated taxes and exclusive versus shared taxes
- A study of the design and formulas for financial transfers from the central government to the subnational governments, including general or specific grants, incentives, and equalization grants
- An examination of budget balance and debt, should specific provisions set this theme apart from the third item above
- An assessment of the revenue and expenditure statistics available to analysts.

This list of themes has been cross-linked with various analytical questions and objectives to produce the analytical guide presented here. The chapters are all structured along the same lines, primarily to facilitate a thematic comparison of decentralization across the four countries, as presented in chapter 6 ("Decentralization: A Comparative and Cross-Cutting Analysis of the Stakes"). The aim is to bring to light the convergences, lessons, and perspectives drawn from the implementation of decentralization in developing countries in Sub-Saharan Africa.

The Institutional Approach to Decentralization

The two first steps in the analytical guide, as mentioned earlier, address the history and institutional design of decentralization as outlined in each country's national constitution or legislation. The constitution and laws define the institutional framework and the normative principles for decentralization—its design—not in terms of an ideal but as a manifestation of the aspirations or intentions of the national legislature. The analytical method draws on the teachings of institutional economy and public choice theory applied to fiscal federalism.

To analyze decentralization and assess its performance, a crucial preliminary step is to understand how the decentralization process has been designed at the institutional level and then to determine the gap—sometimes substantial—between the practical, on-the-ground organization and the organizational frameworks set out in the constitution and legal texts. In this area, the analytical guide allows the coherence of government choices to be analyzed with respect to the multiple implementation phases of the decentralization process. The analysis starts with the assumption that the government's choices of decentralization policies are coherent with and correspond to the institutional framework and objectives explicitly stipulated in the texts.

Yet everywhere—and not just in the developing countries that opt for decentralization—there are clear discrepancies between the design of decentralization and its implementation on the ground at the grassroots level. This analytical guide and cross-country comparison should help to gauge this gap and understand it as representing a learning process. What comes to light are the choices made implicitly because they are too difficult to explain or justify openly; the resistance caused by power sharing; and the delays and misunderstandings needing to be flushed out and corrected. The following four chapters thus try to explain the informal relationships that shape and sometimes distort the institutional design. Figure 1.1 illustrates this approach, as further explained later.

Figure 1.1 Possible Interrelationships in a Decentralized System of Government

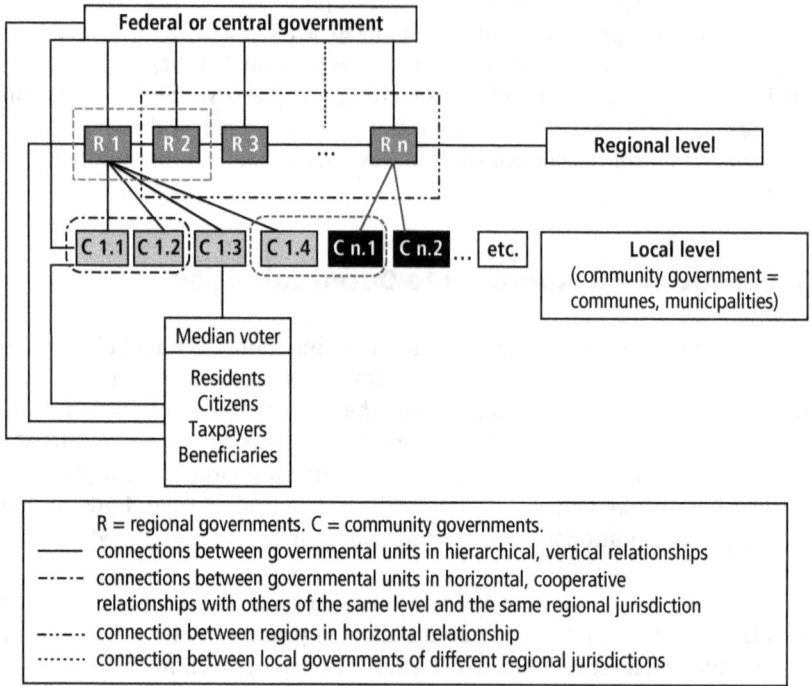

Source: Dafflon 2010a.

According to the traditional tenets of fiscal federalism (bottom-up) or decentralization (top-down), there is a vertical hierarchical structure within a three-tier system of government—layered on a central-regional-local authority basis. Moreover, for the electorate (the voters), the exercise of democracy translates into a threefold relationship: with the municipality (commune), with the region, and with the center.

But in reality, the situation is somewhat more complex. A federal or decentralized model implies recognizing and giving decision-making powers to subnational government entities. However, economic logic (economies of scale, spillover effects, standard service requirements, and macroeconomic or redistributive considerations) and bureaucratic practices tend toward centralized governance (Dafflon and Madiès 2008, 21ff.). Figure 1.1 shows the possible interrelationships between central and subnational government levels in a three-tier system, not only for government units but also for citizens.

Interrelationships of Government Units

A vertical relationship between governments sometimes can "leapfrog" over an intermediate level, such as when local governments address the central government directly without going through a regional jurisdiction. Horizontal relationships between local governments of different regional jurisdictions (see dotted rectangle in figure 1.1) can be problematic if the regions operate under differing legislation (as in the case of the Swiss cantons or the German *Länder*).

Within these government units, the relationship between local elected officials and regional or central government officials must be examined carefully. In particular, the hierarchical links may raise these questions:

- Is the local (regional) government official appointed and paid, appointed only, or paid only by (a) the local (regional) authority itself, or (b) a higher (regional, respectively central) level of government?

- Is the government official subordinated to a local authority in his or her functional capacity while still having the status of a government official through administrative attachment to a deconcentrated unit? If so, the agent's accountability is ambiguous because he or she is responsible for the function relative to the decentralized government unit but administratively depends on a deconcentrated bureau (line ministry).

- In the event of disagreement or conflict, to which authority is the government official accountable?

- How is the shift managed when the status of a delegated government official exercising responsibilities at the local level changes to that of a local government employee?

- What happens when a government official seconded to the local level has managerial and technical skills, whereas the local elected official does not have the knowledge and abilities required for the related responsibility?

New decentralization theories emphasize capacity building to support the decentralization process (which, of course, is necessary), but these theories only rarely address the question of hierarchical positions, the status of government officials, and their loyalty to line ministries rather than to local authorities—all of which are potential sources of conflict. Country studies should take these aspects into consideration.

Interrelationships of Economic Agents

Figure 1.1 employs the terms "median voter," "residents," "citizens," "taxpayers," and "beneficiaries" because they are not synonymous. Each category is likely to be affected differently by the decentralization of responsibilities and resources. Traditional theory does not make such distinctions: it simplifies the situation by claiming to address a rational and informed "median voter" who does not behave strategically.

Bearing in mind Olson's (1969) theory of the equivalence principle regarding the division of responsibilities among different tiers of government—which posits that the circle of deciders, the circle of payers, and the circle of beneficiaries should, as far as possible, coincide—an analogy would be that the citizens decide and the taxpayers pay, while the residents, or users, benefit. However, this is a far cry from reality. The perimeters of these circles may overlap in part only or even not coincide. At the local level, for example, foreign residents rarely have voting rights (thus no power of decision), but they are taxpayers (thus they pay). If they are residents, they may enjoy benefits, or not, depending on whether they use those benefits (for instance, all taxpayers contribute to financing compulsory education, even if they have no school-age children). Because all residents have civic rights, they can solicit the municipality, but they can also bypass this tier and directly solicit the regional or even the central government. Of course, leapfrogging a government level makes exercising one's right to democratic participation more costly, but this path is not systematically blocked.

Figure 1.1 only partially covers the intricate networks of relationships between public authorities or between economic agents belonging to one or the other government level. It simply shows that decentralization takes economic theory into a web of highly complex interrelations that are certainly far more complicated than the simple "state-economic agent" relationship predominant in public finances. Adding one or two government tiers (local, regional) between the citizen and the central government does not simply amount to adding one or two vertical relationships. It superimposes a web onto a more elaborate institutional framework. In line with Lockwood (2006, 33), if the democratic institutions (elections, votes, referendums) and institutional processes through which these relationships play out are taken into account, they will exert a decisive influence on outcomes—in this case, on decentralization.

Evidently, the content of these intertwined relationships is not confined to economic matters. The powerful worldwide shift toward federalization and decentralization is clearly not determined by considerations of economic efficiency alone (Bird and Ebel 2007). Other factors in play are linked to

- The fight against poverty (in Africa, the Balkans, and Latin America);
- The response to globalization and competition (in Europe and Latin America);
- The drive to improve governance (in Africa, the Balkans, and Eastern Europe);
- The effort to address minority issues or fragmented societies (in the Balkans); and
- The will to return control of development to local communities (in Africa, Latin America, and India).

As a result, analysts are facing a twofold challenge: they must simultaneously take into account (a) the network of possible institutional links; and (b) a set of arguments grounded not just on purely fiscal and economic criteria but also on country-specific historical, social, and institutional dimensions. This binomial approach is what establishes and characterizes a "European" (as opposed to classical) vision of fiscal federalism and decentralization.

The European Approach to Analysis

The positive approach first used by European researchers[1] has grown into a movement with global reach that today characterizes a large body of research on decentralized systems.[2] It involves a global dialogue as well as the sharing of experiences and best practices in the area of federalism. Its underpinnings can be summarized in four dimensions: temporal variation, spatial variation, conflicts between economic goals, and conflicts with noneconomic goals (Blindenbacher and Koller 2003; Tóth 2007).

Temporal variation   Any intergovernmental system evolves dynamically, either as a result of or depending on changes in the political and socioeconomic environment. Externalities such as the liberalization of domestic or international markets, competition from new economies, and globalization generate and strengthen financial externalities, affect the streams of tax revenues, and broaden the circle of the potential beneficiaries of public services.

Technological advancements step up the demand for additional public spending (in health care, for example). Demographic trends or changes in labor-market behavior modify public policies, which then become either more centralized (such as in social security or care for dependent elderly persons) or strengthened at the local level (for example, early-childhood care facilities to reconcile work and family life).

The rules of budget discipline and debt capping pressure national governments to monitor public budgets and debt accumulation across all government levels. Likewise, endogenous factors such as changes in citizens' preferences (the choice between efficiency and equity, for example) influence political arbitrations with respect to interregional redistribution or public service financing models.

Spatial variation   As a direct consequence of temporal variation, different countries follow extremely diverse road maps and trajectories, which explains some of the cross-country disparities in intergovernmental relations. Variations in the degree of decentralized responsibilities and resources, to a large extent, reflect the different objectives and norms concerning the role of equalization transfers. The perception of local autonomy or the degree of taxpayer mobility explains the diversity of political attitudes toward fiscal competition, which is viewed as either beneficial or harmful.

The spatial dimension of decentralized public service provision takes different forms: *territorial mobility, fiscal competition,* and *yardstick competition* (comparing services and tax prices from one jurisdiction to another). In developing countries, *mobility of individuals across subnational territories,* most often to urban centers, is spurred more by economic survival strategies than by conscious tax-related choices. Decentralization is thus seen as an instrument for controlling urban growth. *Fiscal competition* is reduced or even nonexistent because tax base mobility is automatically limited by the lack of opportunity to find alternatives (unless the tax residence is established in a place other than the place of production—which can prove highly problematic for shared taxes). What then counts is not spatial mobility but a *yardstick competition* between decentralized authorities, which can prompt a search for better value-for-money (taxes) in service delivery. This comparison does, however, suppose that the local authorities' management of service delivery and their accounting systems are adequate and that they provide the necessary information for comparisons to be made—which is rarely the case in developing countries.

Conflicts between economic goals   Decentralization does not depend solely on economic efficiency criteria for provision of local public services. As regions and municipalities enjoy some degree of autonomy, their viewpoints often differ from those of the central government in the area of redistributive and macroeconomic policies (for example, in favor of local and regional stabilization and growth as opposed to national growth, natural resource use, and environmental protection). In addition, interregional individual mobility is rarely a choice or a usual behavior pattern as it is in the United States, and it is certainly less frequent in Europe, transition economies, and developing countries (the precise subject of the present study). Consequently, redistributive policies implemented by decentralized authorities are unlikely to distort how factors of production are distributed or to lead to an implosion of the redistributive system.

Conflicts with noneconomic goals   Public policies based on purely economic objectives (allocative and productive efficiency, macroeconomic stability, and so forth) may be at odds with the noneconomic objectives of decentralization, such as autonomy, solidarity, or protection of minority interests. Politicians are frequently forced to arbitrate—the best-known scenario being a choice between efficiency and equity.

The choices are most often normative, guided by value judgments rather than purely economic, rational criteria. This is not to say that some choices are better than others; it merely reinforces the need for an analytical guide (and then a decision-making algorithm) that incorporates noneconomic and economic criteria into a cross-cutting, multicriteria approach that ensures the coherence and coordination of the choices adopted (Dafflon 2006, 301). Using the same analytical guide, it should then be possible to (a) measure the performance of the systems and mechanisms set up to achieve the objectives, and (b) if necessary, identify the weaknesses that need correcting.

Defining Terms

Given the diversity of approaches just mentioned, one major stumbling block to the concrete implementation of decentralization hinges on the terminology used—words being laden with symbolic and emotional values and also having a "historic density." This is the case for the term "decentralization," which translates into three modalities (Gauthier and Vaillancourt 2002): deconcentration, delegation, and devolution.

Deconcentration   The central government retains its responsibilities and competences for some specific functions but mandates that its regional or local departments, much like branch offices, carry them out. These deconcentrated offices operate within a vertical hierarchy, sometimes called "line ministries."

Delegation   Through delegation, local governments become direct agents with a mandate to act in place of the central government. They are assigned delegated powers and resources. This arrangement is, strictly speaking, a principal-agency relationship, in which the central government has the role of principal and the local government is the executing agency in compliance with the terms of the "contract."

The norms and standards set for delegated functions should be within reasonable limits, particularly with respect to the resources allocated. If the minimum thresholds for delivery of local goods and services are high but resources are insufficient, the local governments do not have the means to do more or better. Delegation thus gives rise to a de facto form of deconcentration.

Devolution   Devolution effectively transfers powers and responsibilities to local governments. They become (partially or wholly) responsible for formulating, implementing, and financing policies.

Singularity of Country Perspectives

To draw a midway conclusion, it would thus be an oversimplification to think that decentralized institutions are organized on the basis of rational economic criteria. The web of vertical and horizontal relationships also accommodates a country's historical developments and its sociocultural and ethnodemographic dimensions (for example, Dafflon 2010b and 2011). Herein lie the singularity of each country and the stumbling blocks to implementing decentralization.

We thus understand how vital it is to review the historic events that have shaped the institutional mold or pattern for decentralization in each country—and how this history has spawned a country-specific institutional design, constitution, and body of decentralization laws. This dual vision—of norm versus reality—corresponds to the first two sections of the following chapters, each of which covers the recent history and organization of decentralization in one of the four countries studied in this volume. The fundamental question here is this: Are you doing what you said you would do? The analytical guide proposed earlier helps to identify the gaps between the institutional norm and the reality on the ground, which also comes down to assessing the institutional risks associated with the shortcomings and lags in the decentralization process.

Decentralized Budgets

The autonomy of decentralized public entities—which directly reflects their authority to decide and act within the context of the devolution of powers—raises some thorny conceptual problems. The definitions are diverse and often refer to specific aspects of autonomy. Because autonomy can only be relative, some clarification is called for.[3]

Autonomy has two aspects: (a) *financial autonomy*, which concerns local government resources, and (b) *budget autonomy*, which concerns spending decisions. The relation between financial autonomy and budget autonomy is not straightforward. On the one hand, financial autonomy conditions budget autonomy by virtue of the budget responsibility principle: that local governments either must bear the costly (fiscal) consequences of their spending decisions or cannot finance assigned responsibilities unless they have the resources to do so. On the other hand, the nature of the functions performed by decentralized local governments also determines the type of revenues that finance them, the logical sequence being first to define the powers devolved to local governments, and then—also—to give them the means to exercise those powers. Figure 1.2, showing the decentralized budget framework, illustrates this logic in the two upper boxes indicating the assignments of responsibilities and resources.

The Responsibility-Resource Gap
Beyond the assignment of responsibilities and powers (discussed in the next section), the reference "decentralized budget" is intended to provide a benchmark for comparing the financing systems of the four countries studied. This benchmark makes it possible to specify their revenue categories and assess their respective degrees of financial autonomy (revenue side) and budget autonomy (expenditure side).

The comparison between the real situation of local government finances and this budget overview should also give an insight into the problem of eventual vertical gaps between the allocation of own resources to local governments and the responsibilities assigned to them ("gaps between functions and resources" in figure 1.2). The question of the vertical gap has an impact on

- The effective budget autonomy of local governments or, in other words, their discretionary powers as well as the possibility of escaping from vertical

Figure 1.2 The Decentralized Budget: Responsibilities and Gaps

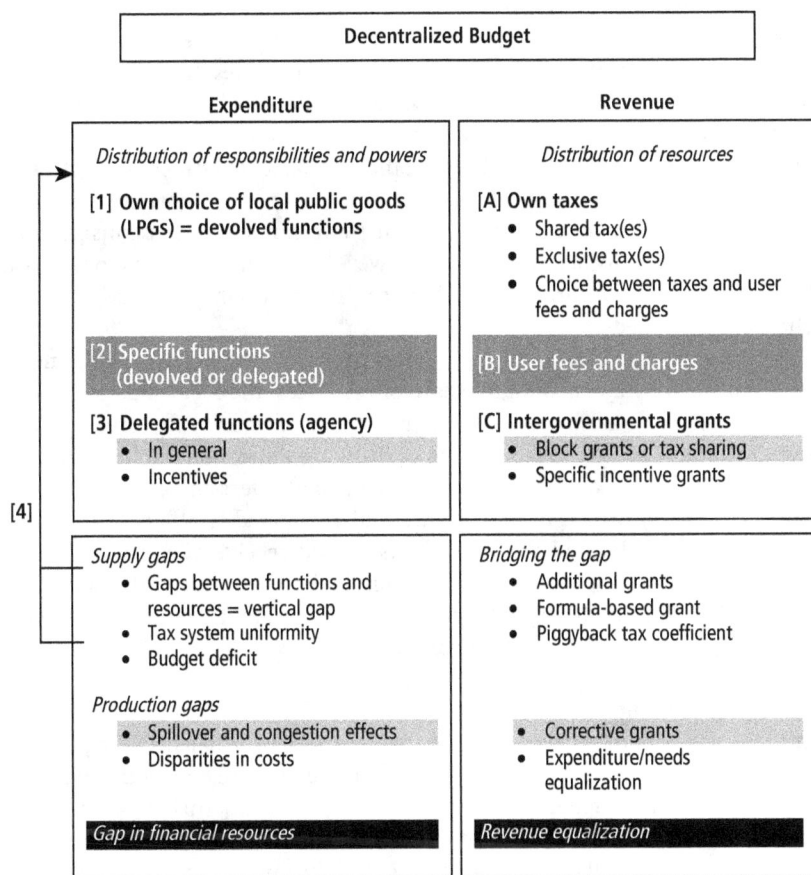

Decentralized Budget	
Expenditure	**Revenue**
Distribution of responsibilities and powers	*Distribution of resources*
[1] **Own choice of local public goods (LPGs) = devolved functions**	[A] **Own taxes** • Shared tax(es) • Exclusive tax(es) • Choice between taxes and user fees and charges
[2] Specific functions (devolved or delegated)	[B] User fees and charges
[3] **Delegated functions (agency)** • In general • Incentives	[C] **Intergovernmental grants** • Block grants or tax sharing • Specific incentive grants
Supply gaps • Gaps between functions and resources = vertical gap • Tax system uniformity • Budget deficit	*Bridging the gap* • Additional grants • Formula-based grant • Piggyback tax coefficient
Production gaps • Spillover and congestion effects • Disparities in costs	• Corrective grants • Expenditure/needs equalization
Gap in financial resources	Revenue equalization

[4]

Source: Dafflon 2010a; adapted from Dafflon and Madiès 2008, 65.
Note: LPG = local public goods.

supervision—a normative "principal-agent" or "line ministries" type of control—that mainly materializes as a form of deconcentration or delegation rather than genuine devolution; and

• The balancing of central and local government risk, because the size of the budget gap and the type of vertical bridging transfer will determine whether donors assume the risks of local government and central government.

Following the comparative method, one also must examine whether the "decentralized budget" is an overall budget (that is, a current and capital budget) or whether it is split into one budget for operating and another for investments, each with separate decision-making and accounting procedures and budget responsibilities. In developing countries, this decoupling often stems from the low level of own revenues or transferred financial resources that only just suffice to cover current expenditures. Other valid explanations include local governments' lack of access (intentionally so?) to capital markets (thus no borrowing); the lack of local managerial skills to see through large investment projects; the technical complexity of such investments; and, even more important, the reluctance of line ministries to relinquish their powers, make concessions, or give prerogatives to the local governments. However, all of these justifications, apart from the question of borrowing and the controversial subject of budget discipline, can be remedied.

In the logic of the decentralized budget, the devolved responsibilities need to be matched by a concomitant share of resources, the ideal situation being that of [A] = [1], as shown in the upper boxes of figure 1.2. Some specific responsibilities, such as the provision of drinking water, household waste collection, or sewage disposal could be subjected to user fees and charges ([B] for [2] in figure 1.2), which in practice are underexploited (Dafflon and Madiès 2008, 56–60). Delegated responsibilities should receive adequate financial support through budget appropriations, preferably as nonearmarked or block grants ([C] for [3] in figure 1.2). Specific earmarked grants should be reserved for incentive or corrective programs.

Bridging the Gap

The question of budget balancing is crucial. Which type of balance is required: a balanced current (operating) budget, or a balanced overall budget that encompasses current and capital items? In developing countries, this question seems to have a self-evident answer: given the inadequacy of financial resources, the requirement of overall budget balance is out of the question because it is virtually impossible to marshal sufficient cash flow to fund investments—a situation, moreover, that is not specific to developing countries.

The key issue, however, is that, given the difference between operating and investment expenditures, it is vital to clearly define the latter and implement a debt-servicing and management policy.[4] These considerations are at the core of the financial system and also define the degree of budget constraint and, ultimately, budget autonomy (Dafflon 1998; Dafflon and Beer-Tóth 2009). Note that figure 1.2 does not include loans as financial revenue because they are a means of paying for investments on the pay-as-you-use principle, but one day, real financial resources must be generated through taxation and assigned to debt servicing and reimbursement.

The two lower boxes of figure 1.2 illustrate imbalances leading to a deficit in the budget or the current account balance (spending in excess of revenue). If the situation persists, the appropriate response is to review the assignment of responsibilities or resources across the different government tiers, as indicated by the arrow [4] in figure 1.2. Financial transfers are only an alternative means of bridging the recorded gaps. In developing countries, budget deficits occur, above all, because general budget transfers fail to cover the expenses incurred by delegated responsibilities, which means that local governments are obliged to eat into their own or shared modest fiscal resources to bridge the gap. A second reason is that the central government sets excessively high standards for the provision of local public goods (LPGs); in this case, the delegation of responsibilities absorbs the financial capacity of local governments, which then have insufficient resources to discharge their devolved responsibilities.

The decentralized budget is the outcome of an iterative and sequential procedure that can be summarized as follows:

1. Assignment of responsibilities across government tiers
2. Inventory of delegated and devolved responsibilities
3. Evaluation of the expenditure incurred by these responsibilities
4. Assignment of concomitant resources
5. Discharge of responsibilities and taxation
6. Estimation of the result: a budget in balance or a budget deficit.

In the case of a deficit, the process is reinitialized, addressing these questions, related to the above sequence as follows:

1. Are the responsibilities truly devolved, or is it only the funding that is decentralized?
2. Are the standards set for delegated responsibilities too high?
3. Are the budget appropriations adequate?
4. Are "own resources" sufficient, or are they used up by having to comply with standards?

The next several sections of this chapter address these questions.

One key point mentioned just above needs particular attention. This relates to the practicalities of the budgetary, fiscal, accounting, and administrative systems used to classify the different financial operations resulting from local public expenditures (reflecting the services provided) and revenues. Decentralization can be managed successfully only if the accounting system is properly organized, provides verified and verifiable information, and enables an accurate breakdown of expenditure and revenue—classified not only according to the delegated and devolved responsibilities (functional classification in the budget and account; see table 1.1) but also according to the actual type of accounting operation (economic classification of outlays and revenues).

Table 1.1 Matrix of Functional Decentralization

Functions (1)		Central (2)	Regional (3)	Local (4)
0 Administration				
01	Municipal assembly (legislative)			
02	Municipal council (executive)			
03	Standing committees			
04	General administration			
1 Law and public order				
10	Legal protection			
11	Police			
12	Justice			
14	Fire services			
15	Army			
16	Civil protection			
2 Education and training				
20	Infant school			
210	Primary school			
212	Secondary school			
217	School transport			
22	Special needs schools			
23	Vocational training			
29	School administration			
3 Worship, culture, and recreation				
30	Culture			
31	Protection of monuments and sites			
32	Mass media			
33	Public parks and pedestrian areas			
34	Sport			
35	Other recreational activities			
39	Worship, churches			
4 Health				
40	Hospitals			
41	Nursing homes			
42	Psychiatric hospitals			
44	Outpatient care			
45	Disease prevention			
46	School health service			
47	Food control			

(continued next page)

Table 1.1 (continued)

Functions (1)		Central (2)	Regional (3)	Local (4)
5 Social services				
50	Social security benefits, old age pensions			
52	Sickness and accidents			
53	Other social insurance			
54	Youth protection			
55	Disabled care			
56	Construction of social housing			
57	Homes for the elderly			
58	Individual aid, social assistance			
6 Transportation and communications				
61	Roads			
62	Road works			
620	Pavements, pedestrian areas			
621	Parking facilities			
622	Maintenance center			
65	Regional traffic			
650	Public transport			
652	Tourist traffic			
66	Navigation			
67	Airports			
68	Communications			
7 Environment				
70	Water supply			
71	Sanitation			
72	Household waste			
73	Slaughterhouses			
74	Cemeteries			
75	Flood protection			
78	Protection of nature			
79	Town and country planning[a]			
8 Economy				
80	Agriculture			
81	Forests and vines			
82	Hunting and fishing			
83	Tourism			
84	Industry, crafts, and trade			

(continued next page)

Table 1.1 (continued)

Functions (1)		Central (2)	Regional (3)	Local (4)
9 Finances and taxes				
90	Taxes			
92	Financial equalization			
93	Revenue sharing			
94	Asset and debt management			
942	Management of financial assets			

Sources: Dafflon 1998, 46–47; Conference of the Cantons' Finance Ministers, Bern (harmonized public accounting system, 2008).
a. Decentralizing town and country planning raises the question of land-use management on two levels: (a) It involves ownership or access to ownership of land used for infrastructures, required both for construction (ownership of land on which a school building or town hall will be built) and civil engineering works (for example, roads and right of way for routing pipes for water supply or sewage). (b) It involves the real estate registry: although property rights are defined at the national level, the cadastral boundaries must be registered and known at the local level without ambiguity; this is necessary for development programs (Rochegude and Plançon 2009) and local tax collection.

The accounting system should also be able to provide statistics for measuring how decentralization is progressing. Finally, the system must be institutionalized so that it is simple enough to encourage democratic participation at the local level and lay the foundations for budget responsibility. As such, the institutionalization of an accounting system for subnational governments is not merely a technical exercise (see also the "Statistical Data" section). These requirements are paramount and must be integrated upstream of the decentralization process.

Assignment of Responsibilities between Tiers of Government

Genuine decentralization can be deployed only if local governments at least have the leeway, at the margin, to make decisions about the local public services they choose to provide on the basis of their own preferences. It is on this point that the distinction between devolved responsibilities and delegated powers takes on full meaning. The approach proposed here is based on an inventory of decentralized responsibilities and an institutional economy analysis of their decentralization that considers the following questions:

- Which responsibilities are decentralized? Are these listed in the constitution or in legal texts on decentralization, or else is delegation or devolution set out, responsibility by responsibility, in specific laws?
- What criteria are used for the vertical assignment of responsibilities?

- Can a distinction be made between delegation and devolution?
- Are the terms used to define the delegated or devolved functions precise, explicit, and common to the stakeholders of decentralization?
- What is the nature of each decentralized function: exclusive, competitive, or shared—and in what way?
- Have local governments been involved in the decentralization process, or have they been presented with a fait accompli?
- How does decentralization translate into budgets or accounts? In other words, do the accounts provide a functional classification of the cost centers, thus making it possible to measure the extent to which functions delegated or devolved to the local governments are decentralized?
- What statistical data on decentralized responsibilities are available to understand, measure, and steer the decentralization process?
- Is it standard practice to differentiate between current and capital expenditure, and for which responsibilities?
- Which responsibilities could be funded by user fees?
- Can "hidden transfers" be identified—that is to say, arrangements that provide transfers "in kind" for delivery of an LPG (by supplying a production input, such as personnel seconded by the central government to the local government and who remain on the central government's payroll)?

Table 1.1 should be viewed as an indicative list of decentralized functions. Its purpose is to compare two levels of information: The rows break down the functional classification of decentralized areas of competence. The columns show the administrative mapping of institutional divisions.

Functional Classification

By way of example, for the row headings, we use the functional classification that has been widely applied by Swiss local governments for some 30 years and stands as the harmonized public accounting system (2008 version). Needless to say, the nomenclature varies from one developing country to another and must be tailored to the national setting under study. We simply wish here to show that a domain-based logic should underpin the breakdown of decentralized responsibilities. This logic not only makes it easier to study the political economy of decentralization but also helps to structure the accounting system used for budgets and accounts. It facilitates the transfer of results in coherent statistical series to enable macroeconomic steering of decentralization programs and measurement of results. At the local level, it guarantees transparency and availability of information on spending, which are key qualities for good local governance (accountability) and participative democracy (acceptability).

Institutional Mapping of the Territory

Here, the scope must be explicitly defined in advance. The proposed starting point is to take the government tiers defined in the constitution or national legislation. For the sake of simplicity, we have taken here (as in table 1.1) the three traditional tiers of decentralization (central, regional, and local), but there may be intermediate situations: for example, intermunicipal cooperation may be recognized as a functional territorial unit if individual municipalities are too small to perform a function that is nonetheless devolved to the local level (see figure 1.1). In this case, an extra column would need to be inserted between the columns 3 and 4 in table 1.1 to cover "intermunicipal cooperation," specifying its legal status.

One important and troublesome aspect of this table is the distinction between decentralized territorial organization and deconcentrated organization. This distinction must be pinpointed and made explicit. In fact, in many developing countries, a "region" is sometimes the middle tier of the decentralized organization and sometimes the result of deconcentrated administrative mapping; this therefore needs to be indicated. Confusion may arise if, within the same country, the same term denotes at the same time a decentralized local government unit and a deconcentrated entity. The type of territorial unit concerned must thus be clarified each time.

Analytical method   This part of the study aims to build a comprehensive picture of decentralization both at an institutional level and in practice. The process breaks down into three steps:

1. Table 1.1 is completed strictly on the basis of the legal texts governing decentralization. Using institutional political economics, it is then possible to analyze the coherence of the decentralization process, verify that there is no confusion in the terms and descriptions used, check on the use of decentralization criteria, and ensure that stated objectives match the recommended institutional approach.

2. The completed "institutional matrix" is compared with its implementation on the ground at the grassroots level. The method uses interviews and the analysis of documents (particularly accounting and statistical documents) that enable verification. One can then measure the convergence between the intentions entered into the institutional matrix, the way they are perceived by the actors of decentralization, and actual achievements.

3. Statistical expenditure data are collected (as discussed in the "Statistical Data" section) on the basis of a functional classification to measure the degree of decentralization by function. Time series data, if available, are used to track and analyze the evolution of the decentralization process.

Shared responsibilities   One of the foremost problems in decentralization involves "shared" responsibilities. This term is imprecise and needs clarification, especially because this situation is frequently found in developing countries. The term can encompass several realities that need some explanation: Does "shared" mean a joint decision about which public service to deliver; joint responsibility for implementation; or simply cofinancing?

Saying that a function—state-funded primary education, for instance—is a responsibility shared between the local and central levels under the supervision of the Ministry of Education, with no further explanation, leads to difficult and eventually conflicting situations. For example, if the responsibility is "shared," each government level may wait for the other level to take the initiative and ensure implementation and financing: as a result, either nothing gets done or, in the end, the central government takes everything in hand, which de facto creates a deconcentrated function. Or each level may act on its own count, leading to overlaps and waste. One way out of this situation is to not view the task as a whole and instead disaggregate the production function to identify the different inputs and assign exclusive responsibility for each of them to one government level. The result is a shared responsibility that is not imprecise and indeterminate but rather clearly specified for each input.

This analytical approach also makes it possible to flush out implicit transfers that may be linked to a function. "Implicit transfer" is understood to mean that the central government supplies the local government with centrally funded resources (both human and material). This is equivalent to services in kind, which leave no financial trace in the local governments' budgets. In table 1.2, the domains in columns 3, 5, 6, and 7 are potential recipients of implicit transfers. The objective for case studies is not to establish an exhaustive list of implicit transfers but to draw the budgetary authority's attention to the fact that explicit financial transfers do not cover the whole range of vertical financial relations between central and local governments.

Table 1.2 takes the example of compulsory primary education. Following the same logic of the institutional economy analysis described earlier in table 1.1, the matrix in table 1.2 uses two inputs. The rows show the institutionally recognized tiers of government. The columns show the inputs of the production function for a specific task. Using this method, the analysis can be replicated for almost all functions likely to be delegated or devolved.

In addition to the central, regional, and local tiers used earlier, we have added a row titled "intermunicipal syndicate." This is intended as a reminder that if municipalities are too small to assume some of the functions assigned to the local level or if economies of scale can be made, institutional solutions exist in the form of intermunicipal cooperation. Rather than add another layer to the decentralized institutional design, local service provision is rationalized. It thus

Table 1.2 Sample Matrix of Shared Governmental Responsibilities and Implicit Transfers in Primary Education

Assignment of responsibilities (government level) (1)	Teacher training (2)	Salaries and employment status of teachers (3)	School curriculum content (4)	Teaching materials (5)	Technical equipment (6)	School buildings • maintenance • construction (7)	School management and organization (8)
Central							
Regional							
Intermunicipal syndicate[a]							
Local							
Implicit transfers[b] identified							

Source: Dafflon 2006, 296–98.
a. "Intermunicipal syndicate" designates an arrangement of two or more small municipalities that join responsibility (cooperate) to successfully assume certain functions or to achieve economies of scale.
b. "Implicit transfers" are centrally funded resources (both human and material) that the central government supplies to local governments. Such transfers, like in-kind services, leave no financial trace in the local governments' budgets.

becomes unnecessary, and inappropriate, to transfer this responsibility to the government tier immediately above.

The production function of compulsory education (in the strict sense) can be split into the seven components shown in table 1.2, each characterized by its own degree of decentralization, described either as delegation or devolution. Although the responsibility for education is "shared," it is not shared overall but rather should be exclusive for each component. It is the combination of these exclusive responsibilities that makes it possible to say that the two government tiers (in this case, central and local) jointly share responsibility for the function. This requires that they set up joint decision-making and coordination procedures. The central government can retain its authority over teacher training for reasons of national unity, subsequent mobility of teachers, and the homogeneity of school curricula, while the other tasks can be decentralized. However, for each of these tasks, both centripetal and centrifugal arguments can be put forward, with the final outcome and degree of decentralization dependent on the weight assigned to each argument in the production function. Thus, the school production function can be entirely decentralized except for the tasks relating to teachers' professional status and salaries—which remain under central authority and paid for by the central government, both to ensure equal treatment and a homogeneous distribution of teaching skills and to avoid strategic behavior by local governments (the wealthier local governments being able to attract better teachers by offering higher salaries).

Budget Decentralization versus Decision-Making Autonomy

With respect to decentralized budgets, the example discussed serves to highlight the distinction between the measurement of budget decentralization and local government budget or decision-making autonomy. In the area of expenditure, budget decentralization is measured by calculating the share of expenditure (the overall total or by function) for each government tier in the aggregate public expenditure of all government tiers. Thus,

$$\text{Budget decentralization ratio} = \frac{\text{total municipal expenditures}}{\text{total public expenditures}} \quad (1.1)$$

gives the expenditure of all municipalities (communes) as a share of total public sector spending (central, regional, and local [municipal] levels).

Local government decision-making autonomy in spending is measured by the proportion of own functions compared with delegated functions. In the decentralized budget, this proportion corresponds to the numerical elements ([1], [2], and [3]) previously shown in figure 1.2:

$$\text{local decision–making autonomy} = \frac{[1] + [2 \text{ in part (financed through user fees)}]}{[3] + [2 \text{ in part (total 2 minus that part financed through user fees)}]} = \frac{[1] + [2 \text{ in part}]}{[3] + [2 \text{ balance}]}. \quad (1.2)$$

This proportion can reveal a high level of expenditure decentralization in the sense that the weight of local public budgets in the total public budget (central government + local governments) is increasing. Yet, it may well be that local-level spending follows the rules and standards set by the line ministries. In this case, local governments become the executing agents in a principal-agent relationship, with no power to decide which policies they wish to adopt. (The following section addresses by analogy the distinction between fiscal sovereignty and financial autonomy.)

An analysis of the distinction between budget decentralization and decision-making autonomy is performed in two steps. The first step is to assess—sometimes even cursorily if statistical gaps exist—the share of local expenditure over which local governments in developing countries have some discretion. Ideally (but in practice still far from achievable, even in advanced economies), the second step would entail identifying for each function the residual responsibilities that genuinely belong to the local governments by assessing the density of legal standards with which they must comply.

Revenue Structures and Systems

The Principle of Concomitance

In public finance, two maxims of fiscal federalism and decentralization serve as basic principles: (a) "finance follows functions," and (b) "the one who decides must also pay." The sense of the first should be limpid, at least in concept if not in application: levying taxes is not an end in itself but serves to finance local public goods and services. It should thus first be decided which functions will be assigned to local governments, and then financial resources should be adjusted accordingly. This holds particularly true for developing countries: given their weak tax bases—and hence the crucial role of financial transfers—decentralization would be no more than wishful thinking if the maxim were turned on its head and decentralization tailored to fit the local governments' available own resources. Decentralization laws listing the functions to be assigned to local governments often mention a *concomitant* transfer of financial resources. What thus needs to be verified is the extent to which this principle is respected in the institutional design and in practice.

The second maxim is a two-way street. On one side, local governments that choose to provide their own public goods and services must bear the financial consequences of their decisions—more precisely, they must also decide which taxes will finance them. On the other side, if a higher tier of government imposes rules and standards for the provision of some local services (mandated functions), this same tier must bear the costs by ensuring equivalent financial transfers. In the decentralized budget (again following the taxonomy in figure 1.2), this means setting out expenditures and revenues in parallel as follows:

- [1] ≅ [A] for own choice spending, at the level of taxes;
- [2] ≅ [B] for those specific functions funded by user fees; and, above all,
- [3] ≅ [C] for financial transfers.

A widespread problem in developing countries, and directly related to this principle, stems from the fact that mandatory spending needs [3] are often too high compared with the transfers received [C]. The result is that the local governments either cannot deliver local public services in line with quantity and quality requirements or are forced to draw on their own resources [A], which leaves them with insufficient resources to fund their own choices. The difficulty lies in balancing these two aspects: the standards imposed by a supervisory central authority must not be too high and, at the same time, the corresponding transfers must be commensurate with the costs originating from this oversight. The *principle of concomitance* expresses this equilibrium and, during case studies, it is therefore paramount to check whether it is respected.

BOX 1.1

Tax Terms Defined

The definitions presented below do not preclude other definitions and must therefore be seen more as conventions that enable us to know we are talking about.

Exclusive Tax
A tax for which only one tier of government can exploit the tax base and collect all of the revenue.

Shared Tax
Several tiers of government have access to the same tax base.

If each government has *full fiscal sovereignty*, each can define the tax base, and there will be as many definitions as government units, with obvious coordination and harmonization problems.

A government has *partial fiscal sovereignty* when it can set part of the taxation criteria (for example, the tax base, exemptions, deductions, tax spending, and tax rate schedule). Taxes that have the same base but are shared by several tiers of government, each of which freely sets the tax rate, enter into this shared-tax-base category.

Fiscal flexibility means that a government sets only the tax coefficient (the base, deductions, and schedules remaining identical). Also in this category are systems that apply additional levies (piggyback taxes).

Finally, *mandatory taxation* means that a government is not free to choose and must levy a tax in compliance with the rules set by a higher tier of government.

Revenue Sharing
Generally, the tax base and the tax rate are set by the higher-tier government that collects the tax, but a fixed share of the tax revenue is apportioned to the government units belonging to the lower tier.

Two methods of revenue sharing exist, depending on whether sharing is based on

- The amount of tax revenue collected in the local government unit concerned, according to the origin criterion (also called the "principle of derivation"); or
- A distribution formula that includes various criteria (such as population size) or is designed to reduce disparities in fiscal capacity ("revenue equalization").

Source: Dafflon and Madiès 2008, 44.

Inventory of Resources

The approach to resource inventory is based on three matrices, each organized along the lines of table 1.3, in this proposed sequence:

- *Matrix 1*: an inventory of institutional and legal provisions
- *Matrix 2*: an account of on-the-ground practices
- *Matrix 3*: available figures and statistical data.

The purpose of Matrix 1 is to list the institutional and legal basis for each resource—constitution, laws, ordinances, and implementing regulations—if necessary, including a history in the event of recent or ongoing changes. The legal inventory must make it possible to identify the basis for each local resource and then to construct the institutional economy analysis, notably the match between the stated goals and the mechanism chosen.

Matrix 2—which replicates Matrix 1—gives an account of practices on the ground and reflects the current state of play in (a) the local implementation of

Table 1.3 Sample Matrix of Financial Resources, by Government Tier

Resources (1)	Central (2)	Regional (3)	Local (4)
Fiscal resources			
1.0 Taxes			
1.1. List of taxes…			
1.2.			
1.3. Property tax[a]			
… (1 to G tax in the equation [1.4])			
2.0 User fees and charges			
2.1			
2.2			
… (G+1 to K in equation [1.5])			
Municipal assets and property			
3.0 Income from municipal assets and property			
3.1. Income from rental, rents			
3.2 Disposals (one-off proceeds)			
… (K+1 to P in equation [1.6])			
Intergovernmental transfers			
4.0 Intergovernmental transfers and grants			
4.1. Block, unconditional			
4.2. Specific, earmarked for a function			
4.3. Equalization (to be specified: own; in addition to 4.1. or 4.2)			
… (P+1 to Z in equation [1.7])			
External transfers			
5.0 External transfers			
5.1. International aid			
5.2. Nongovernmental organizations			
5.3. Pool of financial aid			
5.4. Donations from expatriates, former residents			
… (P+1 to Z in equation [1.7])			

Source: Dafflon 2010a.
a. See note (b) under table 1.1.

the legal provisions listed in Matrix 1, and (b) the review of financial practice at local level (that is, how the resources allocated to the local governments are actually paid). The aim is to pinpoint the gaps between the local governments' objective circumstances and actual practice in the areas of taxation and transfers. These gaps enable an initial assessment of the financing risks, notably with regard to the consequences for the local governments' long-term solvency and thus their decision-making capacity.

Matrix 3 contains straightforward statistical data, on the same lines as the expenditure allocation between functions, for two or three tiers of government: respectively, for the source of own, transferred, shared, and external resources. The analysis must carry out sample checks to ensure the selected year is representative. Insofar as tax data and transfers are subject to large annual fluctuations, the analysis must try to examine a multiyear period, to be defined depending on the context.

The inventory of resources must first make the distinction between tax revenues and the intergovernmental financial transfers received. For tax revenues, a distinction will be made between own exclusive resources and shared taxes. Own resources will, as far as possible, be divided into three categories: (a) taxes, (b) user charges and fees, and (c) proceeds from commercial activities and municipal assets and properties. For transfers in the case of developing countries, it is imperative to separate "intergovernmental" transfers and "external" transfers. Table 1.3, indicating the different resources, serves as a general framework for this inventory. The classification of transfers as general or specific grants or as matching project grants is important and must be informed.

It should be specifically noted that loans do not constitute real revenues but are simply a financial resource for funding investments or providing cash resources to temporarily bridge a financing gap. The loan must be repaid later from fiscal revenue, which is real revenue. By the same count, it should be noted that each loan-financed capital investment will give rise not only to debt servicing (interest and principal) but also to recurrent expenditures related to running the infrastructure (for example, energy, maintenance, or caretaking services) and to the new or additional service supported by this investment (Dafflon and Beer-Tóth 2009). This observation also holds for local investments financed by central government transfers (in the "Financial Transfers" section, see the last paragraph, on risk).

Measurement of Financial Autonomy

A frequent complaint from local authorities in developing countries—justified in the context of the devolution of powers to local governments—concerns the lack of financial autonomy. These stakeholders are nonetheless much less precise, and often in disagreement, about how to define this autonomy. Once again, it is not in itself surprising that definitions diverge; what matters is that the stakeholders in the decentralization process start by agreeing on what they mean by "financial autonomy" and on how it is to be measured, so that they can then use a common language.

Let us consider the following series of equations representing a total of (Z) origins of resources (R) of a local government, namely taxes (T), user charges (UC), revenues from municipal assets (MA), and financial transfers (TRANS):

$$R = T + UC + MA + TRANS, \tag{1.3}$$

$$T = \sum_{i=1}^{G} T_i, \tag{1.4}$$

$$UC = \sum_{i=G+1}^{K} UC_i, \tag{1.5}$$

$$MA = \sum_{i=K+1}^{P} MA_i, \tag{1.6}$$

$$TRANS = \sum_{i=P+1}^{Z} TRANS_i, \tag{1.7}$$

or, for each tax,

$$T_i = t_i \times [B_i - \sum_{j=1}^{n} D_{ij}] \times K_i, \tag{1.8}$$

where i = the tax involved in the 1-to-G taxes assigned to local governments;
t = the tax rate schedule;
B = the tax base;
D_j = the possible j tax adjustments, deductions, and expenditures; and
K = the annual tax coefficient required for a balanced budget.

This formulation raises a series of questions that give insight into the structures and systems of decentralized resources and their actual scope. These are pivotal questions for decentralization because, without adequate means, local governments are powerless in relation to the central authority, and "decentralization" then becomes more akin to "deconcentration."

The question could also be raised as to whether local own resources are appropriate. In other words, does TRANS cover funding of the centrally mandated standardized functions, while T covers the local government's own spending decisions? UC revenues are of limited availability as they are earmarked exclusively for the services for which they are collected. This means that a UC levied, for example, on drinking-water consumption must be used to finance the water services and cannot be treated as a profit accruing to the municipality's general budget. Otherwise, this would qualify as a hidden consumption tax, which would distort the price signaling that underpins the "user pays" or "polluter pays" principle (Dafflon and Madiès 2008, 56–60). Similarly, the MA resources should first be used for the maintenance of the municipal assets and property that generate these resources before any surplus is allocated to the municipality's general budget.

How do the various tax bases (B_i) evolve: in line with local economic development or with the functions assigned to local government? The theory of fiscal federalism holds that the property tax is a "good" tax because its base is fixed, thus guaranteeing a regular yield, and it can neither disappear nor be exported. Yet, aside from the technical resources needed to manage this tax (Dafflon and Madiès 2008, 54), it is clearly a far-from-perfect option as far as yields and tax revenue growth are concerned: once cadastral values have been assessed, the tax base barely expands (unless land use is modified and values are adjusted accordingly).

What parameters have an impact on local autonomy? Here, the measurement of fiscal sovereignty and financial autonomy must not be confused:

- *Fiscal sovereignty* exists when a local government has the discretionary power to design its tax structure and freely set the calculation formulas. This is tantamount to examining which of the variables in equation (1.7)—t, B, D, or K—can be defined and modified by a local government, but also which combination of the various taxes (from 1 to G in T) and user charges and fees (from $G+1$ to K in UC) it can decide on.

- *Financial autonomy* is expressed as the proportion of own revenues in the total resources of local governments—or in other words, the revenue sources in equations (1.4), (1.5), and (1.6) in proportion to total revenues (equation 1.3), that is:

$$\frac{(1.4)T + (1.5)UC + (1.6)MA}{(1.3)R}. \tag{1.9}$$

Thus, the local governments may enjoy a large degree of "sovereignty" in setting the local property tax. Yet we know that, once introduced, this tax generates scant revenue, and the annual growth of this resource is low compared with the pace of growth of the local economy or decentralized functions. The outcome is a high degree of fiscal sovereignty that fails to bring with it a high degree of financial autonomy. The pattern of local revenues must be carefully examined because this is an important piece of the tax puzzle: How does this pattern compare with that of the fiscal revenues assigned to the central government and with the variations in gross domestic product?

Financial Transfers

In developing countries, financial transfers are the backbone of decentralization. At the outset, local governments have only limited own resources. This means that decentralization can only be implemented if the assignment of functions is backed up by an adequate level of intergovernmental grants, not only for recurrent operating expenditures but also for spending on investments and equipment. Hence the importance given to this part of the analysis, which, is again based on three matrices (each modeled on table 1.3), with no change in the sequencing:

- *Matrix 1*: an inventory of institutional and legal provisions
- *Matrix 2*: an account of on-the-ground practices
- *Matrix 3*: available figures and statistical data.

Current State of Play
The first step in establishing the inventory of financial transfers is to identify their legal basis and the existing transfer mechanisms. The transfers are then organized according to their economic justification or on the basis of a grant typology combining five criteria (Dafflon and Madiès 2008, 74–85). This information is found in columns 2 (design) and 3 (benchmark) of the analytical matrix in table 1.4.

The first type of classification—according to the economic justification—must

- Specify the objective of the transfer, analyze whether the amount is appropriate to the objective, and assess performance;
- Following the typology, distinguish operating transfers from those linked to investment; and
- Depending on the use, successively calculate
  - the specific formulas and measurements for the indicators of the different types of transfers,
  - the availability of funds, and
  - the expected result.

Institutional Economy Analysis

The gathered information is then examined from a political economy standpoint and compared with the situation on the ground. To simplify and frame the institutional analysis, we have established a "decide-implement-control-sanction" chain:

- Who *decides* what, how, and when?
- Who *implements* what, how, and when?
- Who *controls* what, how, and when?
- Who *sanctions* what, how, and when?

The field analysis adds the issues of capacity and managerial constraints: Did the local government participate in the design of objectives and means, and are they able to understand them (that is, to relate the macroeconomic objectives to their local interests)? Do they have the resources to manage the toolkit?

The proposed analytical matrix is organized as shown in table 1.4.

Columns 4 and 8 contain the findings of the institutional analysis and the verification on the ground. The gap between the legal basis (design) for the financial transfer and the benchmark is primarily used to establish whether the organizational arrangements for these transfers (that is, the amount available, the distribution formula, and the implementation arrangements) match the objectives and mechanisms stated in the design. In a nutshell, is the legislation well or poorly designed with respect to the targeted objective? This is not a measurement of monetary value but an assessment based on the benchmark economic justifications summarized by Dafflon and Madiès (2008, 74–85).

Table 1.4 Sample Analytical Matrix of Financial Transfers

Type of transfer (1)	Legal basis (design) (2)	Benchmark (3)	Gap between columns 2 and 3 (4)	Other type of intervention (5)	Opportunity cost (6)	Field analysis (7)	Gap between objective and situation on the ground (8)
Transfer 1 decide implement control sanction							
Transfer 2 decide implement control sanction							

Because the same benchmark is used across the four countries studied, the specific situations must then be contextualized in columns 5 and 6, which are explicitly for this purpose. Which reasons are given to depart from the announced legal objectives or economic justification of the transfers? Column 8 describes the divergences between design and practice: More simply, is the law effectively enforced on the ground? To what extent do achievements match expectations? How do local governments assume ownership of the objectives and mechanisms in view of their own preferences? Are the goals and resources hijacked by local strategies?

Information Asymmetry, Moral Hazard, and Risk Assessment

The assessment in column 8 of table 1.4 must be coordinated and harmonized for the four countries under study. Three questions need to be addressed—concerning information, moral hazard, and risk—from a fourfold perspective: decision, implementation, control of performance, and sanction. This nomenclature is not exhaustive: it can be reviewed, completed, or corrected for each case study in line with the experience acquired in the field. Table 1.5 serves as a framework and would be completed on the basis of the data gathered in table 1.4.

Information   Information is understood to mean the information available and required to implement the transfers and the strategies used for this purpose. The experience acquired in other assessments of decentralization shows, for example, the following:

- The objectives of financial transfers are only vaguely specified by the legislator, which creates a gray area, leaving a wide margin of maneuver for subsequent implementation.

- The objective is not necessarily stated but has been adjusted (and justified a posteriori) more or less appropriately to match the resources and distribution formulas put in place.

- The transfers are not based on formulas that meet explicit criteria or are safe from manipulation but rather on ad hoc calculations.

Moral hazard   By moral hazard, we refer to the temptation for different tiers of government to rationally take advantage of the fact that the other

Table 1.5 Sample Matrix for Intergovernmental Financial Transfer Issues

	Information	Moral hazard	Risk
Decision			
Implementation			
Control			
Sanction			

government tiers are not aware of their behavior. There is obviously a direct and proportional inverse relationship between the availability of information and moral hazard. Moral hazard is greatly reduced if the design of transfers has been clearly defined and grounded in verifiable data that is not open to manipulations by either the grantor or recipient local government. Conversely, the hazier the transfer design, the more exposed its implementation becomes to strategic behavior. Here again, experience shows that it is the "offices" (line ministries and departments) that take advantage of the situation, producing a result that is closer to deconcentration than devolution.

Risk   Risk is taken to mean the observed and foreseeable variability in the financial transfer amounts (risks linked to a poor transfer design, economic activity, capture by higher government tiers, politics, and so forth). For instance, a risky transfer design is one in which an investment grant contributes substantially to funding an infrastructure but then fails to take into account the recurrent costs generated by the infrastructure (maintenance costs and the costs of local public services generated by the new infrastructure).

In the case of financial transfers for investment operations, the analyst's reflex is to check whether these transfers are coordinated with operating transfers over the long run because the latter are directly linked to subsequent recurrent costs. If no coordination exists, two situations may arise: either (a) the local government does not commit to the investment, knowing that later it will not have the resources to operate the infrastructure—and the intended incentive policy fails; or (b) the local government commits itself blindly, knowing that it can then force the central government to cover the resulting budget shortfall, which completely negates the notion of budget responsibility that goes hand in hand with decentralization.

Statistical Data

The reliability of statistics, whose time series data can be used to measure the decentralization of responsibilities and resources, is a tricky issue in developing countries. When statistical data exist, even plentifully, it is difficult to exploit them because they are poorly organized from a decentralization perspective. It is difficult at this stage to obtain a relatively precise picture of the true extent of decentralized responsibilities or to measure the performance of institutional devolution or the relative financial autonomy of local governments. The reasons for this state of affairs are many and will be mentioned later in the country-specific chapters.

The basis of statistics is a properly kept public accounting system, which must satisfy at least four requirements:

- Integrate and classify in a budget, then in the accounts, all the financial operations of a government unit, using a classification by both function and type.
- Enable public services costs to be calculated for management purposes, and, where possible and adequate, account for earmarked revenue under the functional head it concerns.
- Enable forecasting and planning.
- Supply the information needed for political decision making within a democratic system.

At the central level, the statistics from the local governments make it possible to

- Steer the macroeconomic aspects of local public policy in a coordinated manner.
- Steer decentralization through the assignment of functions and the allocation of resources.
- Measure the results of decentralization as a process stretching over several years.
- Correct budget imbalances through institutional reorganization.
- Correct budget disparities through equalization.

Classification by Function

Functional classification indicates the local governments' areas of activity and functions. It should distinguish not only the different functions but also the different subfunctions that may exist within each function, if necessary subdividing them into cost centers.

The benchmark for this study is table 1.1, which previously showed the functional classification of expenditures for government levels over one year: it provides a snapshot of decentralization. If decentralization is recent or ongoing, it is crucial to have access to time series data giving the circumstances *before* and *after* the start of decentralization and thereafter the changes from year to year.

It should be noted that the statistical tables of expenditures by function and by government level, even when time series data are used, provide information only on the degree of decentralization but reveal nothing about the decision-making autonomy of local governments. One of the key difficulties in this respect is distinguishing between delegated and devolved functions or, for shared functions, identifying which responsibilities are exclusively assigned to one level or another. A further difficulty stems from the fact that the principle of inclusive accounting (all accounting items in one book) is not observed. In developing countries, one frequently finds that the local expenditures funded by transfers from the central government are recorded in the budget line of the ministry or department concerned but not in the municipal accounts—where the transferred revenue does not appear, either. As a result, it is difficult to retrace and reconstruct the overall financial flows affecting the municipality.

Classification by Type

Accounting classification serves to clarify the content of the budget operations recorded in public accounts: revenue or expenses, book entries for current or capital accounts, and those entries that concern the closing or balance sheet. It must also provide information showing whether the entries record purely accounting transactions—that is, with no cash receipts or payments (such as internal charging)—or financial transactions. If well organized, classification by type also shows the economic content of expenditures and revenues (table 1.6).

Table 1.6 Economic Classification of Public Expenditure and Revenue

Expenditure	Revenue
Current	
30 Wages, personnel expenditures	40 Revenues from taxation
31 Material and equipment, services	
32 Interests on debt	42 Revenues from properties, sales
33 Amortization[a]	43 User charges, fees, sales
34 Block (nonearmarked) grants	44 General block grants, revenue sharing
35 Reimbursement and participation in other jurisdictions	45 Reimbursement from other jurisdictions
36 Earmarked grants-in-aid	46 Subsidies received
37 Transfers redistributed	47 Earmarked grants-in-aid received
38 Reserve funding	48 Levy from reserve funds
39 Internal charge recording	49 Internal revenue recording
Capital	
50 Own investments	60 Disposal of property
	61 Access charges
52 Loans and participation in other jurisdictions' capital expenditures	62 Repayment of loans
	63 Capital payments from third parties
	66 Grants-in-aid for investments
57 Transfers redistributed	67 Transfers for redistribution

Sources: Dafflon 1998, 50–51; harmonized public accounting system in Switzerland.
a. Amortization corresponds to the pay-as-you-use principle for financing capital expenditures. It corresponds to the span of economic use of the investment. For example, if a school building is financed by a loan and can be used for 25 years before heavy maintenance costs, then the linear rate of amortization would be 4 percent. Effective reimbursement of the debt, through annual installments, should also correspond to the amortization in the books. See Dafflon and Beer-Tóth (2009).

Classification by type is the most commonly used system at the local level in the developing countries. This is partly useful in the sense that it provides information about the nature of the expenditures. In particular, the size of personnel-related expenditures says a great deal about the nature of decentralization—centered primarily on consumption rather than policy programs and, if this category of spending is predominant, centered on bureaucracy rather than functions. Combined with a functional classification, it becomes highly useful for assessing decentralization. By crossing this reading with an institutional approach, one can fine-tune the question of shared responsibility (for example, in the case of state education; see table 1.2). This also means that one can establish the relation between user fees or charges levied for a given function and the assignment of these revenues.

Resources

The statistical needs regarding resources were fully explained previously in table 1.3, which listed the nomenclature for revenues. This nomenclature also corresponds to the classification by type shown in table 1.6 but in greater detail. This information is vital for analyzing the decentralized budget, measuring local government financial autonomy, and assessing how decentralization is performing.

Although economic logic places the assignment of responsibilities across government tiers ahead of revenue sharing, it is obvious that, in practice, budget constraints on the revenue side are vital if policies for the delegation and devolution of powers are to succeed. To steer and successfully implement decentralization, it is crucial to be fully informed of the values of these indicators.

Conclusion

The six sections in this chapter—the institutional approach to decentralization, the decentralized budget, the assignment of responsibilities across levels of government, revenue sharing, financial transfers, and statistical data—provide the scaffolding for the country studies presented in the following chapters on Burkina Faso, Ghana, Kenya, and Senegal. The developments and comments that this chapter has proposed as an interpretive guide are by no means exhaustive. The study by Dafflon and Madiès (2008) on these same issues addresses the question in greater depth.

The choices made here were guided by the study mandate from AFD for these four Sub-Saharan African countries and also, to a large extent, by preliminary feedback from the local missions. The authors of the following chapters drew substantially but not exclusively from this feedback. The ambition is to provide the reader with a logically structured comparison of the problems encountered in these countries, while at the same time giving each group of authors sufficient leeway to describe and analyze the specific institutional design and practices of the countries visited, as federalism is first and foremost a respect for differences.

Notes

1. This vision is said to be "European" because it is in Europe that the first theoretical and practical doubts emerged as to the assertions and conclusions of the classical model. The pioneer contribution was that of Wiseman (1989).
2. In a discussion paper published in 2006, Weingast concurs with the view of the European school and points out that second-generation fiscal federalism must reverse the thinking on this subject. Thus his introduction:

   Much fiscal analysis of developing countries is on the following pattern: the academic literature is drawn on to construct a model fiscal system; the existing situation in a particular country is examined to determine how it diverges from the model; and a fiscal reform is then proposed to transform what is into what ought to be. This approach is deficient because it does not require sufficient detailed examination of existing reality to ensure that the assumptions postulated in the model are congruent with reality, that the recommended changes can in fact be implemented, or that, if implemented, they will in fact produce the desired results.

   In contrast, my approach is first to study in detail exactly how the existing system works, and why it works that way, in order to have a firm basis for understanding what changes may be both desirable and feasible. My emphasis has thus always been more on what can be done than on what should be done. (Weingast 2006)

3. Here, we will mention only the best-known political definition of autonomy, commonly accepted by developed countries and transition economies: that provided by *The European Charter of Local Self-Government* and its *Explanatory Report* (Council of Europe [1986] 1996).
4. The distinction between current and capital budgets is not simply an accounting and operational issue for the decentralization of functions. The ownership of the public infrastructures that ensure local service provision goes hand in hand with the decentralization of functions: if the local authority is to deliver a service, it should also own the infrastructure (building and equipment) underpinning this service provision.

References

Bird, R.-M., and R.-D. Ebel, eds. 2007. *Fiscal Fragmentation in Decentralized Countries: Subsidiarity, Solidarity and Asymmetry.* Cheltenham, U.K.: Edward Elgar; Washington, DC: World Bank.

Blindenbacher, R., and A. Koller, eds. 2003. *Federalism in a Changing World: Learning from Each Other.* Montreal and Kingston: McGill-Queen's University Press.

Council of Europe. (1986) 1996. *The European Charter of Local Self-Government* and its *Explanatory Report.* Strasbourg: Council of Europe Publishing.

Dafflon, B. 1998. *La gestion des finances publiques locales.* Paris: Economica.

———. 2006. "The Assignment of Functions to Decentralized Government: From Theory to Practice." In *Handbook of Fiscal Federalism*, ed. E. Ahmad and G. Brosio, 271–305. Cheltenham, U.K.: Edward Elgar.

———. 2009. "Strengthening Fiscal Decentralization at the Local Level in India." In *Final Report on Local Governance in India*, Swiss Agency for Cooperation and Development, New Delhi. http://www.unifr.ch/finpub/fr/research/publications/gouvernance-locale.

———. 2010a. "Fédéralisme financier et décentralisation." Master's course, University of Fribourg, September 2010. http://www.unifr.ch/finpub/fr/studies/courses/master/federalisme_financier.

———. 2010b. "Strengthening Gram Panchayat Planning and Budgeting in Sikkim." Report on Village Action Development Plan for Sikkim for supporting the Rural Management and Development Department (RMDD) in preparing guidelines for grassroots planning. Gangtok, Sikkim and Indo-Swiss Mission to Sikkim, Swiss Agency for Development and Cooperation (SDC) Swiss Embassy, New Delhi. http://www.unifr.ch/finpub/assets/files/RecherchesPublications/GouvernanceLocale/Sikkim2.pdf.

———. 2011. "Conceptual Problems in the Assignment of Functions in SEE: The Case of Albania." In *Decentralization in Developing Countries: Global Perspectives on the Obstacles to Fiscal Devolution*, ed. J. Martinez-Vazquez and F. Vaillancourt, 23–81. Cheltenham, U.K.: Edward Elgar.

Dafflon, B., and K. Beer-Tóth. 2009. "Managing Local Public Debt in Transition Countries: An Issue of Self-Control." *Financial Accountability and Management* 25 (3): 305–33.

Dafflon, B., and T. Madiès. 2008. "Décentralisation: quelques principes issus de la théorie du fédéralisme financier." ["Decentralization: A Few Principles from the Theory of Fiscal Federalism."] Notes and documents 42, Agence Française de Développement, Paris.

Gauthier, I., and F. Vaillancourt. 2002. "Déconcentration, délégation et dévolution: nature, choix et mise en place." Unpublished manuscript, World Bank Institute, Washington, DC.

Lockwood, B. 2006. "The Political Economy of Decentralization." In *Handbook of Fiscal Federalism*, ed. E. Ahmad and G. Brosio, 33–60. Cheltenham, U.K.: Edward Elgar.

Olson, M. 1969. "The Principle of 'Fiscal Equivalence': The Division of Responsibilities among Different Levels of Government." *The American Economic Review* 59 (2): 479–87.

Rochegude, A., and C. Plançon. 2009. "Décentralisation, acteurs locaux et foncier." In *Foncier & développement* Web portal, Fiches pays, Comité technique, Ministère des Affaires Etrangères et Européennes, Paris. http://www.foncier-developpement.org/outils/cadres-legislatifs-et-institutionnels/.

Tóth, K. 2007. "Fiscal Decentralisation in Transition Economies: The World Bank in a Learning Process." In *The World Bank and Governance: A Decade of Reform and Reaction*, ed. D. Stone and C. Wright, 247–67. London: Routledge.

Weingast, B. R. 2006. "Second Generation Fiscal Federalism: Implications for Decentral-ized Democratic Governance and Economic Development." Working paper, Hoover Institution on War, Revolution, and Peace, Stanford University, Stanford, CA. http://ssrn.com/abstract=1153440 or http://dx.doi.org/10.2139/ssrn.1153440.

Wiseman, J. 1989. "The Political Economy of Federalism: A Critical Appraisal." In *Cost, Choice, and Political Economy*, ed. J. Wiseman, 71–111. Aldershot, U.K.: Edward Elgar.

Chapter 2

Local Public Finance of Territorial Collectivities in Burkina Faso

Bernard Dafflon and Thierry Madiès,
in collaboration with Abraham Ky

History of Decentralization in Burkina Faso, 1991–2011

In the history of Burkina Faso, the "new" decentralization process began in the 1990s (Champagne and Ouegraogou 2011), as it did in most African countries that embarked on such reform. The backdrop to the process was a dual crisis: (a) a sociopolitical crisis marked by open contestation of the single-party system or authoritarian regimes and by a rejection of political and administrative centralization; and (b) an economic crisis that had led to the implementation of structural adjustment programs as a corrective response (Mback 2003, 32).

The novelty of the process lies in the challenges at stake, which involve two different dimensions:

- *Introduction of pluralist local democracy*, in a break from former practices, through the election of bodies to manage decentralized local governments, which are authorities elected by universal suffrage

- *Local development* following a widely shared observation in the late 1980s that the African state was apparently "bankrupt" (Sawadogo 2001, 15).

For some, this bankruptcy of the central authority and a lack of awareness of the role of local-level involvement are key reasons behind the continent's lagging development (Mback 2003, 37).

From this perspective, decentralization is intended to be a decisive factor for local development as a driver of local community participation in the formulation and implementation of public programs that directly benefit these communities. In other words, the underpinnings of the new Burkinabé decentralization process are of two kinds: promoting grassroots development and strengthening local governance.

Another novel aspect of the process is that, for the first time, decentralization reforms were enshrined in the constitution,[1] which gives official status to the territorial collectivities (*collectivités territoriales*; CTs) that are now recognized as legal entities, financially autonomous, and administered by elected bodies. It should be noted (along with Mback 2003, 65), however, that this step forward sprang from a general consensus of public opinion that from the outset had converged around the need for such reform. So much so that, following the constitutional referendum of June 11, 1991, the Assembly of the People's Deputies (*Assemblée des députés du people*)[2] adopted a package of five laws in 1993 to establish the process within a stable legal framework. This package included, inter alia, laws relating to municipal structure, the specific statuses of the Bobo-Dioulasso and Ouagadougou communes (or municipalities), and the system for electing councillors.

Moreover, that same year—and with a view to injecting momentum into the process—a National Commission for Decentralization (*Commission nationale de la décentralisation*) was set up to advise the government and propose realistic and consensual institutional arrangements to further the rollout of the reform. The process was translated into concrete form in 1995 with the election of the deliberative and executive bodies of the first 33 fully autonomous communes.

In August 1998, four more laws were adopted to replace the 1993 laws, their foremost objectives being to provide a more coherent legal framework for the decentralization process[3] and a programmatic implementation strategy.[4] It is within this new institutional framework that the second round of municipal elections was organized in May 2000.

The years 2001 and 2004 laid further milestones on the path to greater decentralization. In July 2001, the country's administrative mapping was modified: with the creation of the regions, a third tier was added to the two existing tiers of local government (provinces and communes). However, before the provinces and regions had time to implement their elected bodies, the legislature adopted the General Code of Territorial Collectivities (*Code général des collectivités territoriales*; CGCT) in December 2004, bringing the levels of local government back down to two (communes and regions) and "communalizing" the whole country. It was thus under the 2004 CGCT and the 2001 electoral law that local elections were organized in 2006 to elect the first councillors for the 13 regions (referring here to the "regional governments"), the rural communes, and the second generation of urban communes—excluding the councillors of the first 33 "experimental" communes, which were into their third election.

Viewed as a whole, the decentralization process initiated in the 1990s differed from previous attempts on several counts:

- Elaboration of institutional arrangements and a strategic framework for decentralization
- Division of the entire country into communes
- Organization of three local elections (in 1995, 2000, and 2006)

- Formal transfer of responsibilities and resources to urban communes
- More or less smooth functioning of the communal and regional management bodies.

It is also useful to highlight the reasons that prompted Burkina Faso to initiate decentralization in the 1990s:

- The first reason probably hinges on the fact that the country did not wish to have decentralization imposed on it by foreign donors (mainly the World Bank and the European Union) in the form of aid conditionality.
- Second, Burkina Faso drew on the experiences of neighboring countries, especially Mali.
- Finally, decentralization was a means of associating the country's vital stakeholders with the electoral process.

Whatever the ultimate reasons may have been (for example, "tying up" the legislative elections), the first local elections unquestionably found a resonance within the female population (10 percent of elected officials in the first elections were female, 20 percent in the second, and 30 percent in the last municipal elections—which certainly indicated a good mobilization of female voters), as well as among young people and the non-Francophone Burkinabé. Table 2.1 gives a summary timeline of this period.

Organization of Decentralized Local Government and Deconcentration in 2011

According to the first chapter of the CGCT (2004), titled "On Territorial Organisation," Burkina Faso is organized into CTs.[6] In reality, the administrative network of the territory is not structured around CTs alone. Taken in its broad sense, territorial organization includes not only the CTs but also the administrative units. This means that two dimensions are present: a "decentralized" level comprising regional and local government units (CTs) and a "deconcentrated" level comprising administrative units (regions, provinces, departments).

Figure 2.1 summarizes this architecture but also goes a step further,[7] revealing the tension inherent to any decentralization process within a particular national setting. The left-hand box ("Local Authorities") shows the decentralized structure promoted by the institutional design; this is contrasted with the right-hand box ("Administrative Units") containing the deconcentrated structure. Seen from this angle, resistance to decentralization is not, and cannot be, regarded as an anomaly that simply needs correcting. What is involved is a tension between two conceptions—deconcentration and devolution—that must be turned to the best advantage and balanced out over the long run. In the case

Table 2.1 Timeline of Key Decentralization Legislation in Burkina Faso, 1991–2011

1991	Adoption by referendum (June 2) and promulgation (June 11) of the Constitution of the Fourth Republic, setting out the main principles of decentralization in three Articles:
	Art. 143: " Burkina Faso is organised into local authorities."
	Art. 144: " The creation, abolition and division of local authorities shall be defined by law."
	Art. 145: " Democratic participation of the populations in the administration of local authorities shall be organised by law."
	Order No. 91-0048/PRES of August 7 on territorial organization during the transitional phase
	First presidential election of the Fourth Republic on December 1, 1991
1992	First legislative election of the Fourth Republic and setting up of the Assembly of the People's Deputies (ADP) on May 24
1993	Law No. 03 of May 7 on the organization of territorial administration
	Law No. 04 of May 12 on the organization of municipalities
	Law No. 05 of May 12 on the special status of the province of Kadiogo and the city of Ouagadougou
	Law No. 06 of May 12 concerning the special status of the city of Bobo-Dioulasso
	Law No. 07 of May 12 on the electoral system for village, communal, department, and province councillors
	As is apparent from Laws No. 04, 05, and 06, there are three types of communes: self-governing communes, partly self-governing communes, and special-status communes—the partly self-governing communes having the possibility of becoming fully self-governing.
	Creation of the National Committee for Decentralization (CND) pursuant to Decree No. 93-350/PRES/PM of November 16
1995	Organization of the first municipal elections on February 12 in the 33 self-governing communes
	Creation of the Association of the Mayors of Burkina Faso (*Association des maires[5] du Burkina Faso*; AMBF) pursuant to Decree No. 95-0364/MATS/SG/DGAT/DELPAJ of December 2
1996	Creation on April 3 of the Initiative and Development Financing Fund for Municipalities (*Fonds d'appui au démarrage et au développement des communes*; FODECOM) and the Support Service for the Management of Municipal Development (*Service d'appui à la gestion et au développement des communes*; SAGEDECOM)
1998	Law No. 040 of August 3 on the guidelines for decentralization
	Law No. 041 of August 6 on territorial administration
	Law No. 042 of August 6 on the organization and functioning of local governments
	Law No. 043 of August 6 on the programming for implementing decentralization
2000	Decree No. 163-2000/PRES/PM/MEF of April 28 on the arrangements and conditions for granting cash advances to local governments
	May: second municipal election of the Fourth Republic in 49 urban communes
2001	Modification of the administrative divisions pursuant to Law No. 13-2001 of July 2 relating to the creation of the regions
	Law No. 014-2001/AN of July 3 on the electoral code: Articles 236 *ff.* relating to the election of municipal councillors and municipal bodies
2004	Adoption of Law No. 055-2004 of December 21 on the General Code on Territorial Collectivities (*Code Général des Collectivités Territoriales*; CGCT) as the reference standard for decentralization matters
	Creation of two levels of local government: communes (urban and rural) and regions

(continued next page)

Table 2.1 (continued)

2005	Decree No. 045-2005/PRES/PM/MATD of February 3 on the competences of the regional governor, the provincial high commissioner, and the departmental prefect
	Law No. 024-2005/AN of May 25 on the amendment to the electoral law (No. 014-2001/AN) to take into account the election of the regional bodies
2006	April 23: third municipal elections of the Fourth Republic and first elections for the rural communes
	Law No. 014-2006/AN of May 9 on the determination of local government resources and expenditure in Burkina Faso
	Decree No. 204-2006/PRES/PM/MFB/MATD of May 15 on the local government financial and accounting system in Burkina Faso
	Decree No. 208-2006/PRES/PM/MFB/MATD of May 15 on the standard rules of procedure for local government councils
	Decree No. 209-2006/PRES/PM/MFB/MATD of May 15 on the transfer of powers to the urban communes in the areas of preschool and primary education, health, culture, sports, recreation, and youth
	Law No. 021-2006/AN of November 14 concerning the amendment to Law No. 055-2004 (CGCT) and the extension of the institution of the Village Development Councils (*Conseils villageois de développement*; CVDs) to villages falling within urban communes
	Law No. 027-2006/AN of December 5 on the legal framework applicable to the employment and agents of local government
2007	Decree No. 032-2007/PRES/PM/MATD of January 22 on the organization, composition, and functioning of the CVDs
	Decree No. 069-2007/PRES/PM/MFB/MATD of February 9 on the local government budget nomenclature in Burkina Faso
	Decree No. 095-2007/PRES/PM/MATD/MFB of March 1 on the adoption of the Strategic Framework for the Implementation of Decentralization (2006–2015)
	Decree No. 254-2007/PRES/PM/MATD/MFB of April 11 on the approval of the special status of the Permanent Funding for the Development of Territorial Collectivities (*Fonds permanent pour le développement des collectivités territoriales*; FPDCT)
	Decree No. 287-2007/PRES/PM/MFB/MATD of May 18 on establishing the arrangements for the distribution of taxes between the communes and regions
2009	Decree No. 105-2009/PRES/PM/MATD/MCTC/MJE/MSL/MEF/MFPRE of March 3 on the transfer of central government competences and resources to the communes in the areas of culture, sports, recreation, and youth
	Decree No. 106-2009/PRES/PM/MATD/MEBA/MASSN/MEF/MFPRE of March 3 on the transfer of central government competences and resources to the communes in the areas of preschool and primary education and literacy
	Decree No. 107-2009/PRES/PM/MATD/MAHRH/MEF/MFPRE of March 3 on the transfer of central government competences and resources to the communes in the areas of safe water supply and sanitation
	Decree No. 108-2009/PRES/PM/MATD/MS/MEF/MFPRE of March 3 on the transfer of central government competences and resources to the communes in the area of health
2010	Decree No. 2010-670/PRES/PM/MATD/MEF of October 22 on the budgeting and accounting nomenclature of Territorial Collectivities in Burkina Faso
	Ordinance No. 2010-054/MATD/CAB of May 31 on the organization, attributions, and functioning of the permanent technical Secretariat of the National Conference on Decentralization

(continued next page)

Table 2.1 (continued)

2011	Directive No. 01-2011/CM/UEMOA of June 24 concerning the financial regime of Territorial Collectivities within the West African Economic and Monetary Union (*Union Economique et Monétaire Ouest Africaine*; UEMOA)
	Annex: (1) Accounting system of Territorial Collectivities within UEMOA
	(2) Budget Nomenclature of Territorial Collectivities within UEMOA
	Decree No. 2011-319/PRES/PM/SGG-CM of June 6 concerning the attributions of government members
	Decree No. 2011-707/PRES/PM/MATDS of September 26 on the organization of the Ministry of Territorial Administration of Decentralization and Security

Source: Compiled in Ky 2010 and completed by the authors, updated to the end of 2011.

of Burkina Faso, the role of customary chieftaincies must also be taken into account when organizing decentralized powers. Of course, their role can be sidelined, thus heightening the risk of failure, or the customary power structure can be integrated into the process of stakeholder participation: it serves little purpose to advocate civil society participation if one of its influential components is left out.

Local Authorities

The region   The region is the intermediate tier of local government. Its institutional coverage comprises all the communes within its boundaries and coincides with the territory of the "regional administrative unit." At the end of 2011, Burkina Faso had 13 regional authorities.

The commune   The commune is the basic unit of local government, organized into arrondissements, sectors, and villages. There are three types of communes: rural communes, urban communes with an ordinary status, and two special-status urban communes (Ouagadougou and Bobo-Dioulasso). These types are further described as follows:

- *The rural commune* is a group of villages with a population of at least 5,000 and economic activities generating annual own resources of at least CFAF 5 million. The rural commune's territory includes three distinct spaces: (a) a residential space that is "a permanent human settlement mainly intended for housing, trade, industry, handicrafts, [and] the setting up of public services"; (b) a production space intended "mainly for agriculture, livestock farming, forestry, fish farming and more generally for all activities linked to rural life"; and (c) a conservation space made up of "areas for the protection of natural resources. [They] notably include areas for the protection of flora and fauna."[8] There were 302 rural communes at the end of 2011, each including 25 villages on average.

Figure 2.1 Organization of Decentralized Territorial Collectivities and Deconcentration in Burkina Faso, 2011

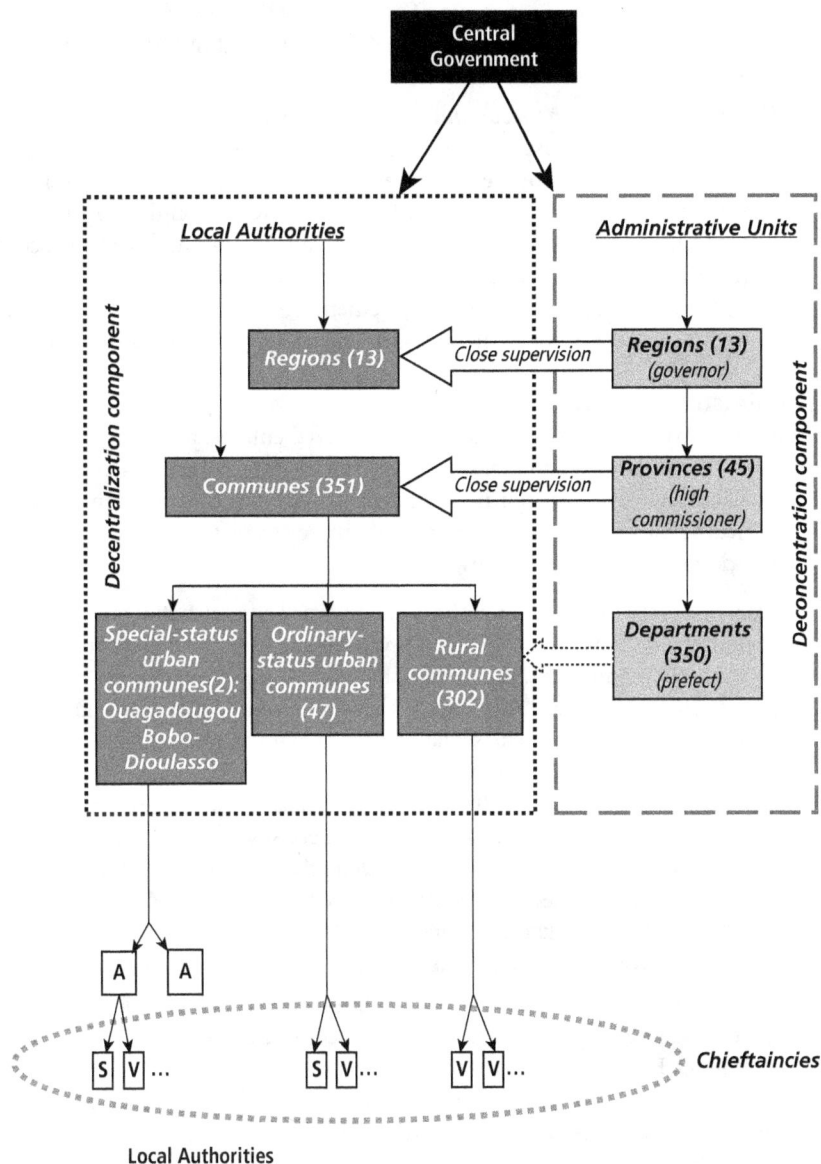

Sources: Data compiled by the authors based on legislation in force in 2009.
Note: A = arrondissement; S = sector; V = village.

- *The ordinary-status urban commune* is a territorial unit that includes a permanent agglomeration with at least 25,000 but fewer than 200,000 inhabitants and annual own resources of at least CFAF 25 million. It is divided into sectors and may also contain villages. At the end of 2011, there were 47 ordinary-status urban communes.

- *The special-status urban commune* is a territorial area that has a main agglomeration of at least 200,000 inhabitants and economic activities generating annual own resources of at least CFAF 500 million. It is organized into arrondissements that are subdivided into sectors and may include villages. Ouagadougou (the political capital) and Bobo-Dioulasso (the economic capital) are the two special-status urban communes. At the end of 2011, Ouagadougou had 12 arrondissements, 55 sectors, and 17 villages; and Bobo-Dioulasso had 7 arrondissements, 33 sectors, and 36 villages.

Administrative Units

Administrative units are deconcentrated territorial entities, all of which represent the central state on national territory. They are not legal entities but simply territorial frameworks for coordinating the activities of the central administration's local agencies. They are organized into three layers: the region, the province, and the department, as follows:

- *The region* is the highest layer in the deconcentrated administrative architecture. Territorially, it comprises one or more provinces. Like the regional authorities, there are 13 administrative units whose boundaries are identical to the regional authorities. The deconcentrated region is administered by a governor who "is the Government delegate and representative for each minister in the region."[9] In addition, each governor serves as the judicial police officer and authorizing officer for the budget grants allocated to the region by the central government. The governors are responsible for ensuring the close supervision of their corresponding regional authorities. The responsibilities include giving approval and prior authorization to the acts and decisions of the regional council and its president as well as performing legality checks on the region's decisions and activities. They also have a support and advisory role for the administrative organs of the regional authorities.

- *The province* is the intermediate layer of administrative unit, of which there are 45 in Burkina Faso. The province's territory comprises either departments or communes. Kadiogo Province is the only one whose territory matches the territory of a commune—namely the capital, Ouagadougou. The provinces are also electoral circles for the national parliamentary elections. The province is headed by a high commissioner, who is appointed by the central government. Representing state authority in the province, the high commissioners are responsible for executing the central government's decisions on their territories and coordinating the activities of all the deconcentrated provincial public administrations. The high commissioners also serve as the judicial police officers and authorizing officers for the budget grants allocated to their provinces by the central government. Finally, the high commissioners are responsible for ensuring the close supervision of the urban and rural communes within their province's jurisdiction, acting under delegation from the ministers responsible for territorial administration and finance. As such, they approve the budgets and administrative accounts of the urban and rural communes. They also have the authority to grant prior authorization for various communal acts.[10]

- *The department* is the bottom layer of the deconcentrated administration. Each of the 350 departments is administered by a prefect who is appointed by the central government. Prefects are responsible for overseeing the enforcement of government laws, regulations, and decisions within the departmental jurisdictions. In addition, they perform the duties of registrar and judicial police officer. The prefects report to their respective high commissioners and represent the latter within their departments.

The Political and Administrative Design of the Commune

Each commune, whatever its status, has a municipal council (deliberative body) elected through direct universal suffrage by its citizens or electors; a mayor (executive body) elected through indirect universal suffrage by the municipal council; and administrative services, as shown in figures 2.2 and 2.3.

The municipal council   The municipal councils of ordinary-status urban communes and rural communes are made up of directly elected councillors who serve an unpaid five-year term of office. In its capacity as a deliberative body, the council's main responsibility is to discuss and decide on "communal matters" and see to their implementation: for example, they define the main guidelines for communal development, discuss and adopt communal development plans, oversee the implementation of these plans, direct the mayor and technical committees, and oversee their respective actions.

The council is explicitly required to set up four permanent committees:[11]

- General, social, and cultural matters
- Economic and financial matters
- Environment and local development
- Land zoning and management.

Municipal councils are required to oversee the setting up of the Village Development Councils (*Conseils villageois de développement*; CVDs).[12] Initially the CGCT provided for CVDs only in the villages within rural communes, but they were extended to villages in urban communes after the CGCT was amended on November 14, 2006.[13] The CVD is a "grouping of all the village stakeholders"—endowed with a deliberative body called "the general assembly" and a management body called the "bureau."[14]

Figure 2.2 Political and Administrative Structure of Rural and Ordinary-Status Urban Communes in Burkina Faso, 2011

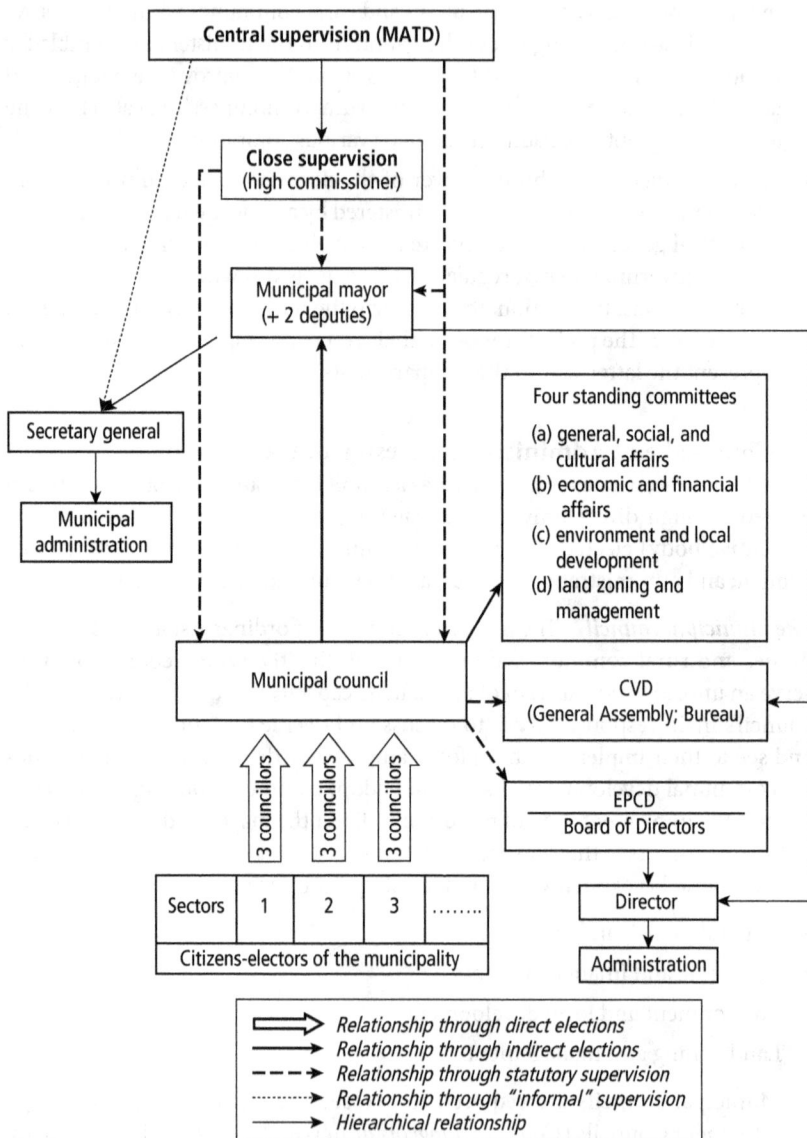

Source: Data compiled by the authors based on legal structures in force in 2011.
Note: CVD = Village Development Council (*Conseils villageois de développement*); EPCD = Municipal Development Unit (*Établissement public communal pour le développement*); MATD = Ministry of Territorial Administration and Decentralization.

Figure 2.3 Political and Administrative Structure of the Special-Status Urban Communes in Burkina Faso, 2011

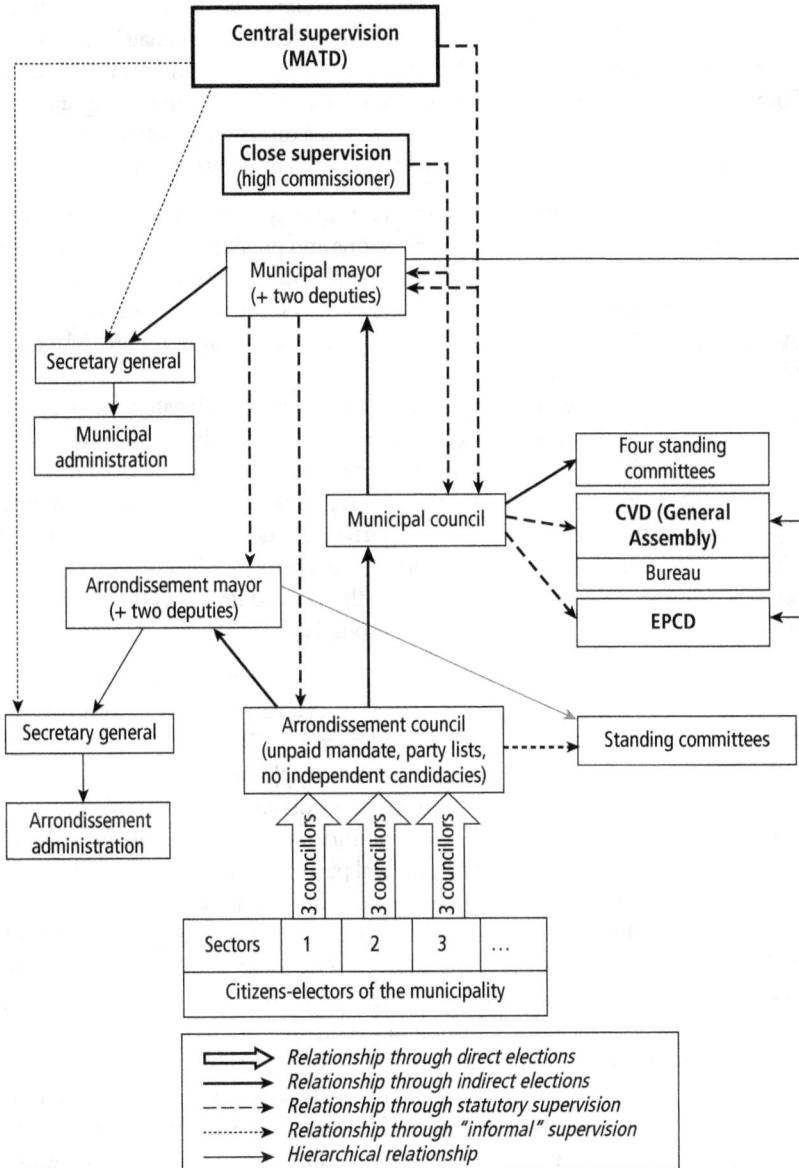

Sources: Data compiled by the authors based on the legal structures in force in 2009.
Note: CVD = Village Development Councils (*Conseils villageois de développement*); EPCD = Municipal Development Unit (*Établissement public communal pour le développement*); MATD = Ministry of Territorial Administration and Decentralization.

Municipal councils can create, with the central government's agreement, public services with a distinct legal identity such as the Municipal Development Units (*Établissements publics communaux pour le développement*; EPCDs). From an administrative and functional point of view, an EPCD has a management board chaired by the mayor, with seats for municipal councillors and representatives from lead trade associations. The council adopts the EPCD's activity program and oversees its implementation, which is ensured by a director recruited by the commune. However, administratively the EPCD reports directly to the mayor's office.

The mayor   As the commune's executive authority, the mayor is responsible for enforcing the municipal council's decisions and presides over its deliberative sessions. In addition, mayors act as communal budget authorizing officers and heads of the communal administration. They also serve as the communes' registrars and judicial police officers, but both these responsibilities are delegated by the central government.

The mayor is assisted by two deputies to whom are delegated some of the mayor's tasks.[15] The mayor also heads the communal administration, which is, however, managed by a centrally appointed secretary general. It is largely this situation that results in a certain ambiguity regarding the central government's supervision of the commune. The secretaries general provide the communes with real technical and logistical support. As government officials from the Civil Service administrative corps—often from the B (middle) or C (lowest) grade but rarely from grade A—their function is purely executive.

The arrondissement council   The two special-status communes, Ouagadougou and Bobo-Dioulasso, have a specific political and administrative regime involving arrondissement councils (as shown in figure 2.3). These councils include all of the arrondissement councillors, who are directly elected for a five-year unpaid term of office. Any person residing in the arrondissement and entitled to vote can be elected councillor. Independent candidates are not eligible because all candidates must be put forward by a political party or group of parties. The election is organized based on "a single-round election using party lists, with filing of the complete list, using proportional representation that applies the rule of the highest average, without vote splitting or preferential votes."[16] The number of councillors varies depending on how many sectors the arrondissement covers, each sector being an electoral constituency returning three councillors.

The arrondissement council is responsible for "all the particular or specific affairs of the arrondissement, except for any matter that is of general interest for all or part of the special status commune."[17] It can deliberate on all affairs concerning the arrondissement, but these deliberations "can in no event be contrary to the deliberations of the municipal council, under penalty of being declared void by the mayor of the special status commune."[18]

Thus, the arrondissement council deliberates on the arrondissement budget before it is reviewed and integrated into the communal budget. Finally, the commune must solicit the opinion of the arrondissement council regarding any project to be implemented wholly or partly within the arrondissement boundaries.

Once in place, the council elects from its members the mayor of the arrondissement and two deputies, and it can also set up standing committees. The mayor presides at the council meetings and is also responsible for implementing council deliberations. In addition, he or she acts as authorizing officer for the grants in the communal budget that concern the arrondissement and as head of the arrondissement administration. Finally, the arrondissement may be "delegated powers by the mayor of the special-status commune, after deliberation of the municipal council" to perform tasks that are of interest to the arrondissement but that legally fall under the municipal mayor's jurisdiction.[19]

Thus, each arrondissement is required to put in place a minimum level of administrative services. The law mentions, for example, a "civil registry," "social welfare," and "revenue authorities."[20]

Institutional Issues

If the texts governing the organization of local authorities in Burkina Faso are carefully analyzed from an institutional economy perspective, and if the legal architecture is compared with realities on the ground, at least eight issues can be identified:

- *The unclear link between decentralization and deconcentration.* This question is paramount, particularly at the regional level because regions have a dual status: they are both central government agencies (in other words, deconcentrated entities) and territorial collectivities. The functions of the decentralized regions do not seem clear despite a list of devolved responsibilities. In fact, according to those to whom we spoke, no task has so far been formally devolved to the decentralized regions.

- *Democratic legitimacy, or lack thereof, of the regional assemblies.* Because the regional assemblies are made up of municipal councillors elected by their peers (indirect elections), there is the risk that the regional authority may be seen as simply an offshoot of the communes, whereas the separation of these two tiers of local government is written into the constitution. This risk is heightened, as will be seen later, by the fact that six of the main local taxes are shared with the communes, which collect the taxes and then transfer only a small share (1.5–3 percent) of the receipts to the regions.

- *The unsettled roles of the departments, provinces, and regions in decentralization, as follows:*

   o At the department level, it is generally admitted that the prefect's role has become obsolete, which raises the question of whether this function and even the department should be abolished.

- o Opinions differ concerning the rest of the institutional architecture. The provinces seemingly have no role in decentralization (either through delegation or devolution), but they do form electoral constituencies for the legislative elections. It is thus unlikely that they will disappear, even if keeping them poses a problem in the institutional design.

- o Should the regions be abolished as a deconcentrated authority? This would seem difficult, mainly because of the political position of the governors and the coordinating function assigned to the deconcentrated regions, underlined by the budget grants they receive. On the other hand, the role of the decentralized regional authorities has so far been completely sidelined. In the long run, a single regional entity should be envisaged, on a decentralized basis—incorporating not only the functions of the deconcentrated region but also those to be devolved. Formation of this unified entity would help to avoid administrative overlaps and enhance the efficiency of the coordinating function. The governor's role would then need to be further defined.

- *Classification of the rural and urban communes based on population and the division of special-status communes into arrondissements.* First, the decision-making role of arrondissements in implementing the decentralization process is not adequately informed. Second, the arrondissements can apparently be subject to boundary changes depending on electoral criteria—which, if so, would have an adverse impact on the institutional design of a genuine devolution.

- *The ambiguous role of the chieftaincies (as noted in figure 2.1) and their ties with elected officials.* No massive involvement of customary chiefs in municipal elections has been visible. Yet at the same time, as our interlocutors pointed out, they are represented on the municipal councils. What is clear is that two forms of legitimacy exist side by side: one through election and the other through succession. The mayor has no choice but to take the customary chiefs into account. The draft bill on land tenure appears to confirm this observation.

- *A line organization of the ministries and departments that encourages deconcentration rather than devolution.* In this situation, the Ministry of Territorial Administration and Decentralization (MATD), which is the cross-cutting ministry, should coordinate government action in favor of devolution. But it comes up against the other ministries on which it depends, not only for the technical competences to implement the government's decentralization policies but also for the budget lines that must be secured for each devolved function. In this situation, the MATD finds it difficult to establish its legitimacy and thus to play an effective lead role in the government's decentralization policy.

- *Insufficient administrative and management capacity of the commune's secretary general and the government officials working for the commune.* To build up the capacity necessary for genuine devolution, priority should be given to creating a corps of local and regional government officials. The job of training could be entrusted to a national higher education institution in a form jointly defined by the stakeholders (the central government, the CTs, and the institution's management). But a first step would perhaps be to incorporate central government officials into the local civil service while guaranteeing them their present salary and employment status.

• *Imprecise definition of the relationships between multiple parallel communal institutions concerning appointment, responsibility, and control.* Figure 2.2 clearly shows that the municipal council appoints the standing committees but that the mayor can also intervene in these committees and the CVDs— which are thus hierarchically under both the legislative and executive authorities of the commune. Figure 2.3 shows further complications in the relations for special-status communes. Here, there is real risk of diluting powers and political responsibility.

The Decentralized Budget

Figure 2.4 summarizes the main provisions of the law regarding the list of expenditures and revenues of the CTs.[21] The budget and accounts comprise two sections: current and capital. Because figure 2.4 is easy to understand without additional comments, this analysis will focus only on some of the more controversial points:

• *The constraint of budget balance* is prescribed by law (Art. 8; see box 2.1), but this needs qualifying because the text is ambiguous and certainly not easily understood on a first reading, for at least five reasons:

   ○ The current (operating) account is expressed as *actual* expenditures and revenues rather than *accrued* expenditures and revenues; thus what counts are actual cash movements, with no possibility of making pure accounting entries for the calculation of costs per function.

   ○ Current expenditures include amortization in the sense of loan repayments (to date, the CTs do not have access to loans).

   ○ The "balance" is asymmetrical and is understood to mean that only a current account deficit is forbidden. In reality, the current account needs to show a surplus because 20 percent of own current revenues must be transferred to fund the capital budget. However, practice deviates from the rule: although this transfer is duly entered at the time budgets are approved (and many CTs make efforts to respect this ratio), examination of the accounts after budget execution shows that this is rarely respected.[22]

Figure 2.4 The Decentralized Budget in Burkina Faso

Current Budget		Capital Budget	
Actual expenditure	Revenue	Actual expenditure	Revenue
Mandatory expenditure 1. Councillors' and council's expenses 2. Municipal personnel 3. Pensions 4. Maintenance of territorial administration headquarters 5. Administrative expenses 6. Utilities, telecommunications 7. Civil registry service 8. Legal costs 9. Contribution to the National Fire Protection Service 10. Library 11. Local hygiene and disinfection services 12. Streets, roads, and public squares 13. Cemeteries 14. Alignment and grading plans 15. Tax collection 16. Cost of debt, interest, and amortization 17. Levy on CT property and revenues 18. Building maintenance 19. Legally devolved local services 20. Expenditure incurred by the transfers of powers Nonmandatory expenditures ... ... *Transfer for the benefit of the "capital" section = at least 20 percent of own revenues*	A. Taxes *"The six taxes"* a. Business licenses b. Residency c. Mortmain d. Firearms e. Land f. Informal sector contribution *"The other taxes"* g. Entertainment h. Gambling i. Advertising j. Carts B. Revenue from communal service provision ✓ Equipment rental ✓ Fee for issuance of administrative documents ✓ Health inspection fee ✓ Revenue from maternity and health centers ✓ Street sweeping fees ✓ Refuse collection ✓ Funeral services ✓ Slaughterhouse tax ✓ Service provision ✓ Sale of products C. Revenue from communal property ✓ Stall placement fees: markets, fairs, stockyards ✓ Rentals ✓ Fees for occupation of public spaces ✓ Cemetery concessions ✓ Parking fees ✓ Tax on degradation ✓ Other revenues D. Miscellaneous revenue ✓ Police fines ✓ Reimbursement of expenses ✓ Income from services under concession or leased ✓ Nonreinvested profits from industrial or commercial operations ✓ Contributions to parcelization operations ✓ Financial income ✓ Sponsorships and voluntary contributions ✓ *DGF (grants for recurrent expenditures)* ✓ *Revenue from shared taxes*	Mandatory expenditure ✓ *Implementation of investment programs* ✓ *Development actions* **Art. 23:** *Capital expenditure must be equivalent to at least one-third of the total amount of the estimated budget.*	I. Own revenues ✓ Proceeds from disposals (movable and immovable property, securities) ✓ Unclaimed impounded animals ✓ Other own revenues ✓ *Grants for investment (DGE)* ✓ *Transfer from "current" section of the budget* II. Other funding ✓ Grants from the center ✓ Grants from other national or foreign CTs ✓ Aid, gifts, bequests III. Borrowing Borrowing is subject to prior approval of the supervisory authority.

Sources: Data from Law No. 014-2006 of May 9, 2006, on the determination of local authority resources and expenditures in Burkina Faso: notably, excerpts from Articles 8 (20 percent rule), 15 (current revenue), 17 (capital revenue), 20 (expenditure), and 23 (one-third rules for investment).
Note: CT = territorial collectivity; DGE = block grant for investment (*dotation générale d'équipemet*); DGF = block grant for current expenditures (*dotation générale de fonctionnement*). **Bolded italic text** represents the direct intervention of the central government in the CT's budget. *Shaded italic text* represents an obligation forced on CTs from the national legislation.

BOX 2.1

Constraint of Budget Balance in the Decentralized Budget in Burkina Faso: Article 8 of Law No. 014-2006 of May 9, 2006

The budget is voted in respect of "real" balance by the local authority's council. The accounts are in real balance when (a) the "current" and "capital" sections, respectively, are approved "as in balance" (the revenues and expenditures having been evaluated in all transparency); and (b) the transfer of revenues from the "current" to the "capital" section (excluding proceeds from borrowing and eventual depreciation, amortization, and provisions) provides sufficient resources to cover the repayments of loan capital falling due within the financial year.

The transfer of revenues from the "current" to the "capital" section must be equivalent to at least 20 percent of the collectivity's own budget revenues.

However, a budget is **accepted as being in balance if** the "current" section includes or carries forward a surplus and the "capital" section shows a real balance of accounts after each section has integrated the results of the administrative account of the previous financial year.

- o The principle of annuality is not respected because a current budget "surplus" can be carried forward.
- o "Own" resources are not defined as such in law. One has to refer to another text of the Ministry of Economy and Finance (MEF)[23] concerning the CTs' financial functioning to find the term "own" attached to the groups A, B, and C in figure 2.4.

- *Capital expenditures* must represent at least one-third of total budgeted expenditures. The text does not specify whether this total amount includes both "current" and "capital" sections or simply the "current" section. If the reference amount comprises only current expenditures, this works out to the equivalent of 33⅓ percent of the current budget or, if the reference amount is the sum of both current and capital budgets, 50 percent of current expenditures.[24] This ratio seems to be a disproportionate requirement in a country where decentralization is ongoing; even well-established federal and decentralized systems cannot meet it. This requirement also raises the issue of the sustainability of investment decisions with respect to the recurrent costs incurred by such decisions (Dafflon and Beer-Tóth 2009): Who will bear these costs, and through what type of financing?
- *External financial aid* is not included in the current budget, but it appears in the capital budget in figure 2.4 under the heading "II. Other funding."

However, each year, the CT budgetary circular (the MATD and MEF Inter-ministerial Order) draws the attention of the authorizing officers to the requirement of entering all resources, be they current or capital, in a single document: the budget. The CTs' budget classification has a line item in the current section for this category of current revenue, referred to in Chapter 73 "Recoveries and participations" (Article 734, "Grants").[25]

- *The accounting classification of itemized expenditures* determines the expenditure nomenclature. However, elements are present that could herald the emergence of a functional classification (for instance, categories 10, 16, and 17 of current expenditure in figure 2.4). The absence of functional classification of expenditures poses a real problem because, as will be seen later, the text of the law devolves responsibilities, not expenditures, to the CTs. However, to date, no government finance statistic gives a functional classification of expenditures.[26] And without a functional classification in the budget and account, it is impossible to trace the delegation and devolution of responsibilities to the CTs and to measure the evolution in time and the performance of decentralization. How, then, can decentralization be steered and its progress measured?

- *Several provisions liable to diverse interpretations*[27] could usefully be revised, addressing the following:

  o If the actual balanced budget is approved, what about the accounts?

  o "Own-source" budget revenues are not defined.

  o Certain tax receipts are entered under general revenue, whereas they are in fact a form of "user pays" charges, normally subject to precise cost-recovery and allocation rules (the refuse collection tax, for example).

  o The listed current revenues are not always "revenues" or even "current" in the sense of an "annual" budget. Thus, the "ordinary surplus from the closings of previous budget periods"—already recognized as revenue in a previous budget period—cannot be recognized as such twice over; these are carryovers and not revenues, which moreover contradict the principle of annuality prescribed by law.

  o The "contributions to parcelization operations" are reported as ordinary revenue, whereas they should appear as extraordinary revenue: once the zoning and parcelization are completed, this revenue disappears (unless there are a series of plots to be developed in a large urban commune).

  o In the capital section, transfers from the current section or capital account surpluses brought forward are well and truly carryovers and not revenue as such. This is also the case for the borrowed funds listed as revenue, which are unquestionably financial resources but not revenue because real revenues must be raised quickly thereafter for capital repayments.

Assignment of Responsibilities

To begin with, we summarize the 10 areas of competence that have been transferred in compliance with the 2004 law. The criteria that determined this transfer to the regional and local authorities are not explicated in the legislation or the accompanying documents apart from the subsidiarity principle and the so-named rule of "progressiveness." Because this rule is specific to Burkina Faso, we will examine this aspect later (in terms of definition and implementation) before addressing the issue of devolution through the prism of institutional economy.

The Areas of Transferred Responsibilities
The functions assigned to the CTs are listed in CGCT Articles 85–105 of Law No. 055-2004 of December 21, 2004 (these are the main references in matters of decentralization). Table 2.2 recapitulates the functions involved and the level of CT to which they are transferred, including the following:

1a. Land management[28]

1b. Territorial development and urban planning

2. Environment and natural resource management

3. Economic development and planning

4. Health and hygiene

5. Education, employment, vocational training, and literacy

6. Culture, sports, recreation, and youth

7. Civil defense, social welfare, and emergency relief

8. Funeral services and cemeteries

9. Water and electricity

10. Markets, fairs, and slaughterhouses.

The Principle of Progressiveness
Article 5 of the 2004 CGCT stipulates that "the implementation of decentralisation is carried out according to the principle of progressiveness," but it gives no details on the actual term, the method, the content, or the timing. Theoretically, the progressive approach guiding a decentralization implementation strategy cuts across three dimensions:

- *Functional.* Implementing decentralization involves successive transfers of responsibilities, which means creating *packages of tasks* to be decentralized in successive steps.
- *Territorial.* The process is *experimental*: by selecting CTs where resistance to change is the weakest, depending on the negotiating model used, a

Table 2.2 Decentralized Functions in Burkina Faso[29]

Function	Devolved responsibilities		
	Region (A)	Urban commune (B)	Rural commune (C)
Mandatory expenditures[a]			
1a. Land management 1b. Territorial development and urban planning	1. Opinion on the regional development plan (SRA) and the urban planning master plan (SDAU) 2. Support for regional public transport 3. Land occupation permit 4. Construction, maintenance of rural roads	1. Opinion on the SDAU 2. Formulation and implementation of subdivision plans 3. Assignment of plots, land titling 4. Building permits 5. Certificate of compliance 6. Street addressing and naming 7. Participation in managing national land 8. Permits for the occupation of public land 9. Traffic police 10. Creation and maintenance of roads and signage 11. Designation of sites for railway stations and parking areas 12. Construction and maintenance of gutters, railway stations, and parking areas 13. Initiatives and support for public transport 14. Initiatives and support for school bus services	1. Opinion on the housing land-use plans (SAEDH) 2. Formulation and implementation of subdivision plans 3. Participation in drafting plans to develop productive space and conservation areas (SAEPC) 4. Participation in the building and maintenance of rural roads 5. Assignment of plots, land titling 6. Building permits 7. Certificate of compliance 8. Street addressing and naming 9. Participation in managing national land 10. Permits for the occupation of public land 11. Traffic police 12. Creation and maintenance of roads and signage 13. Designation of locations for railway stations and parking areas 14. Construction and maintenance of gutters, railway stations, and parking areas 15. Initiatives and support for public transport 16. Initiatives and support for school bus services

(continued next page)

Table 2.2 (continued)

	Devolved responsibilities		
Function	Region (A)	Urban commune (B)	Rural commune (C)
Mandatory expenditures[a]			
2. Environment and natural resource management	5. Creation of woods and forests 6. Participation in the protection and management of classified and protected forests 7. Participation in the protection of watercourses 8. Prevention and response to bush fires and excessive woodcutting 9. Protection of the fauna and fishery resources 10. Participation in the management and exploitation of the aquaculture areas of economic interest (PAIE) 11. Formulation and implementation of action plans for the environment 12. Woodcutting permits 13. Participation in formulating programs and plans for waste collection and disposal	15. Preparation of communal environmental action plans 16. Participation in the protection and management of ground and surface water and fishery resources 17. Sanitation 18. Prevention and response to poor hygiene, pollution, and other nuisances 19. Creation, management of green spaces and municipal parks 20. Prevention and response to free grazing, and livestock regulations 21. Waste management 22. Woodcutting permits 23. Participation in renewable resource conservation and management 24. Prevention and response to bush fires and excessive woodcutting 25. Participation in the protection and management of fauna in classified forests 26. Protection and management of fauna in protected forests 27. Opinion on the setting up of unhealthy, dangerous, and incommodious establishments of first and second classes	17. Preparation of communal environmental action plans 18. Participation in the protection and management of ground and surface water and fishery resources 19. Sanitation 20. Prevention and response to poor hygiene, pollution, and other nuisances 21. Creation, management of green spaces and municipal parks 22. Prevention and response to free grazing, and livestock regulations 23. Waste management 24. Participation in renewable resource conservation and management 25. Prevention and response to bush fires and excessive woodcutting 26. Participation in the protection and management of fauna in classified forests 27. Protection and management of fauna in protected forests 28. Opinion on the setting up of unhealthy, dangerous, and incommodious establishments of first and second classes 29. Management of the production zone developed by the commune

(continued next page)

Table 2.2 (continued)

Function	Devolved responsibilities		
	Region (A)	Urban commune (B)	Rural commune (C)
Mandatory expenditures[a]			
			30. Management of the production zone developed by third parties on communal territory
			31. Creation of conservation areas
			32. Participation in renewable resource conservation and management
			33. Participation in the protection and management of natural forests, wildlife, water resources, and fishery resources
			34. Woodcutting permits
			35. Small game licenses for conservation areas
			36. Sport fishing licenses
3. Economic development and planning	14. Formulation and implementation of development policies and plans in line with national guidelines	28. Formulation and implementation of development policies and plans in line with national guidelines	37. Formulation and implementation of development policies and plans in line with national guidelines
	15. Contracting with central government or legal entities for plans or programs to achieve development objectives	29. Contracting with central government or legal entities for plans or programs to achieve development objectives	38. Contracting with central government or legal entities for plans or programs to achieve development objectives
4. Health and hygiene	16. Participation in constructing and managing primary health centers	30. Construction and management of primary health centers	39. Construction and management of primary health centers
	17. Construction and management of second-level health centers	31. Organization of pharmaceutical supplies and measures for disease prevention	40. Organization of pharmaceutical supplies and measures for disease prevention
	18. Organization of pharmaceutical supplies	32. Hygiene and sanitation measures	41. Hygiene and sanitation measures

(continued next page)

Table 2.2 (continued)

	Devolved responsibilities		
Function	Region (A)	Urban commune (B)	Rural commune (C)
Mandatory expenditures[a]			
	19. Regulation and measures for hygiene and sanitation, and disease prevention	33. Enforcement control of sanitation regulations	42. Enforcement control of sanitation regulations
	20. Promotion of the traditional pharmacopoeia	34. Participation in solving health problems	43. Participation in solving health problems
	21. Participation in solving health problems	35. Participation in drafting the communal part of the national health map	44. Participation in drafting the communal part of the national health map
	22. Participation in drafting the regional part of the national health map		
5. Education, employment, vocational training, and literacy	23. Participation in the responsibility for preschool education	36. Responsibility for developing preschool education: acquisition, construction, and management of schools	45. Responsibility for developing preschool education: acquisition, construction, and management of schools
	24. Participation in responsibility for developing primary education	37. Responsibility for developing primary education: acquisition, construction, and management of schools	46. Responsibility for developing primary education: acquisition, construction, and management of schools
	25. Participation in constructing and managing secondary schools	38. Contribution to developing secondary education: acquisition, construction, and management of schools	47. Contribution to developing secondary education: acquisition, construction, and management of schools
	26. Responsibility for developing higher education		
	27. Responsibility for promoting employment, vocational training, and literacy	39. Responsibility for developing vocational training and literacy	48. Responsibility for developing vocational training and literacy
	28. Participation in drafting the regional part of the national education map	40. Participation in drafting the communal part of the national education map	49. Participation in drafting the communal part of the national education map
6. Culture, sports, recreation, and youth	29. Construction and management of cultural, sports, and youth infrastructure	41. Construction and management of social, cultural, sports, and youth infrastructure	50. Construction and management of social, cultural, sports, and youth infrastructure
	30. Promotion of cultural, sports, and youth activities	42. Promotion of cultural, sports, and youth activities	51. Promotion of cultural, sports, and youth activities

(continued next page)

Table 2.2 (continued)

Function	Region (A)	Urban commune (B)	Rural commune (C)
		Devolved responsibilities	
Mandatory expenditures[a]			
	31. Construction and management of museums and libraries	43. Construction and management of communal museums and libraries	52. Construction and management of communal museums and libraries
	32. Promotion of tourism and crafts	44. Promotion of tourism and crafts	53. Promotion of tourism and crafts
	33. Development of traditional cultural and artistic potential	45. Development of the commune's traditional cultural and artistic potential	54. Development of the commune's traditional cultural and artistic potential
	34. Management and conservation of archives	46. Management and conservation of communal archives	55. Management and conservation of communal archives
		47. Creation and management of sites and monuments	56. Creation and management of sites and monuments
		48. Monitoring of the restoration and rehabilitation of historical sites and monuments	57. Monitoring of the restoration and rehabilitation of historical sites and monuments
7. Civil defense, assistance, and emergency relief	35. Participation in the protection and promotion of human rights	49. Participation in the protection and promotion of human rights	58. Participation in the protection and promotion of human rights
	36. Participation in the advancement and social protection of individuals and groups	50. Participation in the social advancement of individuals and rights	59. Participation in the social advancement of individuals and rights
	37. Participation in the organization and management of emergency relief for vulnerable groups and disaster victims	51. Participation in the organization and management of emergency relief for vulnerable groups and disaster victims	60. Participation in the organization and management of emergency relief for vulnerable groups and disaster victims
	38. Participation in the organization of civil defense and fire fighting: creation and management of fire brigades	52. Participation in the organization of civil defense and fire fighting: creation and management of fire brigades	61. Participation in the organization of civil defense and fire fighting: creation and management of fire brigades
	39. Participation in disaster control		

(continued next page)

Table 2.2 (continued)

	Devolved responsibilities		
Function	Region (A)	Urban commune (B)	Rural commune (C)
Mandatory expenditures[a]			
8. Funeral services and cemeteries		53. Regulation of funeral services and cemeteries	62. Regulation of funeral services and cemeteries
		54. Installation and management of cemeteries	63. Installation and management of cemeteries
		55. Issuance of inhumation permits or authorization for transfer of mortal remains	64. Issuance of inhumation permits or authorization for transfer of mortal remains
		56. Enforcement control of regulations on funerals and mortal remains transfer	65. Enforcement control of regulations on funerals and mortal remains transfer
		57. Creation and management of funeral services	66. Creation and management of funeral services
		58. Construction, maintenance, and management of morgues	67. Construction, maintenance, and management of morgues
9. Water and electricity	40. Opinion on national water supply programs	59. Opinion on the water supply master plan	68. Opinion on the water supply master plan
	41. Participation in formulating the regional water supply master plan	60. Formulation and implementation of the local plans for producing, distributing, and managing energy	69. Formulation and implementation of the local plans for producing, distributing, and managing energy
	42. Participation in maintenance and conservation of watercourses	61. Creation and management of energy infrastructure	70. Creation and management of energy infrastructure
	43. Participation in construction and maintenance of reservoirs, dams, wells, and boreholes	62. Production and distribution of drinking water	71. Production and distribution of drinking water
	44. Opinion on electrification plans in the region	63. Construction and management of wells, boreholes, and standpipes	72. Construction and management of wells, boreholes, and standpipes
	45. Participation in formulating the regional electrification master plan	64. Participation in formulating the regional electrification plan	73. Participation in formulating the regional electrification plan
			74. Installation and management of public lighting

(continued next page)

Table 2.2 (continued)

| Function | Devolved responsibilities | | |
	Region (A)	Urban commune (B)	Rural commune (C)
Mandatory expenditures[a]			
	46. Participation in formulating the national electrification plan	65. Installation and management of public lighting	
10. Markets, fairs, and slaughterhouses	47. Creation, development, and management of sites for fairs	66. Creation, development, and management of markets	75. Creation, development, and management of markets
	48. Organization of regional fairs	67. Construction and management of slaughterhouses	76. Construction and management of slaughterhouses
	49. Participation in construction and management of regional slaughterhouses		

Sources: Data compiled from the legal bases (Law No. 005-2004, Art. 85–105) in effect in 2009.
Note: PAIE = Aquaculture zones of economic interest (*Périmètres aquacoles d'intérêt économique*); SAEDH = Zoning Plan for Housing (*Schéma d'aménagement de l'espace d'habitation*); SAEPC = Plan for productive space and conservation areas (*Schéma d'aménagement de l'espace de production et de conservation*); SDAU = Urban Planning Master Plan (*Schéma directeur d'aménagement urbain*); SRA = Regional Development Plan (*Schéma régional d'aménagement*).
a. Within these functions that have been transferred to the CTs, some expenditures are totally mandatory (delegation); some are mandatory only in part (delegation up to the norm required by the central government, devolution for the extra expenditure if the CT so chooses); and some are not mandatory (devolution: CTs are free to decide and offer the service or not).

demonstration effect can be triggered. Such cases are considered to be "pilot communes" (or, respectively, "pilot regions").

- *Managerial.* Implementation is gradual to take into account the *political capacity* to absorb decentralization (playing a lead role in local goods and services provision) and the *management capacity* to roll out the decentralized policies (managing the production function of local public goods and services).

Although not mentioned in the legislation, the principle of progressiveness in the Burkinabé setting is specified in the Strategic Framework for the Implementation of Decentralization (*Cadre stratégique de mise en œuvre de la decentralisation*) adopted by the central government in March 2007.[30] According to this document, the principle of progressiveness signifies that the transfer of powers to local governments "is carried out gradually depending on the level of ownership of the local authorities and implementation capacities of the (central) State."

In the same document, the central government explains that the notion of ownership is twofold: *Social ownership* "consists in ensuring that the population and civil society organisations become involved as responsible citizens in the management of local affairs." *Political ownership* "concerns the major role that political parties are called on to play so that the democratic rules of the game are strictly respected and local populations encouraged to consciously participate in the political arena." However, no further details are given on the "implementation capacities of the [central] State."

These specifications for a progressive rollout based on political ownership by the various stakeholders of decentralization (such as local governments, civil society, and political parties) furnish little concrete information on how this devolution is to be implemented and operated. As a result, we had to abandon our institutional economy analysis and instead use an interview approach. Based on our field visits and exchanges on this subject, we suggest that the principle of progressiveness be applied in the three above-mentioned dimensions in the following ways:

- *In the functional dimension*, as decentralized responsibilities
- *In the territorial dimension*, as limited to selected communes
- *In the managerial dimension*, as managerial capacity (from deconcentration to devolution).

Decentralized responsibilities   The transfer of responsibilities was not to come into effect at the time that Law 005-2004 entered into force in 2006, but rather on a step-by-step basis. A first package of responsibilities was selected relating to 4 of the 10 areas of competence to be decentralized—even if implementation was still not fully operational because the assigned financial resources were not commensurate (not by a long way) with needs. Thus, in late 2009, the implementation of decentralization involved four areas of competence (and in only some of the communes, not yet including the regions in the process):

- Culture, sports, recreation, and youth (function 6 in table 2.2)
- Preschool, primary education, and literacy (part of function 5)
- Drinking water supply and sanitation (relating to functions 2, 4, and 9)
- Health (part of function 4).[31]

However, apart from subsidiarity and progressiveness, there was no mention of the criteria used to determine which central government responsibilities were to be decentralized or the criteria used to select the responsibilities included in the four areas of competence that made up the first package.

The communes involved   The decentralization process is being carried out selectively in a limited number of communes. The choice of communes was not based on a concept of "experimental decentralization" or on the rule of least resistance but on an institutional approach: initially 33, then 49, urban communes are mentioned, followed by the 13 communes that are regional capitals.

The rural communes appear as, and when, they sign the agreements with their supervisory authority for the transfer of responsibilities. For the time being, the decentralized regions are not included in this process.

Nonetheless, the transfer of resources—which is supposed to go hand in hand with the transfer of responsibilities—has not followed suit. For 2009, only two ministries—Basic Education and Literacy (MEBA) and Agriculture (MA)—earmarked budget grants for transferred equipment and made the corresponding disbursement onto the account opened by the MATD:[32]

- From the MEBA—(a) CFAF 2.8 billion to 49 urban communes for recurrent primary school expenses; and (b) the grants to 13 regional-capital communes for each existing or planned school within their jurisdiction
- From the MA—CFAF 200 million to rehabilitate boreholes located in a first group of 100 rural communes, with CFAF 2 million for each commune (Delegation of the European Commission to Burkina Faso 2009, 56).

Managerial capacity: From deconcentration to devolution   The question of managerial capacities has taken a specific route in the Burkinabé context because there was a phase in which the responsibilities due to be decentralized were first entrusted to the deconcentrated government agencies—for learning purposes. However, in this case, the learning phase did not strengthen CT managerial capacities but rather detoured in a direction that makes it difficult to judge whether the detour is a sincere effort toward decentralization or a form of resistance to devolution.

During the learning phase, deconcentrated government officials can gain knowledge and control of decentralized files before handing them over to equivalent-level CTs. Yet the transfer of responsibilities from the deconcentrated to the decentralized level, in terms of human resources, is a far-from-settled issue. This is mainly because the principle of progressiveness—in its definition, content, and scope—was not jointly developed by the partners of the decentralization process. There are at least three approaches to this process:

- The first approach, recommended and promoted by the central government, involves an initial phase of deconcentration designed to build up managerial and technical skills through a learning process. Government officials in deconcentrated services do not yet master the problems linked to implementing the devolved responsibilities—far from it. Devolution is supposed to follow once deconcentrated capacities have been consolidated, and these are then intended to support the CTs.
- The second approach takes the same progressive route—deconcentration, then devolution—but involves incorporating the deconcentrated government officials into the CTs. This approach entails defining their professional status and compensation as well as their terms of employment. This system

could avoid the problem of duplicate staffing (which would certainly result from the first approach), and the question of staffing needs of small communes would be raised.

- The third approach argues that the deconcentration phase could be eliminated if the CTs were given the financial resources to hire and pay government officials with the skills required by the devolved functions.

Devolution Issues

Four devolution issues come to the fore at this stage of the analysis: (a) coherence in the classification of responsibilities by area of competence; (b) imprecise headings for responsibilities; (c) confusion between responsibility transfers and financial transfers; and (d) need for a more detailed breakdown of devolved responsibilities, as these are too broadly defined.

Coherence in the classification of responsibilities   Each of the functions listed in the left-most column in table 2.2 should correspond horizontally to local responsibilities of the same nature. This is not always the case. Thus, implementing responsibilities B14 and C16 ("initiatives and support for school bus services") brings into play a production function (organization of schooling) that is inconsistent with function 1, which concerns land management and urban planning. School bus services are a factor of production in education (taking children to school, whatever the distance between home and school) and should therefore appear under function 5. Introducing greater coherence would make it possible to identify the exclusive responsibilities falling to each CT and at the same time clearly distinguish which responsibilities are shared by the regions, urban communes, and rural communes.

Imprecise headings for some responsibilities   The headings of some responsibilities are imprecise and ambiguous, which may lead to confusion. Thus, the heading for responsibility C4 ("participation in the building and maintenance of rural roads") for rural communes is found alongside responsibility A4 ("construction, maintenance of rural roads") for the region. What does the addition of "participation" imply? Does it mean participating in decisions on a road project, awarding contracts, comanaging the production function, or only contributing financially without having any say in the matter? Depending on the answer, the implications for the responsibilities of the contracting CTs are not the same. Moreover, if the term "participation" simply refers to a financial contribution (see the following point), then these two headings should not appear under the transfer of responsibilities but under the transfer of resources. The same remarks apply to the terms "initiatives and support for school bus services" mentioned above.

Finally, can a mere "opinion" be considered to be a devolved responsibility? Are the responsibilities A1 ("opinion on the SRA/SDAU"), B1 ("opinion on the

SDAU"), and C1 ("opinion on the SAEDH") not simply administrative proce-dures? In any case, these headings do not allow a clear understanding of the offers and production functions of these responsibilities.

Confusion between responsibility transfers and financial transfers   Some of the competences listed in table 2.2 can, reasonably speaking, refer only to the transfer of funds, not responsibilities. This is notably the case for the regional responsibilities A16, A23, A24, and A25. For instance, given that the acquisi-tion, construction, and management of schools are the exclusive responsibility of the commune (see B38 and C47), the responsibility A25 ("participation in constructing and managing secondary schools") can denote only a participation in the costs.

Need to disaggregate devolved responsibilities that are too broadly defined   The fourth issue stems from the overbroad definitions of devolved responsibili-ties. A responsibility cannot be devolved without first analyzing its production function in detail. The traditional example of this—and this is an acid test of devolution—is compulsory education. Under function 5, the areas devolved to the communes are the "responsibility for developing preschool education: acquisition, construction, and management of schools" (respectively, B36 and C45) and the "responsibility for developing primary education: acquisition, building, and management of schools" (respectively, B37 and C46). But, as we have seen (see chapter 1, table 1.2), the production function for primary educa-tion has several components (Dafflon 2006, 271–305):

- Teacher training, in terms of both an initially recognized diploma and con-tinuous training
- Teachers' employment status (such as salary and social conditions)
- Curriculum content
- Teaching materials
- Buildings and technical educational equipment
- School buildings: construction and maintenance
- School organization (length of the school year, organization of school terms, the school week and day, school transport, and possibly school meals).

It is immediately obvious from this breakdown into seven factors of produc-tion that the mix and degree of deconcentration, delegation, or devolution are probably not uniform. There needs to be an interpretative guide to clarify the criteria underpinning choices and to explain the weight given to each of them by the stakeholders in decentralization. It is thus somewhat misleading to speak of the "devolution" of compulsory basic education. And this analysis can most likely be repeated for other responsibilities.

Local Taxation

The "revenue" column of the current budget (figure 2.4) takes four sources of revenue into account for decentralized CTs:

A. Taxes

B. Revenue from communal service provision

C. Revenue from communal property

D. Miscellaneous revenues.

This corresponds to the nomenclature under Law No. 014-2006 of May 9, 2006, on determining the revenues and expenditures of Burkinabé CTs. It should nonetheless be noted that there are a certain number of "false friends" in this list and that the grants for recurrent expenditures (*Dotation Globale de Fonctionnement*; DGF) such as the tax revenue sharing are, in fact, transfers (as further discussed in the "Intergovernmental Transfers" section, later) and not the CTs' own fiscal resources (as shown in table 2.3). Later, table 2.4 will detail the

Table 2.3 Classification of CTs' Own Revenues in Burkina Faso, 2009

Taxes ("*impôts*") (A)	Revenue from communal service provision (B)	Revenue from communal property (C)	Miscellaneous revenues (D)
• *Business license contribution*	• Slaughterhouse tax	• Stall placement fees: markets, fairs, stockyards	• Reimbursement of expenses
• *Residency tax*	• Revenue from sale of services	• Property rental	• Revenue from leasing/ *affermage* and services under concession or lease contracts
• *Mortmain tax*	• Tax on services rendered	• Other income from communal property	
• *Firearms tax*	• Revenue from maternity and health clinics	• Fees for occupation of public spaces	• Nonreinvested industrial or commercial earnings
• *Land tax*	• Equipment rental		
• *Informal sector contribution*	• Health inspection tax	• Cemetery concessions	• Financial revenue
• Entertainment tax	• Other operating revenues	• Parking charge	• Revenue from sponsorship and voluntary contributions
• Gaming tax	• Fees for issuance of administrative and civil registration documents	• Tax on damage to communal property	
• Advertising tax			• Contingent or nonrecurring revenues
• Cart tax	• Funeral tax		• Revenue from police fines
• Municipal development tax	• Street sweeping and refuse collection fees		• Contribution to parcelization operations

Source: Law No. 014-2006: Art. 13 for the regions, Art. 15 for the communes.
Note: CT = territorial collectivity. Those sources of revenue shown in italics are identical for the regions and the decentralized communes. The others are revenues of communes only. All revenues designated as a tax are referred to in the French nomenclature by the term "*taxe*," but they are, in fact, "*impôts*" in reference to their characteristics.

six main municipal taxes (shown in italics in column A of table 2.3) whose receipts are shared with the regions.

A reading of table 2.3 may lead to confusion because the terms used for tax revenues do not correspond to conventional public finance nomenclature, and the classification into four categories (A to D) is based on the source of the revenues. This makes a comparative reading difficult and lacking in coherence from the point of view of local public finance management. Given the importance of budgetary constraint resulting from available resources—and thus the CTs' financial leeway depending on their own tax-raising capacities—it is crucial that, first of all, fiscal resources be correctly defined and that decentralized own resources then be listed under the correct categories. The next two subsections ("Categories of Tax Revenues" and "Local Leeway in Tax Matters") address this confusion, while the third section ("Revenue and Expenditure Statistics") analyzes the situation at the end of 2009 from the point of view of financial statistics.

Categories of Tax Revenues

The first issue involves the distinction between the different types of revenue in the Burkinabé fiscal system: "*impôt*," "taxe," and "*redevance*" (which translates as tax and user fee or user charge, in English vocabulary).[33]

"Impôt" (nonbenefit-related tax)   This type of tax corresponds to a levy that is

- *Mandatory* by virtue of the state's sovereign powers
- *Not a consideration for services* rendered to the taxpayer or, in other words, the taxpayer can in no way claim a particular service in return
- *Unearmarked*, that is, entering into the CT's general budget or account for the general funding of local public policies and services.

From a public finance point of view, designating these taxes as "contributions" or "taxes for services rendered" is a misnomer.

"Taxe" (benefit-related tax)   This tax is *mandatory* and paid to the CT by virtue of its *monopolistic position in exchange for a service rendered*. The proceeds of such taxes go to the CT's general budget with no obligation to earmark them. In other words, to benefit from a service, the economic agent has no choice but to solicit the CT, which delivers the service against payment.

Contrary to the first category of taxes, benefit-related taxes are payable only by the economic agent (individual or enterprise) that uses the service. Such a tax is not paid if the service has not been requested: concretely, this means that the economic agent can *opt out of the service* (if he or she has no use for it or finds a private solution). In this case, he or she does not pay. Like "*impôts*," benefit-related taxes are set at the full discretion of the local authority that grants right of use; they do not depend on the volume of service provided to the agent or on operating costs.

"Redevance" (user fees and charges)   User fees and charges are the price of a service rendered to an economic agent that uses the service, the amount payable being proportionate to the benefit that the agent derives from the service rendered. There is thus a relationship of equivalence between the service and the price paid. In concrete terms, this means that a user fee

- *Is earmarked*: its proceeds must be assigned to the task for which it is levied (which also means that a functional classification of tasks is required in the local accounting system, at least for those financed on the basis of the "principle of equivalence").

- *Must obey the cost-covering rule*: because the service and payment must show equivalence, the sum of individual payments cannot exceed the total cost of the task financed.[34] Any surplus revenue is considered as hidden taxation. This implies two specific accounting arrangements: First, it is necessary to ensure that all costs actually appear under the functional heading (interest and amortization of the investment used to produce the service, production facility maintenance costs, and recurrent operating costs). Second, if there is a surplus, a corresponding reserve account must be set up at the level of the surplus amount (annual surpluses fuel the reserve, which can then be drawn upon in case of shortfalls). However, if imbalances persist, they should be corrected by adjusting the pricing for the service.

The coupling of these two criteria (earmarking and cost covering) means that user fees constitute a source of funding for specific tasks (see, in chapter 1, figure 1.2, the equivalence between [B] and [2]). *Redevances* cannot be used to increase general revenue or a CT's overall financial elbow room.

It should be pointed out that a CT cannot levy user fees and charges unless a certain number of technical conditions are met (Dafflon and Madiès 2008, 56–59):

- The beneficiaries must be identified and personalized.
- Individuals can be excluded through prices (someone who does not consume does not pay and, conversely, someone who does not pay cannot have access).
- Capacity limits must be taken into account for price setting.
- Mild externalities or spillover effects must be integrated (which means attempting to make the three circles of deciders, beneficiaries, and payers coincide).

Tax categories in practice   In table 2.3, the revenues designated as *"taxes"* (in French) in column A all belong, in fact, to the *"impôts"* category. They meet the three defining criteria: the obligation to pay, no entitlement to anything in return, and no assignment of the revenue to a specific task. The other columns of table 2.3 (B, C, and D) do not include "*impôts*."

It is important to note that the fact that a tax base is personalized does not make it a benefit-related tax. For example, the tax on carts (*taxe sur les charrettes*) is not benefit related. Of course, only cart owners pay this tax, and the tax base is thus selective. But payment of the tax does not entitle them to claim a particular service; they receive nothing in return. These tax receipts go into the communal budget and are not assigned to a specific task.

The revenues in column B break down into benefit-related taxes and user fees. But they cannot be immediately categorized without a detailed examination of the bases of calculation—which is not treated here but could be undertaken in a subsequent step. At first glance, the items listed seem to correspond to user fees (or "prices") if they meet the following criteria:

- Service is received in exchange for payment.
- Equivalence or proportion exists between the payment and the service rendered.
- Receipts are assigned exclusively to funding the task.
- Pricing does not overstep compliance with the cost-covering principle.

Drawing on European practices, the most telling example is certainly the fee for household refuse collection: this is paid in exchange for a service; it should be proportionate to the volume of waste (the bigger the volume, the higher the payment); it should be reported under a functional cost center ("refuse collection") to ensure the equivalence between service and payment; and, finally, it should comply as far as possible with the cost-covering rule.

Category C revenues are more akin to benefit-related taxes. It is clear from the levies described that these apply only when a service is rendered in exchange. But the likeness to benefit-related taxes stops there. It is difficult to say how and to what extent the levy is proportionate to the service provided, and in most cases the revenue is assimilated into the CT's general budget without being earmarked for a specific task. Yet, as in the listing in column B, the frontier between the two categories is not a sharp line. For example, if the "parking charge" involves paying for the right to park a vehicle in a public space and the revenues accrue to the general account, it is a benefit-related tax. On the other hand, if the parking is within a bounded area (such as a car silo, a specially designed enclosed space, perhaps with surveillance) and the receipts are used solely to finance the amenity's operating costs (capital outlay and operating expenses), then this implies a price—in other words, a user fee. And here the difference is clear to see: A benefit-related tax corresponds to a policy on the use of public space—for example, the closer one gets to the urban center, the more expensive the parking is—with no other consideration apart from the right to park one's vehicle. A user fee varies from one parking space to another, depending on the quality of the service provided, to separately finance each structure (here considered as a dedicated property and not as an open public space).

As for the "tax on damage to communal property," this seems to us more akin to a sanction for damage caused or for an offense: one is not "paying" ex ante for damage, but if one is identified ex post as the perpetrator, one has to pay for repair. Here, we have the notion of a fine rather than a benefit-related tax.

Local Leeway in Tax Matters

Two key questions for devolution concern (a) the assignment of tax powers to decentralized local governments; and (b) the full authority to adjust devolved taxes to local needs in the decentralized budget (either to finance own expenditure decisions or to supplement inadequate budget grants). What is involved, of course, is not total sovereignty in tax matters but rather a certain flexibility to maneuver at the margin.

The theoretical concepts of fiscal sovereignty and fiscal flexibility   The conceptual definition of fiscal sovereignty is a government's capacity (in this case, the CT) to create, set, and levy a tax. The following synthetic formula presents the general arrangement used for a direct levy, such as the business license contribution:

$$T = t \times [B - D_j] \times K_{CTi}, \qquad\qquad (2.1)$$

where T = tax yield,
$\quad t$ = tax rate,
$\quad B$ = gross tax base,
$\quad D$ = possible deductions or adjustments (here j possibilities),
$\quad [B - D]$ = net taxable base,
$\quad K$ = annual tax coefficient at the decentralized authority level, and
$\quad CT$ = territorial collectivity "i."

Full fiscal sovereignty means being able to decide B, D, and t. *Partial fiscal sovereignty* is limited to one or two components. *Fiscal flexibility* is represented by the ability to vary K, whereas t, B, and D are set by the central government (Dafflon and Madiès 2008, 44).

In the theory of fiscal federalism and decentralization, a CT should enjoy a margin of maneuverability to enable it to balance its current budget and finance its own choices. This leeway can be achieved in two ways:

- *Balanced sharing of tax sources.* The CTs have access to several tax sources, some of which are raised entirely at their own discretion. The CTs can levy them or not, depending on their needs. These taxes, however, must yield a decent, and not insignificant, share of the CTs' fiscal resources. The tax base also needs to grow in line with economic conditions so that it is buoyant over time.

- *Fiscal flexibility.* Each individual CT is given the ability to adjust the coefficient K in equation (2.1).

It should also be mentioned that the territorial boundaries of the base B rarely come under discussion in the theoretical model. It is assumed that the base is taxed in the place where the created value is produced. The place of production, the producer's registered offices, and the tax base are presumed to be situated in the same CT. Yet, national practices in tax law diverge from this ideal scenario. There may be a legal decoupling between the place of production and a company's registered offices. This then raises the question of the right to tax: To which CT should the tax resource be attached—the legal domicile or the production site? Or, again, how should the right to tax be shared between the CT where the company is registered and the CT where value is produced? These questions are not minor ones in terms of capturing fiscal resources, for various reasons or under various circumstances:

- Natural resources are found in rural areas, whereas the operating companies are headquartered in the capital.
- A mismatch exists between places of production and the commune in which the company is registered.
- There is a disparity of needs between CTs: the CT where production is located has to bear the infrastructure costs of economic activity zones and environmental protection, but it will not collect the tax if this is assigned to the CT hosting the company's registered offices.
- Tax competition is easier between communes where companies are registered than between communes where production is located because, theoretically, it is easier to change a headquarters' location than to move production facilities.

Local fiscal sovereignty in practice   What is the situation on the ground in Burkina Faso? The local government tax system identifies "six taxes" (first listed at the top of column A in table 2.3) assigned to the communes but subject to a rule for sharing the tax receipts between the communes and regions (further discussed in the "Shared Taxes versus Tax Revenue Sharing" section later) as well as five other exclusive communal taxes (whose receipts are not shared with the regions), as follows:

- Six "shared" taxes
  - Business license contribution

- ○ Residency tax
- ○ Mortmain tax
- ○ Firearms tax
- ○ Land tax
- ○ Informal sector contribution
- Other local taxes
  - ○ Entertainment tax
  - ○ Gaming tax
  - ○ Advertising tax
  - ○ Cart tax
  - ○ Communal development tax

Table 2.4 provides more detail on the six main communal taxes that involve revenue sharing with the regions. For those six taxes, the communes have no fiscal sovereignty: t, B, and D are set by the central government. $K = 1$, which translates into an absence of fiscal flexibility. There is thus no institutional margin of maneuver.[35] Therefore, the communes have to turn to other solutions if they wish to increase their fiscal resources. Only two avenues are open to them:

- Mobilize the "other local taxes" if sufficient bases for these exist.
- Verify that the tax bases estimated and taxed by the central government have been correctly identified and quantified, as the Burkinabé communes are not tasked with managing tax collection and litigation. This option is not practicable for the time being because the communes do not receive the nominal list of tax debtors within their territories.

It should also be noted that the current practice of taxing the base in the commune where a company is legally registered rather than in the commune hosting the place of production obviously leads to tax bases being concentrated in Ouagadougou, where the main registered offices are located.

Box 2.2 describes the territorial divisions of tax collection through the General Directorate of Taxation.

Shared Taxes versus Tax Revenue Sharing

The six decentralized "direct" taxes are communal, but their revenue is shared in the proportions given in table 2.5. First, however, it would be useful to recall the two definitions that distinguish a *shared tax* from *revenue sharing*:

- *Shared tax.* Several tiers of government have access to the same tax base. If each government has full *fiscal sovereignty*, each can define the tax base, and

Table 2.4 The Six Main Local Taxes in Burkina Faso, 2011

Tax	Base	Tax Rate and Schedule	Exemptions	Remarks	Reference
Business license contribution	Business tax based on the turnover of a company or an independent profession (fixed part) and on the rental value (RV) of fixed assets used for the business (variable part)	Fixed component: rate based on turnover band, differentiated by business category Variable component: 8% of RV	..	A proportional business tax on public markets exists, applied to firms that have no permanent establishment in Burkina Faso	Tax Code (*Code des Impôts*; CI), Art. 238–253
Residency tax (TR)	Any person with an income, for the occupation of premises used for habitation or any household residing in a developed urban area	Rate differentiated by category depending on geographic criteria and level of comfort (water connection and electricity meter amperage); minimum: CFAF 2,000	Married woman living with her husband; state and local governments; diplomatic and consular agents; the elderly, infirm, and indigent	None	CI, Art. 219–236
Mortmain tax (TBM)	RV of ground, property, and land of unlimited-life legal entities	Percentage of RV of buildings: 10% for hard-wall buildings and 2.5% for semi-hard-wall or mud-and-thatch buildings	State, rural communities, communes Companies with activities in social housing, farm credit, or medical assistance	Deduction of 40% or 50% of RV	CI, Art. 199–210
Firearms tax	Any holder of a firearm or air gun	Rate depends on type of arm, from CFAF 600 to CFAF 5,000.	Armed forces' and ceremonial weapons	Annual tax based on self-declared ownership	CI, Art. 282–290

Land tax	Any occupation and use of land or assets incorporated into a company or property transfer	Rates vary depending on locality and land zoning. Minimum: 2% Maximum: 25% of the cadastral value	..	As of January 1, 2009, an unspecified share of receipts from this tax is assigned to the central government and accrued to a special Treasury account known as the "parcelization operations fund."	Not mentioned in the CI
Informal sector contribution (CSI)	Business tax payable by private or legal persons operating an informal itinerant or home-based activity, applied to businesses whose annual turnover does not exceed the following: Purchase-resale: CFAF 30 million Others: CFAF 15 million	Eight categories based on a flat-rate scale: by zone (by locality) and depending on how the business is run by turnover band	—	Collected by the DGI since 2007: specific tax arrangement for itinerant businesses	Article 371 ter of the CI

Sources: Data from DGI, December 2009; Ky 2010, 189.
Note: DGI = General Directorate of Taxation; .. = negligible; — = not available.

BOX 2.2

Territorial Services of the General Directorate of Taxation

The territorial services of the General Directorate of Taxation (*Direction Générale des Impôts*; DGI) are organized into Regional Directorates (*Direction Régionale des Impôts*; DRIs) for 13 regions (6 DRIs are still to be set up) and into tax divisions (*Divisions Fiscales*; DFs) at the provincial level. Each DF is responsible for the local tax base and tax collection. A specialized local tax service was created at the DRI level for Ouagadougou and Bobo-Dioulasso. The DFs receive financial aid from the communes, the contributions varying in line with a commune's financial capacity and the degree to which local elected officials are involved. Most often, this aid involves making transport (motorbikes) available and supplying fuel coupons. In some cases, the communes also provide communal staff to help.

Much more rarely, the communes agree to actively participate in the job of broadening the tax base. Yet, pooling files and cross-comparing records would produce a wealth of information to be exploited. During our interviews, we were informed that the commune of Ouagadougou had signed an agreement with the Ministry of Finance whereby the latter would give the commune information on tax debtors (especially for the business license contribution). The commune plans to use its own administrative resources to support the central government tax collector in managing taxation. For the informal economy contribution, the communal administrator accompanies the tax collector, who is a central government official—first, because he or she is more familiar with the informal economy environment, and second, to check that all the bases have indeed been taxed. In another commune, this was also the practice for collection of the cart tax.

Table 2.5 Tax Revenue Sharing of CTs and Regions in Burkina Faso, 2010

Tax concerned	Special-status communes	Other communes
Business license contribution		
Residency tax	98.5% to the communes	97% to the communes
Mortmain tax	1.5% to the region	3% to the region
Firearms tax		
Informal sector contribution		
Land tax	75% to the communes	
	25% to the region	

Source: Compiled from DGI fiscal data valid in 2010.
Note: CT = territorial collectivity.

there will be as many definitions as government units, resulting in obvious coordination and harmonization problems. Taxes that have the same base but are shared by several tiers of government, each of which freely sets the tax rate, enter into this category (*shared tax base*).

- *Revenue sharing.* Generally, the tax base and tax rate are set by a higher tier of government. When the higher tier of government collects the tax but a fixed share of the tax revenue is assigned to lower-tier government units, the sharing is *vertical.* When a CT collects the revenue but must share the receipts with another CT at the same level, sharing is *horizontal.* Two methods of revenue sharing exist, depending on (a) the tax revenue collected within the CT in question according to the origin criterion (also called the "principle of derivation"); or (b) a distribution formula that includes various elements, such as population size, or that aims to reduce potential fiscal disparities (in this last case, we refer to "revenue equalization").

In the case of the CTs in Burkina Faso, tax sharing is based on the derivation principle. In other words, the region receives 1.5 percent of the receipts from the first five taxes and 25 percent of the receipts from the sixth tax levied by all the communes located within its jurisdiction. For the regions encompassing the two special-status urban communes, the latter transfer only 1.5 percent of the revenue of the first five taxes listed in table 2.5. There is no equalizing distribution.

Problem Areas in Local Taxation
In the context of the tax situation described, several problem areas need to be addressed:

- *Are taxes appropriately shared between the central government and the CTs?* In other words, are the tax bases for the current six mandatory taxes plus those for the other taxes sufficiently responsive to local economic development? Is this also the case with respect to the growing budgetary needs of CTs within the context of progressive decentralization?

- *Where should the business license tax be levied?* What about the revenue sharing between the commune where the company is legally registered and the commune where production takes place, and what is the distribution formula? Should an equalizing distribution formula for these tax receipts be envisaged in the medium run between the commune hosting a company's registered offices and those communes that host its production facilities?

- *If a communal official has to accompany the tax collector (central government official) to ensure efficiency, would it not be better to transfer the management of these (six) taxes to the local authorities?* Can this transfer be carried out in compliance with the rule of progressiveness, commune by commune, based on a contract signed between the commune and central government, provided that there is an adequate guarantee of their fiscal management capacity (in terms of billing, collection, litigation, and so on)?

- *What fiscal flexibility should be granted to the CTs?*
- *What place should be given to user fees, and for what tasks?*

- *The tax recovery rate is calculated using the budget forecast and not the issued tax rolls, raising a twofold problem*: First, because the rate forecast for one year is increased incrementally over the previous forecast, the eventual omission of tax bases (for lack of information or incentives) to some extent favors a low recovery rate forecast; it is thus quite easy to achieve a high recovery rate. But, second, although the recovery rate must be calculated based on the tax rolls, it must also be ensured that each roll includes an exhaustive list of the taxpayers, which does not appear to be a straightforward matter. According to the DGI, the forecasts made by the different communes provide no guarantee of homogeneity. Consolidating them is therefore a hit-and-miss exercise. Observed recovery rates are often close to 100 percent and sometimes even higher. However, such a rate is not in itself indicative of a truly high-performing recovery system if it is not established that the whole tax base has been taken into account.

- *How can a CT accounting system be put into place so that budgets and accounts classify expenditures?* The classification should not simply be on an accounting and economic basis but also according to function, with revenues organized by type as individualized items. Bear in mind that, for user fees and charges, the accounting system must allow traceability—or, in other terms, tracking—of the equivalence between expenditure and revenue for a given function.

Intergovernmental Transfers

Financial transfers are a crucial source of communal funding, not only because own fiscal resources are insufficient but also because there is a need for policy incentives and corrections to support the production of delegated local goods and services. Without transfers, urban and rural communes could not fulfill their expenditure obligations, and the decentralization process would completely unravel.

To give a clearer picture of the current situation, we have depicted the technical-economic architecture of the system of financial aid provided by the central government to decentralized government units, excluding external sources such as aid from international donors and nongovernmental organizations (NGOs). We have also omitted the budget lines to the deconcentrated levels of government, even though—as we have already seen—deconcentration is part of the rationale behind the decentralization process during the initial phase of application of the progressiveness rule. This architecture is explained later and summarized in figure 2.5. The "Revenue Sharing" subsection establishes indicative amounts for financial aid based on the 2009 administrative budget. The "Importance of Intergovernmental Transfers" subsection highlights the issues that are still outstanding under the present system.

Figure 2.5 Central Government Transfers to Decentralized CTs in Burkina Faso, 2009

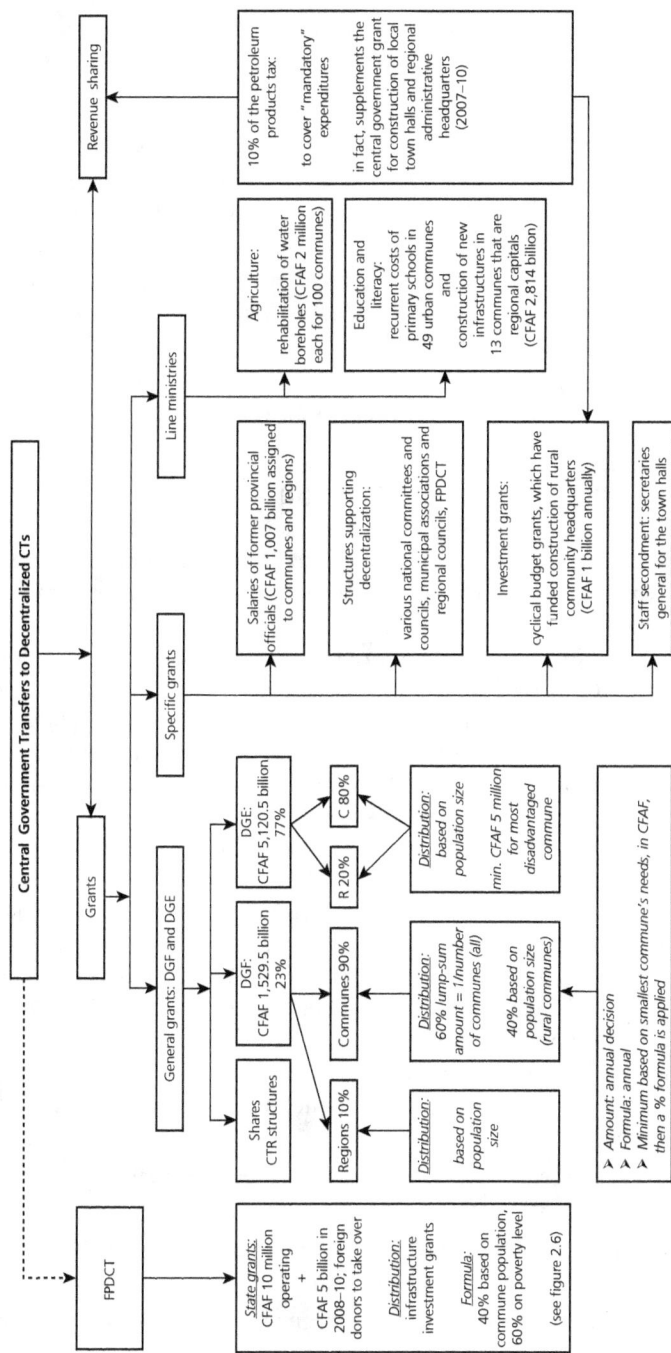

Source: Data from ministries and departments visited by the authors, October 2009.
Note: C = commune; CT = territorial collectivity; CTR = Regional Technical Committee (Commission technique régionale); DGE = Block grants for investment expenditures (Dotation générale d'équipement); DGF = Block grants for current expenditures (Dotation globale de fonctionnement); FPDCT = Permanent Development Fund for Territorial Collectivities (Fonds permanent pour le développement des CT); R = region.

Central Government Transfers to the CTs (2009)

The central government's transfers to the CTs (as shown in figure 2.5) can be analyzed on three levels:

- *Categories*: investment grants allocated by the Permanent Development Fund for Territorial Collectivities (*Fonds permanent pour le développement des collectivités territoriales*; FPDCT), grants, and revenue sharing
- *Types of grants*: (a) general grants, with two components (the DGF grants for recurrent expenditures and the DGE general grants for investment); (b) specific grants; and (c) specific budget lines allocated through the MATD by line ministries to support the decentralization of responsibilities
- *General grants*: split between DGF and DGE categories, allocations between regions and communes, and distribution formulas.

FPDCT transfers   Created by decree (254) in 2007,[36] the FPDCT is an autonomous body distinct from the central state (while being an emanation of the central government), with a legal identity and separate budget. In figure 2.5, the FPDCT connects to the title box with a broken line to underline that, despite its legally independent status, for the time being its funding still depends mainly on the state budget.

The FPDCT's mission is to mobilize resources to support funding for the development programs of local authorities and to strengthen their operational capabilities. The financial aid it delivers can be of three kinds (although, at the end of 2009, options [b] and [c] were not yet operational): (a) grants dedicated to investment, in the strict sense of the term; (b) loans; and (c) loan guarantees.

Two types of resources are available: (a) an annual budget envelope, capped at CFAF 10 million, to cover the Fund's management and administrative costs; and (b) an annual appropriation of CFAF 5 billion (currently guaranteed for 2008 to 2010) to finance local authority investment. For the time being, the Fund's financing comes from the state budget, but its sustainability is not guaranteed. As long as this situation persists, the Fund is under the technical supervision of the MATD and financial supervision of the DGF. Ultimately, the objective is to group together external and NGO financial assistance to avoid the proliferation and overlaps of similar projects and to coordinate external aid for the sake of regional efficiency (performance measurement) and equity. State aid should then gradually disappear.

In the long run, the logic behind separating the FPDCT and DGE furthers the pursuit of a dual objective:

- To avoid mixing different kinds of investment—using the Fund to support only new infrastructure investments
- To avoid discouraging foreign donors by giving the impression that their aid is used to replace financing of the DGE from the state budget.

The CTs can implement three types of investment: (a) replacement invest-ments to maintain their production capital (for example, major renovation of an existing school building); (b) investments to ensure the economic frame-work conditions for the CTs (for example, building a communal dirt track or road to facilitate communication between small villages in a commune); and (c) new investments geared toward the potential for economic development. The FPDCT is exclusively targeted at the third type of investment. Following this logic, categories (a) and (b) should be funded by the DGE.

Proposed projects must undergo a technical and financial feasibility study along with a cost-efficiency analysis. This is financed by the FPDCT, which can also furnish technical support. The communes have full discretion over which priorities they decide on. The Fund intends to set up a system of bonuses and penalties after three to four years of the functioning of the investment, account-ing for its use and maintenance.

For purposes of equity—in the sense that was reported to us—40 percent of infrastructure investment aid is allocated according to the number of inhabit-ants in the commune and 60 percent following a criterion that factors in the poverty level as defined and calculated by the official statistics. Figure 2.6 shows the distribution formula envisaged in the longer term. (At the end of 2009, the bonuses and penalties reserve was not funded: the basic drawing right is thus 100 percent.)

The synthetic index (*IS*) of the commune *j* is calculated using the following formula:

$$IS_j = \left(0.60 \times \frac{H_j}{\sum\limits_{i=1}^{349} H_i} \right) + \left(0.40 \times \frac{IP_j}{\sum\limits_{i=1}^{349} IP_i} \right), \qquad (2.2)$$

that is, 60 percent prorated on population *H* of the commune *j* in the total popu-lation of the 349 communes, and 40 percent prorated on a predefined "poverty depth" index (*IP*) (see table 2.6).

The amounts *M* received by each commune *j* are calculated as follows:

$$M_j = \text{CFAF 10 million} + \left(\frac{IS_j}{\sum\limits_{i=1}^{349} IS_i} \right) \times \text{remainder}. \qquad (2.3)$$

Grant allocations   General grants are distributed in three unequal amounts: grants for structures providing technical support to the communes, operat-ing grants, and investment grants. The first (and smallest) grant finances the

Figure 2.6 Distribution Formula of the Permanent Development Fund for Territorial Collectivities (FPDCT) in Burkina Faso, 2009

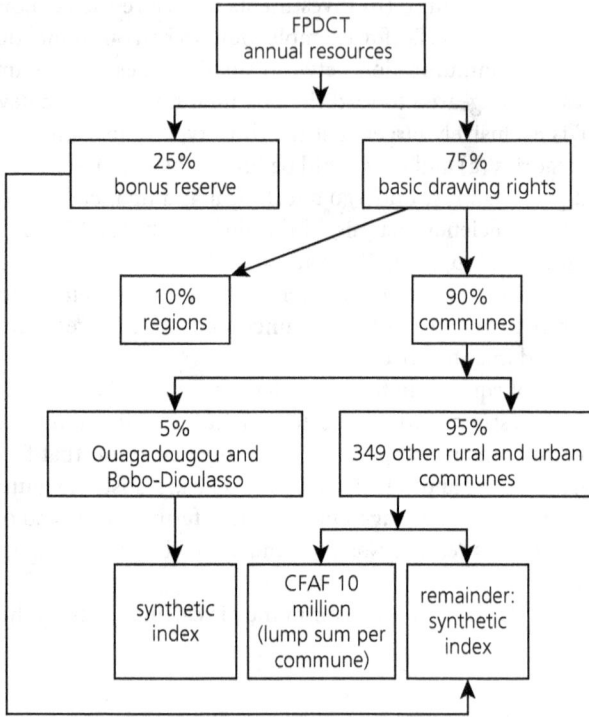

Source: Data from the FPDCT, October 2009.

Table 2.6 Regional Poverty Depth Index in Burkina Faso, 2009

Region	Number of communes	IP	Region	Number of communes	IP
Boucle du Mouhon	47	21.30	Est	27	12.3
Cascade	17	14.60	Hauts-Bassins	32	10.6
Centre	6	7.10	Nord	31	24.7
Centre-Est	30	19.97	Plateau Central	20	20.3
Centre-Nord	28	8.20	Sahel	26	12.6
Centre-Ouest	38	14.10	Sud Ouest	28	17.5
Centre-Sud	19	26.00			

Source: Data from FPDCT, October 2009.
Note: IP = poverty depth index. The higher the index of poverty depth, the more the local government will receive in relative proportion of its index in the total IP.

day-to-day running costs of the regional technical committees, which are pre-sided over by the governor and responsible for examining local budgets in view of their approval (see figure 2.1—here, it involves the "deconcentrated region").

The arrangements for the proportions allocated between the DGF and the DGE are set by joint ministerial decrees of the MATD and the Ministry of Finance. In 2008, for example, 23 percent of the allocation went to the DGF and 77 percent to the DGE.[37] Thereafter, the regions receive 10 percent of the DGF's portion and 20 percent of the DGE's portion, while the communes obtain 90 percent and 80 percent, respectively.[38]

The distribution formulas for grant allocations vary depending on (a) whether they concern the regions or the communes and (b) the type of grant. For the regions, the distribution rule depends on their respective population size, that is:

$$(DGF + DGE)_{region\, i} = \frac{H_{region\, i}}{\sum_{r=1}^{13} H_r} \times [M],$$

(2.4)

where the amount to be distributed is $M = (0.10 \times DGF) + (0.20 \times DGE)$.

The distribution of the DGE among the communes has the same form as equation (2.2): it is proportional to the population size.

$$(DGE)_{commune\, j} = \frac{H_{commune\, j}}{\sum_{c=1}^{151} H_c} \times [0.8 DGE]$$

(2.5)

The minimum DGE amount allocated to a commune is CFAF 5 million. This has been decided on as the basis for calculation because Article 27 of the CGCT specifies the following (emphasis authors'): "The rural commune is a group of villages with a population of at least 5,000 inhabitants and economic activities generating annual own resources of *at least CFAF 5 million (5,000,000)*."[39]

On the other hand, the distribution of the DGF has two components: a lump-sum component (60 percent of the total) and a component based on the each commune's population. The formula used is

$$(DGF)_{commune\, j} = \left(\frac{1}{351} \times 0.6 \times 0.9 \times DGF \right) + \left(\frac{H_{commune\, j}}{\sum_{c=1}^{351} H_c} \times 0.4 \times 0.9 \times DGF \right).$$

(2.6)

The grant amounts and formula percentages in equations (2.2) to (2.4) above are decided upon within the annual budgetary procedures by the two competent ministries, depending on the funds available. They have changed from year to year since 2007, yet this should not be seen as an ad hoc adjustment: the rates are subject to change to take into account the local authorities' actual situation. The calculation takes as its starting point the commune with the weakest fiscal and financial capacity and assesses what minimum grant would be required to reach a minimally acceptable level in its administrative management. The grants to the other communes are then adjusted accordingly.[40]

Earmarked financial aid allocations   Four types of financial aid are allocated to the CTs (Delegation of the European Commission in Burkina Faso 2009, 56) and earmarked. Two of them (types A and C below) are provisional. Type B aid should not be counted as decentralized aid to the CTs but rather as aid to the MATD for decentralization. Finally, the DGF should eventually take over type D aid because expenditures on staff salaries and social security are recurrent and fall under the CT current budget. The four types are as follows:

A. *To remunerate a number of government officials* who had been employed in the former provinces and are now seconded to the regions and communes. The central government continues to bear the costs of their salaries until they retire.

B. *To finance the structures that support decentralization* (six national or inter-ministerial committees or commissions, the association of municipalities, and the association of regional councils, as well as the FPDCT for the administrative part). It could indeed be wondered why the financial aid channeled through these structures and funded out of the MATD's budget is considered as a transfer to the CTs since this aid is clearly linked to steering and implementing the decentralization process, which comes under the responsibility of the MATD, not the regions or the communes.

C. *To build town halls and regional headquarters.* A building program spanning 2006–10 is still under way to provide each of the 351 communes and 13 regions with a fully equipped communal administrative center. The grant amounts to CFAF 1 billion annually, supplemented by funds from the communes' share of the tax on petroleum products (*Produit de la taxe sur les produits pétroliers*; PTPP), further discussed below.

D. *For the secretaries general seconded by the central government to town halls.* In 2009, the 49 urban communes, the arrondissements of Bobo-Dioulasso and Ouagadougou, and 282 of the 302 rural communes had a secretary general. Twenty communes still lack one.

Resource transfers associated with responsibility transfers   In 2009, four areas of responsibility were transferred to the CTs (as previously discussed in the "Assignment of Responsibilities" subsection on "Decentralized Responsibilities"). From then on, the communes were also to receive transfers of the resources associated with the exercise of these powers. The transfers have three characteristics:

- *At a budgetary level*, they should not be earmarked but added to the budget grants.

- *At a technical level*, they should match the transfer of the infrastructures (recurrent costs or capital investments to be made) and the supply of staff who have been assigned to the transferred responsibilities (mainly health workers, school teachers, and principals, whose salaries will continue to be paid by the central government—but whose monetary value must be attributed to decentralization).

- *At an operational level*, they are progressive and follow the pace of implementation (over three years).

The amounts budgeted for the first year of implementation raised several problems: (a) they only partially covered the decentralization measures taken in 2009; (b) they were far from concomitant with the needs linked to the transferred responsibilities; and (c) they were partly tied by spending guidelines decided on by the line ministries and not by the CTs. As a result,

- The Ministry of Agriculture budgeted CFAF 200 million to rehabilitate the boreholes to supply water for an initial group of 100 communes—CFAF 2 million per commune.

- The Ministry of Basic Education and Literacy budgeted CFAF 2.8 billion to cover the recurrent costs of primary schools in the 49 urban communes and school facilities in the 13 communes that are also regional capitals. The transfers in individual communes did not fit the definition of an untied general grant (as discussed further below).

There is controversy as to whether these financial transfers are actually earmarked. We have included the "line ministries" (for the moment, the MEBA and MA) on the earmarked grants side. However, according to the Delegation of the European Commission in Burkina Faso (2009, 55), "although these financial transfers are linked to the exercise of new powers, they are not legally assigned: they are absorbed into the budget of the communes." Nonetheless, considering the precise nature of their allocation—based mainly on what we were told during our visit to the commune of Ouagadougou—these transfers seem more akin to earmarked grants than to unearmarked ones.

In the capital, these transfers were specified under four headings for 2009: (a) school supplies for transferred schools (budget line 605); (b) other supplies for transferred schools (608); (c) maintenance of transferred schools (631); and (d) classroom construction (232).[41] The amounts under the four headings must comply with the criteria for qualitative and quantitative specificity (Dafflon

1998, 52). They are not substitutable: 1 franc not spent under one heading cannot be spent under another heading. Moreover, an Interministerial Circular of June 4, 2009, clearly stipulated which expenditures were eligible for funding through transferred resources.[42] The conditions tied to the transfers set the policy lines desired by the ministries and limited the choices open to the CTs.

In 2009, budget grants linked to the assignment of powers were directly transferred by each ministry (MA and MEBA) to each commune's treasury account, pursuant to a decree on how the said grants were to be distributed among the beneficiary communes.

For 2010, a special budget line was created under the Budget Law to lodge the grants from the ministries whose powers have been transferred (Section 98). This section is managed by the General Directorate of the Budget, which is the authorizing authority and which must unlock and replenish the CTs' accounts. It must also monitor and evaluate the execution of the said resources and, in the light of observations on the ground, propose the necessary readjustments for the following years.

Revenue Sharing

Sharing the Proceeds of the Petroleum Products Tax (PTPP)   The communes and regions receive 10 percent of the PTPP levied the previous year. This tax revenue accrues to the MATD. This type of revenue sharing is referred to as "vertical" because the state has fiscal sovereignty; only the tax revenues are shared. As previously discussed, there is also "horizontal" tax sharing between communes and regions (see the "Local Taxation" subsection, "Shared Taxes versus Tax Revenue Sharing").

The revenue distribution formula among the communes is rather vague. Initially it was prorated based on the number of registered cars (principle of derivation) because the tax replaced the motor vehicle tax. However, abolition of the vehicle tax made it impossible to count the vehicles concerned, with the result that the distribution formula, which was seen as unverifiable and inequitable, had to be abandoned.

The new distribution should enable all the communes to cover "at least their mandatory expenditures," even though the scope of obligation is not really delimited in terms of devolved responsibilities. As of 2009, the amount recorded under this item in the state budget was used to fund the construction of municipal and regional headquarters under a program that was due for completion in 2010. Thereafter, the share of the PTPP was to be effectively disbursed as a grant to the CTs—but the distribution formula had not been finalized.

The Importance of Intergovernmental Transfers (2009)

In the government budget forecast for 2009, financial support for decentralization was to amount to CFAF 17.99 billion, according to the distribution reported

in table 2.7. The table shows that grants represent 30.4 percent of the financial support to the communes, higher than the FPDCT share (27.8 percent).
Added to this are 5.6 percent for the construction of town halls and, currently,
14.4 percent for the PTPP.

The breakdown of financial aid between recurrent and capital expenditures
raises the question of consequential costs and gives some cause for concern. In
effect, as previously seen in figure 2.5, 77 percent of the general grants to communes must go toward investments (that is, 0.77×30.4 percent = 23 percent).

Table 2.7 State Budget Financial Support for Decentralization in Burkina Faso, 2009

Central Government Funding Sources (1)	CFAF (millions) (2)	Percentage (3)
Permanent Development Fund for Territorial Collectivities (FPDCT)	5,000	27.8
General grants		
Grants for structures providing technical support to communes	170	0.9
Grants to communes	5,473	30.4
Grants to regions	1,177	6.5
Remuneration of former provincial government officials	310	1.7
Structures supporting decentralization	254	1.4
National Twinning Committee (*Comité national de jumelage*)	4	—
Interministerial Technical Committee (*Commission technique interministérielle*)	40	—
National Commission for Decentralized Cooperation (*Comité national de coopération décentralisée*)	4	—
National Commission for Decentralisation (*Conseil national de la decentralisation*)	31	—
National Local Finance Commission (*Comité national des finances locales*)	10	—
Association of Municipalities of Burkina Faso (*Association des municipalités du Burkina Faso*)	50	—
Association of Regional Councils of Burkina Faso (*Association des conseils régionaux du Burkina Faso*)	15	—
National Monitoring and Evaluation Committee (*Comité national du suivi-évaluation*)	15	—
Permanent Development Fund for Local Authorities (*Fonds permanent pour le développement des CT*)	85	—
Construction of local government headquarters	1,000	5.6
Rehabilitation of boreholes	200	1.1
Infrastructure and recurrent school costs	1,814	10.1
Shares in revenue from the tax on petroleum products	2,597	14.4
TOTAL	**17,995**	**100.0**

Source: Delegation of the European Commission to Burkina Faso 2009, 53 and 56.
Note: — = not available. Corrections in the totals made by the authors.

In addition, 20 percent of own resources in CT budgets must go into the capital budget (see figure 2.4 on decentralized budgets). In other words, during this first ongoing phase of progressive devolution, an extraordinarily large part of local expenditure is devoted to infrastructure and investment. Will the communes' future budgets be able to bear the maintenance costs for this infrastructure and the operating costs of their decentralized responsibilities?

Revenue and Expenditure Statistics

Although the statistical data on CT expenditures and revenues in Burkina Faso are relatively abundant, they are poorly organized for measuring decentralization.[43] It is currently impossible to gain a precise picture of the real extent to which competences are decentralized, to measure the performance of the institutional devolution process, or to assess the relative financial autonomy of the CTs. There are many reasons for these shortcomings. We will return to these in the rest of this section.

Expenditure Data

Time-series expenditure data exist for the period 1996–2006 and have been published. Table 2.8 summarizes the data for the years 2004–06. Several remarks are necessary here:

- The data are taken from the administrative accounts and thus represent budgetary data and not the results of accounts based on actual expenditure.
- The classification of expenditure headings by line item corresponds to an accounting classification. As far as we know, there is no functional classification of expenditure. This naturally means that it is impossible to measure the decentralization of responsibilities.
- Decentralization was made progressive in 2006, yet current data do not allow assessment of the changes that have occurred since 2006, which is nonetheless a critical year in the targeted process in Burkina Faso.

Aside from these reservations, it can be observed that almost 70 percent of both current and capital expenditures are implemented in the two special-status communes, and 25 percent in the 49 urban communes. For 2006 (the last column in table 2.8), this proportion reaches 93.55 percent for current expenditure (line 10) and 96.52 percent for capital expenditure (line 11). The same information is given separately for Ouagadougou, Bobo-Dioulasso, and the other 49 urban communes. The spending power of the rural communes is virtually absent.

The ratios between capital expenditures and current expenditures are high—at 64 percent, 56 percent, and 87 percent, respectively, for the three reference

Table 2.8 Communal Expenditures in Burkina Faso, 2004 and 2006
CFAF, billions

	Expenditure type	2004	2005	2006	2006 Ouaga-dougou	Bobo-Dioulasso	49 urban communes	Ouagadougou + Bobo-Dioulasso + 49 urban communes
	Current expenditure							
1	Personnel expenditure	2.549	2.828	3.151	1.336	0.609	1.036	2.981
2	General management and transport	1.267	1.214	1.610	0.696	0.279	0.496	1.471
3	Goods and supplies	1.377	1.417	1.825	0.826	0.380	0.449	1.655
4	External works and services	1.633	2.064	2.570	1.685	0.462	0.357	2.504
5	Financial expenses	0.258	0.281	0.315	0.092	0.051	0.125	0.268
6	Transfers and grants	0.635	0.736	0.814	0.537	0.076	0.152	0.765
7	Other expenditure	0.326	0.338	0.499	0.102	0.106	0.236	0.444
8	Total I	8.043	8.878	10.784	5.273	1.963	2.852	10.089
9	Capital expenditure	5.217	5.026	9.419	5.843	1.018	2.231	9.091
	Total II (line 8 + line 9)	13.260	13.904	20.203	11.116	2.981	5.083	19.180
10	Ratio of commune(s)/total recurrent (%)	—	—	—	48.90	18.20	26.45	93.55
11	Ratio of commune(s)/total capital (%)	—	—	—	62.03	10.80	23.68	96.52
12	Ratio of capital/recurrent (%)	64.87	56.61	87.34	110.80	51.84	78.21	90.11

Source: MEF 2009, 49, 110–12.
Note: — = not available.

years 2004–06. Ouagadougou stands out, with a ratio of 110 percent in 2006. This situation heightens the concern about assuming the recurrent expenditure incurred based on the volume of investments (as discussed previously in sub-section on "The Importance of Intergovernmental Transfers").

Revenue Data

The figures for CT revenues, available over the period 1996–2006, are also inconsistent with the listing of CT resources as it appears in the legislation (as discussed in the "Local Taxation" section) because the available tables do not respect the categories listed under the law. Moreover, the terms used do not match. Table 2.9 lists five revenue categories, given in lines 11 to 15.

Table 2.9 Communal Revenue and Budget Ratios in Burkina Faso, 2004–06
CFAF, billions except where noted

Revenue type and budget ratio		2004	2005	2006		
1	Own revenue from state budget	344.8	365.2	391.9		
2	CTs' own revenue	13.5	14.0	16.6		
3	of which communes	9.7	11.0	13.8		
4	of which provinces	4.0	3.0	2.5		
5	Public sector total	358.3	379.2	408.5		
6	Ratio 2/3 (%)	3.9	3.8	4.2		
7	GDP in current prices	2,698.0	2,961.0	3,017.6		
8	Ratio 5/7 (%)	13.3	12.8	13.5		
9	Ratio 1/7 (%)	12.8	12.3	13.0		
10	Ratio 3/7 (%)	0.4	0.4	0.5		
Sources of communal "own" revenue					2006 Ouaga-dougou	2006 Bobo-Dioulasso
11	Direct taxes and contributions	5.588	6.822	7.966	4.877	1.419
12	Indirect taxes	0.320	0.370	0.459	0.197	0.073
13	Operating revenue	1.060	1.097	1.317	0.617	0.130
14	Revenue from communal property	1.791	1.606	2.266	0.430	0.630
15	Miscellaneous revenue	0.929	1.020	1.741	1.173	0.067
16	Total communal own revenue	9.688	10.915	13.749	7.293	2.319
17	Other revenue (external sources: international aid, NGOs)	4.419	4.232	6.946	4.002	0.761
18	Total communal revenue	14.107	15.147	20.695	11.295	3.080
19	Ratio taxes/total own revenue (%)	0.610	0.659	0.613	0.696	0.644
20	Ratio taxes/total overall revenue (%)	0.419	0.475	0.407	0.449	0.485
21	Ratio line 16 Ouagadougou + Bobo-Dioulasso/total of communes (%)	n.a.	n.a.	n.a.	53.05	16.86

Source: Ministry of the Economy and Finances 2009, 26, 53.
Note: CT = *collectivité territorial;* GDP = gross domestic product; NGO = nongovernmental organization.

The text of the MEF (2009, 20) sets out the following categories:

- Taxes and other levies approved by the National Assembly
- Taxes approved by the CTs' deliberative bodies, including
    - Revenue from communal property or infrastructures (markets, slaughter-houses, bus stations, and so on); and
    - Revenue from provision of local services (such as issuance of civil status documents and licenses.
- Central government grants: all financial resources transferred from the central government to the CTs
- Other revenue: loans, donations and bequests, and aid from decentralized cooperation (for example, NGOs and foreign local authorities).

Here, there is a real difficulty in interpreting the data:

- If we compare the categories and definitions in table 2.3 (in the "Local Taxation" section), which reports the legal provisions, with the definitions given above; and
- If we compare the categories of revenue in table 2.3 with the definitions given on lines 11 to 15 in table 2.9;
- Then the explanations provided in the MEF (2009, 2025) document are equally vague and fail to furnish the necessary detail.

Over and above the stand-alone interpretation of table 2.9, there is thus no possibility of gaining a real perspective on statistical revenue data within the context of decentralization. As with expenditure, this knowledge gap needs urgent attention: the statistical classification should at least comply with the categories provided for by law with regard to the details of each source of revenue.

The Issue of Statistical Data

The issue of data is relatively simple: it comes down to setting up a local accounting system that enables full control of budgets and expenditure forecasting at the CT level as well as the development of functional statistics to ensure proper steering of local public policies.

On the expenditure side, there is no functional classification, which means that there is currently no possibility of evaluating decentralization "performance." The appropriate form to adopt is a classification based on the budgetary and accounting heads "FFF.CCC," where FFF corresponds to a functional classification, with F being the function given by the areas of decentralized responsibilities (see chapter 1, table 1.1). The other FF digits are used to specify cost centers. CCC corresponds to the accounting classification as shown in the line items in chapter 1, table 1.6.

On the revenue side, what is needed is information based on precise definitions that make a distinction between taxes in the strict sense of the term and benefit-related taxes and other revenues from administrative and financial assets. The accounting system must also specify the cost centers financed by revenue from user fees and charges to ensure transparency in the application of the "user pays" principle. Approximate wording, such as in table 2.9 (lines 11 and 12), and aggregate data are not sufficient. What is required is a classification that gives details on the type of taxes and other resources that are consistent with the presentation in table 2.3, although this must itself be adjusted—as we saw in the "Categories of Tax Revenues" section for own resources and the "Central Government Transfers to the CTs" section for financial transfers.

Notes

1. Articles 143, 144, and 145 of the Constitution of the Fourth Republic.
2. The current National Assembly (AN).
3. Law No. 040/98/AN.
4. Programme Law No. 043/98/AN.
5. Now the Association of the Municipalities of Burkina Faso (AMBF).
6. CGCT, Art. 7.
7. In institutional economy, the 'economic-technical design' (created by Dafflon) is not simply a practical method of presenting state institutions. Of course, its main purpose is to simplify the sometimes difficult interpretation of the legislation governing the organization of local authorities. But the method has two further important advantages: first, it requires that the legal texts exhibit a coherence when cross-compared, by shedding light on the hierarchies, the channels of command and subordination; and, second, it is the only method that allows the formal design to be compared against the reality on the ground or, in other words, to confront what should exist with what exists.
8. CGCT, Art. 28–31.
9. Decree No. 2005-045, Art. 2.
10. Art. 54 of Decree No. 045-2005.
11. Law No. 055-2004, Art. 221; (d) added in 2011, Art. 221 new.
12. In most villages in the rural communes, the CVDs have taken over from the Village Land Management Commissions (*Commissions villageoises de gestion des terroirs*; CVGTs) that had been set up with the Community-Based Rural Development Program (*Programme national de gestion des terroirs*). Decree No. 032-2007 on the functioning of the CVDs specifies in its final provisions that the assets of the CVGTs are to be transferred to the CVDs as soon as these have been set up.
13. Law No. 021-2006/AN.
14. Decree No. 032-2007 of January 22, 2007.
15. CGCT, Art. 265.
16. Electoral Law No. 014-2001 of July 3, 2001, Art. 239.
17. CGCT, Art. 325.
18. CGCT, Art. 330.

19. CGCT, Art. 321 and 333.
20. Article 324 of Law No. 055-2004/AN on the CGCT.
21. Law No. 014-2006 of May 9, 2006, determines the resources and expenditure of the CTs.
22. An analysis of the 2007 administrative accounts shows that out of the 351 communes, only 95 carried out a transfer. Of these 95, only 32 made a transfer of at least 20 percent as legally required (information provided by the General Directorate of the Budget, December 9, 2009).
23. MEF (2009, 20).
24. If the "capital" section represents one-third of the total amount of both sections, the "current" section then corresponds to two-thirds of 100 percent, or 66⅔ percent. This comes down to saying that the proportion (capital/current) = 33⅓ percent over 66⅔ percent = 50 percent.
25. In practice, it is difficult to keep a check on these funds, and a great many CTs do not record them. They involve, for example, funds from decentralized cooperation (town-twinning and other initiatives), which are managed by local twinning committees. At the end of 2009, the legislation organizing these committees was still under second reading. There will probably be a move toward the fungibility of resources in CT budgets (information provided by the General Directorate of the Budget, December 9, 2009).
26. Note, however, that the Ouagadougou commune has trodden new ground in its 2010 budget by presenting a functional classification of current expenditures. In one of the communes we visited, the accountant kept an admittedly informal functional classification system using an Excel spreadsheet—allocating accounting expenditure categories (rows) to functions (columns). It would seem that a real need is emerging, at least at the local authority level, to have access to a tool for steering local policies. In both cases, the commune also has the necessary technical capacity to meet this need. Moreover, the functional budget was used to inform and explain the links between the required fiscal resources and communal responsibilities.

    Since the redaction of this chapter, Burkina Faso has adopted the budget and account nomenclature of the UEMOA, which is still to be translated into a proper budgeting and accounting system. (See the 2010 entries in table 2.1 in the first chapter section, "History of Decentralization in Burkina Faso.")
27. As classified in Law No. 014-2006.
28. We distinguish between land management and territorial development because, although 10 functions have, in effect, been transferred to the CTs, some speak of 11, referring to 1a and 1b, which they consider as separate functions.
29. Law No. 005-2004, Art. 85–105.
30. Decree No. 095-2007 of March 1, 2007.
31. The legal references for implementation are Decrees 209-2006 of May 15, 2006, for the urban communes and Decrees 105-, 106-, 107-, and 108-2009 of March 3, 2009, for the four areas of competence and the other communes. See table 2.1 for details.
32. Decentralization is not implemented directly through the line ministry to the local authorities but is channeled through the MATD, which is the body that coordinates

and drives the process. This situation creates the cross-cutting problems referred to previously in the "Institutional Issues" section. The biggest stumbling blocks are found in the area of health care, particularly given the relative weight of the Ministry of Health compared with the MATD.

33. This section is reorganized because of the distinction in French between "*impôts*" and "*taxe*," which are translated in English by the single word "taxes." The confusion arises in French with the term "*taxe à valeur ajoutée*" (TVA, or value added tax [VAT]). Despite its wording, it is indeed an "*impôt*" on the consumption of goods and services. Certainly, one has to consume to become liable for a VAT, and one can avoid it by consuming nothing or only exempted goods and services, but its characteristics are those of a nonbenefit-related tax: mandatory, nothing in return, and incorporated into the Treasury's general budget. This section distinguished between nonbenefit-related and benefit-related taxes, on the one side, and user charge and fees on the other side.

34. In some countries, case law recognizes that a user charge can be lower than the average cost of producing the service. This gives rise to an asymmetric situation: the charge cannot exceed the cost, but it can be lower—there is no profit or hidden tax, but there may be a deficit and thus a need for funding from another source. There is a cross-subsidization from taxpayers to users if the gap is funded through taxation and a redistributive subsidy benefiting the user, who is paying a less-than-cost price. This situation does not respect the "user pays" rule and poses production efficiency problems because the charge no longer sends the correct "price signal."

35. At present (end of 2009), the General Directorate of Taxation considers that the current tax base for the different taxes is underexploited and that, without changing the law, thought must be given to how to optimize these resources. This is the subject of a study now being conducted by a private firm based on a field survey covering three communes.

36. Article 141 of the CGCT adopted by the National Assembly in December 2004 and enacted in April 2005 (see table 2.1): "1) In the framework of the technical and financial support to local authorities, a Permanent Development Fund for Local Governments is to be created. 2) The missions, organisation and functioning of the Fund are to be set by decree by the Council of Ministers."

37. Source: *Le Territorial* No. 00, October 2008, p. 4. A joint MEF-MATD decree initially set the annual allocation percentages at 20 percent for recurrent expenditures and at 80 percent for investment. The proportionality is arbitrary. At the outset, it was thought that the central state support should go primarily to projects that would be visible to the population because it was expected that all locally collected revenues would be fed into the CTs' current budgets. The group that worked on the file thus proposed these percentages, at the same time underlining that the central government could revise them year on year depending on the realities on the ground. Thus, in 2008, following complaints from two communes experiencing problems in ensuring their staff's salaries, the MEF-MATD adjusted the rates to 23 percent for the DGF and 77 percent for the DGE—that is, for expenditures and investment, respectively (information provided by the General Directorate of the Budget, December 9, 2009).

38. There are two ministerial decrees: one specifies how the DGF is to be shared between the communes and regions, the other how the DGE is to be shared between the communes and regions. The rates are arbitrary, but the share for recurrent expenses is kept to a marginal amount. A first proposal of 30 percent for the regions and 70 percent for the communes was put forward. But in the distribution (based on an iterative process), the regions' share was high compared with the share given to the communes, so this was adjusted until the 20/80 ratio was reached, and it seems acceptable. This is how the decrees were drafted. The same gymnastics were applied to the DGF to arrive at a 10/90 ratio. Note that as of 2011, a committee, in collaboration with the *Institut national de la statistique et de la démographie* (INSD), was to propose a distribution formula that integrates the poverty index of each authority as well as each one's absorption capacity and population.

39. Law No. 055-2004/AN of December 21, 2004, on the General Code for Local Governments in Burkina Faso.

40. This approach corresponds to the Rawls "maximin" criterion. It refers to Rawls's difference principle in *A Theory of Justice* (1971, p. 152). Social and economic inequalities should be corrected so that the least-advantaged members of society should obtain the greatest benefit, or that redistributive policies should maximize the minimum benefit ("maximin") of those with the lower allocation of resources. What should be avoided is generation of a leapfrog effect in which the local authority with the weakest capacity exceeds the one preceding it; otherwise the system will be disrupted by a disincentive effect.

41. Note given to us by the Directorate of Financial Affairs and the Budget of the commune of Ouagadougou during our discussion of November 5, 2009.

42. Interministerial Circular 381-2009/MEF/MATD of June 4, 2009.

43. In this section, we draw upon two documents: MEF (2009) and Delegation of the European Commission to Burkina Faso (2009).

References

Champagne, E., and B. M. Ouegraogou. 2011. "Decentralization in Burkina Faso: The Slow March towards Devolution." In *Decentralization in Developing Countries: Global Perspectives on the Obstacles to Fiscal Devolution*, ed. J. Martinez-Vazquez and F. Vaillancourt, 303–26. Cheltenham, U.K.: Edward Elgar.

Dafflon, B. 1998. *La gestion des finances publiques locales*. 2nd ed. Paris: Economica.

———. 2006. "The Assignment of Functions to Decentralized Government: From Theory to Practice." In *Handbook on Fiscal Federalism*, ed. E. Ahmad and G. Brosio, 271–305. Cheltenham, U.K.: Edward Elgar.

Dafflon, B., and K. Beer-Tóth. 2009. "Managing Local Public Debt in Transition Countries: An Issue of Self-Control." *Financial Accountability and Management* 25 (3): 305–33.

Dafflon, B., and T. Madiès. 2008. "Décentralisation: quelques principes issus de la théorie du fédéralisme financier." [Decentralization: A Few Principles from the Theory of Fiscal Federalism.] Notes and documents 42, Agence Française de Développement, Paris.

Delegation of the European Commission to Burkina Faso. 2009. "Programme d'appui à la gouvernance locale et à la décentralisation – 10e FED." Étude d'identification, ARS Progetti SPA, Rapport provisoire 2, European Commission, Rome.

Ky, A. 2010. "Décentralisation au Burkina Faso: une approche en économie institutionnelle." Doctoral thesis, Faculty of Economics and Social Sciences, University of Fribourg, Switzerland.

Mback, C.-N. 2003. *Démocratisation et décentralisation: genèse et dynamique comparées des processus de décentralisation en Afrique subsaharienne.* Paris and Cotonou: Éditions Karthala.

MEF (Ministry of the Economy and Finance). 2009. "Les opérations financières des collectivités territoriales." Rapport 2006, Secrétariat général, Direction générale du budget, Ouagadougou, Burkina Faso.

Rawls, J. 1971. *A Theory of Justice.* Cambridge, MA: The Belknap Press of Harvard University Press.

Sawadogo, R.-A. 2001. *L'État africain face à la décentralisation.* Paris: Karthala.

Chapter **3**

Local Public Finances in Ghana

Guy Gilbert, Réjane Hugounenq, and François Vaillancourt

History of Decentralization in Ghana: From Independence to 2010

In Ghana, as in many African countries, the first forms of local government date back to the colonial period. Three hundred fifty-five native authorities had thus been created, mainly in rural areas, and organized around the traditional chieftaincies. Meanwhile, in urban areas, the Municipal Ordinance of 1859 had established the first municipalities in the coastal cities of the Gold Coast. However, it was not until the 1950s that elected town and municipal councils were set up. The legal foundations for these councils' activities (the Ordinances of 1943 and 1953) were developed over the two decades or so prior to the country's independence on January 6, 1957 (Ahwoi 2010a; Fischer 1957).

Immediately following independence, and despite the federalist demands of the Ashanti Confederacy and the Northern State, Ghana became a unitary republic.[1] The Independence Constitution (1957) divided Ghana into five regions that initially had assemblies elected by universal suffrage. However, these survived no more than a year. The 1960 Constitution increased the number of regions to eight but did not grant them any substantive power.

On the whole, Ghana's regions were to remain, at best, deconcentrated levels of government with no real powers. This can be explained by the overriding goal of building national unity, as well as by the fear that a power-sharing process could exacerbate territorial divisions in a context of ethnic fragmentation (Asante 2007; Jacquemot 2007). For the same reasons, the first president, Kwame Nkruma (1957–66), centralized power within the Office of the President, as did his successors, at least until the 1980s.

1957–66: A Strong Central Government
To all extents, right after independence, Ghana's territorialized public institutions were characterized by a dual hierarchical pyramid: central government institutions were powerful and present at the local level as deconcentrated

administrative units, while local authorities (for example, the elected municipal councils in Accra, Cape Coast, Kumasi, and Sekondi-Takodari) were clearly separate from the deconcentrated structures but had little democratic legitimacy, a narrow range of competences, and limited financial and human resources. The whole system operated in a national territory where the power of traditional chiefs was still strong, with the result that public action at the local level was nonexistent or redundant.

The first Local Government Act relating to the various municipal councils was adopted in 1961 but ended in 1966 following a first coup d'état.

1967–80: First Attempts at Deconcentration

Various investigative commissions (the Mills-Odoi Commission in 1967 and the Siriboe and Akufo-Addo Commissions in 1968) and several reports on the subject led to the Local Administration Act (Act 359) of 1971, implemented in 1974 following a change of government in 1972 (Lt. Col. Acheampong's administration).[2]

The 1971–74 system aimed to abolish the dual institutional pyramid inherited from the colonial period and to replace it with a single local public institution: the district council (DC), which was to have full responsibility for public policy in its territory. The DCs were to be assigned the ministries' deconcentrated responsibilities, notably those of the ministries in charge of agriculture, education, planning, social affairs and community development, public health, industry, and sports.

The new system's territorial network was fairly extensive and comprised 65 districts. Two-thirds of the DC members were appointed directly by the government, and the remaining third were designated through the chieftaincy system (Asante 2007).

This reform—which sought to rationalize deconcentrated structures while keeping intact the concept of a local structure with an assembly—was a failure. It led to the creation of 65 monolithic administrations that had a hybrid status, were too large, had no decentralized responsibilities in the strict sense of devolved responsibilities, lacked autonomous financial resources, and were staffed by personnel hired in haste and often directly tied to local interests. The attempt to integrate and steer deconcentrated government services within these councils effectively failed. The DCs were simply added to the local and regional deconcentrated central government services, and all were placed under the exclusive supervision of the central government's financial administration. Asante (2007) notes that, at this time, the central government recentralized in Accra various competences that had thus far been held by the districts: education (the Ghana Education Service) and transportation (the Omnibus Services Authorities).

1980s: A Mixed System of Subnational Governance

The next stage in the organization of subnational government dates from the 1980s under President Rawlings's Provisional National Defense Council (PNDC) government. It was in this setting of a strong, centralized government—little inclined to power sharing—that the "decentralized" local government structure was established. For the most part, it is still in force today. This change resulted from the 1988 adoption of Local Government Law 207, whose provisions were to be taken up and consolidated in Chapter 20 of the 1992 Constitution and later in the Local Government Act (Act 462) of 1993. These last two legislative texts still constitute the mainspring of decentralization in Ghana.

The reasons behind these reforms were both economic and political (Ahwoi 2010b). To begin with, the 1980s was the decade of structural adjustment policies (in the framework of Economic Recovery Programs [ERPs]) imposed by donors. The leitmotif of these ERPs was economic liberalization and the concurrent goal of reducing government involvement in running the economy. Although ERP I (1982–86) focused on economic stabilization policies (fighting deficits and inflation), ERP II (1986–92) was more oriented to structural policies such as infrastructure investments and improved efficiency in the public sector, which gave rise to the reforms to rationalize the functioning of the subnational institutions that had been in place since 1974.

When Rawlings's government came to power in 1981, it immediately adopted the catch phrase of "give power to the people" and pledged to ensure "participatory development" (Lentz 2006; Ayee 1997). In this setting, such slogans can be interpreted more as a desire to seat the government's power on popular support than as a true intent to share political power with the local levels of government. The PNDC thus set up a mixed system of subnational governance that relied both on (a) local-level institutions with legal status and assemblies of elected councillors (to listen to grassroots demands), and (b) government-appointed councillors and government officials.

During a first phase, new districts were created, rising in number from 65 to 85 in 1988 and to 110 in 1992. The setting up of these new districts raised numerous issues relating to the delimitation of their borders and, thus, to the position of traditional chiefs. Overall, however, the borders of the new districts broadly mirrored those of the colonial chieftaincies (Lentz 2000).

In 1988, the DCs created by the 1974 reform were replaced by district assemblies (DAs). Whereas DC members had been appointed officials,[3] the PNDC introduced a degree of representation by holding elections for two-thirds of DA members. The remaining third were chosen by the government from among civil society members, in consultation with the district secretary (who was appointed to head the DA by the president) and the traditional chiefs.

The first local elections were held under this system in 1988–89. They were nonpartisan: candidates ran as individuals in each ward; if elected, they would represent their wards' interests in the DA. These candidates could not, at least officially, be backed by political parties. In the single-party regime of the 1980s, this practice was in line with the populist and nonpartisan philosophy of the Rawlings administration, which aimed to mobilize initiatives and foster local consensus, transcending ideological divisions (Ayee 2008).

Today, local elections are still formally nonpartisan, although a multi-party system was introduced at the national level in 1992. In reality, however, starting with the 1994 local elections and then under the Kufuor administration (2001–08), national political parties have indeed given their backing to candidates in local elections (Asante 2007; Ayee 2008; Crook 1999).

The government's nomination of one-third of DA members can be justified in different ways. For Kwamena Ahwoi, then minister of local government, these appointments were seen as a way of balancing the necessarily partial vision of elected members—who needed to satisfy their constituents and thus were potentially subject to pressure—against a more global vision of the district's interests (Crook 1999; Ahwoi 2009). The vision of the national interest was carried by the district secretary (and later by the district chief executive [DCE] as of 1993).[4]

For political scientists, a totally different interpretation may be given: these appointments and the role assigned to the district secretary or DCE indicated a takeover of the DAs. Using case studies of how the DAs operated, Ayee (1996) and Crook (1994) have shown how difficult it was for DA members to oppose the DCE's position in case of conflict because the latter enjoyed PNDC protection and ultimately retained control over the allocation of resources to the district. Furthermore, many authors have also shown how the DCEs were able to play an active local role during national elections.

In addition to these operational modalities—which, with a few minor changes, are still in force today (as further discussed in the next section on local government organization in 2010)—in 1988, the DAs were assigned legislative and executive functions, responsibility over all matters pertaining to local development, the local delivery of infrastructure and essential services, and the task of ensuring security and local resource mobilization.[5] In all, 86 specific (deconcentrated, delegated, and devolved) responsibilities were assigned to the DAs, from road construction and maintenance to ensuring health services and the supervision and control of slaughterhouses.

In connection with the transfer of deconcentrated responsibilities, the DAs—as had already been planned in the 1974 reforms—were also to supervise the administration of 22 ministerial departments deconcentrated to the district level with a view to forming a governmental and financial system integrated with the districts. As a result, the DAs were also made responsible for establishing "composite" budgets, a process allowing all expenditures for a given responsibility (by the districts and as well as within the districts through ministerial budgetary lines, whether or not these expenditures transit through the national budgeting processes) to be synthesized so that the consolidated information could be transmitted to the Ministry of Finance.

As of 2010, the use of this approach was still pending. The text of the Comprehensive Decentralization Policy was discussed before the cabinet but was sent back to the Ministry of Local Government and Regional Development and Environment (MLGRDE), which has now been asked to conduct additional consultations. The deconcentrated offices in the districts thus continue to record their spending separately from the DAs' accounts.

The DAs were also given powers for local planning, with overall coordination to be provided by a regional coordinating council (RCC), an administrative structure also created in 1988 to head each of Ghana's 10 regions.[6]

Finally, before the reform, the DAs had available a certain number of financial resources: taxes, license fees, voluntary contributions from wealthy members of the community, and external aid. The reform granted them "ceded" taxes from seven different sources, notably taxes on entertainment (casinos and gaming), business, and transport. All of these ceded revenues were to be officially shared among the DAs based on population density and level of development (Ayee 1996). These ceded taxes are said to have yielded ¢ 204 million, ¢ 594 million, and ¢ 2.1 billion (old cedis) (or ¢ 20,400, ¢ 59,400, and ¢ 210,000 [new cedis])[7] in 1990, 1991, and 1992, respectively (Ayee 1996). Payment of these ceded taxes to the DAs came to a near halt in 1994 with the creation of the District Assembly Common Fund (DACF), as will be further discussed in the "Intergovernmental Transfers" section.

1990s: A New Pluralist Democracy

The year 1991 marked a turning point in Rawlings's philosophy on government. Under pressure from donors, Ghana reinstated the principle of respect for civil rights and adopted a multiparty electoral democracy as the basis for its new constitutional government. Ghana thus switched from the PNDC's military regime to a pluralist regime governed by President Rawlings and his National Democratic Congress.

The DAs were introduced into the 1992 Constitution of the Fourth Republic in the local government clauses.[8] The DAs became metropolitan, municipal, and district assemblies (MMDAs), and the new legislation confirmed and strengthened their principal characteristics.

The Rawlings government—which remained in power until 2000 following its successive reelections (in 1992 and later in 1996 under the multiparty regime)—consolidated the legal framework for decentralization throughout the 1990s. Additional sources of funding were granted through the DACF from 1993 on, thanks to the Local Government Act (Act 462).[9]

For all that, not all of the measures taken necessarily worked toward clarifying the functions assigned to these assemblies and improving the financial and human resources that would enable them to perform these functions. Similarly, the governance framework of districts (DAs) and various ministries, departments, and agencies did not lessen the overlaps between devolved and deconcentrated entities.

Ayee (2008) cites the laws passed in 1995 and 1996 on the organization of health and education services as examples of this lack of clarity about the assemblies' roles and funding sources. Whereas the DAs had been responsible for providing education and health infrastructures since 1988, these laws[10] placed the administrative personnel in charge of delivering these district services under the authority of the ministry and, at the district level, under the authority of the DCE. The activities and salaries of these personnel were financed directly by ministerial budget lines. The DAs were thus, in practice, deprived of the financial information and the authority over the personnel needed to accomplish their tasks.

2000–10: Toward a Renewal of Reform

From 2001 and throughout its term of office, Kufuor's New Patriotic Party (NPP) administration, aware of the failings in local government structure, attempted to revive the reform by proposing plans to improve its functioning. The National Decentralization Action Plan in 2003, amended by the Growth and Poverty Reduction Strategy (GPRS) II for the years 2006–09, was supposed to help relaunch the process. In March 2007, the MLGRDE declared that it wished to deepen political, administrative, and fiscal decentralization in Ghana and reaffirm the government's commitment to a decentralization policy (MLGRDE 2007a, 7). Yet, at the same time, the NPP's proclaimed determination to put an end to the central appointment of DCEs and make the office elective never materialized, running counter to the stated objective of the decentralization policy.

In 2007, the Ghanaian Parliament adopted a rise from 5 percent to 7.5 percent of the portion of tax revenue ceded by the central government to subnational levels, thereby manifesting the will to transfer greater resources to the local level.[11] Additionally, the government, in conjunction with donor partners, concurrently put in place a new grant to districts: the District Development Facility (DDF) (further discussed in the "Intergovernmental Transfers" section). Finally, in May 2008, the intent to implement measures to put decentralization into effect was reiterated at the cabinet level through the adoption of a framework document (which so far, however, has not been presented to parliament).[12] At the same time, the number of districts rose from 110 to 138 in 2003, and from 138 to 170 in 2008 (see "The Regions" subsection later), which potentially weakens their economic viability.

The December 2008 elections marked the return to power of the National Democratic Congress with the election of John Atta Mills. For Ahwoi (2010a), who was the minister in charge of the 1988 reform under Rawlings and now adviser to President Mills, decentralization needed to take on a new face and move decisively toward a real devolution of powers to the DAs. As in the past, it was reaffirmed that the regions and the RCCs, which have neither a legal status nor resources of their own, were not destined to play a prominent role. This stance (as had already been the case under the PNDC) was justified, in a context of ethnic fragmentation, by the threat of secession that had been fostered with the creation of the regions on account of their boundaries and size.

The path to decentralization, however, may still be long. The minister of the MLGRDE declared the following in a June 2009 press briefing:[13]

> The functions and responsibilities under the [decentralization] policy are articulated under three levels:
>
> 1. The central government ministries and departments are responsible for policies, standard setting, and monitoring and evaluation.
>
> 2. RCCs are responsible for coordination and monitoring of activities of MMDAs in their regions.
>
> 3. The implementation function is discharged by the MMDAs.

This description of decentralization coincides equally well with the definitions of deconcentration, delegation, or devolution—depending on how one chooses to interpret "policies and standards." This decentralization policy can therefore lead to three different outcomes. In the same declaration, the minister pointed out the importance of creating ongoing interaction between the government and the districts through the role of the DCE. As Ahwoi (2010a) notes, there are multiple conceptions of decentralization in Ghana.

Organization of Decentralized Local Government and Deconcentration in 2010

Decentralized Components

The meaning given to "decentralization" in Ghana covers, in fact, all territorialized public institutions or, in other words, both the deconcentrated institutions and the decentralized ones. The former correspond to the administrative agencies that execute the policies of the central government and its line ministries and thus embody deconcentrated public policy in the strict sense of the term (Dafflon and Madiès 2008). The latter are truly decentralized local authorities (in this chapter, the terms "local authorities" and "local government" refer to all decentralized tiers of government), with elected assemblies and autonomous powers devolved to them by law. They thus embody the decentralization of public policy—or what is also referred to as devolution.

The confusion between these two types of administrative units is all the greater in Ghana given that the DAs, which are the main tier of subnational government, are established and operated on a mixed basis. They function not only as management bodies for deconcentrated central government services but also as decentralized local government bodies for the districts. There has been constant debate between the more powerful deconcentrated government agencies (endowed with longer-term and better-quality human and financial resources) and the more recent decentralized local authorities, which dispose of fewer resources. Yet the confusion between decentralization and deconcentration remains (Ahwoi 2010a).

The institutional framework for the overall system of local government institutions is defined in Chapter 20 of the 1992 Constitution and by the Local Government Act of 1993 (Act 462). The former stipulates that "Ghana shall have a system of local government and administration which shall, as far as practicable, be decentralised."[14] It also stipulates that the state shall "make democracy a reality by decentralising the administrative and financial machinery of government to the regions and districts and by affording all possible opportunities to the people to participate in decision-making at every level."[15]

The objectives showcased by the Ghanaian government in this constitution give top priority to (a) local democracy building, (b) the territory's economic and social development, and (c) poverty alleviation. The principles and arrangements for the process are also specified:

- Functions, powers, responsibilities, and resources must at all times be transferred to local authorities in a coordinated manner.
- The capacity of local authorities to plan, initiate, coordinate, manage, and execute local public policies must be built with a view to ultimately achieving the localization of these activities.
- There shall be established for each local authority a sound financial base with adequate and reliable sources of revenue to allow each to make the local public investments that they will vote for.
- Persons in the service of local authorities shall be subject to the direct control of their supervisory local authorities.

For its part, the Local Government Act (Act 462) of 1993 describes the "decentralization policy" as a solution to

- Transfer functions, resources, means, and powers from central government ministries and departments to the districts
- Merge the government institutions in each subnational unit into a single administrative entity by integration of the institutions and the human resources and through the budgetary consolidation of government grants (which fund concentrated services) and local resources

- Transfer responsibility for implementing public policies to the districts
- Assign functions and competences to each level of government
- Encourage citizen participation in the planning, implementation, provision, and maintenance of the public services that drive improved standards of living and ordered, equitable, and well-balanced development.

Development, in fact, is the core concept that summarizes the aspirations, objectives, and priorities of citizens; it is a responsibility that is basically shared between central government, local government, parastatal public institutions, and nonprofit organizations.

Table 3.1 summarizes all the laws and implementing decrees voted into force by successive Ghanaian governments and that give substance to the country's structure of decentralized government.

Table 3.1 Timeline of Key Legislation and Other Legislative Instruments[a] on Decentralization in Ghana, 1971–2009

1971	Local Administration Act
1988	Local Government Law (PNDCL 207)
1990	Local Government (Amendment) Law (PNDCL 235)
	Local Government (Amendment No. 2) Law (PNDCL 246)
	Local Government (Amendment of Sixth Schedule) Instrument (LI 1508)
	Local Government (District Tender Board) Establishment Instrument (LI 1503)
1991	Local Government (Urban, Zonal, Town Councils and Unit Committees) Establishment Instrument (LI 1514)
1992	Local Government (Amendment of Sixth Schedule) Instrument (LI 1530)
	Local Government (Amendment of Sixth Schedule) Instrument (LI 1531)
	Constitution of the Republic of Ghana
1993	Local Government Act (No. 462)
	• Tasks the MLGRDE with creating (through LIs) municipalities, which are called "districts" (MMDAs) and RCCs.
	• Describes the political and administrative relationships between the MMDAs and RCCs.
	• Defines the scope of the districts' exercise of their executive and legislative powers by specifying the activities of their assemblies, their areas of competence—notably their responsibilities as local development agencies—and the fiscal and audit requirements. An LI referring to this law specifies, for each district, its scope of intervention and responsibilities. The planning functions devolved respectively to the MMDAs and RCCs, as well as to the MDAs, are specified in the National Planning System (National Planning [System] Act of 1994). To this end, regional and district development coordination units (RPCUs and DPCUs, respectively) were created (Act 462); their activities are governed by the guidelines issued by the MLGRDE and the National Development Planning Commission. These guidelines cover, among other things, the coordination between MMDA and RCC budget decisions and national-level budget planning. These texts place the RPCU in charge of coordinating all MMDA and RCC activities within the regional territory.

(continued next page)

Table 3.1 (continued)

	District Assembly Common Fund (DACF) Act (No. 455)
	Stipulates parliament's annual obligation to transfer to the districts a minimum of 5 percent of the fiscal resources collected by central government. A specific public establishment—the Office of the District Assembly Common Fund—is in charge of allocating this grant and monitoring its use.
	Local Government Service Act (No. 656)
1994	National Development Planning System Act, 1994 (No. 480)
	Local Government (Urban, Zonal, and Town Councils, and Unit Committees) (Establishment) Instrument
1997	Financial Administration Regulations (LI 1234)
	Financial Administration Decree (SMDC 221)
2000	Audit Service Act (No. 584)
	Assigns the responsibility for auditing public accounts to the auditor general. See also the Internal Audit Agency Act (No. 658), passed in 2003.
	Public Procurement Act (No. 663)
	Sets the rules and thresholds in regard to public procurement.
2003	Financial Administration Act (No. 654) and its implementing decree, the Financial Administration Regulations (LI 1802), establish the rules for the public accounting system and the modalities for preparing the budgets of districts and deconcentrated government administrative units (MDAs).
	Internal Audit Agency Act (No. 658) tasks an agency with establishing internal audit standards and procedures within the districts.
	Local Government Service Act (No. 656)
	Distinguishes between the district and regional staff, on the one hand, and the central government staff, on the other. It describes the functions and organization of the Local Government Service, its technical support and MMDA and RCC support functions, and the auditing of MMDAs and RCCs to improve efficiency. A government undersecretariat (Local Government Service) is entrusted with developing training programs for these staffs.
2004	Financial Memoranda for MMDAs
	Financial Administration Regulations (LI 1802)
2008	Comprehensive Decentralization Policy Framework: Intergovernmental Fiscal Decentralization Framework
2009	A new text, LI 1961 (Local Government Service), was adopted in December 2009. This provides for formal—if not very substantial—amendments to the administrative regime for some government officials working in the MMDAs. Thus, there will be a change in the employment framework of around 30,000 government officials, who will continue to be recruited by the MMDAs: they will be transferred from the civil service to the Local Government Service managed by the MLGRDE, which will then be administratively responsible for paying their salaries. This does not, therefore, seem to evidence the creation of a genuine local government civil service, which does not exist in Ghana.

Note: DPCU = district development coordinating councils; LI = legislative instrument; MDA = ministries, departments, agencies; MLGRDE = Ministry of Local Government and Regional Development and Environment; MMDA = metropolitan, municipal, and district assembly; PNDCL = *Provisional National Defense Council Law*; RCC = regional coordinating council; RPCU = regional development coordinating council; SMDC = submetropolitan district council.
a. Legislative instruments (LIs) belong to the category of "subsidiary legislation" (which also includes executive instruments, constitutional instruments, and regulatory notices), which must be the subject of prior submission before parliament and published in the *Ghana Gazette*. They come into force after 21 sitting days of parliament (which can vote to reject them with a two-thirds majority).

Structure of Local Government Institutions

The system of local government institutions in Ghana is summarized in figures 3.1 and 3.2. On paper, it comprises three main institutions of a relatively

Figure 3.1 Organization of Decentralized Authorities and Deconcentration in Ghana, 2010

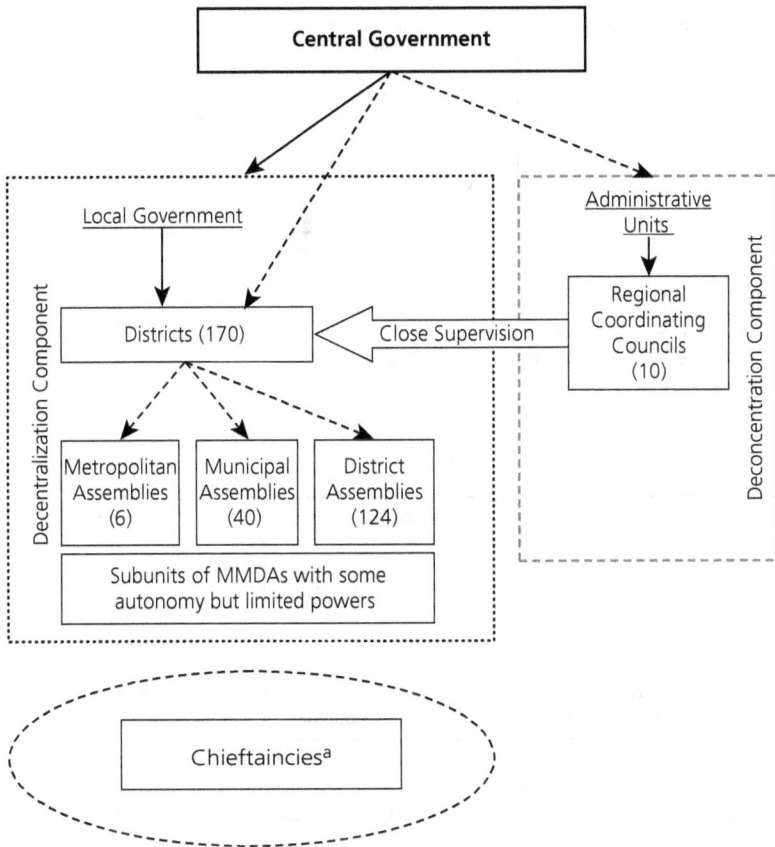

Source: Data compiled by the authors based on legislation in force in 2010.
Note: MMDA = metropolitan, municipal, and district assembly.
a. See box 3.2.

different nature: on the regional level, the RCC; on the intermediary district level, the DAs; and on the subdistrict level, the unit committees (UCs). Figure 3.1 shows the links between the central authorities, the deconcentrated bodies (RCCs), and the MMDAs. Figure 3.2 shows intra-MMDA deconcentration.

The Regions

Ghana's 10 regions are deconcentrated administrative institutions. Their decision-making body is the RCC governed by Article 255 of the Constitution and Article 141 of the Local Government Act. Each RCC has a chairman and

Figure 3.2 Organization of Local Public Institutions in Ghana, 2010

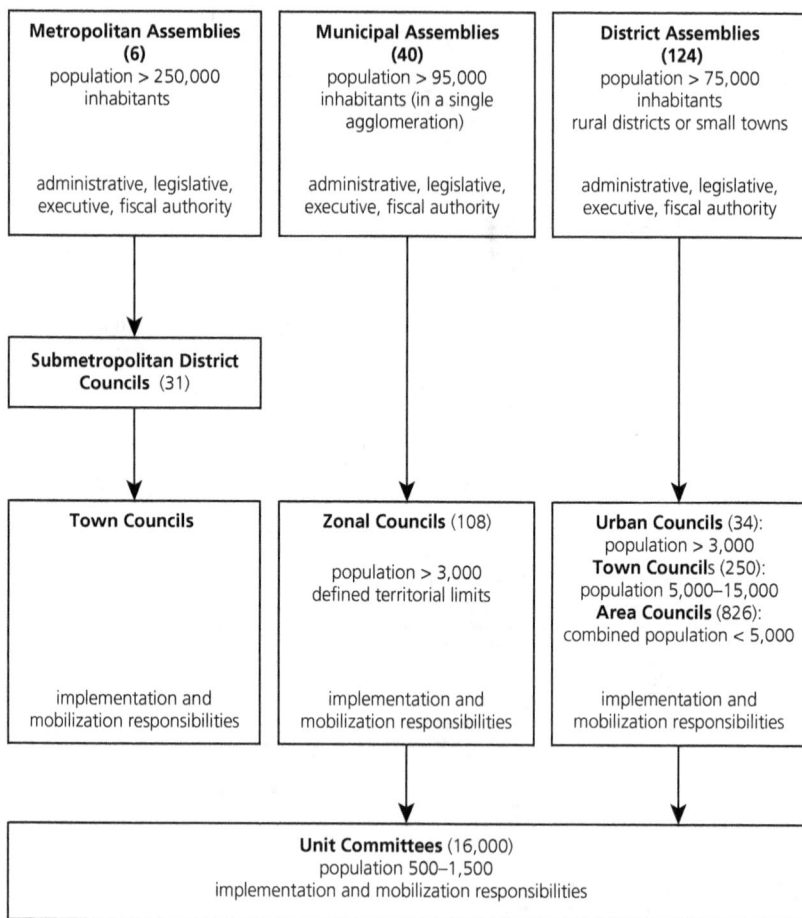

Metropolitan Assemblies (6) population > 250,000 inhabitants	Municipal Assemblies (40) population > 95,000 inhabitants (in a single agglomeration)	District Assemblies (124) population > 75,000 inhabitants rural districts or small towns
administrative, legislative, executive, fiscal authority	administrative, legislative, executive, fiscal authority	administrative, legislative, executive, fiscal authority

Submetropolitan District Councils (31)

Town Councils	Zonal Councils (108) population > 3,000 defined territorial limits	Urban Councils (34): population > 3,000 Town Councils (250): population 5,000–15,000 Area Councils (826): combined population < 5,000
implementation and mobilization responsibilities	implementation and mobilization responsibilities	implementation and mobilization responsibilities

Unit Committees (16,000)
population 500–1,500
implementation and mobilization responsibilities

Source: Data compiled by the authors based on legislation in force in 2010.

a presiding member elected with a two-thirds majority by the RCC, which is made up of

- The regional minister, a minister of state appointed by the president of the republic with the approval of parliament, who acts as chairman;
- One or more deputy ministers (appointed by the president of the republic);
- The (elected) presiding member of each DA within the region;
- The DCEs (appointed by the president of the republic);

- Two representatives of the (traditional) chiefs from the Regional House of Chiefs; and
- The regional heads of the deconcentrated services of line ministries (appointed by the president of the republic or the ministers), as nonvoting members.

The RCC is therefore heavily dominated by members appointed by the president or by the central government. In parallel to the RCC, the president appoints a regional minister for each "region" from among members of parliament and after prior approval of parliament.[16] Furthermore, the president has the power to appoint one or more deputy ministers, also chosen from among the members of parliament.[17] These deputy ministers are more directly in charge of running and coordinating deconcentrated government services within the regions.[18]

The RCCs monitor, coordinate, and evaluate the performance of the districts within their regions. They check on the use of the material, financial, and human resources made available to the districts by the central government agencies. They examine the action of public services in the region.[19] They coordinate, notably through the regional planning coordination unit, the districts' planning activities with those of the central government in the framework of the National Development Planning Commission (NDPC) of 1994. Overall, the RCC's functions thus basically involve administration and coordination. The RCCs are not political bodies that drive and produce autonomous and decentralized public policy. Their democratic legitimacy is at best indirect. Their action is thus best qualified as deconcentrated.

The Districts

In compliance with the Local Government Act (Art. 162), the term "district" designates the geographic zone over which an eponymous *elected assembly*, the DA, has jurisdiction. These DAs take on different names depending on their demographic and rural or urban characteristics (metropolitan assembly or municipal assembly, respectively). On paper, they represent the tip of a four-tier metropolitan or three-tier municipal or DA institutional pyramid (see figure 3.2 and box 3.1).[20] None of these subdistrict structures have an independent legal status; they are simply administrative subdivisions.

Changes in institutional divisions since 1993   In 1993, there were 110 districts. This number rose to 139 in 2004. In the early 2000s, Ghana thus had 139 "municipalities" (MMDAs), ranked by population size: 4 metropolitan district assemblies with populations over 250,000 inhabitants (Accra, Kumasi, Shama Ahanta East, and Tamale); 11 municipal district assemblies (with populations over 95,000); and 124 DAs (with populations over 75,000).

These divisions were again modified in 2007–08, when two municipal assemblies were transformed into metropolitan assemblies (Cape Coast and Tema)

BOX 3.1

The Operating Modalities of Subdistrict Structures

At the base of each pyramid, there are, in principle, *unit committees* (as shown in figure 3.2). The UCs are composed of an assembly of, at most, 15 representatives elected or appointed for a four-year term. Ten of these are elected during a meeting (called an "electoral commission") of all residents in the UC's territory (in practice, groups of residents [500–1,000 in rural areas and 1,500 in urban areas]), and five other members (maximum) are appointed by the DCE. These UCs do not have an independent legal status. Their functions are described by the LI 1589 (5th Section), to which can be added the functions delegated to them by bodies higher up the institutional pyramid (the town, submetropolitan, zonal, and area councils). The 15 functions assigned to a UC by law primarily concern the census of taxpayers and assistance with tax collection within its territory, pest control, the organization of communal labor, waste collection, civil status records, civic education, and general control of MMDA staff activities within its territory. The UCs are accountable for their actions before the DA through the *urban, town,* or *zonal councils*.

The second tier of the institutional pyramid comprises the *urban, zonal, and town councils*, created by decree by the MLGRDE. Urban councils, zonal councils, town councils, or submetropolitan district councils (13 of the latter existed in 1996) are created depending on the local context. Their assemblies (elected for four years on a similar basis to the UCs) comprise 25 to 30 councillors in the urban councils and 15–20 councillors in the town and zonal councils. At most, one-third of their representatives are the elected members of the metropolitan assembly from the respective submetropolitan district council's area; a maximum of half their representatives are from the UCs within that area, and the remainder are appointed by the DCE from among the inhabitants residing in the area and after consultation with the DA and the traditional authorities.

The submetropolitan district councils (SMDCs) were established because of the complexity and size of some agglomerations. As of 2007, the Metropolitan Assembly (MA) of Accra comprised 11 SMDCs, compared with 6 previously, and the MA of Kumasi has had 10 since 2003, relative to an earlier 4.

In smaller cities (population usually agglomerated in several centers and more than 15,000 inhabitants but without the complexity of metropolitan areas), *urban councils* (34 in 1996, excluding Accra) can be created under the same conditions.

Town area councils are created for the municipal assemblies that have only one agglomeration with an identifiable local interest, communication infrastructure, cadastral elements, district limits, and a population of more than 3,000 inhabitants. These councils are intended as structures for mobilizing local democracy. Town councils also exist in metropolitan assemblies, but in this case they cover a larger population (sometimes more than 50,000 inhabitants).

None of these subdistrict structures are independent legal entities; they are simply administrative subdivisions, their personnel appointed by the DA. They are structured

(continued next page)

Box 3.1 (continued)

in subcommittees, mainly including a services and development subcommittee and a finance and administration subcommittee. The list of their functions was established by law.[a] In principle, they are in charge of forecasting fiscal revenues at the rates set by the DA or at area-specific rates (if applicable), collecting taxes, preparing the current and capital budgets to be approved by the DA, and any other tasks that the DA delegates to them. They do not have the right to levy taxes. They may each have their own bank account, funded by their zone's specific taxes, and approved by the DA to finance projects in their territories; a portion (50 percent) of the district taxes collected in their territories; and funds allocated by the DA, notably from central government grants and subsidies. They provide the DA with quarterly reports on their activities and accounts.

a. LI 1589, Art. 34–35.

---

and 31 new districts came into being. This involved both new entities—as in the case of the four municipal assemblies created in the Greater Accra region (Adenta, Ashaiman, Ga South, and Ledzokuku-Krowor)—and the splitting up of existing DAs to create 26 new DAs. Overall, in 2008, Ghana had 170 districts (6 metropolitan assemblies, 40 municipal assemblies, and 124 DAs).

The mushrooming of new districts in 2008 can be explained by a combination of factors of varying importance, depending on the case:

- Demand for more self-governance by an ethnic group that felt it was a minority within a district
- Presidential favor for this group, which would thus have its share of the DACF funding
- Improvement in the quality of local services.

District bodies   The DAs are composed mostly of elected representatives (70 percent), with the president appointing the remaining 30 percent after consulting the traditional chiefs and other local interest groups. The members of parliament elected in the district also sit on the DA but do not have voting rights. DA elections are held every four years. The presiding member of each district is elected for a two-year (renewable) term by the DA from among its members. Apart from presiding over the DA, the presiding member's functions are only honorary and ceremonial.[21]

Within each district, the executive and administrative functions are performed by an executive committee whose members (numbering no more than one-third of the total number of assembly members, excluding its president) are elected by the DA members.[22]

The executive functions are performed not by the presiding member but by the DCE. "District chief executive" is the generic term to designate the executive head of a district, municipality, or metropolis. The DCE is appointed for four years by the president with the approval of two-thirds of the assembly's voting members. He or she represents the central government within the district.[23] As such, the DCE is the head of the district's general administration and is assisted in this function by the district coordinating director and two deputies (the deputy directors of finance and budget and of general administration).

In addition to functioning as head of the general administration, the DCE automatically chairs the executive committee, which confers considerable power on him or her.[24] Thematic subcommittees are created (development planning, social welfare, works, justice and security, and finance and general administration). The executive committee coordinates the work of the subcommittees, executes the decisions made by the assembly, supervises the running of district services (with the DCE), and executes the development plans of the district substructures (the UCs, areas, towns, and submetropolitan districts).

The district services are required to be organized as departments, the list of which is set by law (12 services including administration, finance, education-youth and sports, public health, agriculture, land registry, social welfare, natural resources, forestry-hunting, works, industry and trade, and risk prevention). These services correspond to the departments that structured the central government services before decentralization. De facto, they continue to report to RCC units and operate as deconcentrated departments within the districts.

District functions   In addition to the packages of responsibilities transferred under the decentralization laws, the districts are assigned limited functions that are listed by law. The districts are responsible for

- Development and planning within their territories;
- Infrastructure development;
- Delivery of local public goods and services;
- Environmental improvement;
- Ownership of public infrastructure construction in the district; and
- Action as agents of central government for certain functions (such as regulating public auctions or alcohol licenses).

Local development plans (and the associated budgets) are prepared in collaboration with the regions (RCCs) and then submitted to the NDPC for approval, with the budgets being submitted to the Ministry of Finance.[25] The district development plans summarize and coordinate the plans of the subdistrict entities. The district is assisted in its planning task by a structure

BOX 3.2

The Local Role of Chieftaincies in Modern-Day Ghana

The chieftaincy institution in Ghana is, to some extent, a construct of the Anglo-Saxon colonial system—yet only to a certain degree because the introduction of the hierarchical chief system (head chief, divisional chief, and so on) at the time the Native States Authorities were created was largely based on precolonial political structures (Lentz 2000). After independence (despite the determination of various administrations to lessen their role, above all their political role), the chieftaincy system persisted and adapted. Far from being eliminated on independence, the system was given representative institutions. For instance, the National House of Chiefs, which brings together the delegates from all the regional houses of chiefs, dates from the end of the 1960s, as does the title of paramount chief (Jacquemot 2007).

Although the chiefs no longer have as much power as they did under the colonial regime—mainly due to the arrival of competing structures (districts and other public institutions)—their influence is still far from negligible at the local level, particularly in rural areas. They are, of course, active in the public institutions. When the local government councils were created, the chiefs appointed under the colonial regime were assigned a fixed quota of seats in the assemblies. Although ineligible, they are still present today in the RCCs and DAs, primarily because they participate in the appointment of one-third of assembly members.

However, the chiefs draw their prestige not so much from their presence in these institutions as from the social and economic role they play. They have relatively strong judicial power, notably in civil affairs (for example, inheritance and family law) and land tenure matters, even though a state tribunal system is in place. They are called on, for example, to resolve conflicts over land and between individuals (conflicts between family members or neighbors). They also have redistributive obligations toward their communities and, for this, have access to financial resources primarily from land (stool/skin lands)[a] and natural resources (mines), which may also prove to be sources of conflict with the local authorities (Rochegude and Plançon 2009).

Today, the strength of the chieftaincy system paradoxically lies in the fact that it dovetails the role of preserving the traditions it personifies (essentially cultural ones) with the role of an educated elite well acquainted with development issues—a role that many chiefs assume more than adequately. Lentz (2000) explains how the first generation of (traditional) chiefs chosen by the colonialist power from among traditional figureheads was replaced in the 1950s by a second generation of chiefs who had been educated in schools for chiefs' sons and were thus familiar with how the colonial authorities functioned. Along the same lines, Jacquemot (2007) explains how today's chiefs have adapted to the changes in modern society, how they are educated, how they monitor development projects, and, depending on their abilities, how they mobilize their networks (even internationally) and resources for such projects—in the best cases, in collaboration with the district authorities. It is probable, however, that the chiefs' still-influential role is simply the counterpart of the local authorities' current weakness in terms of both funding and human resources.

a. Stool/skin lands are customary lands owned by stools, skins, clans, and families.

that brings together all central government services in the district for this purpose.

Issues and Questions about the Institutional Framework

The institutional framework elicits four major issues—the first two of which touch on the management of the MMDAs, and the second two of which relate to their number, their structures, and their relationships with other entities:

- *The position and power of the DCE and, more generally, of appointed DA members in a local authority that, as a decentralized entity in principle, has direct democratic legitimacy.* On paper, the president proposes a DCE nominee, but this proposal must be ratified by two-thirds of the DA council members. If the proposed candidate obtains less than 50 percent of the votes in the first round, the candidacy is usually withdrawn. In practice, several cases of such withdrawal were reported to us. Yet, also in practice, after a presidential election, all DCEs can be replaced and sometimes are. The presidential will seems to be a decisive factor, in seeming contradiction with the texts, which theoretically give the DAs substantial power. For instance, following the presidential elections in December 2008, the new president, sworn in in January 2009, replaced the DCEs in April–June 2009 as well as the appointed members of the MMDA councils. President Kufuor, who was in power from 2004 to 2008 and replaced by Mills in 2009, had, during his campaign, proposed to make the position of DCE elective. At the end of his term of office, however, he indicated that he had no regrets in not having carried this through.

- *The efficiency of a tight pyramidal network of nested district-level institutions (akin to the Russian matroichka dolls), which are intended to facilitate the bottom-up expression of grassroots democracy.* The second issue is directly connected to the first. Because the district executive has no direct democratic legitimacy, Ghanaian legislators have deemed it necessary to cover the districts with a close network of interconnected institutions. Yet this system is not delivering results, largely because it relies throughout on voluntary and unpaid work. Moreover, the number of actors foreseen by law in these substructures' assemblies is very (excessively) high. A proposal, currently under study, would reduce the number of elected UC members from 15 to 5 plus eventually two appointed members. On an even broader scale, it is hard to understand how these subdistrict institutions can be made operational. In other words, how can functions be delegated to these structures if they are not given the authority (and responsibility) to take on the financial consequences of their decisions—or, more explicitly, if they do not formally hold some fiscal responsibility? Yet in the current state of affairs, the DAs cannot delegate the power to legislate, levy taxes, or contract loans to the subdistrict entities.

- *The delimitation of district and constituency boundaries.* There are 230 elected members of the national parliament (MPs), or 1.23 MPs per district. In addition, each electoral constituency is, by design, contained within a single district, which itself may comprise several constituencies. These divisions raise the issue of the interactions between the MMDAs and the MPs, who receive a small development grant (see the subsection under "Intergovernmental Transfers": "Direct Financial Transfers: DACF and DDF"). One possible reform would be to redraw the boundaries of both the districts and constituencies so that (ultimately) the two converge toward an identical mapping of districts and constituencies. A tailored solution would need to be found for the metropolis of Accra, as is always the case for capital cities.

- *The creation of new local authorities.* The creation of new districts is explicitly provided for in the Local Government Act. The executive power can create new local authorities or redefine existing ones using the available executive instruments and legal instruments. However, parliament's role in this process is relatively vague (Ferrazzi 2006), which further weakens a local government network that is already fairly permeable to presidential intervention. Many of our interlocutors spoke, often somewhat negatively, about the recent sharp increase in the number of districts and the ensuing consequences, more specifically, the financial ones. This proliferation has sometimes been described as opportunistic and unrelated to the need for effective and efficient delivery of local public services or to what is required for the deconcentration of central government services.

The Decentralized Budget

Legal and Regulatory Framework
The Constitution of Ghana provides a solid, if not comprehensive, foundation for the budgetary and financial construction of local governance. It notably stipulates that each local authority must have "a sound financial base with adequate and reliable sources of revenue."[26] The DACF is one tool used for this purpose.[27] The constitution also mandates that parliament annually allocate at least 5 percent of total government revenues to the DACF.

Yet the pivotal law in this area is the Local Government Act 462 of 1993, which lays down the districts' budgetary and financial framework, including the description of 10 sources of internally generated funds (IGF), which are equivalent to "own resources"; the regulatory budget framework; rate setting for taxes and fees (including the possibility for the government to set guidelines in this area [Art. 100]); and the regulatory framework for local government borrowing, financial control, and the DACF.

In addition to the LG Act, the following two laws establish key aspects of the legal and regulatory framework for local finance:

- The District Assemblies' Common Fund Act (Act 455) of 1993, which sets out the conditions for sharing and distributing the DACF among the districts (according to a distribution formula approved by parliament [Art. 2]), providing that the local authorities supply the data required by the DACF's administrative services

- The National Development Planning (System) Act of 1994 (Act 480), which provides the legal bases for the oversight, particularly budgetary and financial oversight, of district and RCC planning activities (through guidelines).

It would, however, be an overstatement to say that the decentralized local authorities benefited from an adequate budgetary and financial framework right from the mid-1990s and that the related laws immediately produced their full effects. The central government was aware of the existing shortcomings and began therefore to tackle this issue in 2000 and especially 2003. It came up with quite a considerable number of legislative texts and innovations conducive to more effective financial decentralization.

For example, although the 1992 Constitution[28] placed the auditor general in charge of verifying that the MMDAs keep their accounts, use their funds, protect assets, and conduct their financial operations in an appropriate manner, it was not until 2000 that the Ghana Audit Service Act (Act 584) defined the procedures for auditing the MMDAs' books.

The Public Procurement Act (Act 663) of 2003 defines the conditions for public procurement procedures applicable to the MMDAs. These procedures allow the MMDAs the freedom to undertake works projects valued at under ₵ 2 million and make purchases of less than ₵ 1 million for goods and services but oblige them to consult with the central government for operations over these thresholds.

The Internal Audit Agency Act (Act 658) of 2003 defines the standards and procedures applicable to MMDA internal audits.

The Financial Administration Act (Act 654; FAR) of 2003, the Financial Administration Regulations (LI 1802), and the Financial Memoranda for District Assemblies of 2004 make up the core texts defining the MMDA budgetary and financial framework. The Minister of Finance and Economic Planning is responsible for presenting fiscal policy to parliament.[29] The Controller and Accountant General's Department (CAGD) is the chief disbursement agency. These texts also define the procedures for preparing and presenting MDA and MMDA budgets. Articles 186 and 1802 of the FAR require that accounting be carried out on an "accrual" basis and not according to cash-based accounting. The various offices of CAGD provide support to ensure compliance with accounting standards and procedures.

The FAR also specifies the responsibilities of the staff involved in the financial management of the MMDAs and the corresponding obligations, notably in terms of reporting requirements. In addition, it describes the adjustments necessary to ensure harmonization between the MMDAs' annual accounts and the multiyear accounts relating to the financing and execution of multiyear activities undertaken within the medium-term development policy framework. It specifies the respective responsibilities of the persons charged with financial management of the MMDAs as well as those in the MDAs, mainly with a view to ensuring that the decentralized authorities comply with the procedures, reporting, and supervision imposed by the Receiver General. The accounting frameworks and classifications required by the auditing procedures for local government finance are also described. The FAR and its regulations are intended to serve as the benchmark in the area of public financial management. Yet the information collected in the field would seem to indicate that most MMDAs fail to comply, albeit without incurring any penalties in practice.

The Internal Revenue Act, Registration of Business (Act 684) of 2005 reviews the list of revenues, defined by the Local Government Act of 1993, that are collected by the central government and shared with the MMDAs.

Finally, legislative and regulatory production in recent years has chiefly focused on the question of "composite budgeting"—an innovative reform intended to synthesize within a single document the budgets of local authorities (MMDAs) and the central government services located in the same administrative unit. This reform, planned for rollout in 2008, is slow to enter its decisive phase, and although some local authorities have already adopted it, this by no means is the case everywhere.

MMDA Budgets and Accounts

The DAs vote on their own budgets. They thus have a certain degree of autonomy over expenditure in the sense that, even though a large part of their spending is constrained by central government decisions, they still retain some residual power to allocate expenditures funded by their own resources, over which they have some discretionary power (see, in the "Local Taxation" section, the subsection on "Internally Generated Funds").

The districts are responsible for preparing and approving "their" annual budgets.[30] The district budget contains the revenues and expenditures not only of the district *stricto sensu* as a decentralized local authority—that is to say, including those of all departments and organizations under its control—but also those of the District Coordinating Directorate, mainly covering the revenue and expenditure of the annual investment programs of the departments and organizations under the DA's authority.[31] The entire district budget, in a broad sense, is prepared by the district bodies, notably the budget committee, which takes into account the guidelines issued by the Ministry of Finance and the

DACF administration. The budget is submitted to the RCC before the end of the financial year (that is, before the end of the calendar year). The RCC collates and coordinates the budgets of the districts (broadly speaking) within its regional jurisdiction, then submits the aggregate budget to the Ministry of Finance as well as to the Ministry of Local Government and the NDPC.

As a result, the budgetary autonomy of subnational government units, guaranteed by Article 11 of the Local Government Act of 1993, is—both in practice and in law—heavily constrained not only by the consolidation process at the regional level but also by the ex ante endorsement required from the Ministry of Finance.

Budget construction is subject to the following presentation rules and procedures (MoFEP 2004):

- The financial statement, as of December 31, must show the total variation in the surplus balance over the year; under revenues, it must report "own" revenues and transfers received and, under expenditures, recurrent expenditures and capital expenditures. It must be linked to previously approved budgets.
- The DA must approve the initial budget before the start of the financial year (January 1). It must contain the following items:
  - Summary of revenue for the year
  - Summary of expenditure for the year
  - Estimated revenue for the coming year
  - Estimated expenditure for the coming year
  - Receipts and payments recognizing loans.
- Budget revisions may be voted on during the financial year, but they are subject to constraints imposed by the finance authorities (current expenditure and revenue) and the DACF administration (investment spending).
- The budget must be presented using the classification given in table 3.2.

The monitoring of budget execution relies on the monthly comparison of the budgeted expenditure and revenue with actual expenditure and revenue. It should be mentioned that in Ghana, the "single account" rule does not exist. Each district is authorized to open bank accounts for its revenues (minimally one account for own revenues, one for transfers from the central government, one exclusively reserved for receipt of revenues from the DACF, and so on). In practice, local authorities have many separate bank accounts. The number of accounts held depends in part on the requirements of donor partners, who often find it more convenient to open a specific account for each project.

A monthly balance is established to check for consistency and to consolidate the ledger balances, and the resulting items are compared against the corresponding budget items. Any observed divergence must be accounted for by the

Table 3.2 Budget Structure of Local Government Units in Ghana
(Estimated Revenue and Expenditure), 2009

Revenue	Expenditure
• Rates	*Personnel emoluments*
• Lands (stool lands and royalties)	• Salaried posts
• Fees and fines	• Assembly's direct employees
• Licenses	• Social contributions
• Rent from DA-owned property	• Assembly members' allowances
• Transfers and grants (DACF, ceded revenues, salaries, donor support, transfers)	• Other allowances
	Administration
• Revenue from the rental of assets and investment income (equipment rentals, capital income)	• Utilities
• Miscellaneous	• Office cleaning
	• Consumables
	• Printing and publications
	• Rent
	• Travel and transport
	• Maintenance
	• Financial charges
	• Other allowances
	Service activity
	• Training
	• Consultancy
	• Materials and consumables
	• Printing and publications
	• Rent of plant and equipment
	• Travel and transport
	• Maintenance
	• Financial charges
	• Other allowances
	Investment
	• Construction works
	• Rehabilitation
	• Purchase of plants, equipment

Source: Local Government Act 1993 and related Acts and implementation decree up to and including 2008.
Note: DA = district assembly; DACF = District Assembly Common Fund.

heads of the departments concerned and may (under fairly strict conditions) give rise to budget revisions approved by the DA and transmitted to the RCC and the relevant ministries.

Expenditure is controlled by a six-stage administrative chain, beginning with the approval of the DCE, then the district coordinating director, the district finance officer, the district budget officer, the internal auditor, and the department heads.

The books of accounts for local government include a treasury cash book (to be balanced at every month's end) and a treasury ledger comprising four subheads (revenue; expenditure; revenue, expenditure, and balance; and "below the line" accounts for other operations). All of these documents, classifications, and accounting conventions are defined by the Financial Memoranda for District Assemblies of 2004.

The revenue and expenditure statement for the financial year and the balance sheet as of December 31 are produced annually, published, and sent to the offices of the Auditor General by March 31 following the close of the financial year, as well as to the Ministry of Local Government.

The central Auditor General is responsible for verifying the MMDAs' financial statements and reporting to parliament. The Auditor General verifies, above all, that the DACF funds are properly used, as specified by law, for investment expenditure and not for "recurrent" expenses.

MMDA Borrowing and Debt

The MMDAs hold accounts with private banks, which may be interest bearing. At year-end 2006, bank deposits amounted to ₵ 12.1 million, and at year-end 2007, ₵ 4.3 million. In total, the MMDAs' net financial assets minus liabilities were ₵ 13.3 million in 2006 and ₵ 5.7 million in 2007. An examination of the data indicates that for the two years in which the MMDAs ran deficits (expenditure exceeded revenue), the deficit at the national level was ₵ 4.1 million in 2007. This corresponds to excess spending of 1.7 percent over revenues, but this national figure hides wide disparities between regions. For instance, expenditure in the Upper West region exceeded revenues by 68 percent, whereas the Accra region had a surplus balance of 13 percent.[32]

Furthermore, the MMDAs cannot freely dispose of their physical assets and cannot transfer them without prior authorization from the Ministry of Local Government.

The MMDAs can raise loans or obtain overdrafts after approval from the Ministry of Local Government in consultation with the Ministry of Finance.[33] This authorization is not required if the loan amount is less than ₵ 20,000, a ceiling that has not been revised since 1993 and that is now derisory relative to the MMDAs' financing needs. A loans register is kept, showing the year-end outstanding balance. In fact, it appears from consulting the accounts of a few MMDAs that they borrow primarily to meet cash-flow needs while awaiting DACF disbursements, which are late and irregular.

Recent initiatives have been documented (Government of Ghana and Development Partners 2007, 61) that seem to indicate that the two ministries directly involved (Finance and Local Government) are envisaging setting up a long-term credit market to facilitate the MMDAs' access to long-term financing. We saw no concrete signs of this initiative in the field.

Issues Related to Financial Autonomy, Balanced Budgets and Accounts, and Arrears and Debt

There are four issues to examine under this heading:

- The conditions for balanced budgets and accounts are, in principle, clearly defined by law. Should there be an imbalance between actual revenue and actual expenditure, this situation requires decisions to revise the budget and restore balance. Divergences between estimates and actual execution, as previously noted, serve as early indicators of such imbalances. In fact, it was reported to us that divergences between projected and actual revenue and expenditure are apparently frequent, most often because of delays in revenue collection and overspending. At the end of the financial year, any deficit (or surplus) is carried over to the next year, and these operations have seemingly not been formally prohibited. Arrears in settling MMDA expenditures are, it would seem, common practice. This appears to corroborate the fact that the auditor general also ensures that there are no arrears for pensions, electricity, and suppliers. Faced with such practices, certain suppliers sometimes demand payment in advance, which goes against the "payment after delivery" rule. Stricter supervision in this field is undoubtedly desirable as a prerequisite for deepening decentralization.

- Local expenditure autonomy is guaranteed by law.[34] We have seen, however, that this autonomy is in fact limited by the supervisory powers (guidelines and formal auditing) of the Ministry of Finance, the DACF administration for capital budgets, and the NDPC. The MMDAs complain less about this supervision than they do about the lack of synchronization between the cycle for their current budgets (which must be presented as early as September–October, even before the national budget has been approved) and the cycle for presenting their capital budgets to the NDPC. This means that they are virtually bound, by the institutional process, to submit supplementary budgets (mainly for development plans) mid-year (around April or May) to factor in the realities of the financial year that stem from the national budget and NDPC decisions. This mismatch in financial programming makes it nearly impossible to integrate the notion of "recurrent expenditures" into budget planning. In the present setting, it is hard to envisage the introduction of financial forecasting systems aimed at making the MMDAs aware of the long-term financial consequences of their decisions. Very likely, raising an awareness of this type of approach—which is probably a precondition for developing a dialogue with donors—can only realistically be envisaged with a small number of MMDAs (probably starting with the MMDAs in the capital region).

- The MMDAs have greater autonomy in the use of their internally generated funds (IGF). They can use these resources as they wish, and they are subject only to ex post control for compliance (and occasionally to controls as to the appropriateness of use if actual expenditures are substantially higher than budgeted expenditure). Expenditures that draw on resources from government transfers are more restricted because line-to-line transfers must receive prior approval from the central government.

- Finally, discretionary decisions by the central government regarding transferred resources are not uncommon (for example, in the case where the central government decides to use transfers initially planned and approved in the framework of the DACF for expenditures of its own choosing).[35]

Assignment of Responsibilities

The Responsibilities Transferred

The Local Government Act of 1993 remains relatively silent on the modalities for exercising the powers transferred to the MMDAs. According to Article 245 of the Constitution, "Parliament shall, by law, prescribe the functions of District Assemblies which shall include (a) the formulation and execution of plans, programmes and strategies for the effective mobilisation of the resources necessary for the overall development of the district; (b) the levying and collection of taxes, rates, duties and fees."

The Local Government Act lists the functions of the MMDAs, some of which involve the provision of essential services, but no law provides for the explicit devolution of responsibilities from the central government to the MMDAs, even though the constitution views this assignment of responsibilities as a necessary step in decentralization. Many official texts refer to the "decentralized departments" (sic) of the MMDAs; however, they do not give a precise description of the responsibilities but refer rather to "the distribution among administrative sub-units of material, financial and human resources."

This legislative gap probably explains the frequently mentioned (and deplored) overlap of responsibilities between the central government's deconcentrated services (MDAs) and the "decentralized departments" of the MMDAs mentioned in the Local Government Act (see box 3.3). Identical responsibilities can be attributed to these two providers of public services; this is the case notably in the fields of education and health (Ferrazzi 2006; Government of Ghana and Development Partners 2007, 15).

BOX 3.3

Overlapping Responsibilities between the MMDAs and Central Government Offices: The Case of Health and Education Services

The legal instrument (LI) that established the District of Accra (LI 1615 of 1995) assigns it, first, the responsibility to "promote and safeguard public health and for this purpose the Ministry of Health shall assign Medical Officers of Health, health inspectors and other staff . . . to the [district] for the proper discharge of this duty." At the same time, the legal instruments that established the public health service and hospital regime (the Ghana Health Service and Teaching Hospitals Act 525, 1996) states that the Ghana Health Service shall "ensure access to health services at the community, sub-district, district and regional levels by providing health services and contracting out service provision to other recognised health care providers," and shall "plan, organise and administer comprehensive health services." These latter texts establish a vertical hierarchy for the provision of health care services, in blatant disregard of the functions decentralized to the MMDAs by their legal instruments.

In the field of education, the MMDAs were tasked with "build[ing], equip[ping], and maintain[ing] all primary, middle and special schools as are in the opinion of the Minister for Education, after consultations with the Minister responsible for Local Government; to advise the Minister for Education on all matters" and notably on teacher postings and transfers, discipline of teachers, opening and closing primary and middle schools, and payment of teachers' salaries. At the same time, however, the legal instrument defining the Education Service's (ES) responsibilities (GES Act 506, 1995) stipulates that the ES is to provide and oversee basic education, secondary education, technical education, and special education as well as to register teachers. Once again, there are considerable overlaps between these functions devolved simultaneously to the MMDAs and the Ministry of Education. These overlaps were evoked during meetings with the Ministry of Education (secondary education department) and reported in the *Decentralisation Policy Review, Final Report* (Government of Ghana and Development Partners 2007).

The Local Government Act stipulates that a specific decree (a "legislative instrument") attributes a territory and responsibilities to each MMDA. In fact, these responsibilities are nearly always the same and grouped into 88 different functions (many of which are shown in table 3.3). In the case of the Metropolitan District of Accra, the tasks of maintaining order and safety within the metropolitan territory have been added to the functions listed in table 3.3. On the other hand, the tasks assigned respectively to the DAs and municipal assemblies are strictly identical.

Table 3.3 Functions Assigned to the MMDAs in Ghana

Health: hygiene	• *Assignment and provision of medical and health personnel to the MA (by the Ministry of Health)*
	• Construction, maintenance, and operation of clinics, dispensaries, and first aid stations
	• Detection and treatment of health and hygiene problems (relating notably to food, economic activities, and insect eradication)
	• Issuance and supervision of hygiene regulations (economic activities, foodstuffs, industrial products, and so on)
	• Construction and maintenance of public health and hygiene equipment (such as wash places and urinals)
	• Provision and maintenance of slaughterhouses
	• **Collection of household waste**
	• Well capping, pond draining
	• Regulation and control of brush clearing on private property
	• Domestic animal control
	• **Regulation, control, and surveillance of meeting halls, restaurants, and hotels**
	• **Control over the banning of the production and distribution of fermented beverages harmful to health**
Cemeteries, crematoriums	• Construction and maintenance
Roads, public lighting	• Construction, maintenance, clearing, and sweeping of roads other than main roads
	• Identical responsibilities for main roads, *in the capacity of government agents*
	• Public lighting (in conjunction with the Ghana electric company)
	• Planting trees along roads
Urban planning and construction	• Issuance of building regulations, demolition, safety, and outside maintenance of buildings; verification of compliance with these rules; destruction of dangerous buildings; upkeep and maintenance of MMDA buildings; *and (as agents of the central government) public buildings*
	• Urban plans and rules
	• Regulation and control of mines and other excavations
	• Regulation and control of advertising space
Markets	• Construction and maintenance of markets, **parking lots for heavy vehicles**; layout and control of commercial spaces; and collection of stall and market tolls
Education	• Construction, equipment, and maintenance of nursery schools, primary schools, **junior secondary schools**, and special schools according to the metropolitan population school coverage plan
	• Appointment and assignment of teachers in the metropolitan territory, oversight of teacher discipline *(in accordance with the discipline code issued by the Ministry of Education)*, appointment and remuneration of head teachers, granting of study-leave for teachers, payment of teachers' salaries (using resources transferred from the Ministry of Education), and payment of the salaries of school welfare officers
	• Oversight of the functioning of primary and secondary teaching establishments
	• Setting up of education committees
	• Ongoing education for teachers
	• Ordering and provision of school books
	• Award of teaching grants

(continued next page)

Table 3.3 (continued)

Sports, cultural, and recreational activities	• Regulation and control of cultural and recreational activities (theater, cinemas, fairs, circuses, and so on), except for charity events
	• Construction and maintenance of cultural, sports, and recreational facilities
	• Promotion of sporting activities, construction of sporting facilities, and organization of events, *as recommended by the authorized central government organizations and as the latter's agent*
	• Creation and ongoing support of musical groups and ensembles
	• Creation and upkeep of libraries in cooperation with the Ghana Library Board
	• Oversight of the circulation and exhibition of antiques and works of art
Rural and community development	• Organization of educational activities for people in rural areas, support for community development work (such as water supply systems, construction of roads, schools, and community centers)
Childcare services	• Provision of shelters and health care centers for orphans and disadvantaged children
Rescue services	• Provision of rescue and relief services in the case of floods, earthquakes, and accidents
Agriculture	• Support for agricultural development, land allocation, property fencing
	• Improvement of farming and stock-rearing techniques, prevention and treatment of cattle diseases
	• Control of hunting, fishing
	• Implementation of soil conservation and water quality measures, support of forest planting, creation of nurseries (including the commercial sale of their output)
Promotion of economic activities, tourism, public parks	• Encouragement, creation, and commercial operation of very small enterprises and farms in rural areas
	• Tourism promotion in collaboration with the region and the Tourist Development Board
	• Construction and maintenance of public parks
Civil registry	• Provision of civil registry services *under the direction and control of central government services*
Support for traditional authorities	• Financial support to maintain traditional authorities in the metropolitan territory
Land registry	• Creation and maintenance of a registry of landowners and tenancies granted
Road traffic, transportation, fuel	• Issuance of traffic and vehicle identification rules in compliance with the Motor Traffic Ordinance
	• Establishment of circulation licenses and collection of license fees for taxis, bicycles, and motorcycles
	• Acquisition and maintenance of public transit vehicles for land, rivers, and sea
	• Construction and maintenance of parking lots
	• Provision of licenses for fuel distribution stations
Postal services	• Creation and maintenance of post offices *in agreement with the Ghana Postal Services Corporation*
Fire prevention	• Enforcement of fire prevention regulations and implementation of relevant activities
Information	• Setting up of information centers (*in consultation with the Ministry of Information*)

Sources: Legislative Instruments of the Tamale Metropolitan Assembly, Ho Municipal Assembly, and Ejisu-Juaben District Assembly and documents given by the Ministry of Local Government and Regional Development and Environment in the beginning of 2009.
Note: Functions shown in italics are those similar or equivalent to deconcentrated or delegated functions. Functions shown in bold are those specific to metropolitan areas. MA = municipal assembly; MMDA = metropolitan, municipal, and district assembly.

Issues Relating to the Responsibilities Transferred to the MMDAs
Six issues should be raised here:

- The responsibilities transferred to the municipal assemblies and the DAs are identical. Yet it is highly unlikely that the types of responsibilities involved are totally unaffected by the characteristics (land area, population, geographic situation, potential resources, and so on) of the local authorities concerned.

- Moreover, what is striking is the long list of responsibilities transferred to the local authorities relative to how these responsibilities are effectively performed, as was described to us. For instance, the MMDAs seem to play no more than a marginal role in the sectors of water, sanitation, electricity, health, education, and roads—all of these being areas in which the deconcentrated central government agencies and public sector enterprises intervene almost exclusively. This observation is found in all recent reports on the subject. Yet, these areas of responsibility are clearly specified in law as belonging to the MMDAs. Therefore, there seems to be a discrepancy between the legislative texts and what is happening on the ground.

- This discrepancy springs from two phenomena: First, there is persistent confusion perpetuated by the legislative texts themselves between deconcentrated responsibilities and delegated or devolved responsibilities. It is true that some clarification is required in this respect, but such a clarification is directly at odds with the central government's reaffirmed determination to make the district level into "composite" (that is to say, consolidated) entities for territorialized public action. Ghanaian legislators thus wish to make the same territory into a unit of deconcentrated public action and, at the same time, into a space of decentralized local governance. This can only lead to a second point of confusion as to the central government's and the MMDAs' respective responsibilities, and thus entail higher costs or failure to provide public services.

- As a result, the MMDAs find themselves playing an ambiguous and complex role. On the one hand, they are acting as deconcentrated agents for the central government, without however receiving additional resources, as for the upkeep of public edifices. On the other hand, they are the providers of services that complement centrally delivered services in sectors for which the central government has exclusive responsibility. (Numerous examples of this are found in the areas of health services, education, agricultural equipment, water, tourism promotion, and so on, where some of the central government transfers to the MMDAs are channeled to bolster these sectors.) Additionally, the MMDAs are service providers in the areas devolved to them by law (local development, mobilization and management of financial resources, construction and maintenance of local communication networks, construction and urban planning, and spatial planning).

- The texts on responsibilities neither mention mandatory functions nor clearly divide responsibilities between the central government and the MMDAs on this point (Ferrazzi 2006).
- Finally, any expansion of the MMDAs' scope of responsibilities is severely constrained by the lack of resources, as further discussed below.

Local Taxation

The fundamental distinction between the different types of local government resources in Ghana is between "internal" resources and "outside" resources (as from the state or international aid). The legislation provides no substantive definition of "own resources" but gives a restrictive definition of "internally generated funds" (IGF). The scope of IGF would seem to coincide relatively well with "own resources" as defined by Dafflon and Madiès (2008).

Internally Generated Funds

The MMDAs' IGF comprise fiscal resources (property rates, that is, property taxes); royalties from natural resources; levies collected on the exercise of a commercial activity or profession (business licenses) or for the construction of buildings' fines and fees; rent from MMDA-owned property; and other miscellaneous revenues.

With the exception of natural resources, the rates, fees, charges, fines, and rents are fixed and approved annually by each MMDA assembly in its fee-fixing and rate imposition resolutions. These resolutions seem to comply relatively closely with the guidelines set annually by the MLGRDE. The guidelines, which proved difficult to obtain, seem to change little from year to year. (According to our interlocutors at the MLGRDE, the 2008 guidelines were largely based on those for 2006.) The legal status of the guidelines is fairly imprecise, as it is not clear whether they are legal standards or "good practices." In fact, they were often mentioned to us in the field and, in practice, seem to be well followed.

The Accra District Assembly Resolution for 2008 states the rate-setting principles and mentions meetings with professional groups before the MMDA Finance Committee examined the resolution and submitted it to the assembly. Various reasons were evoked in the resolution to explain how each amount or rate was set:

- The need to collect funds
- Taxpayers' and users' ability to pay
- The need to cover the cost of providing local public services
- Equity ("as near as practicable, groups with equal incomes should be made to pay equal fees")

- The need to discourage certain activities ("deterrence of quacks or incompetents")
- The rationale for using charges, conducive to economic efficiency
- Environmental factors
- Encouragement of certain private sector activities
- Business registration.

Property rates   Property taxes constitute the major component of the local tax system.[36] Land is not taxed; only real property is. However, certain categories[37] are exempt from taxation: places of worship, cemeteries, charitable or public educational institutions registered with the MMDAs, public hospitals and clinics, and foreign embassy premises approved by the Ministry of Foreign Affairs (on the basis of reciprocity). The MLGRDE 2008 guidelines on local taxation also exempt the palaces of traditional chiefs with reference to Local Government Act Article 99—which makes no mention of them. Apart from this exemption, the chiefs receive the same treatment as all other taxpayers.

The basis for rating property is the replacement cost (Article 96) of buildings, appurtenances (such as parking areas and drainage systems), and other fixed assets (for example, a large underground fuel reservoir is taxed, but a small propane tank at ground level is exempted). From this cost is deducted an amount equivalent to the cost (expressed as a percentage of the property value and estimated by the valuer) of restoring the premises to a condition in which they would be as serviceable as they were when new. Incomplete buildings and buildings under construction are not valued and therefore not taxed. Government buildings (except those of the decentralized ministries), quasi-governmental buildings, and public companies are subject to the tax on developed property, according to the law and the MLGRDE 2008 guidelines on local taxation.

The valuation is carried out by the Land Evaluation Board, which is a central government institution with 44 offices nationwide. It can call on private contractors and invoices the MMDAs for its services on a time-spent basis when its staff performs a complete valuation, but it provides yearly updates (termed "supplementary rolls") free of charge. The statutory period between two valuation rolls is five years. In practice, more than 20 years may pass between two valuations (for example, the last two valuation rolls for Accra were prepared in 1984 and 2006).

The method used to establish the rateable value is known as "quantity surveying," whereby appraisal is carried out by a certified valuer or, in some cases, an expert (a mechanical engineer for a complex industrial valuation, for example). The value is established with respect to the prices recorded by the valuers for the MMDA in question: the prices in effect in the year (t) during which the general roll was established are used to prepare the supplementary rolls (*t*+1, *t*+2, and so on) until a new general roll is established.

A reduction is applied to the replacement value if the housing is occupied: a 50 percent reduction if the housing is owner-occupied, and a 75 percent reduction in all other cases. Taxpayers who are dissatisfied with their valuation or the rate levied can appeal before a five-member district committee and subsequently a tribunal.

Local rates are collected by the MMDAs, which can call on private collectors paid on commission. The rates of commission mentioned by our interlocutors were 20 percent for individual collectors and 30 percent for collection companies.

When building permits are issued for extensions or renovations, the Town and Planning Departments do not seem to require proof that property rates have been paid. The same holds true when property transactions are registered by the competent authorities.

For example, the rates fixed in Accra in 2006 were 0.46 percent for a residential property in a "first class" zone, 0.35 percent in a "second class" zone, 0.30 percent in a "third class" zone, and 0.27 percent in a "fourth class" zone, whereas the rating for commercial property was 1.2155 percent, and the rate for government buildings was 1 percent. In Agona West, the 2009 residential rates were 0.3 percent, 0.2 percent, and 0.15 percent for property in first-, second-, and third-class zones, respectively.

Also, an annual poll tax may be levied on individuals, with exemptions for students and people over the age of 70. In practice, the amounts levied are very low: ₵ 0.20 in Bia and ₵ 0.10 in Agona West in 2009. In addition, MMDAs may reduce the amount payable for people on low incomes.

Royalties from the sale of natural resources   The rates applied to mineral products amount to 3 percent of the proceeds from gross sales, divided as follows:

- To the central government, 80 percent
- For mineral development (central government), 10 percent
- For other bodies, 10 percent, specifically
  - For the agency administering chieftaincy revenues (the Stool Agency), 1 percent
  - For the MMDAs, 4.95 percent (55 percent of 9 percent)
  - For the paramount chiefs (196 in January 2010), 2.25 percent (25 percent of 9 percent)
  - For the traditional authorities, 1.80 percent (20 percent of 9 percent).

Ground rent   Ground rent is a flat-rate land tax per acre of land (₡ 1 per acre), designed as a way of controlling land use. The revenue from ground rent is shared in the following way: 10 percent to the Administrator of Stool Lands, 49.5 percent for the MMDAs, 22.5 percent for the paramount chiefs, and 18 percent for the traditional authorities.

Fees for the exercise of business activities, fines, and rents   The ratings for businesses, fines, and rents are fixed by the assembly councils. Nonetheless, the MLGRDE 2008 guidelines on local taxation[38] divide the current 138 MMDAs into four groups and set a maximum rate for each group. The four groups are composed as follows:

- *Group A:* the four metropolitan assemblies and Tema
- *Group B:* 28 MMDAs, specifically the other regional capitals (6), 3 other municipalities, and 19 districts (including Ga East and Ga West, located on the outskirts of Accra)
- *Group C:* 32 districts with populations of 10,000–20,000
- *Group D:* 73 districts with populations of less than 10,000.

A maximum rate for the various taxes and charges is established for each category, as shown in table 3.4.

The districts collect many of the fees, such as those levied on poultry farming (a varying amount depending on size); financial institutions (per establishment); civil status activities (marriages); funerals; building permits (fixed amount or per square meter); street closures for ceremonies; and so on. For example, Agona West's Fee-Fixing Resolution for 2009 contains 365 different types of fee. Table 3.5 summarizes the extent to which districts have authority to set their own tax bases, rates, and ceilings.

Table 3.4 Sample Guidelines for Rate, Fee, and License Charges in Ghana, 2008
Cedis

Object	Group A[a]	Group B[b]	Group C[c]	Group D[d]	Frequency
Second-class residence, unassessed	25	10	5	3	Yearly
Class A business, unassessed	1,000	600	300	200	Yearly
Market stall	20	15	10	10	Monthly
Taxi stand	0.40	0.40	0.40	0.40	Daily
Property transfer document	30	25	15	10	Per act

Source: MLGRDE, January 2008 Guidelines.
Note: MMDAs = metropolitan, municipal, and district assemblies.
a. Group A = four metropolitan assemblies and Tema.
b. Group B = 28 MMDAs (6 regional capitals, 3 other municipalities, and 19 districts).
c. Group C = 32 districts with populations of 10,000–20,000.
d. Group D = 73 districts with populations of less than 10,000.

Table 3.5 Degree of Fiscal Autonomy of MMDAs in Ghana, 2007

Tax	Authority to set tax rates and ceilings	Authority to set tax base	Collection
Rates	MMDA and central government (for ceilings and guidelines)	MMDA, following LG Act rules and central government general valuation rules	MMDA
Land taxes	Central government	MMDA	MMDA
Fees and fines	MMDA and central government (ceilings and guidelines)	MMDA	MMDA
Licenses	MMDA and central government (ceilings and guidelines)	MMDA	MMDA

Source: Government of Ghana and Development Partners 2007, table 9.
Note: LG Act = Local Government Act (No. 462) of 1993; MMDA = metropolitan, municipal, and district assembly.

Issues Relating to Local Taxation and the MMDAs' Fiscal Autonomy

There are nine issues of relevance here:

- With the exception of royalties on natural resources, there were no cases in 2009 of taxes shared between the central government and local authorities in Ghana. All local taxes are therefore exclusive.

- The rates fixed by the MMDAs must generally fall within the limits set by the central government guidelines, and these limits depend on the category in which an MMDA has been placed (category 1: metropolitan; category 2: municipal; category 3: urban area; and category 4: rural DA). In practice, it seems that the MMDAs either ignore these guidelines—viewing them as obsolete (a sizable part of these guidelines has not been updated since 1991)—or, in other cases, describe them as mandatory and effective. Some of our interlocutors presented the guidelines as an indispensable tool: first, because they serve as a routine benchmark for local authorities that are little inclined or able to question the guideline rating structure; and second, because they protect local taxpayers from fiscal irresponsibility on the part of the local authorities.

- Internally generated funds (IGF) do not meet recurrent expenditures. The Ghanaian government and its partners outlined this statistical finding for the years 2004 and 2005 (Government of Ghana and Development Partners 2007). The demonstration is not fully compelling because no detailed breakdown of recurrent expenses was provided. However, analysis of the MMDAs' IGF-transfer revenues ratio lends a degree of plausibility to the finding, as does the use of DACF funds, as further discussed below.

- The percentage of IGF in total MMDA resources has grown only slightly in recent years; it rose from 16 percent in 2004 to 18 percent in 2005 and remained at this level in 2007.

- It can be hypothesized that the MMDAs have not mobilized the full fiscal capacity they have available. This is particularly the case with the property rate, for reasons that include the absence of regular property valuation updates, the lack of skilled staff, high administration costs, and no DA control over the activities of the Land Valuation Board (Government of Ghana and Development Partners 2007, 52).

- The incentive from the central government to increase own-revenues generation in the form of grant mechanisms is particularly weak; the "responsiveness" factor is not weighted heavily in the DACF distribution formula (see below).

- Because deconcentrated government units provide most local public services, the MMDAs receive relatively little in the way of payment for services rendered (user fees and charges).

- In all, the shortcomings pointed out by the Government of Ghana and Development Partners report (2007) in the area of mobilizing local fiscal capacity seem to coincide with our own observations in the field. Fiscal revenue mobilization at the local level is low, the legal framework is obsolete because of the infrequency of revisions, and the administrative system for managing the chain of fiscal operations is highly inadequate. The link between the MMDAs and local taxpayers is weak, as is the link between the fees paid and the services provided. The transfer system offers almost no incentive for change in this area, and the central government has not placed improving tax collection high on its agenda.

- The proposals formulated in the joint Government of Ghana and Development Partners *Decentralization Policy Review* (2007) are still relevant:

  ○ Update the property rates guidelines, which date back to 1991, and introduce some leeway for local authorities to set the rates and rules used for assessing tax bases

  ○ Regarding land revenues and use, give the MMDAs land use rights and the right to participate in the preparation of land use guidelines

  ○ Regarding the collection of user fees and charges, fines, and license fees, give the MMDAs the possibility of calling on the Internal Revenue Service (IRS) of Ghana.

Intergovernmental Transfers

Financial transfers can come from either the central government or international donors. Here, we will be dealing only those from the central government—not with the transfers (mainly for projects) from donor partners or the aid (debt cancellation) from the World Bank and the International Monetary Fund under the Heavily Indebted Poor Countries (HIPC) program.[39]

The transfers from the central government operate either as direct payment of expenses incurred by local authorities (notably, transfers for payment of salaries) or as direct financial transfers. In Ghana, a revenue-sharing system on the basis of 5 percent of total national revenues is enshrined in the constitution. An additional 2.5 percent of annual revenue sharing has been in effect as of 2008 through the central government's annual budget.

The overall rationale behind the system of financial interrelationships between Ghana's central government and the MMDAs can be reconstructed as follows: Because the ministries' contributions to MMDA spending carry no particular conditions (except when the centrally paid expense is explicitly defined, as with salaries), de facto they chiefly finance current (or recurrent) expenses to supplement the internally generated funds. The other financial transfers (DACF and DDF) are reserved for "development" expenditure.

Indirect Transfers

Some indirect transfers imply central government funding of expenses paid within the MMDAs. This primarily concerns paying the salaries of a substantial number of central government employees who are nonetheless recruited and working in the MMDAs. This system has been in place since 1995.

An MMDA obtains an increase in the number of staff supplied by the central government in two stages: First, it must submit a request to the Civil Service Commission, which gives its opinion on the appropriateness of the increase. Next, if the commission decides in favor of the increase, the MMDA has to obtain approval from the Ministry of Finance. Approval is often refused at that stage, and a gap often appears between the approved number of positions for government officials employed in the MMDAs and the number actually financed. The MMDAs can also hire staff whom they pay in line with their own salary scale. Each sets its own scale, but in practice these scales seem to be similar to those used by the central government.

The central government may cover other expenditures through budgetary grants. For instance, in 2002, purchases were made at the central level, and equipment (for example, refuse trucks) was transferred to the MMDAs in lieu of monetary transfers.

Direct Financial Transfers: DACF and DDF

The Local Government Act of 1993 guarantees that the districts will have sufficient financial resources to exercise the functions devolved to them. This is explicitly prescribed by the 1992 Constitution (Art. 252-2), which obliges parliament to set aside each year at least 5 percent of total resources for the MMDAs for development purposes. This is operationalized by the District Assemblies Common Fund Act of 1993 (Act 455), which created an administrator's office at the central government level responsible for managing the DACF. Another type of financial transfer from the central government to the districts, the District Development Facility (DDF), was set up in 2009.

The District Assemblies Common Fund (DACF)   The DACF is a conditional grant because use of the funds is earmarked for district "development" expenditures—in practice, infrastructure investments. Use of the funds is governed by guidelines prepared annually by the MLGRDE and approved by parliament. The funds are released only if the development projects are submitted to the DACF Administration and are included in the National DACF Bureau's annual action plans and budgets. In addition, the districts are required to submit monthly reports on the use of the funds to the DACF Administration. The MMDAs are required to adopt a "development" budget, and only items under this budget are eligible for DACF funding. The budget is transmitted to the RCC, which ensures, among other things, that the projects comply with national priorities (such as the Ghana Poverty Reduction Strategy). DACF funding is thus doubly conditional.

The basis for calculating the DACF is a percentage of the aggregate central government resources, defined as follows: "all revenue collected by or accruing to the central government other than foreign loans, grants, non-tax revenue and revenues already collected by or for the District Assemblies."[40] In 2009, the principal elements taken into account as the basis for the 7.5 percent allocated were income taxes (IRS), customs duties, and two-thirds of the value added tax (VAT). Indeed, out of a 15 percent VAT rate, only 10 percentage points are used for the DACF. The remaining 5 percentage points are earmarked for education and health expenditures (2.5 points each through the Ghana Education Trust Fund and the National Insurance Health Scheme).

The DACF calculation is based on fiscal revenues actually collected by the central government, and not on budget projections. Disbursements are made quarterly and are payable in arrears. The January–March payment, for example, is made in April, and the last payment for year t takes place in year $t+1$.

In 2009, the DACF revenue-sharing formula was as follows: the funds were first split between a Reserve Fund (15 percent) and a nonreserve fund (85 percent).

DACF Reserve Fund   The reserve fund divides its 15 percent of DACF revenue sharing as follows:

• Six percentage points of this fund are shared evenly among the 230 parliamentary constituencies. Part of the 6 percent (at most, half) may be used to finance projects managed and evaluated locally. The MMDAs are responsible for overseeing funds for the members of parliament of their constituencies (hence, the interactions between the MPs and the MMDAs mentioned earlier).

- One and one-half percentage points are allocated to the 10 RCCs according to the following formula: half is shared equally among the 10 RCCs, and the other half is shared depending on the number of districts covered by each RCC.
- Two percentage points are used at the Minister of Local Government's discretion.
- One-half of a percentage point is used by the DACF Administration to cover some of its management expenses (the rest is covered by the central government's general budget).
- Five percentage points are devoted to financing the DDF (discussed further below). This is the national counterpart to contributions by donor partners.

DACF Nonreserve Fund   The nonreserve fund divides its 85 percent of DACF revenue sharing as follows:

- One percentage point of the fund's total amount is deducted at the source to finance training activities for DA members.
- Thirty-five percentage points are paid to the fund to fight youth unemployment. The sums reserved for youth employment do not go through the MMDAs but are paid to the Ministry of Labor. These funds are therefore not included in the assemblies' budgets.
- Two percentage points are allocated to spending for the handicapped.
- One percentage point may be used to fight HIV/AIDS and malaria (0.5 percentage point for each).
- Sixty-one percentage points (or 62 if the aforementioned two 0.5 percentage points are not used) finance other MMDA projects covering economic development, social services, administration, and environmental work (such as drainage and waste removal).

This "nonreserve" share of the DACF is distributed among the MMDAs by applying a formula approved annually by parliament. It was cut by 5 percent (dropping from 90 percent to 85 percent) in 2009 to allow the government of Ghana to pay counterpart funds to the DDF (described below).

Determining the DACF Allocation   The decision-making process that establishes the DACF (both reserve and nonreserve) allocation follows these basic steps:

1. The DACF Administration submits a document to the government that normally contains three DACF distribution scenarios.
2. The Council of Ministers chooses one of the scenarios and recommends it to parliament.

3. A parliamentary commission studies the document and proposes a scenario to parliament, usually the government's, which holds a majority on this commission.

4. Parliament votes to approve the DACF revenue-sharing formula for the budget year concerned.

According to the DACF Administration, the comments raised when the formula is under study influence long-term changes, such as the withdrawal of one or another of the factors from the formula.[41] To establish the formula, it is thus necessary to

- List the allocation factors and their indicators;
- Give a weighting to each factor; and
- Measure the various indicators.

The 61 (or 62) percentage points from the DACF nonreserve fund were shared among the MMDAs in 2005–09 using the following four criteria (see table 3.6):[42]

- *Equality.* The allocation of an equal lump sum to each MMDA, regardless of size[43]
- *Needs.* An allocation that takes the following indicators into account (themselves weighted, as discussed in box 3.4):
  - Education (number of schools and the student-teacher ratio)
  - Health (number of facilities and the population-doctor and population-nurse ratios)
  - Percentage of tarred or paved roads relative to the total mileage of the road network
  - Percentage of the population with water service access.
- *Service pressure.* An allocation based on population density as an indicator of pressure on financial needs[44]
- *Responsiveness.* An allocation that takes into account revenue mobilization improvement as a performance indicator[45]

Table 3.6 Weight of Factors in Allocating DACF Nonreserve Funds to MMDAs in Ghana, 2005–09

Year	2005	2006	2007	2008	2009
Equality	60	50	50	50	50
Needs	35	40	40	40	40
Service pressure	2	5	5	6	6
Responsiveness	3	5	5	4	4

Source: DACF annual proposals to parliament, 2010.
Note: DACF = District Assembly Common Fund; MMDAs = metropolitan, municipal, and district assemblies.

BOX 3.4

The Needs Factor for DACF Nonreserve Fund Allocation

In 2009, the formula used to calculate the needs factor, which itself accounts for 40 percent of the District Assembly Common Fund (DACF) nonreserve fund allocation, took into account the following indicators and weightings:

- Number of schools: 5 percentage points (out of 40)
- Student-teacher ratio: 6 percentage points
- Number of health care facilities: 6 percentage points
- Population-doctor ratio: 8 percentage points
- Population-nurse ratio: 8 percentage points
- Percentage of population with access to safe drinking water: 7 percentage points.

The formula uses data from the 2000 population census; the data on health and education are provided by the ministries. When two districts are created out of an existing district, the former's population is evenly divided between the two. The ministries then provide the information for the new districts. Concretely, the process of calculating the data for each indicator is as described below.

For the three health indicators (and the number of schools),

- The ratios of health care facilities, doctors, and nurses in the metropolitan, municipal, and district assembly (MMDA) to the total number of each nationally are computed. In the case of health care facilities in Accra, for example, this gives 44/1,782 facilities, or 0.02469136.
- The population ratio (the MMDA's share of population to total population) is computed. For Accra, this gives 1,105,958/18,912,079, or 0.05847892.
- The location quotient (LQ) is computed by dividing the first ratio by the second: LQ = (1)/(2). This gives 0.42222662 for Accra.
- The value of 1/LQ is divided by the sum of all 1/LQs for all MMDAs, that is, 198.4957187 for clinics, which gives 0.01193173 for Accra. This thus gives the share of the amount of the health and clinic sub-budget received by Accra.

For the student-teacher ratio, total population is replaced by the number of students enrolled in school in each MMDA and the same type of formula applies.

For drinking water coverage, the percentage of the population in each MMDA with access to drinking water is divided by the sum of these percentages. This gives 51.33/9,333.7 or 0.00549943 for Accra. Using the same computations made above for the health indicators using the population of Accra, this gives Accra a share of 0.04909948.

Applying all of these factors means that 62 percent of the DACF is allocated proportionally to population size and to the local authorities' fiscal effort. It should be pointed out that the weightings have changed over time to give a greater preponderance to needs (+9 points, including 5 points for needs and

4 points for service pressure) and responsiveness (+1 point) to the detriment of equality among the MMDAs (−10 points). Overall, however, the rating scale remains basically conservative with regard to offsetting differences across the MMDAs because the needs and responsiveness criteria continue to carry comparatively low weights.

However, once the financing decision has been made, the regularity of the DACF disbursement schedule is not totally guaranteed. It would appear to depend on the Ghanaian state's macro-budgetary situation. The standard schedule provides for payment of the first quarterly installment in April, with the final quarterly installment being released in $t+1$. Yet delays may occur. For instance, the third installment for the year 2009 was not disbursed because of insufficient national revenues—but this third-quarter payment was due to be disbursed in 2010, according to the DACF Administration, as was the payment for the fourth quarter of 2009. A similar problem was seen in 2002 with a missing payment spread out over five years. It should also be noted that all ministry budgets were cut in 2009.

The District Development Facility (DDF)   The DDF, set up in 2009, aims to promote economic development by facilitating public investment funding. Five percent of its total budget comes from the DACF and the rest from a range of international donors.[46] It should be mentioned that the automatic effect of this fund is to reduce (by 5 percent) the DACF funds paid directly to the MMDAs as of 2010. The DDF is composed of three types of grants, broken down in 2009 as follows: (a) 40 percent for the base grant, (b) 40 percent for the performance-based grant, and (c) 20 percent for the capacity-building grant.

The distribution of these grants to the MMDAs is subject to various conditions. Although all MMDAs can receive the capacity-building grant, only the MMDAs that qualify for the base grant can also qualify for the performance-based grant. The MMDAs can therefore only receive all three grants under restrictive conditions. In 2009, 80 percent of the DDF was therefore distributed using incentive-related logic according to the results-based criteria listed below.

DDF Base Grant   The base grant is reserved for local authorities that meet six criteria relating to their operating modalities. Of the 138 districts that existed in 2006[47] and whose applications were analyzed,[48] only 50[49] met all six conditions:

- Hold the number of annual community council (assembly) meetings stipulated by law (41 MMDAs did not meet this condition).
- Prepare and submit an annual statement of account (41 MMDAs did not meet this condition).
- Draw no comments from the Auditor General noting behavior bordering on dishonesty (38 MMDAs did not meet this condition).

- Set up a planning committee (30 MMDAs did not meet this condition).
- Set up the three committees handling calls for tender (11 MMDAs did not meet this condition).
- Prepare an annual plan of action (5 MMDAs did not meet this condition).

For the qualifying MMDAs, 40 percent of the base grant was split equally among the eligible districts; 50 percent was distributed according to each district's share of the 2007 population[50] (in eligible districts); and 10 percent was distributed according to each district's portion of the total land area of eligible districts.

DDF Performance-Based Grant   The MMDAs that fulfill the above six criteria and therefore receive the base grant may also be eligible for the performance grant. An MMDA's performance is assessed using 60 indicators (detailed in the DDF setup guide, grouped into eight main categories, as shown in table 3.7).

The performance-based grant is then allocated to the eligible MMDAs according to the districts' performances relative to other eligible districts. Each district's score is therefore divided by the sum of all eligible districts' scores to calculate its share of this grant.

DDF Capacity-Building Grant   The capacity-building grant is distributed to all MMDAs as follows: 60 percent is divided equally among the 170 districts (as of 2012), and 40 percent is used to fund training courses in basic skills provided by the central government for district staff.

In all, only 50 MMDAs received all three types of grants listed above in 2009, whereas 88 others received only the capacity-building grant. The proportion of districts meeting the required conditions varies considerably from one region

Table 3.7 District Indicators for DDF Performance-Based Grants in Ghana, 2009

Performance measurements	Maximum score / item's % of total (100-point scale)	Average MMDA score	Average score / potential score (%)
Management and organization	15	6.1	41
Transparency, openness, and accountability	10	5.1	51
Planning system	16	7	47
Human resources management	10	4.1	41
Relationship with subdistrict structures	9	2	22
Financial management and auditing	20	10.2	51
Fiscal capacity	10	4	40
Procurement	10	6.8	68

Source: MLGRDE 2009, 10, table 1.
Note: DDF = District Development Facility; MMDA = metropolitan, municipal, and district assembly.

to the next. Table 3.8 lists the number of MMDAs, by region, that received both the DDF base grant and the performance-based grant in 2009.

Finally, the weightings assigned to the three grants were to be modified in 2010—becoming 38 percent, 50 percent, and 12 percent for the DDF base grant, performance-based grant, and capacity-building grant, respectively. The change marked a determination to give heightened priority to local capacity building and performance against a lower weighting for the base grant, which provides no incentive.

Issues Regarding Intergovernmental Financial Transfers to the MMDAs

We note 10 points here:

- Leaving aside the (crucial) subject of indirect transfers—which simply reflects in financial terms the clear demarcation between deconcentration and decentralization—the mechanisms for direct financial transfers between the government of Ghana and the MMDAs seem straightforward, relatively transparent, and, in the case of the DDF, even innovative in their stated determination to provide the MMDAs with incentives. The joint *Decentralization Policy Review* seems to share the same overall assessment, giving this

Table 3.8 Local Authorities in Ghana Eligible for DDF Base Grant and Performance Grant, by Region, 2009

Region	MMDAs in region (number)	MMDAs meeting DDF base grant requirements (number)	MMDAs eligible for DDF performance grant (%)
Ashanti	21	9	43
Brong Ahafo	19	10	53
Central	13	2	15
Eastern	17	7	41
Greater Accra	6	0	0
Northern	18	6	33
Upper East	8	4	50
Upper West	8	4	50
Volta	15	5	33
Western	13	3	23
Total	138	50	36

Source: MLGRDE 2009, 5, table 2.
Note: DDF = District Development Facility; MMDAs = metropolitan, municipal, and district assemblies. All MMDAs have access to the DDF capacity-building grant (20 percent of DDF disbursements). However, only those that meet DDF requirements for the base grant (40 percent of DDF disbursements) also have access to the performance-based grant (another 40 percent of DDF disbursements).

transfer system a score of A (on a scale of A to D, with A being the highest) for the system's transparency. However, it gave D scores for the timeliness of scheduled transfers, the reliability of information given the MMDAs about the size of their grants, and the quality of consolidation between the subnational and central government finances (Government of Ghana and Development Partners 2007, 55).

- In regard to the DACF grant, which is earmarked for development expenditure, an important question arises as to how to distinguish recurrent expenditure from investment expenditure. Several of our interlocutors mentioned cases of DACF-funded expenditures that were clearly similar to recurrent expenses. For instance, the expenditures for a youth employment program were presented as being "an investment in the future of Ghana," and other cases concerning fuel to operate equipment (trucks) were presented as "development" expenditures and thus eligible for DACF funding. The Ghana Audit Service has denounced such practices, although we could not assess just how widespread they were. At the very least, there is a degree of inconsistency between the (legitimate) practices of the DACF (which wants to see the MMDA capital investments generate services) and the (also legitimate) practice of the Ghana Audit Service, which notes that the law prohibits certain uses of the funds but not others. This inconsistency raises the most fundamental point—the lack of a general operating grant for the MMDAs.

- The lack of cost evaluations means that there is no precise link between the DACF amount allocated and the costs generated by investment expenditures to provide services relating to transferred responsibilities. Rising costs probably justify the increase from 5 percent to 7.5 percent of public funds earmarked for the DACF, but the rise in costs have not been evaluated with any precision.

- The reported transfers to the MMDAs sometimes differ by up to 10 percent, depending on the sources. One explanation for these differences is that some sources take into account gross transfers while others refer to net transfers. Certainly, the value of supplies provided directly to the MMDAs by some ministries (the delivery of trucks, tractors, television sets, and so forth) is sometimes deducted from the gross grant amounts. Finally, the accounting systems used for grants are far from uniform across all MMDAs (Government of Ghana and Development Partners 2007, 55–100).

- The DACF distribution factors are not exempt from criticism, either. For example, it is difficult to find any indication of equity considerations. In addition, the currently used "needs" factor may constitute a reverse incentive because an MMDA that provides a service will be less and less encouraged to progress insofar as it will receive smaller and smaller grants for the service delivered. It could be appropriate to review the "needs" indicators (using items such as the literacy rate or public health indicators). Finally, the "responsiveness" factor designed to encourage greater mobilization of local resources receives too small a weighting to have any noteworthy impact. Factoring in population density (the higher the density, the higher the grant) raises an empirical problem because we do not know whether the local service supply-cost curve is continuously decreasing in population or whether it follows a U-shape.

- The narrow earmarking of most funds received from the DACF for very specifically defined uses contrasts with the small share of discretionary funds for local use. The DACF is micro-earmarked, which, in principle, makes monitoring easier but also heightens rigidity and reduces effectiveness. This effectiveness is further eroded in cases where discretionary interventions by the central government's deconcentrated services result in the DACF funds being used for their own purposes. This means that, in practice, the DACF only remotely resembles a general grant that gives autonomous MMDAs the leeway to make budgetary decisions.

- The schedule for submitting documents to the DACF is in no way synchronized with MMDA budget operations. The investment-planning schedule that governs the DACF file submitted to the RCC needs to come much earlier than the current operations schedule, yet the two budgets are tied together.

- In addition, the DACF payment schedule is erratic and makes it impossible to secure equipment financing plans in the MMDAs. Some local authorities told us that they had (marginal) recourse to loans on account of these scheduling uncertainties.

- Finally, in regard to the DDF, the first results show the strong selectivity of the chosen criteria. A simulation run on the year 2006, for instance, showed that less than one-third of the MMDAs were eligible for the DDF's three subgrants, and the remaining two-thirds received only the capacity-building grant, or 20 percent of the total. As elsewhere, the share of this last grant is due to diminish over time (it accounted for only 12 percent in 2010), and one can wonder how realistic this trend is. Is the pressure on local authorities to rapidly meet capacity-building and performance objectives realistic? Would too many requirements regarding incentives not have the effect of concentrating the benefits of the DDF onto a small number of local authorities and ultimately leave out the local authorities that are furthest behind?

- The DACF and the DDF are supposed to cover investment expenses. Accordingly, the question of their overlap—and thus the question of the overall coherence of the transfer system—can be raised.

Revenue and Expenditure Statistics

The statistical data discussed below are intended to provide information on the approximate magnitude of the weight and structure of local-authority expenditures and revenues in Ghana as well as the role that central government transfers play in these expenditures and revenues.

However, care must be taken in presenting and interpreting these data—first of all, because the confusion between decentralization and deconcentration makes the statistical delimitation of expenditures relating to either of these processes a fragile matter. Furthermore, and as various interlocutors indicated to us, the breakdown between recurrent expenditure and capital expenditure is also far from robust because of lack of precision regarding the local expenditures met by the central government (confusion between deconcentration and decentralization) and the DACF's subsidization rules. Moreover, there is no breakdown of local expenditures by function. Finally, during our field visits, we obtained information on MMDA revenues for 2006 and 2007. This implies that we cannot examine separately the ministries, departments, and agencies created in 2008.

Shares of Local Public Expenditure and Revenue in Ghana

Total public sector spending in Ghana represented 25.9 percent of gross domestic product (GDP) in 2005, and the total tax burden represented 22.1 percent (Government of Ghana and Development Partners 2007).[51] The proportion of total public spending and public revenues seemed to remain steady—at close to 27 percent and 22 percent of GDP, respectively—until 2009. Breaking down these figures, MMDA spending accounted for 6.2 percent of total public expenditure in 2005 (6.2 percent in 2004), or 1.6 percent of GDP (Government of Ghana and Development Partners 2007). MMDA revenues amounted to 5.3 percent of total public revenue in 2005 (6.0 percent in 2004). The gap between internally generated public revenues and public spending—0.2 percent of GDP in 2005—is covered by international donors (Government of Ghana and Development Partners 2007).

In the expenditure breakdown, a substantial fraction of spending is shown to be dedicated to investment, as seen in figure 3.3. This particularity may possibly be explained by the breakdown (not precisely measured) between current expenditure assumed by the central government and local current expenditure. Because there is reason to assume that some of the latter is met by the central government, the share of investment spending increases.[52] This characteristic is stable. Already in 1996, capital expenditure accounted for 69 percent of local spending, even rising to 78 percent in 2004. The low level of spending on salaries reflects the assumption of these costs by the central government and

Figure 3.3 Breakdown of Local Public Expenditure in Ghanaian MMDAs, 2007

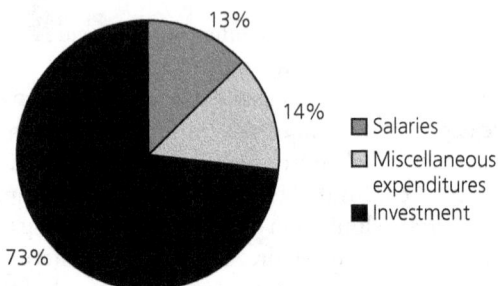

13%

14%

■ Salaries
□ Miscellaneous
   expenditures
■ Investment

73%

Source: Data from MLGRDE.
Note: MMDAs = metropolitan, municipal, and district assemblies.

probably also the small degree of real decentralization of responsibilities or the low level of service delivery.

The MMDAs' total average per capita revenue was ₵ 9 in 2007. This is equivalent to approximately 1.2 percent of 2007 GDP,[53] which is consistent with the numbers reported earlier. This amount drops with the size of the population in the MMDAs: the average nonweighted amount is ₵ 18 for the quintile containing the smallest municipalities and ₵ 8 for the largest. This disparity reflects both the share of the transfers in MMDAs' revenues (see the breakdown by population quintile below) and the weight of the equality criteria in the DACF's formula, which gives the smallest MMDAs an advantage in per capita terms.

In 2007, the MMDAs drew 82 percent of their total resources from the transfers received from the government of Ghana. This amount is similar to the figures for 2004 (84 percent) and 2006 (83 percent). This slight downward trend can be partially explained by the pilot actions in some MMDAs to improve local tax collection.

Ranking the 138 MMDAs in 2007 by population size from smallest (South Dayi, population 42,527) to largest (Accra, population 2,233,865) and grouping them into quintiles yields the following breakdown: The share of direct financial transfers in total MMDA revenues ranges from 93 percent for the first quintile of MMDA (by population size) to 74 percent for the fifth quintile. The second, third, and fourth quintiles' share of direct transfers in MMDA revenues are 91 percent, 88 percent, and 85 percent, respectively.

Statistical treatment of the data grouped by MMDA on the basis of their legal status would yield similar results, since the large MMDAs are metropolitan or municipal assemblies. Thus, for the three largest cities in terms of population, the percentage of transfers in total revenues is as follows: Accra, 59 percent; Kumasi, 68 percent; and Tema, 47 percent.

The share of government transfers in total MMDA revenue also varies among regions (see table 3.9). One can see that the MMDAs' degree of financial dependency (measured as the share of transfer revenue in total revenue) seems to rise with poverty level and fall with higher average income. The correlation coefficient between poverty and dependency on transfer revenues is 0.71, and the correlation coefficient between the share of transfers and per capita revenue is −0.92. There is, therefore, an element of equalization (de facto, but not explicitly indicated in the relevant texts), at least in terms of potential local resources in total transfers to MMDAs in Ghana.

The internal breakdown of total transfers (IGF) received by the MMDAs in 2007 is presented in figure 3.4. We can see that the DACF is the primary source of transfers. The sum of transfers financed by domestic resources is 58 percent (44 + 11 + 3). The "Gov. of Ghana" transfer corresponds to the sum paid by the central government to cover the salaries of municipal staff that are directly remunerated. These percentages are similar to the figures for 2004: 52 percent DACF, 10 percent salaries, 27 percent HIPC, and 11 percent donors (Government of Ghana and Development Partners 2007, 56, table 10).

The breakdown of IGF in 2007 is presented in figure 3.5. The largest source of local internally generated revenues is fees and fines. These fees include business taxes levied on companies. Property rates and revenues from building permits and the payments received for resource exploitation (stool lands) are of secondary importance.

These data are similar to the data for the year 2005 (23 percent for rates; 43 percent for the combination of permits, ground, fees, and fines; 19 percent for licenses; and 15 percent for miscellaneous revenues (Government of Ghana

Table 3.9 Ghanaian Regions by Share of Transfer in MMDA Revenue, Poverty Index, and Per Capita Revenue, 2007

RCC	MMDA revenue from transfers (%)	Poverty (%)	Annual per capita revenue (¢)
Accra	60	12	2,907
Ashanti	78	20	1,967
Brong Ahafo	87	29	1,614
Central	88	20	1,810
Eastern	82	15	1,794
Northern	96	52	1,529
Upper East	96	70	1,066
Upper West	94	88	901
Volta	92	31	1,514
Western	75	18	1,924

Source: MLGRDE 2007b.
Note: MMDAs = metropolitan, municipal, and regional assemblies; RCC = regional coordinating council.

Figure 3.4 Grants to MMDAs, by Grant Type and Donor Category, in Ghana, 2007

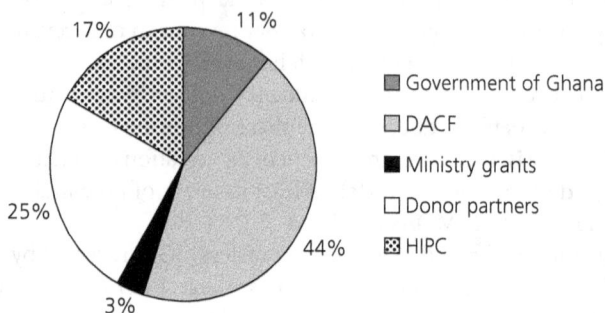

- Government of Ghana
- DACF
- Ministry grants
- Donor partners
- HIPC

11%
17%
25%
3%
44%

Source: Data from MLGRDE.
Note: DACF = District Assembly Common Fund; HIPC = Highly Indebted Poor Countries (program of the World Bank and International Monetary Fund); MMDAs = metropolitan, municipal, and district assemblies.

Figure 3.5 Sources of MMDA Internally Generated Funds, Ghana, 2007

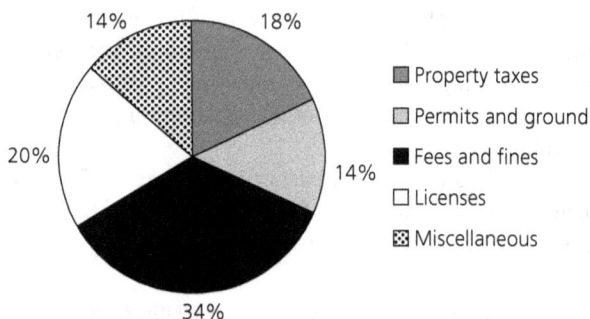

- Property taxes
- Permits and ground
- Fees and fines
- Licenses
- Miscellaneous

14%
18%
20%
14%
34%

Source: Data from MLGRDE.
Note: MMDA = metropolitan, municipal, and municipal assembly.

and Development Partners 2007, 51, table 8). It should be pointed out here that the revenues associated with natural resources are mining royalties, which are mainly concentrated in two regions: Western (50 percent) and Ashanti (25 percent) (Government of Ghana and Development Partners 2007, 51, table 8; Inanga and Osei-Wusu 2004, 87, table 3).

Notes

1. On the eve of independence, Ghana consisted of the coastal region (former colony), the Ashanti Confederacy, the Northern Region, and Togo (under the British protectorate and integrated into the Gold Coast in 1956). On independence, the territory of the former colony was split into two regions, bringing the number of regions up to five.

2. Prior to its application in 1974, the Local Administration Act of 1971 was modified by the Local Administration Amendment Decree, 1972 (NRCD 258).
3. The DCs were steered by the Interim Management Committee.
4. In the 1993 laws, the district secretary was replaced by the district chief executive. In addition to this change in title, the modalities for nominating the DCEs were also modified.
5. PNDC Law 207.
6. Today, Ghana comprises 10 regions, 8 of which were created immediately following independence in 1957 (Ashanti, Brong Ahafo, Central, Eastern, Greater Accra, Northern, Volta, and Western). In September 1960, the Northern region was carved up to create Upper East. In 1983, under the Rawlings regime, the same process was used to create the Upper West region out of the Upper East region.
7. One cedi is worth 0.5 euro.
8. Constitution of 1992, Chapter 20.
9. See the Civil Service Law (PNDC Law 327) of 1993, the Local Government Act (Act 462) of 1993, and the District Assemblies Common Fund Act (Act 455) of 1993.
10. The Ghana Health Service and Teaching Hospitals Act (Act 506) of 1996 and the Ghana Education Service Act (Act 525) of 1995.
11. See "District Assemblies' Common Fund Increased": http://www.modernghana.com/news2/140096/1/district-assemblies-common-fund-increased.html.
12. This document, the Intergovernmental Fiscal Decentralization Framework, proposes the following: (a) a clarification of the responsibilities of the different government tiers when it comes to local public investments, according to the subsidiarity principle; (b) the allocation of resources adapted to these (newly) devolved responsibilities; (c) control over local taxation and the possibility of accessing credit or financial markets within certain set limits; and (d) the implementation of a transparent financing mechanism to build capacities and consolidate good management of the districts.
13. See http://news.peacefmonline.com/meet_the_press/200906/24191.php.
14. Constitution of 1992, Art. 1, Chapter 20.
15. Constitution of 1992, Art. 35d, Chapter 6.
16. Constitution, Art. 78[1].
17. Constitution, Art. 79(1).
18. Constitution, Art. 256.
19. Local Government Act, Art. 142.
20. Their institutions are established by the LI 1589 of 1994.
21. Defined by Art. 244 of the Constitution and Art. 17 of the Local Government Act.
22. Local Government Act, Art. 24–25.
23. Constitution, Art. 243–244, and the Local Government Act, Article 20.
24. Constitution, Art. 243 of Chapter 20.
25. Local Government Act, Art. 10 and 46, and the National Development Planning [System] Act of 1994, Art. 479–480.
26. Constitution, Art. 240[2c].
27. Constitution, Art. 252[1].
28. Constitution Article 187[5]) and Act 584, Section 23[1].
29. Financial Administration Act (654) of 2003, Section 2[a].

30. Local Government Act, Art. 11.
31. Local Government Act, Art. 92.
32. Calculated using MLGRDE data.
33. Local Government Act (462) of 1993, Section 88.
34. Local Government Act (462) of 1993, Art. 11.
35. Thus, the 2007 *Decentralization Policy Review: Final Report* (Government of Ghana and Development Partners 2007, 49) cites cases in which the central government imposed the procurement of a cesspit tanker for a local authority that had no need for one, or the purchase of televisions for distance learning, or vehicles for chief executives, and so on.
36. Articles 94–119 of the Local Government Act define the general framework.
37. Listed in Article 99 of the Local Government Act.
38. Local Government Act, Art. 100.
39. The HIPC funds for MMDAs are not examined in detail in this report. On this point, we refer to the fairly negative judgment of the Government of Ghana and Development Partners (2007, 60–61).
40. District Assemblies Common Fund Act of 1993 (Act 455).
41. The records of the meetings of the parliamentary commission that studies the proposal for the government transfer are useful in the long run; they fuel reflections on modifying DACF distribution parameters.
42. In the past, a share (whose weight varied annually) of the "nonreserve" DACF was earmarked for sanitation, and only for metropolitan and municipal entities. This is no longer the case today.
43. It is to be noted that the equality factor, which apportions an equal sum to MMDAs regardless of their size, results in a different per capita distribution depending on the size of the MMDA. The inhabitants of small MMDAs are mathematically favored by such a system.
44. The ratio for any given MMDA is the population density in 2000 to the sum of all population densities. For Accra, this ratio (rounded to one decimal place) was $4,726.3/40,127.5 = 0.1178$. Accra therefore received 11.78 percent of the monies paid on the basis of this factor.
45. The responsiveness factor for any given MMDA is the ratio of the percentage increase of its revenues (IGF) over two years (for instance, 2007–09 for 2009) to the sum of all percentages. For Accra, this gives (figures rounded to one decimal place) $321.4/10,3521 = 0.0031$. Therefore, Accra received 3.15 percent of the monies paid on the basis of this factor. It should be noted that when more recent data are not available, the computation is based on 2001, the baseline year.
46. International donors include Canadian Agency for International Development (CIDA), L'Agence Française de Développement (AFD), Denmark's development cooperation (Danida), and the German development bank KfW (Kreditanstalt für Wiederaufbau).
47. The new districts created in 2006 from existing districts qualified for the base and performance-based grants. The DDF grants were calculated using 2006 data based on the divisions in effect at that date. These grants were thus equally shared between the new districts and their districts of origin.

48. The 2006 data on the situation for the then-existing MMDAs were used to calculate the sharing of funds in 2009.
49. For the 88 remaining districts, the breakdown is as follows: 38 met five conditions, 33 met four conditions, 10 districts met three conditions, 6 districts met two conditions, and 1 district met one condition.
50. Produced by the Ghana Statistical Service.
51. The *Decentralization Policy Review* (Government of Ghana and Development Partners 2007) is based on Shah 2006. For the same year, the Organisation for Economic Co-operation and Development (OECD) reports the that total public sector spending amounted to 27.8 percent of GDP, and the tax burden amounted to 19.4 percent of GDP.
52. Discussions with representatives of the DACF and the MLGRDE indicated that the definition of "investment" can be broad.
53. Ghanaian GDP was ₵ 18 billion in 2007, equivalent to almost €12 billion (Ghana Statistical Service): see http://www.statsghana.gov.gh/docfiles/GDP/GPD-Real,Nominal,Growth%20Rates%20and%20Percentage%20Contribution%20of%20the%20various%20sectors%20of%20the%20economy(2006-2008).pdf.

References
Ahwoi, K. 2009. "Management, Leadership and Administration: What Type of Chief Executive Does Ghana need?" Talk given at the National Stakeholder Conference on Decentralization, Ghana Institute of Management and Public Administration, Kumasi, September 25–27.

———. 2010a. "Conceptualising Decentralisation in a Unitary State." Talk given at the National Stakeholder Conference on Decentralization, Ghana Institute of Management and Public Administration, Accra, January 19–20.

———. 2010b. *Local Government and Decentralisation in Ghana*. Accra North, Ghana: Unimax Macmillan Limited.

Asante, F.-A. 2007. "Capacity Constraints on Local Government Environmental Policies in Ghana." In *Environmental Governance and Decentralization*, ed. A. Breton et al. Cheltenham, U.K.: Edward Elgar.

Ayee, Joseph R. A. 1996. "The Measurement of Decentralization: The Ghanaian Experience, 1988–1992." *African Affairs* 95 (378): 31–50.

———. 1997. "The Adjustment of Central Bodies to Decentralization: The Case of the Ghanaian Bureaucracy." *African Studies Review* 40 (2): 37–57.

———. 2008. "The Balance Sheet of Decentralization in Ghana." In *Foundations for Local Governance*, ed. F. Saito, 223–58. Heidelberg: Physica-Verlag.

Crook, R. C. 1994. "Four Years of the Ghana District Assemblies in Operation: Decentralization, Democratization and Administrative Performance." *Public Administration and Development* 14 (4): 339–64.

———. 1999. "No-Party Politics and Local Democracy in Africa: Rawlings' Ghana and the Ugandan Model in the 1990s." *Democratization* 6 (4): 114–38.

Dafflon, B., and T. Madiès. 2008. "Décentralisation: quelques principes issus de la théorie du fédéralisme financier." [Decentralization: A Few Principles from the Theory of

Fiscal Federalism.] Notes and Documents 42, Agence Française de Développement, Paris.

Ferrazzi, G. 2006. "Ghana Local Government Act 1993: A Comprehensive Analysis in the Context of the Review of the Act, Local Governance and Poverty Reduction Support Programme (LGPRSP)." Paper prepared for the Ministry of Local Government, Rural Development and Environment/Deutsche Gesellschaft für Technische Zusammenarbeit (GTZ). http://www.gtz.de/de/dokumente/en-Ghana-Local-Governance-Act-Comparative-Analysis-2006.pdf.

Fischer, G. 1957. "Le Ghana, l'indépendance et ses problèmes." *Politique étrangère* 22 (2): 139–50.

Government of Ghana and Development Partners. 2007. *Decentralization Policy Review, Final Report*. http://dege.dk/assets/files/DecentralisationPolicyReview.pdf.

Inanga, E. L., and D. Osei-Wusu. 2004. *Financial Resource Base of Sub-national Governments and Fiscal Decentralization in Ghana*. Oxford and Malden, MA: African Development Bank and Blackwell Publishing Ltd.

Jacquemot, P. 2007. "Chefferies et décentralisation au Ghana." *Afrique Contemporaine* 2007/1 (221): 55–74.

Lentz, C. 2000. "Chieftaincy Has Come to Stay: la chefferie dans les sociétés acéphales du Nord-Ouest Ghana." *Cahiers d'Études Africaines* 159 (XL-3): 593–613.

———. 2006. "La Décentralisation dans le Nord Ouest du Ghana: des frontières contestées." In *Décentralisation et Pouvoirs en Afrique*, eds. C. Fay, F. Y. Kone, and C. Quiminal, 363–83. Montpellier: IRD Editions.

MLGRDE (Ministry of Local Government and Regional Development and Environment). 2007a. "Comprehensive Decentralization Policy Framework." Report, MLGRDE, Accra.

———. 2007b. *Patterns and Trends of Poverty in Ghana, 1991–2006*. Accra: Ghana Statistical Service.

———. 2009. "Consolidated Report on Performance Assessment of MMDAs for the 2006 Fiscal Year." Report, MLGRDE, Accra.

MoFEP (Minister of Finance and Economic Planning). 2004. "Financial Memoranda for Metropolitan, Municipal and District Assemblies." *Ghana Gazette* 35, August 20.

Rochegude, A., and C. Plançon. 2009. "Fiche Pays Ghana N° 12." In *Décentralisation, foncier et acteurs locaux*, http://www.foncier-developpement.org/.

Shah, A., ed. 2006. *Local Governance in the Developing Countries*. Public Sector Governance and Accountability Series. Washington, DC: World Bank.

Chapter 4

Public Finances of Local Government in Kenya

Yvon Rocaboy, François Vaillancourt, and Réjane Hugounenq

History of "Centralization" in Kenya, 1963–2010

At its independence from British rule on December 12, 1963, Kenya adopted a federal constitution known as *Majimbo*,[1] which gave the regions (a total of seven) a significant role. These regions, as true local government units, had assemblies elected by universal suffrage as well as financial resources. In addition to the regions, the system of territorialized public institutions at that time included a second tier of local government—the local authorities (LAs). As in many African countries, these structures did not date from independence but were inherited from the colonial period.[2]

This experience of a highly decentralized state—which resulted from a compromise that developed throughout the interim period (1960–63) before independence[3]—was short lived and, in some ways, never really worked. Just one year after independence, the opposition rallied behind the party in power for want of other options, which allowed independent Kenya's first president, Jomo Kenyatta, to implement a republican constitution (1964) with a relatively free hand. Kenya thus became a unitary republic. The regions, as local governments, were dissolved and regained their former status as "provinces" along with the powers that they had held during the colonial period (Bourmaud 1988). In other words, Kenya returned to the territorial organization set up by the British during the colonial episode—on the one hand, a deconcentrated system structured around the provinces and, on the other, a decentralized system made up of LAs.

At the time, the deconcentrated provincial system was structured around provinces, districts, divisions, locations, and sublocations. In December 1964, supervisory authority for this system was transferred from the Ministry of Home Affairs to the Office of the President, which directly appointed (and still appoints) the provincial commissioners (PCs) and district commissioners

(DCs). The organization of this provincial administration and its various levels (PCs, DCs, division officers, chiefs, and assistant chiefs)—nearly 3,000 people in total—gives the president almost direct control over a large part of the political and administrative spheres of government (Bourmaud 1988).

As for the LA system, this was governed from independence by the Local Government Act Regulation (1963),[4] which recognized two levels of LA: The first tier comprised (a) the municipal councils that operated within urban areas and (b) the county councils that covered rural areas and whose boundaries roughly coincided with those of the districts. These first-tier authorities were divided into area, urban, and local councils, which made up the second tier. The distinction between these two tiers was to disappear during the 1970s. In 2010, just one tier remains, made up of city councils, municipal councils, town councils, and county councils (as further discussed in the next section, "Organization of Decentralized Local Government and Deconcentration").

Throughout the 1960s and 1970s, the scope of the LAs' responsibilities and resources as well as their political-administrative operation became increasingly recentralized. Indeed, shortly before independence—and to contain the anticolonial movements—the county councils and the municipal councils were assigned a large number of responsibilities[5] as well as the right to create public employment. In practice, however, the LAs exercised these functions only since 1964 because the regionalization process of the early 1960s had initially overshadowed these lower-level local government entities. Having removed the regional level, the Kenyatta administration first sought to revitalize the LAs to stimulate the economy by mobilizing the grassroots. The government set up a system of grants and created a local tax for the LAs (the graduated personal tax or GPT) as a complement to the national income tax. The LAs were also able to levy a host of local taxes (rates), user fees, and charges and license fees. At the time, they had relative autonomy in their decision making. This state of affairs was, however, less the result of a real willingness by the central government to share power than a step in building national unity based on a strong state, in line with the wishes of the Kenyatta government. The first years of independence were devoted to setting up control from the center, while the local level was not a political priority (Bourmaud 1988), at least initially.

The operation of the LAs quickly proved to be financially unviable because of the high costs they had to bear with respect to their responsibilities and also because of measures introduced unilaterally by the government (such as free health care and increased salaries for teachers) that put greater strain on the LAs' budgets. At the end of the 1960s and in the early 1970s, many of these local authorities, notably the county councils, were almost bankrupt.

This was also the era of *Harambee*, an ideology promoted by Kenyatta aiming to encourage citizens' direct involvement in financing local infrastructure (schools, health care centers, and the like) through cash donations or contributions in kind, with the goal of boosting the fight against ignorance, poverty, and disease and, ultimately, of stimulating development. This initiative, however, meant that the movement contributed to the implementation of local infrastructures that the local authorities could not afford to operate (Njeru and Njoka 2007). Faced with this situation, but also because of its agenda for political centralization, the government put in place a range of measures designed to curb the LAs' responsibilities and resources.[6]

In 1965, collection of local taxes (notably the GPT) was transferred to the provincial level. In 1970, the Transfer of Function Act transferred the county councils' mandatory responsibilities for primary education, public health, and roadways to the central government through the ministries involved in the deconcentrated administration. The county councils also lost control of the GPT. As for the municipal councils, the adjustments affected resources more than responsibilities. In 1974, they were deprived of the GPT, which was abolished and replaced by a centrally controlled sales tax. In addition, large cuts were made to central government grants.

Overall, the system established between independence and the mid-1970s was run from the center. Many responsibilities and resources fell on ministry offices in the provinces, and spending was carried out through ministry budget lines. In addition, the decision-making autonomy that the LAs had enjoyed was undermined throughout the 1960s. Because of their political and administrative arrangements, the LAs found themselves under the supervision of both the deconcentrated provincial services and the Ministry of Local Government.

In fact, the recentralized powers also rested with the Ministry of Local Government, which inevitably caused problems between the ministry and the deconcentrated structures under direct presidential control. Through its provincial representatives, the Ministry of Local Government was required to approve almost all decisions made at the local government level (see the section later on "The Administrative Units"). It directly appointed a quarter of the LA councillors and had a say in the recruitment of administrative staff such as clerks and treasurers. All local bylaws and budgets were under the ministry's oversight. Finally, the LAs also came under the direct control of the DCs, which were hierarchically linked to the Office of the President and ex officio members of the municipal and county councils.

Kenya was not immune to the movements that emerged in the 1990s under pressure from civil society and donors protesting against the authoritarian and centralized political regimes. As in many African countries, the reforms driven by the international community targeted, among other things, democratization of the political system and improvement of public sector efficiency. The first item involved, at the national level, the reintroduction of a multiparty system into the constitution[7] and, at the local level, the will to encourage civil society participation in formulating the demand for public services. The second item resulted in reforms aimed at promoting budgetary and fiscal decentralization.

In Kenya, however, the issue addressed was merely the question of the resources to be made available to the LAs and not that of the LAs' political-administrative arrangements and their subordination to the central authorities—which nevertheless calls into play the very notion of the LAs' responsibilities and, by extension, the effectiveness of decentralized organization. Table 4.1 summarizes the chronology of constitutional development in Kenya since its independence.

In 1995, the Kenya Local Government Reform Program (KLGRP), steered by the Ministry of Local Government in conjunction with donors, was devised in an attempt to increase the LAs' financial resources, foster citizens' participation in community life, and improve the reliability of budgetary and accounting information. The KLGRP came into its own notably in 1999 with the creation of the Local Authority Transfer Fund (LATF), which gave some financial leeway back to the LAs (as the "Intergovernmental Grants" section will further discuss). In 2002, as part of this program, the Local Authority Service Delivery Action Plan (LASDAP) was created. Its purpose is to encourage citizens to participate more fully in the public decision-making process, particularly concerning the production of local public services. In accordance with LASDAP, investments funded by the LATF first have to be discussed at public meetings

Table 4.1 Constitutional Landmarks in Kenya, 1963–2010

1963	The Independence Constitution: a classic parliamentary system replicating the British model, with a prime minister (Jomo Kenyatta) as head of government and a bicameral parliament (House of Representatives and Senate). The constitution did not make provision for the post of president but included a position—ceremonial in nature—of governor general representing the British monarchy and acting as head of state.
	It includes (a) a federal-style *Majimbo* system, with seven regions having some autonomy; (b) an independent judiciary system; and (c) a charter of rights for minorities.
1964–97	The constitution was amended and the monarchy transformed into a republic. Executive power was vested in a president who held all powers: head of state, head of government, and head of the armed forces.
	The *Majimbo* system was abolished, and power was thus centralized, along with a transition to a unicameral parliament, with the dissolution of the Senate in 1967.
	Period of one-party rule from 1982, which allowed a maximum of two five-year presidential terms.
1998–2009	Constitutional reform process: a new constitution (the Bomas draft followed by the Wako Bill) was proposed in 2005 by the attorney general and rejected by popular referendum in November of that year.
	After the 2007 riots, a new constitution was proposed by a Committee of Experts in 2009 and put to a referendum in 2010.
August 4, 2010	New constitution passed by referendum, with a majority of 66.9 percent of votes in favor. This text came into force on August 27, 2010, but it will be implemented gradually, in line with the transitional procedures set out therein.

and ranked in order of priority, taking into account the available financial envelope. The existence of this scheme is one of the conditions for allocating the LATF "performance" envelope. Finally, the Local Authority Integrated Financial Operations and Management System (LAIFOMS) was established. This is a software application that aims to improve and harmonize the procedures for budget preparation and execution.

The creation of the LATF certainly means that there is greater funding at the LAs' disposal, but the funds cannot necessarily be used as they wish. Supervision by the Ministry of Local Government persists through the setting of rules that strictly limit the LAs' budgetary freedom.

The already relatively opaque system became even more complex with the creation of the Constituency Development Fund (CDF) in 2003 (Kimenyi 2005), which brings the members of parliament (MPs) into play (see the "Constituencies" and "Central Government Financial Aid to the Constituencies" subsections later in the chapter). The CDF is managed by an advisory board that allocates grants to the electoral constituencies. Each constituency has a fund management committee that is responsible for selecting which projects will receive CDF grants. The committee members are appointed by the elected MP according to representativeness criteria (for example, percentages of youth and women).

By providing constituencies with grants and delegating to them the authority to develop local investment projects, the government has weakened the municipal councils' lead role in the provision of local public services. In 2007, the state confirmed the constituencies' role as a major local public stakeholder by authorizing them to recruit project managers, thereby creating a new local bureaucracy that then entered into competition with the LAs' administrative power.

Overall, the local government structure established at independence has actually changed little over the past 30 years. However, the LAs' responsibilities and resources have been recentralized. Between 1963 and 1974, the shift toward centralization was initiated by President Kenyatta, the country's "founding father," and none of his successors seriously challenged it. The weakening of the LAs' responsibilities concerning local public service delivery lessened the financial importance of Kenyan local governments, with their share of spending falling from 3.26 percent of gross domestic product (GDP) in 1969/70 to 1.22 percent in 1999/2000 (World Bank 2002). The measures taken in the 1990s helped to provide the LAs with more resources but did not increase their responsibilities or restore their decision-making autonomy.

Today, this decision-making autonomy is central to the proposed reform of the Local Government Act (LGA).[8] A bill specifically aimed at strengthening local democracy has been submitted to parliament, but its relevance under the new constitution is uncertain. Meanwhile, since the late 1990s, Kenya has committed to a process of constitutional reform,[9] the first stage of which was completed, after 10 years of meanderings, with the adoption of the new constitution by referendum on August 4, 2010. Besides reforming the national institutions—including notably reducing presidential powers, in part because a newly created Senate represents the new local governments[10]—this constitution intends to change the system of territorialized public institutions themselves. As drafted, however, it leaves many issues concerning the operation and financing of the new local system unresolved.

The second stage of the constitutional reform process, that of implementation, is thus likely to prove difficult. These issues are discussed in the last section of this chapter. The following sections of this chapter analyze the local government structure in force in 2010 and through to the implementation of the terms of the new constitution.

Organization of Decentralized Local Government and Deconcentration in 2009–10

The distinction made here between decentralization and deconcentration follows the definitions and criteria outlined in Dafflon and Madiès (2008). Kenya has four types of local-level territorial governments. But, in practice, the territorial administrative network is not only made up of territorial governments. In the broadest sense, territorial organization comprises not only these local governments but also administrative units and electoral constituencies. Local or territorial governance therefore has three components: (a) a decentralized component that corresponds to the LAs, (b) a deconcentrated component made up of the administrative districts, and (c) a component comprising the constituencies.

Decentralization

In 2009, Kenya had just one tier of decentralized entities, namely the LAs, of which there are 175—a number that has remained unchanged since 2000. The LA represents the basic unit of local government, whose territory is divided into electoral wards, numbering 2,850 in 2009. There are four types of LA:

- The county councils (67) for rural areas
- The municipal councils (45)
- The town councils (62) for urban areas
- The capital, Nairobi, which is a city council.

The institutional framework governing the operation of LAs stems from the 1963 LGA Regulation, modified in 1977.[11] This regulation was amended during the 1980s to become Chapter 265 of the Laws of Kenya (or CAP 265), which is in force today. (The terms LGA and CAP 265 are used interchangeably below.)

In compliance with the LGA, the LAs come under the supervision of the Ministry of Local Government. The minister has the power to create new authorities as well as to merge or dissolve existing ones and even redraw their boundaries.[12] However, the LGA does not contain any formal criteria to distinguish between these four types of LAs or to define how an LA could move from one category to another. Informal criteria are mentioned, such as population (depending on whether population is greater than 500,000; greater than 200,000; or greater [or less] than 50,000 inhabitants); the presence of adequate infrastructures (electricity, water, and road networks); budget levels; and cleanliness. These criteria are drawn from a nonpublic report written in 2003 and are included in the LGA revision draft that was unveiled in December 2009.

Finally, there is some confusion over the status of "city." This is not mentioned in the LGA, even though this status is claimed not only by Nairobi but also by the municipalities of Mombasa and Kisumu. By virtue of a special charter that was granted in 1950, Nairobi, unlike the other two municipalities, is formally authorized to call itself a city despite being considered a municipal council in the LGA. However, Mombasa and Kisumu, which are also municipal councils according to the LGA, call themselves cities pursuant to a presidential promise made in the early 2000s relating to the attribution of this status. Formally, therefore, there is just one city: Nairobi. However, some refer informally to Mombasa and Kisumu as presidential cities.

The Administrative Units
The administrative units are deconcentrated territorial entities, which together constitute the central government's representation across the national territory. Lacking legal status, these entities are simply territorial frameworks used to coordinate the activities of the central government's local agencies. These structures come under the authority of the Office of the President as well as the Ministry of State for Provincial Administration and Internal Affairs.

The five levels of administrative districts are province, district, division, location, and sublocation.

The province   The province is the highest level in the deconcentrated administrative network. Its territorial area is divided into several districts. There are eight provinces in Kenya: Central, Coast, Eastern, North Eastern, Nyanza, Rift Valley, Western, and Nairobi.

Each province is administered by a regional prefect or governor, who is also the provincial commissioner (PC) and is appointed by the president. It is at the provincial level that the representative of the Ministry of Local

Government is found: the provincial local government officer (PLGO), who is responsible for closely supervising the local government authorities described below. The PLGO is the secretary of the Provincial Budget Committee that approves the budgets of urban and rural LAs. This committee is chaired by an official from the Ministry of Local Government and, in addition to officials from this ministry, comprises the clerk, treasurer, mayor, and Finance Committee chairman as well as senior officials from the LA whose budget is being examined.

The budget may be modified to ensure compliance with various rules. The municipal council is then informed of these modifications but does not vote on them again. At this stage, the PLGO also approves the number of positions (establishment) in the LA and any increases or cutbacks. In addition, the PLGO approves bank overdrafts, loans, the LA's investment projects, and the rates of various taxes and fees. Finally, the PLGO must give an opinion on the administrative accounts and has the jurisdiction to grant prior authorization for some LA decisions. Formally, approval is given by the minister and not the ministry, but it is the ministry's role to scrutinize everything in advance.

The district   The district is the second level of administrative unit. Between 1999 and 2008, the number of districts rose from 50 to 149 (KNBS 2008b). At the end of November 2009, 174 districts had officially been gazetted (that is, had been officially announced in the *Kenya Gazette*). However, some districts operated without having been gazetted, bringing the total to 214 at the end of November 2009. There is a drive to create new districts by dividing former districts and aligning the borders of these new districts with those of the constituencies (which number 210) or by incorporating them within the borders of these constituencies. These constituencies are the electoral units of the Kenyan National Assembly's MPs.[13]

Each district is headed by a district commissioner (DC), the equivalent of a departmental prefect in France, appointed by the president. The DC, as holder of central government authority in the district, is responsible for enforcing decisions from the central government within the district's territorial sphere as well as coordinating the activities of the provincial deconcentrated public administration as a whole. Moreover, the commissioner is a police officer. The DC does not exercise authority over the urban and rural LAs within the district's territorial sphere. His or her responsibilities are similar to those of a PC but for a smaller territorial land base, and the DC reports to the PC. Last, the Ministry of Local Government does not have representatives in the districts.

The division   Each division is headed by a district officer. The division is primarily a public security structure to support the chiefs and assistant chiefs.

The location or sublocation   The location and sublocation are the basic levels of deconcentrated government unit. In November 2009, there were 2,948 locations and 7,947 sublocations.[14] Their number is increasing over time along with the number of districts. Each of the locations or sublocations in the country is run by a chief or assistant chief appointed by the central government. These positions are generally held by individuals belonging to the community in question. They are above all responsible for resolving conflicts relating to land tenure and maintaining public order.

Ministry of Nairobi Metropolitan Development   The Ministry of Nairobi Metropolitan Development was created in April 2008. It has not been active to date, but its role is supposed to include Greater Nairobi planning and the construction of road infrastructure. It extends beyond the borders of Nairobi Province, covering part of the Rift Valley and Eastern Provinces.

The Constituencies

The constituencies (electoral districts) are now important actors in the process of providing local public services through their involvement in local investment projects. There are 210 constituencies.[15] They are present at the local level through the CDF, a fund created in 2003 when parliament passed the CDF Act. The CDF envelope is equal to 2.5 percent of the central government's ordinary revenue, excluding external aid. The CDF was created to reduce differences in interregional development. It is mainly intended for the implementation of investment projects with a specific focus on poverty alleviation programs.

Within each constituency, there is a Constituency Development Committee (CDC), composed of a maximum of 15 members and chaired by the MP. This committee is responsible for allocating funds to projects selected in theory by the community (a minimum of 5 and a maximum of 25 projects per year). Sitting on the CDC, in addition to the MP, are two local councillors, the district officer, two members of religious bodies, two men, two women, one young person, one member of a nongovernmental organization, and a maximum of three other residents of the constituency. The nature of this structure is not clear: It should not be confused with the deconcentrated administrative structures. It is closer to a devolved structure in the sense that it is steered by an elected representative of the constituency—the MP—and a decision-making council appointed by the MP. At the same time, however, the structure is not fully autonomous or accountable for the decisions made. Projects selected by the CDC must subsequently be validated at a national level by the Board of Management of the CDF. This board comprises, among others, the permanent secretary of the Ministry of Planning (or equivalent) and the permanent secretary of the Ministry of Finance.

Finally, at the district level, there is a District Project Committee that is responsible for ensuring a minimum of coordination between projects funded by the CDF and projects funded by the districts or LAs. More particularly, they must ensure that there is no duplication of projects within any one district. The members of this committee include the MPs from the district's constituencies as well as the mayors or chairs of the local authorities of the district in question.

Table 4.2 summarizes the main organizational characteristics of the local public sector and deconcentration in Kenya.

The Political-Administrative Structure of Local Authorities

Each LA, regardless of its status, has a council[16] (deliberative body)—part of which is designated by a ward electorate through direct universal suffrage and part of which is appointed by the minister of local government. The council is chaired by a mayor, who directs policy decisions but is not the budget authorizing officer. The mayor is chosen by the council, through indirect suffrage, for a two-year term (renewable without limits). Finally, each LA has its own administration.

The municipal council   The municipal councils in urban and rural LAs are composed as follows: three-quarters of LA councillors are elected through direct universal suffrage in each electoral ward for a five-year term, and one-quarter of the councillors are appointed by the Ministry of Local Affairs for five years or less (thus resulting in one appointee for every three elected councillors), with the minister able to revoke this mandate at any time.[17] These appointments are based on each party's share of councillors elected for a five-year term. If, for example, 60 percent of the *elected* councillors belong to party A, then 60 percent of the *appointed* councillors must also come from party A. Initially, in the context of a single-party system, the decision to have appointed councillors was designed to ensure a minimum capacity for good management among the councillors. (See chapter 3 on Ghana for alternative explanations of why some council members are not elected.) Because councillors are appointed contingent on election results, the central government's control over the council can be kept to a minimum.

The councillors are required either to have been residents for at least five years or to be residents who paid the property rates in the year preceding the election. They are also required to be literate, but the electoral committee may suspend this requirement.[18] The number of councillors depends on the size of the LA's population. As a deliberative body, the council's main task is to deliberate on all of the LA's business: define the broad lines for LA development, discuss and adopt LA development plans, monitor the execution of these plans, direct the mayor and technical committees, and scrutinize their actions.

Table 4.2 Organization of Decentralized LAs and Deconcentration in Kenya, 2009–10

Level/ Decentralization	Deconcentration			Devolution	Constituencies
	Line ministries				
Central		Office of the President, Ministry of Provincial Affairs	Ministry of Local Government	n.a.	Constituency Development Fund (CDF)
Noncentral					
Provinces	Representatives	Provincial commissioner (PC)	Provincial local government officer (PLGO)	n.a.	n.a.
Districts	Representatives	District commissioner (DC)	n.a.	n.a.	n.a.
Divisions	n.a.	District officer	n.a.	n.a.	n.a.
National Electoral Constituency	n.a.	n.a.	n.a.	n.a.	Constituency Development Committee (CDC), District Projects Committee (DPC)
LAs	n.a.	n.a.	Executive staff	Four types of LA[a]	n.a.
Location or sublocation	n.a.	Chief or assistant chief	n.a.	n.a.	n.a.

Source: Chapter 265 of the Laws of Kenya (CAP 265, also known as the Local Government Act [LGA] 1977 and updates until 2010).
Note: LA = local authority; n.a. = not applicable.
a. The four types of LA are county councils (for rural areas), municipal councils, town councils (for urban areas), and a city council (Nairobi).

The council should meet at least four times a year. Its meetings are open to the public and the press, which is not the case for the committees. The minutes of their proceedings are available for inspection. The council is explicitly required to appoint a standing financial committee on which sit the mayor or chairman, deputy mayor or vice chairman, and other council members.[19] This committee advises the council on taxation rates, recovery of debts due, and other miscellaneous financial issues.

The mayor or chair   The mayor and deputy mayor are elected by, and from among, the municipal councillors for a two-year renewable term. The procedure is the same for the chair and vice chair in county councils and town councils, but the Minister of Local Government may appoint the chair (although this is rare). In practice, approximately two-thirds of mayors serve only one term.[20] The mayor does not have budgetary authority. He or she presides over council deliberation. In addition, the law stipulates the following: that the budget will be executed by the town clerk, assisted by the town treasurer (or, in, modern parlance, chief financial officer [CFO]). The town clerk is the chief executive officer (CEO).[21] The key role of these senior officials is clearly illustrated in Section 141 of the LGA, which states the following:

• They have the right to attend the meetings of the council, its committees, and its subcommittees.

• They also have the right to demand that their opinion be included in the minutes if it is not followed.

• The council must obtain the Minister of Local Government's authorization to implement a resolution to which a senior public official has recorded his or her objection.

In general, all senior executive staff in every LA provided for in the LGA[22] belong to Kenya's Public Service Commission. They include, for example, the town clerk, the CFO, the medical officer of health, and the town engineer, as well as the other positions rated 1 to 9 in the job classification (out of a total of 20). Their salaries are paid by the LAs that hire them. They alternate postings at the central level and in the LAs.[23] It should be noted here that the job positions held at the local level are less well paid than their equivalents at the central level, which led to discussions in 2009 to review the remuneration policy for these executives. One possible alternative would be for the central government to continue paying these senior staff directly or to transfer funds to the municipalities to cover their salaries.

All of these political and institutional arrangements considerably reduce the LAs' decision-making autonomy. However, giving mayors the possibility of acting as budget authorizing officers and of challenging senior public officials' right to dissent are modifications under discussion within the framework of the reworking of CAP 265.[24]

Institutional Issues

Several types of institutional problems arise from the way the local public sector is organized in Kenya. First, there is some degree of competition between the LAs and the constituencies over the provision of local public infrastructures. They enjoy the same prerogatives, but the law imposes no coordination between the two. The only requirement on this count is under the CDF Act, which makes it compulsory for a District Projects Committee (DPC) to involve the mayors of LAs that belong to a district affected by a DPC project. However, the main responsibility of these committees is primarily to prevent duplication of projects of constituencies belonging to the same district, not to organize cooperation between LAs and constituencies within a given district. It is thus to be expected that this type of organization will engender inefficient public decision making within a particular geographical area. The actors on the ground readily acknowledge this, even though the problem, seen as significant during the CDF's early years, is apparently less acute now that the procedure is well established.

Second, LA mayors have limited powers, as the brevity of their terms of office (two years renewable) and their low renewal rate (barely 30 percent) indicate. They appear to be politically dominated at the local level by the MPs heading the constituencies and, even within the LA, by the town clerks who have considerable administrative power. Moreover, the mayor's office seems to be a stepping-stone used by some to enter parliament. All this weakens the LAs in their role of local governance. In this respect, the LAs' existence seems more akin to a process of deconcentration or delegation than one of devolution.

The Decentralized Budget

The fiscal year starts on July 1 of the year (t) and ends on June 30 of the following calendar year ($t+1$). The LGA provides for an annual budget and, if necessary, supplementary estimates. Budget preparation follows a Ministry of Local Government circular, "Guidelines for Preparing Budget Estimates," which is published at the end of February ahead of the financial year. This circular imposes strict budgetary rules that may vary from one year to another. These rules must be followed to qualify for the LATF "performance" envelope (further detailed later in the "Financial Aid from Central Government to Local Authorities" subsection).

Budgetary Rules

These rules may be of a general nature and apply to either an expenditure section or a revenue section of the budget. The rules for the fiscal year 2008/09 are given here as examples.

General Rules

1. The budget put forward must be balanced (taking into account cash balances and commitments brought forward from the previous year) and provide for the LA's working capital requirements. In practice, budget deficits are common because forecasted revenue tends to be artificially inflated.

2. The budget must be submitted to the Provincial Budget Committee by April 15 of the year preceding the financial year for approval. This committee comprises members of the Office of the Deputy Prime Minister and the Ministry of Local Government as well as municipal councillors and staff from the LA. The budget may then be amended as recommended by the committee and must be submitted by June 5 to the Ministry of Local Government for approval.

3. After approval by the Ministry of Local Government, each municipality must publish its budget in at least two national newspapers (one in English and one in Kiswahili). The chairman of the Finance Committee must present the budget to the LA's citizens in a public meeting, generally held on the last Thursday in June (Local Authority Budget Day).

Rules for the Expenditure Budget Component

4. The share of personnel expenditures must not exceed 45 percent of total expenditure.

5. At least 10 percent of total expenditures must be used for repair and maintenance projects.

6. Capital expenditures must represent at least 65 percent of the LATF allocation for the provision of public services (see the "Financial Aid from Central Government to Local Authorities" subsection).

7. Expenditures equivalent to 20 percent of the total LATF allocation must be assigned to the implementation of antipoverty policies.

8. Expenditures for staff training must be at least 2 percent of total LA revenue.

9. A local government is authorized to contract debts, but in this case at least 10 percent of the LA's total revenue must be used to reduce outstanding debts. Local government debt, as a rule, consists of both bank debt and payment arrears that may or may not bear interest. For arrears due at the end of December 2009, the LATF dictates that payment arrears (amounts due to social security agencies, for example) be cleared by June 30, 2010 (see the "Local Government Expenditure" subsection later). If this seems impossible, the LA must make this known and restructure its debt.

Rules for the Revenue Budget Component

10. Budgeted revenue must not exceed the revenue ceilings set by the Ministry of Local Government. This rule aims to avoid overly optimistic revenue projections. These ceilings are based on past revenues and a growth rate deemed reasonable by the ministry.

11. The Ministry of Local Government must approve any changes to the amount of taxes or charges paid by local taxpayers.

Making the best of strict budgetary rules   Theoretically, the LAs' freedom in regard to expenditure and revenue is extremely limited. Nevertheless, it would appear that a number of them do not comply with these rules. For instance, the municipality of Kisumu's 2007/08 budget shows a ratio of "personnel to total expenditure" equal to 54.3 percent, which far exceeds the authorized limit. Its capital expenditure is also well below the level required by the circular (K Sh 50.5 million instead of K Sh 71.6 million). Moreover, only 5 percent of total spending was allocated to repair and maintenance projects, instead of the required 10 percent. These discrepancies highlight not only the ministry's determination to strictly control the evolution and structure of local government budgets but also the difficulties that LAs have in complying with these rules.

At the same time, the LAs seem to make the best of these stringent rules, which even appear to be popular with all the actors we met. Certainly, the rules enable them to point to external constraints when the pressure from citizens to increase local public spending (especially wages) becomes too strong. The existence of these rules should, in theory, limit any financial irresponsibility of local elected officials.

Table 4.3 provides a general overview of Kenyan local government budgets. Expenditures are listed by type, of which there are three: recurrent expenditures, capital expenditures, and debt repayments. Under revenue, there are transfers from the central government, revenues from international institutions, and local own revenues.

Note that the revenue nomenclature includes loans, which, from both the financial and public finance management viewpoints, are not revenues but sources of funding. Except for bailout situations, the loan must be repaid (expenditure item 3 in table 4.3), which necessitates real revenue—either own revenue or revenue received through financial transfers. The definition of deficit is also skewed by including loans in item 14 under revenues; regardless of how they are used (to cover operating expenses or to finance investment), obtaining a loan is all that is needed to balance the account. A properly balanced budget, as defined by the golden rule of local public finances, should be drawn up without including item 5 (capital projects) under expenditures and item 14 (loans) under revenues in the balance calculations.

Table 4.3 The Decentralized Local Government Budget in Kenya, 2009

Expenditures	Revenues
Recurrent expenditures	*Central government transfers*
1. Councillor expenditures	1. Local Authority Transfer Fund (LATF)
2. Personnel costs	2. Road Maintenance Levy Fund (RMLF)
3. Operations costs	3. Contribution in Lieu of Rates (CILOR)
4. Maintenance costs	
	Local own revenues
Capital expenditures	4. Single business permit
5. Capital projects	5. Property rates
	6. Market and slaughterhouse fees
	7. Vehicle parking
Debt resolution repayments	8. Plot rents and house rents
	9. Cesses (taxes on agricultural products)
	10. Game parks and natural reserve fees
	11. Water supply and sewerage charges
	12. Solid waste disposal charges
	13. Other taxes (Pursuant to LGA Section 148, LAs may create fees or charges in exchange for services to taxpayers—for example, funeral taxes and billboard advertising fees—after approval by the Ministry of Local Government.)
Net Surplus or Deficit	14. Loans (Pursuant to LGA Section 222, LAs may borrow from the Local Government Loans Fund or from any bank after receiving authorization from the Ministry of Local Government.)
Corresponds to the difference between total revenues and the sum of [recurrent expenditures + capital expenditures + debt installments]	*Revenues from international institutions*

Source: LGA, Guidelines for Preparing Budget Estimates and Accessing Local Authorities Transfer Fund Monies, LATF 2009.
Note: LA = local authority; LGA = Local Government Act.

Table 4.4 presents a matrix of the LAs' current budget categories, showing expenditure by function (rows) and by type (columns). The spending by function column breaks down spending by the local government's main departments: municipal council, clerk's department, and treasurer's department. It should be noted that the functional classification (rows) is far from adequate. Indeed, the first functional section includes only institutional references (municipal council, clerk, treasurer, and engineer) but not devolved responsibilities as such. The second functional section shows four specific functions, although some are composite, such as water and sewers, or health and environment—functional areas that don't necessarily go hand in hand.

In addition, it is clear that the responsibilities listed in table 4.4 do not match the transferred responsibilities according to the nomenclature given in

Table 4.4 Organization of Local Operating Budgets in Kenya, by Function and Type, 2009

Spending type / Spending function	Personnel	Operations	Maintenance
Council or civic			
Clerk's department			
Treasurer's department			
Engineer's or works department			
Social services			
Water and sewers			
Public health and environment			
Education			
Other			

Source: Analysis of LGA documents.

the upper section of table 4.4 as well as in table 4.5. For example, in table 4.4, the budget nomenclature combines "health and environment" under the same umbrella, whereas the decentralized responsibilities (shown in table 4.5) lists "health and hygiene" as item 4 and "environment and natural resource management" as item 2, while "sewerage" is item 9—"water and electricity"! With such divergences in classification, it would be reasonable to ask how one can measure both the outcome of decentralization and its progress toward multiyear implementation.

Assignment of Responsibilities

The 10 functional areas of transferred responsibilities according to the Local Government Act (LGA—revised edition, 2010) are as follows:

1a. Land management

1b. Territorial development and urban planning

2. Environment and natural resource management

3. Economic development and planning

4. Health and hygiene

5. Education, employment, vocational training, and literacy

6. Culture, sports, and recreation

7. Civic defense, social assistance, and emergency relief

8. Funeral services and cemeteries

9. Water and electricity

10. Markets, fairs, and slaughterhouses.

Table 4.5 summarizes the responsibilities of LAs' decentralized functions in Kenya in 2010. These responsibilities are fewer than those the LAs exercised at independence. What is involved here, therefore, is not a transfer of responsibilities from the central government to the LAs, but rather the opposite, such as in the field of education. The disappearance of some of the LAs' financial instruments discussed earlier can also be linked to this change.

Table 4.5 Decentralized Functions in Kenya, 2010

Function (A)	Municipalities, counties, and townships (B)	Municipalities and townships (C)	Municipalities (D)
1. Territorial development, land management, urban planning	147 a) regulate fencing, tree, shrub, or hedge overhanging on street	Same as in column 2, and, in addition, the following:	Same as in columns 2 and 3
	154 e) prohibit and control brick-making yards and the quarrying of stone, lime, clay, or other material	161 e) construct footways along the side of any road or street	
	159) control shops (shopping and market areas) in rural areas (county councils)	162 e) control the subdivision of land in building lots	
	166) control the development and use of land and buildings in the interest of the proper and orderly development of its area	177) oversee housing, building plots, and dwelling houses	
	186) establish and maintain ferries and toll bridges	182) build and maintain streets	
2. Environment and natural resource management	147 d) control the cutting of timber and the destruction of trees and shrubs, to prohibit the wasteful destruction of trees and shrubs	179) ensure diversion and canalization of streams and watercourses	
	154 d) ensure prevention and control of bush and forest fires		
	155 e) establish and maintain game parks, including accommodation for visitors		
	155 f) establish and maintain forest		
	162 c) ensure prevention and destruction of insects and pests		
	162 i) provide for the due and proper care of the common pasture land		

(continued next page)

Table 4.5 (continued)

Function (A)	Municipalities, counties, and townships (B)	Municipalities and townships (C)	Municipalities (D)
3. Economic development and planning	153) establish and maintain a public transport system, with a monopoly if desired (outsourcing possible) 155 b) engage in livestock and agricultural undertakings	160 j) establish and maintain aerodromes 162–163) control various types of commercial activities and trades	Same as in column 2
4. Health and hygiene	145 z) establish and maintain welfare centers and regulate such activities aa) provide assistance to the needy ab) establish and maintain day nurseries and clinics and assist such establishments 155 b) take measures for preventing the outbreak and spread of animal disease	160 c) acquire and maintain ambulance services establish and maintain: 160 b) public lavatories, closets, and urinals 160 d) cold storage works and depots for the inspection of meat 160 q) pounds (any article of vehicle apparently abandoned, animals and birds) 161 b) places for the washing of clothes establish, maintain, and control: 161c) lodging houses and boarding houses 161 d) tea rooms, cafes, restaurants, hotels, eating houses, snack bars, bake houses, butchers' shops, grocers' shops, and all factories and places where articles of food or drink are manufactured or prepared for sale or use, or are stored or sold, whether for consumption on or off the premises	i) create and maintain hospitals, maternity services, and dispensaries 160 a) establish and maintain sanitary services for the removal and destruction of all kinds of refuse and effluent 160 h) take measures for the destruction and suppression of rats and vermin 162 j) control swimming bath and bathing in open water 163 j) establish disinfestation services
5. Education, employment, vocational training, and literacy	152 3) grant scholarships		152 1) establish and maintain schools and educational institutions, including boarding blocks and school hostels

(continued next page)

Table 4.5 (continued)

Function (A)	Municipalities, counties, and townships (B)	Municipalities and townships (C)	Municipalities (D)
6. Culture, sports, and recreation	145 o) establish and maintain the following: i) parks ii) boats iii) aquariums and piers iv) recreation grounds v) recreational apparatus vi) cafes s) establish and maintain libraries, art galleries, museums, and botanical or zoological gardens t) establish and maintain musical bands u) establish and maintain radio and television stations subject to national law ac) establish and maintain theaters, cinemas, and concert halls	160 m and o) establish and maintain ornamentation of square and open space, including the erection of statues, fountains, and other structures, trees, flowers, and shrubs 162 d, e , f, and n) control various recreational activities	Same as in column 3
7a. Civil defense	145 l) storage of explosives	160 k) establish and maintain fire brigade	Same as in column 3
7b. Social assistance and emergency aid	155 g) establish, maintain, and control rehabilitation centers for the care, maintenance, and rehabilitation of beggars		No information
8. Funeral services and cemeteries	No information	161 a) establish and maintain cemeteries, mortuaries, crematoria 167) burial of all destitute persons	Same as in column 3
9. Water and electricity	No information	160 p) arrange for the lighting of streets and other public places 178 and 180) drinking water services 181) supply of electricity, light, heat, and power	Same as in column 3

(continued next page)

Table 4.5 (continued)

Function (A)	Municipalities, counties, and townships (B)	Municipalities and townships (C)	Municipalities (D)
10. Markets, fairs, and slaughterhouses	145 p) i) and ii) establish and control public markets 145 r) establish and maintain public weighing machines 147 c) prohibit and control the sale and movement of livestock 155 d) control sales, outside markets establish, maintain, and control: 154 a) cattle cleansing facilities 154 b) premises for the drying, cleaning, and storing of hides and skins 155 a) services, for the inspection, grading, and storing of produce	establish and maintain: 160 e) slaughterhouses for the slaughter of animals and poultry 160 f) plants for the manufacture of by-products and to purchase animals for the purpose of conversion into by-products and to sell them 160 g) depots for the inspection, treatment, distribution, purchase, and sale of milk and milk products 161 l) control the display of advertisements and advertising devices in street or public place	Same as in columns 2 and 3

Source: Local Government Act (LGA), Chapter 265, Sections 145–147, 152–155, 159–163, 166–167, 177–182, 186, revised edition 2010, http://www.kenyalaw.org.
Note: The numbers and letters that precede items in the columns refer to the sections, referenced in the source line, of the LGA, Chapter 265.

Yet by and large, the LAs' responsibilities are adequately defined, at least in the legislative texts. In practice, the demarcation of the LAs' responsibilities is far more blurred. During our interviews, it became clear that the LASDAP mechanisms prompted some LAs to fund projects through the LATF that are not within their areas of competence. Conversely, some services under their responsibility may well, in certain cases, be performed by the deconcentrated administration through ministerial budget lines. Finally, and this explains the previous point, the LAs discharge their responsibilities only as far as resources allow.

Local Taxation

Before turning to the financial aspect of our discussion, it should be noted that in Kenya there is no deconcentrated treasury system, as in the French model, that either imposes or offers tax collection and management services for local authority funds, and thus the principle of a single treasury account does not apply. Local governments deposit their funds in commercial banks such as the National Bank of Kenya or the Kenya Commercial Bank.

Categories of Fiscal Revenue

Except for property rates and agricultural taxes (called cesses),[25] local taxation is based on LGA Section 148, which stipulates that the LAs may charge fees for activities they are empowered to control or license—in practice, all economic activities—and impose fees or charges for any service provided[26] if all fees and charges have the Minister of Local Government's consent. The legal instrument used is publication in the official journal (*Kenya Gazette*) of the LA council's decision, approved by the minister, setting the fees and charges. Because these fees and charges remain in force until modified, they are not necessarily published annually. No political considerations appear to be at play in the granting of the minister's approval, which to all appearances seems relatively automatic.

The principal elements of local taxation are the following:

- The single business permit
- Property rates
- Contribution in lieu of rates (CILOR)
- Cesses.

Table 4.6 lists the LAs' own revenues.[27] Their amounts are later examined in table 4.13.

Table 4.6 Classification of Local Authorities' Own Revenues in Kenya, 2010

Taxes (A)	Operating Revenues from LA Services (User Fees) (B)	Revenues from LA Property (C)
• Single business permits • Property rates • Cesses • Advertising taxes (posters, pamphlets, blimps, sandwich boards, umbrellas, and so on) • Taxes on buses and *matatus* (minibuses) • Taxes on gatherings (sporting, musical, religious, and so on)	• Income from the sale of services: fire brigades (such as bee removal, opening doors) • Income from maternity wards and medical centers • Income from local schools (per-student admissions and transfers) • Equipment rental • Health inspection fees • Processing fees for administrative and civil status records • Funeral taxes	• Permits for markets, fairs, animal parks • Tax on quantities sold at market (per basket, sack, or by weight) • Community property rental fees (receptions, housing, and so on) • Public land occupation fees • Cemetery and burial operation (rates based on death in Nairobi or outside Nairobi) • Parking permits • Taxes on LA property degradation

Source: LGA, Section 148; 1977 and updates until 2010.
Note: LA = local authority. Taxes (category A) are compulsory levies that are paid out of certain described economic activities (the tax base) and sustain the general public budget. User fees and charges (category B) are the prices of services rendered to an economic agent that uses the service, the amount payable being proportionate to the benefit the agent derives from the service rendered. Revenues from public properties (category C) are payments (prices) made by economic agents that are using state properties for their own benefit.

Single business permit   This flat-rate fee was introduced in 1988 and revised in 2008.[28] It is equivalent to a sales tax in a situation where the appropriate information for calculating the amount is nonexistent. The fee payers are the businesses or establishments that are required to register with the LA where they operate by completing a form prepared by the Ministry of Local Government. The fee is payable annually.

The type of permit issued depends on the nature of the business activity and company's size. To determine this activity, the Ministry of Local Government provides a list of 91 possible types of activity, grouped into eight main categories:

- General trade
- Informal sector (small traders and craftsmen)
- Transportation, storage, and communications
- Agriculture, mining, and forestry
- Accommodations and food services
- Professional services
- Education, private health, and entertainment
- Manufacturing.

Within each specific sector, businesses are often ranked by size (small, medium, or large).

The ministry also provides 10 tax scales applicable to different cases. Each LA council has some leeway in the choice of scale, depending on its legal status. Scales 1–5 may thereby be used by town councils and county councils, scales 4–9 by municipal councils, and scales 8–10 by city councils (for example, Nairobi). An LA may, however, request permission to use a lower scale than those proposed by the ministry.

The ministry specifies a total of 910 possible fee amounts. For example, in the hotel industry, for an average-quality hotel with 41–100 rooms, the fee varies from K Sh 17,500 (in scale 1) to K Sh 84,000 (in scale 10). The rate for a street vendor varies from K Sh 250 to K Sh 1,200. Within a single sector, the highest fee is 4.8 times the lowest fee. Across all scales, the lowest fee is K Sh 250 (scale 1: informal sector), and the highest is K Sh 120,000 (scale 10: luxury hotels). The rates in scale 1 range from K Sh 250 to K Sh 25,000, and the rates in scale 10 range from K Sh 1,200 to K Sh 120,000—a ratio of 1 to 100.

The annual fee is payable in full, regardless of the length of time the business has been operating during the (calendar) year. This measure discourages end-of-year business start-ups.

Property rates   This tax is payable by either the owner, a tenant holding a lease of at least 25 years, or, should the title be unclear, the individual with a vested interest in the property.[29] The tax is based on the unimproved site value per square meter, expressed in Kenyan shillings (K Sh). It is based either on assessments by certified valuers from the private sector (in urban areas mostly)—as it is in Ghana—or by LA employees (more often in rural areas).

The valuers in urban areas generally calculate hypothetical values because the land is, in fact, most often developed. In rural areas, the valuation is typically based on an administrative price per square meter in K Sh. In theory, the valuation roll must be updated at least every five years.[30] In practice, the interval seems to be approximately 10 years. Places of worship, cemeteries and crematoria, hospitals and similar institutions, educational institutions including student residences, charitable institutions, museums and libraries, outdoor sports grounds, national reserves, and national parks are exempt from this tax.[31] In addition, agricultural land is not taxed.

In the event of a dispute over how the tax amount was established, the ratepayer may lodge an objection regarding the valuation with the town clerk. If this first solution is unsuccessful, the ratepayer may then appeal to the valuation court set up by the local authority and comprising at least three members. As a last resort, any ratepayer who is dissatisfied with the valuation court's decision may appeal to the High Court.[32]

As for the tax rates, they are set by local governments, subject to approval by the Ministry of Local Government.

As in most African countries, cadastral information is lacking, especially away from the large urban centers, and the collection rate is low.

Contribution in lieu of rates (CILOR)   Publicly owned land that is being used by the central government is subject to a valuation to establish the amount payable by the central government to the LA of the territory in question.[33] Land is excluded if it is used for museums and ancient monuments, botanical gardens, quarantine areas, president's lodges, airport facilities (such as runways and control towers), railway tracks, wharves, streets and roads, and parks.[34]

Cesses   This is a tax on agricultural production equal to 1 percent of the production value.

Fiscal Issues

LAs have some leeway in setting the rates for most of the taxes, especially property rates. These decisions, however, are subject to the minister's approval. In practice, the choices made at the local level do not appear to be challenged by the central authorities, as evidenced by the wide range of rates applied. With regard to the single business permit, LAs can choose a rate scale from the available schedule in line with their legal status, but for the agricultural cess, they have no choice.

As far as property rates are concerned, tax assessments based on unimproved land, particularly in urban areas, could probably be improved in cases where the development value can be evaluated.

Intergovernmental Grants

Central government grants to the LAs make up a sizable share of their budgets. The grants have been growing steadily since 2003/04, reaching nearly 43 percent of the LAs' revenue in 2007/08. Here, we present central government aid to the LAs and, further below, to the constituencies. As for local taxes, the financial volume of these transfers will be reported in more detail in the next section, "Revenue and Expenditure Statistics."

Financial Aid from Central Government to Local Authorities
Financial aid from the central government to the LAs transits through two channels: the LATF and the Road Maintenance Levy Fund (RMLF).

Local authority transfer fund (LATF)   The LATF was created in 1999 (as discussed previously in the "History" section). The total value of transfers to be shared among the 175 LAs amounts to 5 percent of personal and corporate income taxes. In 2008, the LATF alone accounted for almost 35 percent of the LAs' total revenue (as detailed in the "Local Government Revenue" subsection later). Transfers channeled through the LATF are similar to drawing rights that each LA may claim. The formula for calculating each LA's drawing rights from the total amount available is as follows:

- A fixed amount of K Sh 1.5 million per LA
- An amount calculated on 60 percent of the total fund, depending on an LA's population (based currently on the 1999 census)
- An amount calculated on the remainder of the fund, that is, [Total − (1.5M × 175 LAs + 60 percent × Total)] depending on the LA's urban population

For each LA, access to LATF drawing rights is through two accounts:

- A *service delivery account*, representing 60 percent of the drawing rights, is obtained upon submission of LA budgets, which must comply with the guidelines discussed above. In addition, LAs must have paid their statutory creditors (see the subsection on "Local Government Expenditure").
- A *performance account*, representing 40 percent of the drawing rights, is released upon submission, within the prescribed time limit, of information on

the LAs' previous budgets, payables and receivables, a summary of accounts, a LASDAP designed to encourage public participation in the decision-making process, and a revenue-enhancement plan.

Regarding the performance account, only delays in submitting the required documents are penalized. The quality of the documents produced is not verified because of insufficient resources in the LATF's administrative offices. A delay of 1–30 days theoretically incurs a penalty of 15 percent of the LATF performance account, increasing to 40 percent for a delay of 31–60 days and to 100 percent for a delay of 61 or more days. In practice, smaller penalties are applied. Any undistributed amounts are added to the total amount available the following year. For instance, in 2007/08, 26 LAs were penalized by 3.0–22.5 percent of the performance account disbursements due to them. In all, 99.73 percent of the LATF was distributed.

It should be noted, however, that the LATF authorities were attempting to enhance performance criteria for accessing the drawing right as of July 1, 2010. The requirements relating to observing various procedures (compliance criteria) as well as the choice of funded projects should be strengthened. How this will be implemented following the constitutional changes discussed later is unclear.

Road maintenance levy fund (RMLF)   The Kenya Road Board (KRB) is responsible for the major maintenance works on the country's roads. It derives its revenue from three sources:

- The RMLF, funded by a tax on petroleum products (K Sh 9 per liter of gasoline or diesel), which supplies the bulk (more than 97 percent) of the KRB's revenue source
- Toll charges
- An agricultural cess.

Responsibility for implementing road maintenance spending falls to the 175 Kenyan LAs, under the auspices of the KRB. The LAs submit projects to the KRB, which finances them if they are accepted. In 2007/08, the RMLF accounted for approximately 6 percent of the LAs' revenue. Districts (administrative units) are also stakeholders, acting as coordinators in their geographic intervention areas. In this capacity, they receive 24 percent of the RMLF.

Central Government Financial Aid to the Constituencies

The Constituency Development Fund (CDF) was created in 2003 (as mentioned previously in the "History" section). It funds investment projects in the constituencies' territories, which inevitably overlap with all or part of LA territories.

The total envelope to be shared among the 210 constituencies amounts to 2.5 percent of the Kenyan state's ordinary revenues, excluding external aid. In 2008, the CDF amounted to 42 percent of LA resources, which means this mechanism has considerable impact. The formula for dividing the CDF among the 210 constituencies is as follows:

- Seventy-five percent of the net total CDF (net of 8 percent for miscellaneous charges) is distributed equally among the constituencies.

- Twenty-five percent of the net total CDF is allocated on the basis of a national poverty index adjusted by the CDF's own poverty index (see box 4.1).[35]

The CDF distribution formula per constituency is as follows:

$$CDF_i = (75\% \times \text{total net CDF}/210)$$
$$+ (25\% \times \text{total net CDF} \times \text{adjusted poverty indicator}). \quad (4.1)$$

A Kenya National Bureau of Statistics (KNBS) report discusses the consequences of this formula (KNBS 2008a). Over a period of five years, some sparsely populated constituencies received K Sh 18,000 per capita, whereas other more densely populated constituencies received K Sh 900 per capita even though their poverty rates (per capita revenue) were the same. This differential is due to the relatively substantial fraction (75 percent) of the CDF that is distributed equally among the 210 constituencies. The equal treatment of the constituencies receives such importance because each MP has the same political weight in terms of parliamentary vote.

BOX 4.1

CDF Poverty Indicator

The Constituency Development Fund (CDF) poverty indicator combines data from the Welfare Monitoring Survey III (KNBS 1997) and the 1999 population and housing census to obtain the number of poor people per constituency. The procedure is as follows (KNBS 2005, 77):

1. The WMSIII household microdata are used to estimate regressions by province and area type (urban or rural). The variable explained (dependent) is the log of per capita spending, and the explanatory variables are a set of variables shared by the census and the WMSIII. These variables were identified by analyzing the questionnaire from the two data sources and by examining the distribution of potential variables. A stepwise method is used to identify the best set of variables

(continued next page)

Box 4.1 (continued)

for each regression, significant to 5 percent (the best signifying the highest R^2, which ranges from 0.31 to 0.49).The following variables are generally used in these regressions:

- *Household size*: higher household size lowers per capita spending.
- *Education of household members*: a higher level of education among household members increases household spending.
- *A turf roof, mud walls, and the use of wood for cooking* all lower household spending.
- *Access to clean drinking water* increases household spending.

2. These coefficients are used to calculate per capita spending for each household in the census.

3. Poverty lines are then used to determine whether a household is poor (below the line) and to calculate the number of poor households and individuals in each constituency. This number, divided by the national total number of poor people obtained by this method, gives each constituency's contribution to national poverty.

It should be noted that extrapolations are used in the case of the North Eastern Province because it was excluded from the WMSIII survey. Thus, the WMSIII information for Coast Province is used to estimate the coefficients applied to the census data for North Eastern Province. Comparing the constituency estimates with those produced directly with the WMSIII at the province and district level indicates that these estimates are, by and large, precise. A more detailed examination, however, reveals some weaknesses, particularly for small rural constituencies.

Poverty is then weighted by multiplying each constituency's contribution to national poverty, calculated as indicated above by 0.23 for urban constituencies[a] and by 1 for rural constituencies. This increases the rural constituencies' share in the CDF. Finally, the calculation is adjusted so that the sum equals 100 percent (the amounts removed from the urban constituencies' envelope are allocated to the rural constituencies' envelope). The weighting by 0.23 in favor of rural constituencies is justified as follows (KNBS 2005, 40):

- In the country as a whole, the proportion of rural poor (81 percent) is greater than the proportion of urban poor (19 percent), thus giving a ratio of 19/81 = 0.23.
- The KNBS assumes that most urban Kenyans have a rural home that they visit and will occupy in retirement.
- The concentration of migrants in slum settlements indicates that urban economic conditions are better than the conditions in the rural areas they left behind.
- Improving conditions in rural areas will reduce rural-urban migration.

a. According to a graph-based count, 16 constituencies are defined as urban based on a KNBS recommendation.

Issues Relating to Intergovernmental Transfers

LATF transfers to the LAs are, in principle, operating grants. However, the restrictions placed on their use means that they are actually earmarked grants mainly for investment purposes (as previously discussed in "The Decentralized Budget" section). The grant to constituencies (through the CDF) is also intended to fund investment projects. As a result, there is an almost total lack of general operating grants.

The coherence and coordination of the LATF and the CDF across a given area are cause for concern for several reasons:

- The LATF creates an incentive for the LAs, in terms of both spending guidance and compliance with accounting rules (see "The Decentralized Budget" section). Moreover, the associated LASDAP mechanism requires local community participation in investment expenditure choices.
- Projects funded by the CDF are chosen outside the LASDAP because they are implemented in electoral constituencies and not within the LA boundaries even if their territories overlap. In addition, the projects are approved by official bodies that are parallel to the LATF.
- The methods used for distributing the CDF minimize the disparities between the constituencies, understating the size effect even though size is factored in by the LATF as an indicator of needs.

Revenue and Expenditure Statistics

Central Government Revenue and Expenditure

According to the KNBS, Kenya's per capita GDP is K Sh 35,611 (approximately €320). Public spending as a share of GDP was estimated at 35.88 percent for the financial year 2007/08. Table 4.7 describes the trend in central government spending since financial year 2005/06. The increase in spending for the period in question was steep, averaging nearly 24 percent per year. It was greater than 17 percent between the financial years 2005/06 and 2006/07, and it stood at nearly 30 percent between 2006/07 and 2007/08.

Note, however, that the increase in spending in real terms over this latter period was nil because the rate of growth in public spending was identical to the rate of inflation—around 30 percent over the 2006/07–2007/08 period. This high rate of inflation was due to the postelectoral events in 2007 that created significant economic turmoil in the country. Spending, nevertheless, rose much more rapidly than GDP, which averaged only 13 percent growth annually over the same period.

Table 4.7 Central Government Expenditure in Kenya, 2005/06–2007/08

Expenditure	2005/06 (K Sh, millions)	%	2006/07 (K Sh, millions)	%	2007/08 (K Sh, millions)	%
General public services	54,188.20	12.50	52,697.95	10.40	117,320.63	17.80
Public debt transactions	101,472.58	23.50	129,715.33	25.50	135,618.73	20.60
General intergovernmental transfers	5,507.24	1.27	6,865.85	1.35	9,329.67	1.42
Defense	25,608.64	5.90	25,122.90	4.90	36,741.86	5.60
Public order and safety	39,804.15	9.20	41,790.91	8.20	49,825.01	7.60
Economic affairs	49,488.64	11.40	71,420.75	14.00	99,037.84	15.00
Environmental protection	3,764.55	0.90	5,044.94	1.00	5,799.34	0.90
Housing and community amenities	6,107.97	1.40	8,300.86	1.60	13,624.36	2.10
Health	22,963.79	5.30	27,517.68	5.40	30,282.54	4.60
Recreation, culture, and religion	2,948.09	0.70	4,086.57	0.80	5,646.64	0.90
Education	96,027.43	22.20	109,238.90	21.50	124,908.59	19.00
Current account	370,209.34	85.30	402,248.42	79.00	497,634.27	76.60
Development account	63,381.91	14.70	106,597.10	21.00	160,446.11	24.40
Total expenditure	**432,591.25**	**100.00**	**508,845.51**	**100.00**	**658,080.37**	**100.00**
Growth in expenditure (%)	—	—	17.62	—	29.32	—
Rate of inflation (%)	—	—	11.30	—	29.30	—

Source: KNBS 2009.
Note: — = not available.

Spending patterns vary considerably from one year to the next. Investment expenditure grew rapidly, reaching nearly 25 percent of total spending in 2007/08. Debt repayment was the largest item of expenditure, accounting for 20.6 percent of total spending in 2007/08, followed by education (19.0 percent), general public services (17.8 percent), and economic affairs (15.0 percent). Central government transfers to local governments rose considerably, from 25 percent between financial years 2005/06 and 2006/07, to 36 percent between 2006/07 and 2007/08.

The trends and structure of central government revenues are presented in table 4.8. Average annual revenue growth is barely 20 percent, which is less than the growth in spending over the same period, thus widening the central government's deficit. Personal and corporate income taxes, profits, and capital gains accounted for the largest share of central government revenue, at 37 percent in 2007/08. A fraction, representing 5 percent of these taxes, was distributed to the LAs through the LATF. Property rates are mostly local and accounted for only

Table 4.8 Central Government Revenue in Kenya, 2005/06–2007/08

Revenue source	2005/06 (K Sh, millions)	(%)	2006/07 (K Sh, millions)	(%)	2007/08 (K Sh, millions)	(%)
Taxes on income, profits, and capital gains	114,629.06	37.0	130,719.00	35.1	16,515.50	37.3
Taxes on property	189.59	0.1	25,306.00	0.1	301.59	0.1
Value added tax	79,925.91	25.8	96,497.01	25.9	11,501.65	26.0
Taxes on other goods and services	61,709.65	19.9	76,111.19	20.5	88,836.37	20.0
Taxes on international trade transactions	29,861.43	9.7	40,235.00	10.8	46,949.00	10.6
Other taxes	2,353.23	0.8	2,747.87	0.7	4,288.62	1.0
Nontax revenue	20,747.14	6.7	25,425.91	6.8	22,537.89	5.1
Total revenue	**309,416.01**	**100.0**	**371,989.04**	**100.0**	**443,084.97**	**100.0**
Revenue growth (%)	—	—	20.2	—	19.1	—
Rate of inflation (%)	—	—	11.3	—	29.3	—

Source: KNBS 2009.
Note: — = not available.

0.1 percent of the central government's revenue; the value added tax and other taxes accounted for 26 percent and 32 percent, respectively, of the government's total revenue. The CDF accounted for 2.5 percent of the government's ordinary revenue.

Local Government Expenditure

The data presented here are taken from the Ministry of Local Government's LATF database. They are collected every year when the LAs produce the accounting and financial statements required to allocate the performance component of the LATF grant. Table 4.9 presents the trends and pattern of the LAs' spending between the financial years 2003/04 and 2007/08. Local spending amounted to nearly K Sh 23 billion in 2007/08—representing 3.5 percent of central government spending and reaching K Sh 613 per capita (approximately €5.50).

The sharp rise in spending over the period in question was close to the rise in central government spending. The average annual increase was 23 percent but reached very high levels in some years; for instance, the increase was 34 percent between 2005/06 and 2006/07—much higher than the rate of inflation, which was 11 percent over the same period. Personnel expenditure was the largest item, at nearly 40 percent of total expenditure in 2007/08, showing a steady decrease as of 2003/04. This continuous reduction in personnel expenditure is likely linked to LATF allocation conditions that limit the weight of

Table 4.9 Local Authority Expenditure in Kenya, 2003/04–2007/08

Expenditure classification	2003/04		2004/05		2005/06		2006/07		2007/08	
	(K Sh, millions)	(%)	(K Sh, millions)	(%)	(K Sh, millions)	(%)	(K Sh, millions)	(%)	(K Sh, millions)	(%)
Civic expenditure	712	7.01	833	6.24	1,102	7.32	1,315	6.52	1,236	5.42
LA personnel	4,399	43.32	5,770	43.23	6,138	40.77	7,830	38.80	9,047	39.66
LA operations	2,572	25.33	2,203	16.51	3,233	21.48	3,899	19.32	4,008	17.57
LA maintenance	718	7.07	563	4.22	628	4.17	723	3.58	807	3.54
Total recurrent expenditure	8,401	82.74	9,369	70.20	11,101	73.74	13,767	68.22	15,098	66.19
Capital expenditure	1,158	11.40	1,559	11.68	1,511	10.04	3,073	15.23	3,469	15.21
Debt repayment	554	5.46	2,202	16.50	2,268	15.07	3,317	16.44	4,229	18.54
Loan amortization	41	0.40	217	1.63	174	1.16	23	0.11	13	0.06
Total expenditure	**10,154**	**100.00**	**13,347**	**100.00**	**15,054**	**100.00**	**20,180**	**100.00**	**22,809**	**100.00**
Annual growth in expenditure (%)	—	—	31.4	—	12.8	—	34.0	—	14.4	—

Source: Ministry of Local Government data, 2010.
Note: LA = local authority; — = not available.

this expenditure in the LAs' budgets. Capital expenditure rose by an average of 34 percent annually, which is also a major consequence of the measures associated with LATF allocation. The weight of capital expenditure in the LAs' budgets rose from 11 percent in 2003/04 to more than 15 percent in 2007/08.

The constraints imposed by the LATF have also affected debt repayment terms, which was one of the government's objectives. The LAs thus had until June 30, 2010, to clear their local institutional debt arrears. In fact, repayment of these arrears (much of the debt consists of salary and pension fund payment arrears of 11 percent and 30 percent, respectively, in June 2008) increased significantly from 2003/04, by approximately 55 percent per year on average. In 2007/08, it accounted for more than 18.5 percent of total spending by LAs.

Table 4.10 illustrates the outstanding debt of the country's major cities and its evolution between 2006/07 and 2007/08. The city of Nairobi alone accounted for nearly 50 percent of this outstanding debt in 2007/08, rising by 17 percent over the previous year. It therefore seemed highly unlikely that the city would

Table 4.10 Local Authorities' Outstanding Debt in Kenya, 2006/07–2007/08

Council	2006/2007			2007/2008			Change
	(K Sh, millions)	(%)	(cumulative %)	(K Sh, millions)	(%)	(cumulative %)	(%)
Nairobi City	6,177	47.74	47.74	7,241	53.42	53.42	17.22
Mombasa Municipal	2,066	15.97	63.71	2,024	14.94	68.35	−2.03
Kisumu Municipal	529	4.09	67.79	411	3.04	71.39	−22.19
Nakuru Municipal	333	2.57	70.36	312	2.30	73.69	−6.17
Kitale Municipal	167	1.29	71.65	244	1.80	75.50	46.65
Nanyuki Municipal	6	0.05	71.70	231	1.71	77.20	3,757.15
Kisumu County	175	1.35	73.05	175	1.29	78.50	0.18
Kisii Municipal	2	0.02	73.06	149	1.10	79.60	7,363.67
Nakuru County	157	1.21	74.28	135	1.00	80.59	−13.91
Nyando County	73	0.56	74.84	129	0.95	81.54	76.07
Gusii	115	0.89	75.73	114	0.84	82.39	−0.60
Vihiga Municipal	133	1.03	76.76	92	0.68	83.07	−30.48
Eldoret Municipal	420	3.25	80.00	59	0.44	83.50	−85.94
Others	2,587	20.00	100.00	2,236	16.50	100.00	−13.59
Total	**12,940**	**100.00**	**100.00**	**13,554**	**100.00**	**100.00**	**4.75**
Total excluding Nairobi	6,763	52.3	n.a.	6,314	46.6	n.a.	−7.11

Source: Ministry of Local Government data, 2010.
Note: n.a. = not applicable.

Table 4.11 Structure of Expenditure in Kenya, by Local Authority Type, 2007/08

percentage

Expenditure classification	Nairobi city council	Municipal councils	Town councils	County councils	Total
Civic expenditure	0.89	4.07	8.79	11.78	5.42
LA personnel	45.88	42.51	34.16	30.08	39.66
LA operations	12.27	18.90	17.97	22.78	17.57
LA maintenance	0.16	4.87	4.86	6.08	3.54
Total recurrent expenditure	59.20	70.34	65.78	70.72	66.19
Capital expenditure	14.53	13.74	17.05	17.20	15.21
Debt repayment	26.27	15.73	17.17	12.08	18.54
Loan amortization	0	0.19	0	0	0.06
Total expenditure	**100.00**	**100.00**	**100.00**	**100.00**	**100.00**
Total LA expenditure (%)	35.38	29.88	6.84	27.91	100.00
LAs (no.)	1	45	62	67	175

Source: Ministry of Local Government data, 2007/08.
Note: LA = local authority.

manage to pay off its debt by 2009/10. The same is true for Mombasa, whose debt repayment rate was not sufficient to pay off its debt in 2010.

Based on our interviews in June 2010, progress has been made, and the government was still aiming to maintain pressure.[36]

Table 4.11 shows the structure of expenditure by LA type. The city of Nairobi alone accounts for 35 percent of local public spending in Kenya. It stands out from the other types of LAs, particularly in the shares of personnel expenditure and nonrecurrent expenditure (capital expenditure and debt repayment), which are relatively higher for Nairobi than for the other LAs—at 46 percent and 40 percent, respectively, compared with the average of 40 percent and 34 percent. Overall, the weight of maintenance expenditure remains relatively low, averaging 3.5 percent.

Local Government Revenue

Table 4.12 presents the trends and structure of LA revenues. The average annual increase in LA revenue amounted to 14.7 percent, significantly lower than that of central government. This increase was predominantly driven by the rise in central government transfers, averaging approximately 23 percent annually, whereas the increase in own revenue averaged only 10 percent annually over the same period.

The weight of the central government grants thus grew regularly, reaching nearly 43 percent of LA total revenue in 2007/08. The LATF alone accounted for more than 35 percent of LA total revenue. The increase in this grant was linked

Table 4.12 Local Authority Revenue in Kenya, 2003/04–2007/08

Revenue source	2003/04 (K Sh, millions)	(%)	2004/05 (K Sh, millions)	(%)	2005/06 (K Sh, millions)	(%)	2006/07 (K Sh, millions)	(%)	2007/08 (K Sh, millions)	(%)
LATF	3,719	27.40	3,930	30.35	4,986	31.95	7,461	36.19	8,232	35.13
RMLF	323	2.30	524	4.05	506	3.24	869	4.21	1,485	6.34
CILOR	365	2.70	270	2.09	300	1.92	327	1.59	327	1.39
Total transfers from central government	4,407	32.50	4,724	36.48	5,792	37.12	8,657	41.98	10,043	42.86
Single business permit	1,572	11.60	1,674	12.93	1,736	11.13	1,963	9.52	2,232	9.53
Property rates	2,028	14.90	1,840	14.21	2,497	16.00	2,986	14.48	3,067	13.09
Market fees	706	5.20	701	5.41	832	5.33	950	4.61	1,092	4.66
Vehicle parking	615	4.50	973	7.51	1,128	7.23	1,300	6.30	1,452	6.19
House rents	386	2.80	314	2.43	314	2.01	308	1.49	160	0.68
Plot rents	166	1.23	163	1.26	169	1.08	202	0.98	198	0.84
Cesses on agricultural products	440	3.25	494	3.82	569	3.65	569	2.76	755	3.22
Game park fees	458	3.38	688	5.31	729	4.67	1,011	4.90	884	3.77
Water and sewerage fees	1,767	13.05	535	4.13	472	3.02	518	2.51	392	1.67
Other	994	7.34	843	6.51	1,367	8.76	2,156	10.46	3,157	13.47
Total LA revenue	9,132	67.45	8,225	63.52	9,813	62.88	11,963	58.02	13,390	57.14
Total transfers from central government and LA	**13,538**	**100.0**	**12,948**	**100.0**	**15,604**	**100.0**	**20,619**	**100.0**	**23,432**	**100.0**
Annual increase in revenue (%)	—	—	-4.30	—	20.5	—	32.13	—	13.64	—

Source: Ministry of Local Government data, 2010.
Note: CILOR = contribution in lieu of rates; LA = local authority; LATF = Local Authority Transfer Fund; RMLF = Road Maintenance Levy Fund; — = not available.

to the increase in personal and corporate income taxes collected by the central government, with the LATF receiving 5 percent of these taxes. The LAs thus share, with the central government, the macroeconomic risk associated with this tax, and they must use forecasts rather than guaranteed transfer amounts when establishing their budgets. Property rates and single business permits rose annually at a comparable pace of approximately 10 percent, accounting for 13 percent and 9 percent, respectively, of LA total revenue in 2007/08.

The city of Nairobi alone collected 42 percent of the own revenue collected by all LAs in 2007/08. It derives the bulk of its own revenue (nearly 55 percent) from property rates, business permits, and parking fees, as shown in table 4.13. The other revenues, which consist mainly of advertising taxes, also represented an important source of financing for Nairobi (37.3 percent).

The town councils make up 35 percent of the LAs but took only 5 percent of the own revenue collected by all LAs. This raises the question of their capacity to deliver local public services. The county councils collected nearly half of their own resources in the form of taxes on agricultural products (cesses) and entry fees to attraction parks and nature reserves (48.73 percent). They received relatively more transfers from the central government than did the other types of LAs. In fact, they took in 21 percent of all own revenue collected and accounted for 29 percent of total local revenue.

Table 4.13 Structure of Own Revenue, by Local Authority Type in Kenya, 2007/08
percentage

Revenue source	Nairobi City Council	Municipal councils	Town councils	County councils	Total
CILOR	2.60	2.79	2.24	1.38	2.38
Single business permit	13.38	17.61	21.49	18.72	16.27
Property rates	29.82	27.41	4.20	4.79	22.36
Market fees	5.64	9.71	15.07	8.21	7.96
Vehicle parking	11.26	13.65	20.81	2.21	10.58
House rents	0.00	2.70	1.58	1.12	1.17
Plot rents	0.00	1.29	5.41	3.52	1.44
Total cess receipts	0.00	2.80	12.28	18.62	5.51
Game park fees	0.00	0.01	0.22	30.11	6.45
Water and sewerage fees	0.00	5.46	0.74	0.20	1.79
Other	37.30	16.58	15.97	11.12	24.09
Total own revenue	**100**	**100**	**100**	**100**	**100**
Total LA own revenue (%)	42	31	5	21	100
Total LA revenue (%)	34	30	7	29	100

Source: Ministry of Local Government data, 2007/08.
Note: CILOR = contribution in lieu of rates; LA = local authority.

Table 4.14 Evolution of the CDF and the LATF in Kenya, 2003/04–2007/08
K Sh, millions

	2003/04	2004/05	2005/06	2006/07	2007/08
CDF	1,260	5,432	7,029	9,737	9,797
LATF	3,719	3,930	4,986	7,461	8,232
CDF/LATF	0.33	1.38	1.40	1.30	1.19

Source: Ministry of Local Government for the LATF data; CDF 2010.
Note: CDF = Constituency Development Fund; LATF = Local Authority Transfer Fund.

The constituencies may be considered as local government units financed entirely by the central government through the CDF. They receive funds from the central government and provide public services. Table 4.14 shows the amount and relative importance of the CDF and LATF from fiscal year 2003/04 to 2007/08. From 2004/05, the CDF grew at an average annual rate of 21 percent, whereas over the same period the LATF rose by 28 percent per year. In 2004/05, the CDF was 1.38 times larger than the LATF. It was only 1.19 times larger in 2007/08.

These contrasting trends are not a result of central government discretion but of LATF and CDF indexation rules. Income taxes on which the LATF is indexed rose more rapidly than total central government ordinary revenue on which the CDF is fixed. Nevertheless, thanks to the CDF, the constituencies are major providers of local public services on an equal footing with the LAs. On average, their resources amount to 42 percent of the LAs' resources.

Remarks on Statistical Data for Local Expenditure and Revenue

Regarding expenditure, the functional classification remains inconsistent. The decentralized responsibilities, as they appear in CAP 265 (previously shown in table 4.5), do not clearly correspond to items in the budget documents (see table 4.4, for example). As a result, it is difficult to measure the relative weight of the assigned functions.

On the revenue side, however, the main taxes and grants are well documented, although there are still some problems of statistical consistency: the revenue categories listed in table 4.3 do not exactly reflect those in table 4.12; and there is also a discrepancy between tables 4.12 and 4.13, in that revenue sources are not broken down in the same way.

Generally speaking, from the budget documents provided, it is difficult to identify the basic elements of budgetary analysis, such as operating cash flow capacity or working capital variances. This is primarily due to the principle of budget annuality, which is not observed, and the lack of a clear division between the current and capital sections.

Decentralization, the 2010 Constitution, and the Proposed LGA Reforms: Some Remarks

Since the 1990s, Kenya has been committed to a process of institutional reform. This movement has its origins in the democratization of Kenyan society. The introduction of a multiparty system in 1992 has indeed allowed opposition parties to compete in elections, but this has not given them the means to carry out their countervailing role once the elections are over (see Lafargue 2008).

Although the institutional reform movement dates from the 1990s, it was not until 2005 that the Bomas Draft[37] and the Wako Bill were put to a referendum in 2005—unsuccessfully.[38] This process was relaunched shortly after the 2007 general elections. The parliament thus tasked the Committee of Experts on Constitutional Review (COE) with once again formulating reform proposals.[39] The draft, prepared in November 2009 and later revised, was successfully put to a referendum on August 6, 2010.[40]

The new constitution addresses many areas, most significantly the reform of national institutions to reduce the excessive powers held by the president. This legislation also includes a section on the local government system, which is our primary interest here.

In parallel with the constitutional revision process, the government tabled a proposal in parliament in December 2009 to amend the LGA. At the time of writing this chapter, the draft had still not cleared the first of three stages of approval necessary for a draft to be adopted in the Anglo-Saxon parliamentary system (that is, the first-reading and first-vote stage).

Without claiming to be a rigorous analysis of a subject that is beyond the scope of our expertise, the following section outlines the principal amendments relating to local governments under the revised LGA and the new Kenyan constitution. The latter should, in principle, come into effect in 2012.

Draft Reforms to the Local Government Act (CAP 265)

The changes proposed in this draft law are ambitious and, were they adopted, would substantially alter the physiognomy of decision making at the local level. The principal changes are as follows:

- Direct election of (county, municipal, city, and metropolitan council) mayors by the population for a maximum of two five-year terms (Sections 13 and 50)
- Transformation of the mayor's role from simply council chair to budget authorizing officer and CEO (Sections 14 and 53)
- Support to the mayor by an executive committee (Sections 56 to 57) comprising the chairs of the council committees and with the town clerk as secretary

- Composition of the municipal council (Section 26) including elected councillors and one councillor appointed by the minister for every six elected councillors (thus, one-seventh of the council not elected)
- Dissent of senior government officials to be noted in the minutes but no longer allowed to block the process (Section 118)
- Introduction of explicit criteria (Sections 23 and 28) to confer municipal or metropolitan status on a city.

The Constitution of Kenya of August 4, 2010

On November 17, 2009, the COE released the Harmonized Draft Constitution of Kenya. This draft was subjected to public consultation after its publication and was reviewed by a parliamentary committee. The COE produced a revised version, taking into account the work of the parliamentary committee of February 23, 2010. This revised version was put to a referendum on August 4, 2010, and was adopted with 66.9 percent of votes in favor. The themes devoted to the organization of territorialized government structures are discussed below.

Institutional framework   Article 6 and Chapter 11 present two tiers of government: the central government and the counties, 47 in number. These two tiers will be distinct and interdependent, interacting collaboratively and cooperatively. In other words, the counties will constitute a decentralized level. It is, however, specified that the national government will prevail over the counties (Articles 186 and 191).

Article 18 of the Sixth Schedule, which deals with transitional provisions, specifies that all local governments established under CAP 265 will continue to exist. In other words, the current decentralized structures—municipalities, towns, cities, and county councils—will remain but will not be institutionally recognized, as is currently the case. However, there is no mention of deconcentrated structures (such as provinces or districts) accompanying these institutional changes.

National Level   At the national level, the new constitution provides for the transition from a unicameral system to a partly bicameral system. A Senate (lower house) is to be created, with a legislative role limited to county affairs (Article 96) such as equalization, fund allocations to counties, debt levels, and county borders. The Senate will consist of 68 members (Article 98): one per county directly elected by the voters (total of 47) and others designated as per Article 98. The composition of the National Assembly will also be modified: 290 members will be elected from the constituencies and 47 women elected (one per county). The Senate's powers relating to county affairs are specified in Articles 96 and 110. The National Assembly may amend or veto special bills (Article 111) passed by the Senate only with a two-thirds majority. A bill mediation mechanism is planned for ordinary laws.

The new constitution also provides for the creation of a National Land Commission (Articles 61–67) whose responsibility will be to administer the use and ownership of public land on behalf of the central government and the counties. This commission is to conduct a land reform process to end what is judged to be an inequitable distribution of land. This is considered to have been one of the sources of postelection violence in 2007/08.

Local Level   At the local level, the constitution provides for the creation of 47 counties. Their number and implicit boundaries correspond to the historical districts. During the debate surrounding the referendum, some politicians promised postreferendum revisions to increase this number. Articles 94 and 188 stipulate that parliament may alter their number and borders on the advice of a commission set up for this purpose.

Political organization of the counties   The County Assemblies (Article 177) will be elected for five years, composed of the following:

- Councillors elected by universal suffrage in their wards[41]
- Councillors chosen to ensure that no more than two-thirds of councillors are of the same gender, taking into account the proportion of votes for each party in the council elections
- Councillors representing marginalized groups according to procedures to be defined by parliament.

The executive authority of the counties will consist of a governor and a deputy governor, both elected by direct suffrage in a single-round ballot for up to two five-year terms. The governor, deputy governor, and a maximum of 10 members proposed by the governor and approved by the county assembly will form the county executive committee.

Responsibilities   Article 174 specifies the objectives to be attained by the devolution process,[42] and the county's responsibilities are listed in the Fourth Schedule. It indicates that the central government has a general jurisdiction clause, which is somewhat at odds with the objectives of decentralization. Article 191 deals with the procedures for resolving conflicts between levels of government.

According to the Fourth Schedule, the counties will be responsible for the following 14 areas:

- Agriculture, including abattoirs, stockyards, and disease control
- Health services, including ambulances, primary health care clinics, cemeteries, control of undertakings that sell food, and, above all, removal and management of refuse and solid waste

- Control of noise and air pollution and of outdoor advertising
- Cultural activities, including libraries and museums; sporting and recreation activities; and casinos, racing, and control of drinking establishments
- Transportation, including local roads and street lighting; traffic and public road transport; and local ferries
- Animal control
- Trading activities, including markets and trade licenses
- County development and planning, including electricity and gas, statistics, and land surveying
- Preprimary education, including childcare facilities
- Implementation of national environmental policies, including water, forestry, and soil and water conservation
- County public services, including water and sanitation
- Disaster relief and fire fighting services
- Control of drugs and pornography
- Encouragement of communities' and locations' participation in local governance.

Financing   Article 203(2) states that at least 15 percent of the national government's revenue will be paid to the counties, a relatively large amount relative to the amounts currently transferred to the LAs. The sums transferred to the subnational level would be increased at least fivefold relative to 2010 if the LATF is taken to be the transfer mechanism to local entities in 2010. In addition, an equalization fund is to be set up, amounting to 0.5 percent of the national government's revenue.

Article 215 provides for the establishment of a Commission on Revenue Allocation whose composition is a priori primarily political[43] and which will be in charge of making recommendations concerning the vertical (center-to-counties) and horizontal (between counties) distribution of resources assigned to the counties. Regarding vertical distribution, the exact percentage of national revenue allocated to the counties (with the constraint of the 15 percent minimum [Article 218]) will be voted on annually by parliament. The rules for sharing amounts horizontally, previously set by parliament, will instead be the responsibility of the Senate. It will determine the sharing of revenue among counties (Article 217) at five-year intervals (every three years for the first and second times [Sixth Schedule, Section 16]) according to 11 criteria listed in Section 203.

According to Article 209, counties will not have access to income tax, customs duties, excise taxes, or the value added tax. They may, however, levy property rates and entertainment taxes as well as impose user charges for services provided. It is specified that taxation by the counties must not prejudice the mobility of goods and services, capital, or labor.

Counties may borrow only if the national government guarantees their loans (Article 212) according to terms to be prescribed by a law (Article 213) that is required to have been enacted one year after the adoption of the constitution (Fifth Schedule).

Miscellaneous   The structure, content, and conduct of the county budget process are to be set by national legislation (Article 226).

A controller of budget, nominated by the president and approved by the National Assembly, is responsible for overseeing the implementation of national budgets and those of devolved entities (Article 228).

An auditor general, nominated by the president and approved by the National Assembly, is responsible for auditing the accounts of national government and devolved entities (Article 229).

Status of local staff   Devolved entities will likely be responsible for employing, promoting, and dismissing local government officials in compliance with the standards prescribed by an act of parliament (Article 235). A priori, the constitution therefore provides for the creation of a local civil service. At the same time, however, it is specified that a national Salaries and Remuneration Commission will be responsible for establishing recommendations on the levels of compensation for the employees of devolved entities (Article 230). Finally, notwithstanding Article 235, teachers are to be recruited by the Teachers Service Commission (Article 237).

Remarks
The following remarks are limited to comments on local structures:

- The boundaries and number of counties that will constitute the electoral basis for future senators are regulated by the constitution but subject to change. This new territorial structure will be superimposed on the existing LAs. The fate of the LAs is uncertain. For the time being, their sole protection is Section 18 of the Sixth Schedule, which deals with transitional arrangements. Consequently, the question of how existing local structures will be financed remains open. It is likely that matching these structures, through legislation, with entities recognized by the constitution will pose some problems.

- The 15 percent minimum amount of national revenue transferred to the counties is extremely generous, given that their formal responsibilities have evolved little relative to the responsibilities assigned to the current LAs. There is still a great unknown: How will the counties' spending evolve to reflect their greater share of national revenue? Will the counties continue to intervene in their usual areas of responsibility (Fourth Schedule, Part 2), spending more than usual on these, or, to ensure macroeconomic equilibrium, will they assume expenses that have thus far been borne by the central government? Note that primary and secondary education is not a possible area of intervention for the counties.

- What fate awaits the current LATF structure? Will the CDF be continued?
- The fact that the national parliament can legislate on any subject, notwithstanding the distribution of powers between tiers of government laid down in the constitution, could be a serious impediment to decentralization (see earlier, the general jurisdiction clause of the central government).
- The Commission on Revenue Allocation consists of experts appointed by the political parties. It remains to be seen whether the commission will be expert or political. Moreover, its interaction with parliament, and particularly the Senate, will be complex.

The 2011–12 period—which should in theory prepare the new constitution's entry into force with the advent of the national elections in 2013—is full of hopes and dangers for decentralization, given that there are so many issues to be tackled. Clearly, even if the LGA amendments bring about significant changes for the current LAs, the new constitution maintains a relatively centralizing tone. Overall, the text is a potential source of confusion because of the areas of conflict created by various articles, at least from our perspective. For the time being, we can only wait and see.

Notes

1. *Jimbo* means "district" or "administrative region" in Kiswahili. *Majimbo* indicates that there can be many of them.
2. The LAs were set up throughout the colonial period as true local government entities to facilitate administration of the territory. The Ministry of Local Government was created in 1928 to manage their expansion. It is worth noting that the LA structure, unlike that of the regions, was not mentioned in the 1963 Constitution.
3. The influential players present on the eve of independence were the Kenya African National Union (KANU), the Kenya African Democratic Union (KADU), and the British colonial authority. KANU brought together local political parties dominated by the Kikuyu and the Luo and advocated a centralized territorial organization in the name of national unity and the struggle against neocolonialism. Conversely, KADU, which was formed by the ensemble of political parties of ethnic minorities (including the Kalenjin), argued in favor of a decentralized structure for the country, with the creation of regions that had control over lands, to prevent the Kikuyu-Luo alliance from dominating national institutions. This alliance attempted to claim a territorial right to all state property, particularly in the Rift Valley Province where the Kalenjin's principal districts were located (Bourmaud 1988). This federal state, advocated by KADU and based on strong ethnic demand, was called *Majimbo*. The British, meanwhile, backed the formation of a decentralized state. Stamp (1986)

explains that the British position was due to both the belief in the benefits of this form of governance and the desire to curb nationalism and, by extension, anticolonial forces.

4. The 1962 draft code on local governments, adopted in 1963 under the name of the Local Government Act Regulation, had its origins in the Sessional Paper No. 2 of 1961.

5. Responsibilities included primary education, comprising the construction and maintenance of school premises and payment of teachers' salaries, health-care management, maintenance of secondary road networks, and so on.

6. For many authors, including Bourmaud (1988), the government conveniently took advantage of the near-bankrupt state of the LAs.

7. In 1982, Section 2A of the constitution indicated the abolition of the multiparty system. This section was removed in 1992. See Kibwana (1998) for a discussion on the role of civil society and donors in Kenya's democratization process.

8. Or CAP 265 (see the "Decentralization" subsection).

9. As later discussed in detail in the "Decentralization, the 2010 Constitution, and Proposed LGA Reforms" section.

10. The judiciary should be strengthened by the creation of a Supreme Court. Appointments made by the president are now subject to approval by parliament, which may also initiate impeachment proceedings against the president.

11. In 1977, parliament voted in a new regulation that incorporated almost all of the provisions found in the 1963 text.

12. LGA, Art. 5. The only constraint is that an LA may not be located simultaneously within two provinces (administrative units).

13. The National Assembly comprises 225 members, of whom 12 are appointed and 3 are ex officio.

14. President's Office, private communication, December 4, 2009.

15. The draft constitution plans to increase this number to 290.

16. A county council (rural area), municipal council, town council (urban areas), or a city council (Nairobi).

17. LGA, Section 27.

18. LGA, Fifth Schedule, Paragraph 3.

19. LGA, Section 92.

20. According to the Ministry of Local Government.

21. LGA, Section 129.

22. LGA, Sections 129–132.

23. The inter-LA mobility of senior public officials is facilitated by being able to transfer from one pension fund to another (LGA, Sections 139–140).

24. This is further discussed in the section, "Decentralization, the 2010 Constitution, and the Proposed LGA Reforms."

25. The term "cess" is an abbreviation of "assess"; this misspelling is due to a mistaken connection with the word "census" (see http://en.wikipedia.org/wiki/Cess and http://dictionary.reference.com/browse/cess).

26. Some LAs charge for a number of services provided by firefighters, such as removing bees' nests or breaking down doors.

27. Note that the nomenclature in table 4.6 does not exactly correspond to the description of fees and taxes in the text. This type of discrepancy is frequent in countries embarking on a decentralization process and makes the job of understanding them more complicated.
28. Legal Notice No. 146, *Kenya Gazette Supplement 79*, November 14, 2008. This is a fixed business license fee without proportional charges, unlike what is usually found in African countries
29. Valuation for Rating Act, Section 7.
30. Valuation for Rating Act, Section 3.
31. Valuation for Rating Act, Section 27.
32. Valuation for Rating Act, Sections 10–21.
33. Valuation for Rating Act, Section 25.
34. Valuation for Rating Act, Subsidiary Legislation, Rules under Sections 25–26, Rule 4.
35. See *Kenya Gazette Supplement 107* (January 2004), reproduced in KNBS (2005, 40).
36. In addition, estimating these institutional arrears apparently raises issues in some cases because of the overestimation of these amounts by the social agencies, in their favor.
37. The Bomas Draft was the outcome of nearly eight years of discussions; proposed amendments to the constitution dated from 1997, with the creation of the Inter-Parties Parliamentary Group.
38. See Chitere et al. (2006) for a critical analysis of the proposals submitted in 2005.
39. The Constitution of Kenya Review Act.
40. This is the version published by the attorney general in compliance with Section 34 of the Constitution of Kenya Review Act and the subject of a 30-day civic education campaign.
41. The two remaining types of councillors are elected by proportional representation (Article 90) or according to the number of seats obtained by direct election (Article 177). There seems to be an inconsistency here.
42. Note that item (h) in Article 174 specifies that the devolution consists in facilitating decentralization, which raises problems with the definition of these two terms.
43. The chair of this commission is to be nominated by the head of state. The other members are to be designated by the political parties present in the National Assembly (two members), the political parties present in the Senate (five members), and the Ministry of Finance (one secretary).

References
Bourmaud, D. 1988. *Histoire politique du Kenya: État et pouvoir local.* Paris: Karthala Editions.

Chitere, P., L. Chweya, J. Masya, A. Tostensen, and K. Waiganjo. 2006. "Kenya Constitutional Documents: A Comparative Analysis." CMI Report, R 2006: 5, Chr. Michelsen Institute, Bergen, Norway.

Dafflon, B., and T. Madiès. 2008. "Décentralisation: quelques principes issus du fédéralisme financier." [Decentralization: A Few Principles from the Theory of Fiscal Federalism.] Notes and Documents 42, Agence Française de Développement, Paris.

Kenya National Bureau of Statistics (KNBS). 2005. *Geographic Dimensions of Well-Being in Kenya Who and Where Are the Poor?* Nairobi: The Regal Press Kenya Ltd.

———. 2008a. *Constituency Report on Well-Being in Kenya.* Nairobi: KNBS.

———. 2008b. "Statistical Abstract." Page IV, KNBS, Nairobi.

———. 2009. "Economic Survey 2009." KNBS, Nairobi.

Kibwana, K. 1998. "Constitutionnalisme et démocratie au Kenya, 1990–1997." *Politique Africaine* 30/06/1998 (70): 74–81.

Kimenyi, M. 2005. "Efficiency and Efficacy of Kenya's Constituency Development Fund: Theory and Evidence." Economics working paper, Department of Economics, DigitalCommons@UConn, University of Connecticut, Storrs, CT. http://digitalcommons .uconn.edu/cgi/viewcontent.cgi?article=1052&context=econ_wpapers.

Lafargue, J. 2008. *Les élections générales de 2007 au Kenya. Les terrains du siècle.* Paris: IFRA, Karthala Editions.

LATF (Local Authorities Transfer Fund). 2009. "Annual Report, FY 2007–2008." LATF, Republic of Kenya, Nairobi.

Njeru, G.-R., and J.-M. Njoka. 2007. "Political Ideology in Kenya." In *Governance and Transition Politics in Kenya*, eds. P. Wanyande, M. Omosa, and C. Ludeki, 21–54. Nairobi: Nairobi University Press.

Stamp, P. 1986. "Local Government in Kenya: Ideology and Political Practice 1895–1974." *African Studies Review* 29 (4): 17–42.

World Bank. 2002. "An Assessment of Local Service Delivery and Local Governments in Kenya," Africa Region Report 24383, Water and Urban I Africa Region, World Bank, Washington, DC.

Chapter **5**

The Local Government Financing System in Senegal

Guy Gilbert and Emmanuelle Taugourdeau

History of Decentralization in Senegal

Senegal inherited an embryonic system of territorial collectivities (*collectivités territoriales*; CTs) at the end of the 19th century, molded on the national system of the former colonial power, France. In 1873, the country had four fully functioning communes (municipalities): Dakar, Gorée, Rufisque, and Saint-Louis. The year 1903 saw the creation of 20 "mixed communes," where the office of mayor was held by a centrally appointed municipal administrator.

Upon independence in 1960, decentralization gained more of a foothold: the number of communes gradually increased to 37 and then 48, while the special-status communes ("mixed communes") were dissolved. A 1972 law established "rural communities" (CRs) with a view to creating real centers for development. Their management was nonetheless entrusted to a subprefect. Finally, Dakar was given the status of urban community (CU), which was later dissolved in 2001. Since then, Dakar has been a commune. Its territory comprises 19 arrondissement communes (CAs). In addition, since 2004, Dakar is a member of two intermunicipal structures created in lieu of the previous urban community.

Decentralization continued with successive reforms until the watershed year 1996, when 12 new communes were created and, more important, some key legislation was passed, including (a) Law 96-06 of February 5, 1996, on the Code of Local Government (*Code des collectivités locales*; CCL) and (b) Law 96-07 on the transfer of powers to these entities.

The 2001 Constitution enshrined the advances made in 1996 by strengthening their constitutional basis. In particular, it stipulated that the CTs "constitute the institutional framework for citizens' participation in the management of public affairs"; "that they are freely administered by elected assemblies"; and that "their organisation, their composition and their functioning are determined by law."[1] Table 5.1 sets out the chronology of key legislative and regulatory texts on decentralization.

Alongside the creation of these CTs, the central government has set up deconcentrated administrative entities: regions, *départements*, and *arrondissements*.

Table 5.1 Timeline of the Key Legislation on Decentralization in Senegal, 1972–2008

1972	Law 72–02 of February 1, on the organization of territorial administration
	Law 72–59 of June 12, introducing a rural tax
1973	Decree No. 3853/DCPT/PM of May 2, laying down the arrangements for collection of the rural tax introduced by Law 72–59 of June 12, 1972
1988	Decree No. 12248 of October 15, laying down rules for the organization and functioning of the Fund for Local Government Infrastructures (*Fonds d'équipement des collectivités locales; FECL*), a special Treasury account
1992	Law 92–40 of July 9, on the General Tax Code (*Code général des impôts; CGI*)
1993	Interministerial decree 10830 MEFP/M.INT. of December 1, on the nomenclature for local government budgets
1996	Law 96–06 of March 22, on the Code of Local Government (*Code des collectivités locales; CCL*)
	Law 96–07 of March 22, transferring powers to the regions, communes, and rural communities
	Law 96–09 of March 22, laying down the administrative and financial organization of the arrondissement commune (*commune d'arrondissement; CA*) and its relationship to the urban area
	Law 96–11 of March 22, concerning the limitation on accumulating electoral mandates and certain functions
	Decree No. 96–458 of June 17, organizing public accounting
	Decree No. 96–510 of July 4, on the financial regime of local government
	Decree No. 96–1118 of December 27, setting up the National Council on Local Development (*Conseil national de développement des collectivités locales; CNDCL*)
	Decree No. 96–1121 of December 27, setting up the Interministerial Committee on Territorial Administration (*Comité interministériel de l'administration territoriale*)
	Decree No. 96–1122 of December 27, on the standard agreement setting the conditions and arrangements for use of external state services
	Decree No. 96–1123 of December 27, on the use by local governments of external state services in the region
	Decree No. 6–1124 of December 27, setting the amount over which local government procurement contracts must obtain prior approval from a government representative
	Decree No. 96–1135 of December 27, implementing the law transferring powers to the regions, communes, and rural communities in matters of health and social services
1997	Interministerial Decree No. 62 of January 30, on the budget nomenclature for local government
1999	Organic law 99–70 of February 17, on the Court of Accounts
2002	Law 2002–02 of February 15, amending Law 72–02 of February 1, 1972, concerning the organization of territorial administration
2002	Decree No. 2002–550 of May 30, on the Public Procurement Code (*Code des marchés publics; CMP*)

(continued next page)

Table 5.1 (continued)

2003	Decree No. 2003–101 of March 13, on government accounts
	Decree No. 2003–701 of September 26, amending Decree No. 2002–550 of May 30, 2002, on the CMP
	Law 2003–20 of July 23, laying down the rules for the organization and functioning of the Urban Transportation Development Fund (*Fonds de développement des transports urbains*; FDTU)
	Circular 01191/MINT/CAB of January 29, on the exercise of local government budget control
2004	Decree No. 2004–1093 of August 4, creating the *Communauté des agglomérations de Dakar* (CADAK)
	Decree No. 2004–1094 of August 4, creating the *Communauté des agglomérations de Rufisque* (CAR)
	Law 2004–12 of February 6, reforming local taxation (systematic registration of taxpayers, limitations on property tax exemptions, introduction of the combined business tax [*Contribution Générale Unique*; CGU])
2005	Decree No. 2005–876 of October 3, amending Decree No. 2004–1093 of August 4, 2004, creating the CADAK
	Decree No. 2005–877 of October 3, amending Decree No. 2004–1094 of August 4, 2004, creating the CAR
2007	Decree No. 2007–545 of April 25, on the CMP
	Decree No. 2007–546 of April 25, on the organization and functioning of the Public Procurement Regulatory Authority
	Decree No. 2007–547 of April 25, creating the Central Directorate of Public Procurement (*Direction centrale des marchés publics*)
2008	Decree No. 2008–517 of May 20, laying down arrangements for the organization and functioning of the regional development agencies (*Agences régionales de développement*; ARDs)
	Law 2008–14 of March 18, amending Law 72–02 of February 1, 1972, organizing territorial administration (creation of three new regions)

Note: Authors' compilation is based on the situation at the end of 2009. The Senegal legislation uses the term "*collectivités locales*" for all decentralized territorial collectivities. We translate this generic term as "local government" and as specified local government units. The term also corresponds to territorial collectivities (CTs). Local government units or CTs in Senegal include both the regions (first tier) and the communes and rural communities (basic tier)—that is, two levels (as discussed further in the next section).

Organization of Decentralized Local Government and Deconcentration in 2009

Senegal is made up of a territorial network comprising decentralized local government, on one side, and administrative units that are executing agencies for the central state, on the other side. The distinction here between decentralization and deconcentration abides by the definitions and criteria presented in chapter 1.

Structure of Decentralized Local Government

The CCL (Law 96-06) and Law 96-07 on the transfer of powers to the regions, communes, and rural communities (referred to overall as CTs) set forth the arrangements for the free administration of the CTs. This legislation defines the missions and competences of the CTs, their organization, their functioning, and their oversight.

Article 3 of the CCL lays down the fundamental principles of the free administration of the CTs and defines their mission: "the local authorities have the mission to design, programme and implement actions for economic, educational, social and cultural development of regional, communal or rural interest." It also defines their administrative autonomy: "the local authorities are exclusively responsible, in accordance with the laws and regulations, for the appropriateness of their decisions."

Powers are devolved to them in nine sectors: land registry; environment and natural resources management; health, population, and social welfare; youth, sports, and recreation; culture; education; planning; territorial development; and urban planning and housing. "Any transfer of powers to a local authority should, at least, be accompanied by a concomitant transfer from the State of the resources and means necessary for the normal exercise of these powers."[2] The "necessary resources for the exercise of their powers are bestowed upon them either through tax transfers or through grants or through both of them."[3] The state must provide financial compensation for any new cost burdens arising from an amendment by regulation to the rules on the exercise of these powers, including special grants to some CTs if "the lack of resources is likely to compromise the exercise of the public service missions."[4] Other legal characteristics of the CTs include the following:

- Each CT has an executive body, defined by law and elected from the ranks of its council members. It has its own budget (established in compliance with public accounting rules) and own resources. It is staffed by personnel whose status is defined by law.

- The acts of the CTs are reviewed by the state's representatives to ensure they are legally compliant.[5]

- Although CTs are free to cooperate, none has supervisory authority over another.[6] This cooperation can take the form of groups, programs implemented jointly with the central government, or agreements signed with foreign local authorities or public or private international development bodies.[7]

- Finally, the state "guarantees and organises the principle of solidarity between the local authorities. To this end, it creates an allocation fund replenished from its budget."[8]

Senegal has three types of CT: the region, the commune, and the rural community. In urban areas, a commune is referred to as a "town" if its territory is divided into subdistricts (arrondissements), which are called arrondissement communes (CAs). In addition to the CTs, there are intercommunity groups. The CTs are created by decree, which assigns them rural status or otherwise.

The region   The region is the first tier of subnational government. Its territory encompasses two other types of CT: the communes and the CRs. Its boundaries coincide with those of the regional administrative units bearing the same name. As of 2008, there were 14 regions in Senegal, as shown in table 5.2.

The commune   The commune is the basic local government unit. It covers "the inhabitants within the boundaries of the same locality united by neighbourhood solidarity, wishing to manage their own interests and able to find the necessary resources."[9] Only those "localities that are developed enough to have the necessary own resources to balance their budget and that have a combined population of at least one thousand inhabitants"[10] are eligible for commune status. The law imposes no minimum budget requirement to create a commune. Large communes can be divided up (by decree) into CAs (subdistricts) and are then designated as "towns." Only 15 communes have populations of more than 50,000 inhabitants, and fewer than 60 have populations of more than 20,000. Special-status communes no longer exist.

Table 5.2 CTs in Senegal, by Type, 2009

Region	Communes (no.)	Rural communities (no.)	Population from 2002 census (no. and % of total)
Dakar	51 including 5 towns with arrondissement communes • Dakar: 19 • Pikine: 16 • Guédiawaye: 5 • Rufisque: 3 • Thiès: 3	2	2,411,528 (16.26%)
Diourbel	3	34	930,008 (6.27%)
Fatick	7	32	639,075 (4.31%)
Kaolack	7	27	5,128,128 (34.56%)
Kolda	9	31	444,753 (2.997%)
Louga	5	47	559,268 (3.77%)
Matam	10	14	423,041 (2.85%)
Saint-Louis	15	8	863,440 (5.82%)
Tambacounda	7	36	430,332 (2.90%)
Thiès	15	31	1,348,637 (9.09%)
Ziguinchor	5	25	557,606 (3.76%)
Sédhiou	9	29	390,000[a] (2.63%)
Kaffrine	5	21	600,000[a] (4.04%)
Kédougou	3	16	111,207[a] (0.75%)
Total 14	**151**	**353**	**14,837,023 (100%)**

Source: Directorate of Territorial Collectivities (*Direction des collectivités locales;* DCL) 2010.
Note: CT = territorial collectivity.
a. Figures estimated following the creation of three new regions in 2008: Kaffrine, Kédougou, and Sédhiou.

The arrondissement commune   The CAs[11] have exactly the same bodies as the commune: an elected council, though with fewer members; a mayor elected from and among council members; and deputy mayors (fewer in number). The powers of a CA mayor are somewhat narrower in scope than those of a communal mayor. The limits of their powers are defined by law, and their resources are less diversified. For investment projects, coordination is the practice: the town mayor informs the CA mayor about town projects to be carried out within the CA, and vice versa. The CAs are entitled to managerial autonomy in the sense of Article 3 of the CCL.

In all, there are 151 communes in Senegal. Dakar is the region with the highest percentage of population living in communes (or towns): 97 percent in 2006. Elsewhere (except for the region of Fatick), the population is distributed more or less equally between communes and rural communities. At present, the country has five towns: Dakar (19 CAs), Pikine (16 CAs), Guédiawaye (5 CAs), Rufisque (3 CAs), and Thiès (3 CAs).

The rural community   The CR is on the same level of government as the commune, but its economic and demographic criteria are different. It comprises "several villages belonging to the same locality, united by neighbourhood solidarity, having common interests and together able to find the necessary resources."[12] The village consists of several families, parcels of land, or districts grouped into one agglomeration.[13] In 2009, there were 353 CRs. The region of Fatick has the highest proportion of inhabitants living in CRs: 87 percent in 2006.

The CTs' elected bodies   The CTs are administered by councillors elected by direct universal suffrage for five-year terms (as regional councillors or municipal councillors). Each council elects a bureau made up of a president, a first vice president, and second vice presidents, along with two secretaries. A secretary-general, appointed by the president after an opinion from the state's representative, is a government official recruited from among grade A (or equivalent grade) officials. In the case of the communes, the mayor is elected by the municipal councillors. Table 5.3 presents the various government bodies that administer the CTs.

According to the CCL, the elected offices are held for five years, but in practice, these can be extended on a discretionary basis. For example, the mayors of communes and the CRs served seven-year terms between 2002 and 2009.

Grouping of CTs   Grouping of CTs was recognized by a 1983 law on territorial development. The CCL defines four types of grouping, depending on the nature of the activities involved:

• Urban communities, made up of communes
• Community interest groups, made up of communes and CRs

Table 5.3 Local Government Bodies

	Region	Commune	Rural community
Deliberative body	Regional council	Municipal council	Rural council
Term of office	Elected for 5 years by universal suffrage	Elected for 5 years by universal suffrage	Elected for 5 years by universal suffrage
Composition	Bureau:	Bureau:	Bureau:
	• President	• Mayor	• President
	• First vice president	• One or more deputies elected[a]	• Two vice presidents
	• Second vice president		Rural councillors: number ranges from 30 to 80, according to the rural community's population
	• Two secretaries	Municipal councillors: number ranges from 26 to 100, according to the commune's population	
	Regional councillors: number ranges from 50 to 70, according to the region's population		
Decision making	By majority vote (CCL, Art. 47)	By majority vote (CCL, Art. 154)	By majority vote (CCL, Art. 224)
Executive body	President	Mayor	President
Committees	Four statutory committees (CCL, Art. 44)		

Source: CCL 2010.
Note: CCL = Code of Local Government.
a. One deputy mayor for communes with between 1,000 and 2,500 inhabitants; two deputies for communes with between 2,501 and 10,000 inhabitants; and, for communes with over 10,000 inhabitants, one additional deputy per 20,000 inhabitants, with a cap of 18 deputies.

- Associations of CTs (*ententes ou syndicats intercommunaux*), which group several CTs around one or more public services
- Mixed groups, including central government and CTs.

A group of CTs is created or dissolved by decree after deliberation and unanimous decision by the CT councils involved.

In 2004, two urban communities were created within the perimeter of the metropolitan area of Dakar:

- The Community of Agglomerations of Dakar (*Communauté des agglomérations de Dakar*; CADAK), which groups the towns of Dakar, Guédiawaye, and Pikine
- The Community of Agglomerations of Rufisque (*Communauté des agglomérations de Rufisque*; CAR), which groups the town of Rufisque, the communes of Bargny and Diamnadio, and the CRs of Sangalkam and Yene.

Deconcentration and Administrative Units

The deconcentrated administrative units are territorial bodies that represent the central state on national territory. They have no legal identity and constitute the territorial frameworks for public policy. They are organized on three tiers: the regions, the *départements*, and the *arrondissements*, as figure 5.1 illustrates. In this respect, there is a close resemblance with the French organization, in which the map of the administrative units coincides with that of the CTs (except for the *département*, which, in Senegal, is uniquely an administrative unit and not a CT).

These deconcentrated government structures do not appear to have much impact on the financing of decentralized entities, notably on the central government's financial transfers to CTs. In our interviews, the ex ante control of CT budgets by the governor (for the region), the prefect (for the commune

Figure 5.1 Territorial Organization in Senegal

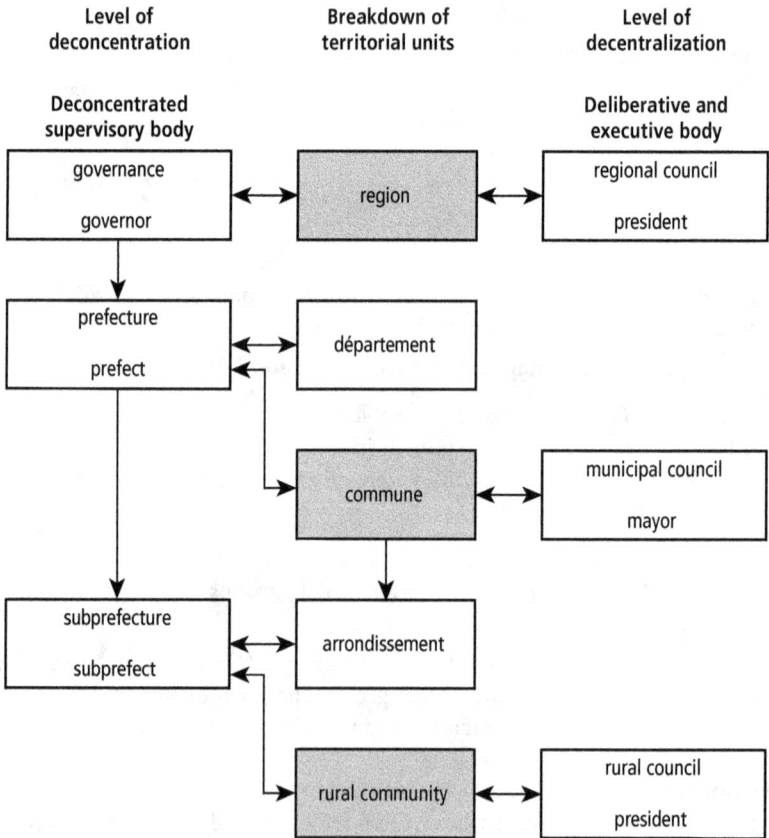

Level of deconcentration	Breakdown of territorial units	Level of decentralization
Deconcentrated supervisory body		Deliberative and executive body
governance / governor	region	regional council / president
prefecture / prefect	département	
	commune	municipal council / mayor
subprefecture / subprefect	arrondissement	
	rural community	rural council / president

Source: Badiane 2004.
Note: The arrows indicate a relationship of supervisory authority.

and the CA), or the subprefect (for the CR) never seemed to be a determining factor in the CT financing system. On the other hand, the state representatives from deconcentrated entities have powers over the provision of state services to CTs, thus over "certain implicit transfers."

Central Government Supervision and Services

Conventionally, relations between central government services and the CTs mobilize a large number of ministries and departments. At the forefront are the Ministry of Finance, the Ministry of the Interior, and the recently created Ministry of Local Government. The research mission focused on these three ministries as well as the Ministry of Education, given the choice to examine decentralization of primary education and its financing. Figure 5.2 summarizes

Figure 5.2 Relations of Central Government, Ministries, Deconcentrated Government Services, and CTs in Senegal

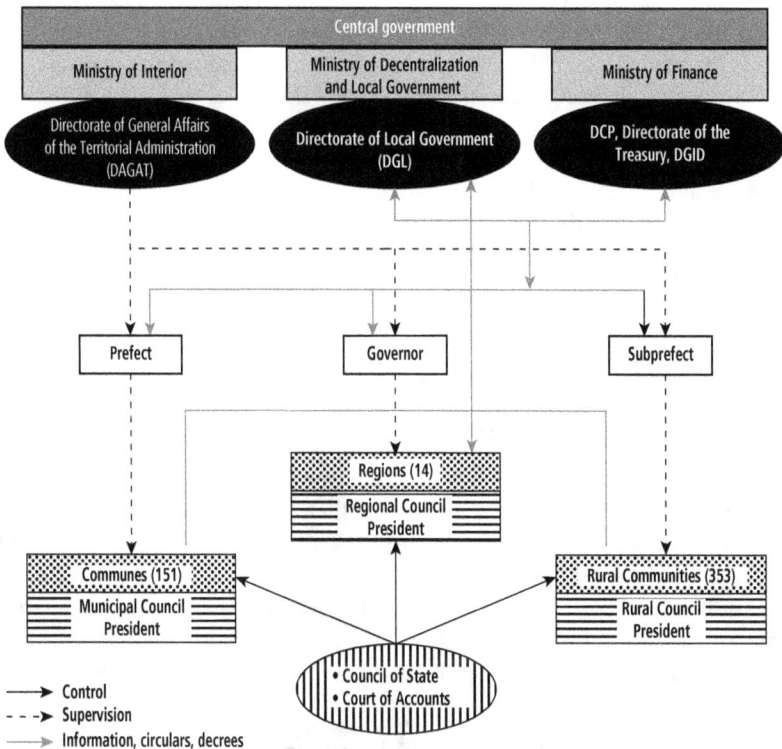

Note: CT = territorial collectivity; DAGAT = Directorate of General Affairs of the Territorial Administration; DCP = *Direction de la comptabilité publique*; DGID = General Directorate of Taxation and Property *(Direction générale des impôts et des domains)*; DGL = Directorate of Local Government.

these relations. The CTs' relationships with the Ministries of the Interior and Finance are further discussed below in the subsection on supervision.

Ministry of local government   Since the 1970s, the department in charge of decentralization and local development has reported to a variety of ministries. The Directorate of Local Government (DCL) is the longest-standing service in the administrative apparatus. In 1872, four communes (Dakar, Gorée, Rufisque, and Saint-Louis) were administered by the communal office attached to the Office of the Governor General of Saint-Louis. The communal office was successively called the Directorate of Communal Affairs (*Direction des affaires communales*), then the Directorate of Local Government Supervision (*Direction de la tutelle des collectivités locales*), and finally the Directorate of Local Government (*Direction des collectivités locales*; DCL).

Before 1980, a state secretariat for decentralization reported to the Ministry of the Interior. Thereafter, several attempts to give it an autonomous status came to nothing. Not until October 2009 was a full-fledged ministry created: the Ministry of Local Government. These various attempts emphasize that the integration of decentralization into the central state's institutional framework is relatively fragile. The DCL comprises four divisions: finance, human resources, structural and planning studies, and archives. There is also the Directorate of General Affairs of the Territorial Administration (*Direction des affaires générales de l'administration territorial*; DAGAT) under the Ministry of the Interior, whose main function, as in France, is to manage relations with the prefectoral authorities and governors.

Supervision and control   The 1996 laws (previously listed in table 5.1) mainly define the operating framework for the CTs, and specifically their relations with the central government. Moreover, the CTs fall within the scope of the organic laws (and are thus governed by their provisions), including those relating to the Court of Accounts, the General Tax Code (*Code général des impôts*; CGI), and the Public Procurement Code (*Code des marchés publics*; CMP).

Reviewing the legality of CT acts   Before Law 96-06 (the CCL), all the acts of the CTs were subject to prior review for their appropriateness by the state's local-level representatives. Since the 1996 laws,[14] all CT acts must be disclosed and transmitted to the local-level state representative who has the authority to review their legality (but not their appropriateness) ex post.[15] By way of derogation, Article 336 of the CCL maintains ex ante supervisory powers in the following six cases, for which CT deliberations are subject to the prior approval of their supervisory authorities:

- Budget controls (initial budget, supplementary budgets, and revenue and expenditure accounts).[16] The state representative attends the regional, municipal, or community councils and may give only an advisory opinion (no voting capacity). He or she is entitled to speak and can oppose any illegal acts, notably those of a budgetary or financial nature at variance with the law. These grounds for intervention give rise to injunctions, followed if necessary by the ex officio establishment of budgets or the issuance of mandatory payment orders. Generally, the reasons are as follows:

o   Budget not approved by March 31

o   A "seemingly balanced" budget (revenue overestimated or expenditure underestimated)

o   "Mandatory expenditures" not entered (see the discussion concerning mandatory expenditures under "Responsibilities Effectively Exercised" and in box 5.2)

o   Excessive deficit in administrative account (of more than 10 percent of operating revenue).

The public accountants for the decentralized administration carry out an ex ante control of expenditure commitments and also make the payments. They are responsible for producing the CTs' revenue and expenditure accounts and report directly to the Treasury.

• Land registry and urban development

• Contracts worth over CFAF 100 million (for the regions); over CFAF 50 million (for communes that are regional capitals with a budget of over CFAF 500 million); or over CFAF 15 million (for the other communes or CRs)

• International cooperation financial agreements over a fixed threshold (variable depending on the type of CT)

• Planning, development plans, and territorial development

• Loans and loan guarantees.

If necessary, the state's representative or any aggrieved party can apply to the administrative court. The Council of State is the judge of any dispute arising from legality controls. Should the state's representative refuse to grant approval, this can be challenged before the Council of State, which has jurisdiction over cases involving the *ultra vires* use of power.

Auditing of accounts   The auditing of accounts is the remit of the state's representatives, the General Inspectorate of Territorial Administration, the General State Inspectorate, the finance services, and the Court of Accounts. The Court of Accounts evaluates all of the CTs' public accountants. The judge carries out an appraisal after hearing the CT's authorizing officer and makes comments to which the CT is invited to reply. The judicial control of accounts is provided for under Articles 342 and 343 of the CCL.

For the smallest communes (with fewer than 15,000 inhabitants and a budget under a threshold set by decree), the clearance of accounts is undertaken by the local-level paymasters, who give full discharge to the accountants or refer contentious matters to the Court of Accounts. For the other communes, the audit by the Court of Accounts is based on supporting documents.

Issues Regarding Local Institutions and Auditing

Based on our field observations, the legality control gives rise to few disputes. Although the prefects' observations are many, shortcomings in transparency seem rare (according to what the prefect of Dakar told us).

Regarding the auditing of accounts, the letter of the law (which is close to the French system) is apparently far from effective on the ground. The Court of Accounts currently has seven magistrates in charge of auditing the accounts of the 503 CTs as well as all other government departments. The presentation of accounts seems to have improved, even though, as of November 2009, the Court of Accounts had not yet received all of the 2007 accounts.

Furthermore, the Court of Accounts magistrates have uncovered several highly specific problem areas:

- Most CTs do not keep administrative accounting records. They produce only revenue and expenditure accounts, and their administrative accounts are little more than "copy-and-pastes" from the revenue and expenditure accounts.

- The absence of supporting documents for revenues complicates the magistrates' auditing task (the CTs do not see the tax rolls).

- The sanctions applied in the event of irregularities lack precise definitions.

The Decentralized Budget

Title V of Law 96-06 of February 5, 1996, concerning the CCL defines the budget framework. The budget is prepared annually by the CT's executive, then voted on by the council and approved by the state's representative, at the latest, by March 31. It must be "complete and detailed (without revenues and expenditures being adjusted or compensated against each other)" (Art. 243–245 and 346). The presentation of the budget is governed by the public accounting rules.

Law 96-06 describes and delimits the CTs' budget resources and expenses (see table 5.5 for the items of expenditure and revenue). The budget and accounts comprise two sections: "ordinary" (including ordinary revenues and operating expenses) and "extraordinary" (including nonrecurrent revenues and investment expenditures). The accounts are recorded in terms of receipts and expenses, thus as actual monetary movements except possibly for balancing operations.

Budget Nomenclature

The Interministerial Decrees No. 10830 of December 1, 1993, and No. 62 of January 30, 1997, lay down the framework for the budget nomenclature to be used by all Senegalese communes, which have no discretion in accounting matters. (This nomenclature predates and differs from that recommended by the West African Economic and Monetary Union, to which Senegal's nomenclature has not been adapted.)

The nomenclature includes a classification by service (functional nomenclature, as shown in table 5.4) and a classification of expenditures and revenues by type (as shown in table 5.5). The classification by expenditure type lists all the expenses traditionally included in public accounts at the international level (the International Monetary Fund's Government Finance Statistics classification, for example).

Budget and Account Presentation Issues

The presentation of the budgets and accounts must combine, without confusing them, the cost centers used for the functional classification (the services) and, at a second level, the classification by type. However, tables 5.4 and 5.5 show a high degree of confusion between these two classification systems. The revenues in table 5.4 follow the system of classification by type, which we find again in table 5.5. These should, in fact, be broken down under the cost centers corresponding to the CT services.

This confusion also appears in the investment expenditure column. For example, the purchase of heavy equipment (item "Chapter 711" in table 5.4) describes the nature of the expenditure: depending on the destination of the equipment, the item should be entered under the relevant cost center (such as in Chapter 371, municipal policing, in table 5.4). What is problematic is the lack of consistency between the operating expenses of cost centers and investments.

Also, the allowances for depreciation (thus the consumption of fixed capital by the CTs)[17] are missing. Gray shaded entries in table 5.5 are neither effective expenditures nor revenues but rather pure internal accounting entries relating to the chosen accounting proceedings. They should not be taken into consideration to fix the final exact result of annual accounts.

It should also be noted that the presentation does not identify the CTs' own resources, only their "ordinary" (operating) revenues. These include revenues from the use of state property and local services; from taxes, including shared-tax revenues transferred from the central government or from other local authorities; the taxes and other levies collected on their behalf; and the annual grants from the allocation fund for local authorities. There is thus no substantive definition of the autonomy of local resources.

Finally, loans are by nature a means of obtaining finance, but they are not capital revenue, at least not revenue in the permanent category. In recording

Table 5.4 Budget Nomenclature of CTs in Senegal, by Service ("Functional" Nomenclature)

Current budget		Capital budget	
Actual expenditure	**Revenue**	**Capital expenditure (classification by service)**	**Capital revenue**
Ch 100 - Excess expenditure at end of year	70 - Revenue from sale of goods and services	Ch 701 - Administrative facilities	10 - Grants
Ch 110 - Debt, dues, insurances	71 - Income from property	Ch 702 - Roads	105 - Allocation fund
Ch 210 - Block shares and contributions	72 - Local taxes	Ch 703 - Protection against accidents and disasters	1050 - Base grant
Ch 313 - President's Office:	720 - Fiscal minimum tax		1051 - State cost-sharing fund
President of the Regional Council, Mayor or President of the Rural Council	721 - Business tax	Ch 704 - Industrial, commercial, or handicraft infrastructure	1052 - Cost-sharing contributions from the Local Government Investment Fund
	722 - Licenses		
	723 - Rural tax	Ch 705 - Health, hygiene, and social welfare	
Ch 313 Bis - Office of the President of the Economic and Social Committee	724 - Tax on developed property		1053 - Local Government Investment Fund
	725 - Tax on undeveloped property	Ch 706 - Education, youth, culture, and sports	1054 - National Solidarity Fund for rural communities
Ch 321 - Secretariat and offices	728 - Ordinary additional taxes		
	729 - Tax shares received from central government	Ch 707 - Information	1055 - Contributions from associations and mutual-aid societies to the construction effort
Ch 322 - Mayor of arrondissement town hall	7290 - Tax on motor vehicles	Ch 708 - Tourism	
	7291 - Capital gains tax on property	Ch 709 - Development actions	1056 - Contribution from properties bordering sidewalk construction
Ch 331 - Regional, municipal, or rural Rates Office	73 - Local taxes		
	730 - Direct taxes	Ch 711 - Purchase of heavy equipment	1059 - Other cost-sharing funds
Ch 341 - Municipal Tax Office	7300 - Additional tax on business tax	Ch 721 - General studies	106 - Capital gifts and bequests
Ch 351 - Slaughterhouses, markets, cold stores			
Ch 361 - Local property	7301 - Tax on horse-drawn vehicles	Ch 731 - Financial operations	107 - Value of properties allocated
Ch 371 - Municipal policing and protection of the population against accidents and disasters	7302 - Sewerage tax	Ch 800 - Excess investment expenditure	108 - Additional nonrecurrent tax
	7303 - Tax on licensed premises		
	7304 - Tax on sewing machines		
Ch 381 - Roads, public squares, and gardens	7305 - Tax on cattle	*Capital expenditure must account for at least one-third of the total amount of estimated expenditure.*	11 - Reserves
	731 - Indirect taxes		115 - Capitalized operating surpluses
Ch 391 - Refuse collection	7310 - Tax on entertainment		
Ch 401 - Workshops and garages	7311 - Tax on night halls		116 - Differences on liquidation of movable and immovable property.
	7312 - Tax on automatic machines		
Ch 411 - Water service	7313 - Tax on advertising		12 - Carry-over
Ch 412 - Sanitation	7314 - Tax on electricity consumption		16 - Long-term loans or debts
Ch 421 - Public lighting			
Ch 431 – Economic intervention	7315 - Tax on water consumption		160 - Government loans
	7316 - Tax on rental of furnished accommodation		161 - Bank loans
Ch 441 - Education, youth, culture, and sports	7317 - Tax on fuel distribution		162 - Loans from foreign or international bodies
Ch 451 - Health, hygiene, and social welfare	74 - Miscellaneous revenues		

(continued next page)

Table 5.4 (continued)

Current budget		Capital budget	
Actual expenditure	Revenue	Capital expenditure (classification by service)	Capital revenue
Ch 461 - Cemeteries and funeral services Ch 508 - Public feasts and ceremonies Ch 509 - Miscellaneous expenditures	75 - Operating grants 754 - Local equalization fund and Intercommunity development fund 755 - Decentralization allocation fund 76 - Reimbursements, cost-sharing contributions, contributions 77 - Interest and dividends received 78 - Capital works under local authority control 79 - Nonrecurrent revenue		

Source: Interministerial Decree No. 10830 MEFP/M.INT. of December 1, 1993, concerning local government budget nomenclature, modified.

Table 5.5 Budget Classification of CTs in Senegal, by Category

Current budget	
Current expenditure	Current revenue
60. Deficit carried over	120. Operating surplus (carried over from t-1)
61. Materials and supplies consumed	70. Revenue from sale of goods and services
62. Transport consumed	71. Income from state property (rental of souks, stands and stalls, restaurants, snack bars, booths and canteens, market stall fees, fees for occupancy of public property, and so on)
63. Other services consumed (works, supplies, and external services)	
64. Miscellaneous expenses and losses (including grants and elected officials)	72. Local taxes
	720. Fiscal minimum tax
65. Personnel expenditure	7202. Household refuse collection charge
66. Taxes and other levies	721. Business tax
67. Interest and other financial expenses (including interest paid, costs of services under concession or leased)	722. Licenses
	723. Tax on developed property
68. Transfer to investment expenditure (operating section balancing operation)	724. Tax on undeveloped property
	725. Shared-tax transfer (taxes shared with central government)
	7290. Tax on motor vehicles
	7291. Capital gains tax on property
	73. Municipal user charges or fees
	74. Miscellaneous revenues

(continued next page)

Table 5.5 (continued)

Current budget	
Current expenditure	**Current revenue**
	75. Operating grants (cost-sharing contributions, Decentralization Allocation Fund, exceptional grants, and so on)
	76. Reimbursements and participations
	77. Financial revenues (including revenue from services under concession)
120. Operating result: surplus	60. Operating result: deficit
Capital budget	
Ch. 20 Expenses and value of intangible fixed assets (cost-sharing contributions, studies, and so on)	
Ch. 21 Land	
Ch. 22 Tangible fixed assets (construction and buildings)	
Ch. 24 Fixed asset losses	
Ch. 25 Loans and other long-term debt	
Ch. 27 Earmarked grants	

Source: Compilation from Interministerial Decree 10830 MEFP/M.INT. of December 1, 1993, on local government budget nomenclature, modified.
Note: CT = territorial collectivity (*collectivité territorial*); gross saving = excess current revenue over "actual current expenditure" (current expenditure less the transfer to the benefit of investment expenditure). Gray shaded entries are neither effective expenditures nor revenues but pure internal accounting entries relating to the chosen accounting proceedings. They should not be taken into consideration to fix the final exact result of annual accounts.

loans as revenue in the capital budget—in compliance with the Senegalese accounting standard—the capital section of the budget is inevitably always balanced. This practice can hide the fact that a loan, which is a financial resource today, implies repayment and thus real revenue tomorrow. It is for this reason precisely that the balanced budget rule requires that a CT's gross surplus (after payment of interest on debt) be at least equal to capital repayment of loans. This means that contracting a loan today is indeed a temporary means of funding that comes with an obligation to raise real revenue tomorrow. We find a similar obligation with respect to accounts, where the closing balance (deficit) must not exceed a certain percentage of current revenues.

Assignment of Responsibilities

A distinction will be made between the responsibilities set out in law and the functions and competences effectively performed by the CTs. Except for some specific cases, the law does not set standards for goods and services provision.

Responsibilities Defined in Law

The CCL confers on the CTs (excluding the CUs) an overall competence defined as the "design, planning and implementation of economic, educational, social and cultural development actions bearing a regional, communal or rural interest."[18] Article 5 assigns and distributes specific responsibilities in nine functional areas. These responsibilities, under common law for the communes, do not apply to the CAs, whose responsibilities are precisely specified by Law 96-09 (Art. 8). Expenditures pertaining to the responsibilities transferred involve both current and capital expenditure.

The responsibilities are outlined in table 5.6.[19] Most of the responsibilities transferred to the CTs concern education and health. This transfer does not lead to the automatic reassignment of staff formerly employed by the central government for managing these functions. Both before and after the laws on decentralization and competences, the communes have had the power to hire communal personnel (for example, a doctor for the communal health center) and keep them on. These employees do not have the status of local government officials because there is no local government civil service. Education is a case apart because all teaching staff are central government officials, the regions and communes being limited to hiring support staff (such as caretakers). Finally, CRs are not empowered to pay salaries, which means that if they wish to recruit a caretaker or gardener, this service must be contracted out to a company that then bills them for the services that they have to provide.

Finally, in the special case of the region of Dakar (see box 5.1), intercommunal structures (the CADAK and the CAR) perform the responsibilities that have been reassigned to them by the member communes. The CADAK has opted to mostly delegate management to private companies to manage its responsibilities, but it retains overall ownership. The CADAK and the CAR are responsible for street cleaning and managing household refuse as well as for building and maintaining part of the municipal roads and public lighting.

Responsibilities Effectively Exercised

Law 96-07 does not always require the CTs to perform some of the responsibilities or tasks that are nonetheless defined as their areas of competence. Furthermore, it only rarely defines standards for the provision of goods and services or the delivery of goods. This is the case, for example, in the areas of education (see box 5.3) and health and hygiene that involve obligations to take in pupils or the sick. Thus, mandatory responsibilities are not defined in terms of what the services must provide but rather in terms of *expenditures*, referred to as "mandatory expenditures."

These mandatory expenditures (set forth in box 5.2) are to be included in the budget either because (a) the law requires all CTs (or those that fulfill certain conditions) to do so; or (b) although the law gives CTs the *option* of providing

Table 5.6 Responsibilities Transferred to the CTs in Senegal[a]

Functions	Regions	Communes	Rural communities
Management and use of state private property, public property, and national property	Nonclassified roads (public domain) Management of zones in the public maritime or fluvial domains, subject to special development plans	Idem.	Idem.
Environment and natural resource management	CCL, Art. 28 13 responsibilities transferred, including the following: Management, protection, and maintenance of forests, protected areas, wildlife, and inland waters; implementation of fire belts and early burning Distribution of forestry exploitation quotas; creation of voluntary brigades for environmental protection	CCL, Art. 29 (Law 2002) 6 responsibilities transferred, including the following: Management of felling, reforestation, waste Fight against insalubrity, pollution, and nuisances; protection of ground and surface water resources Formulation of action plans for the environment	Art. 30 12 responsibilities transferred, including the following: Management of forests, reforestation, waste, and fight against insalubrity Setting up of watchdog committees to combat bushfires; authorization for felling, land clearing, and farm-out Creation and maintenance of woodlands and protected areas and artificial ponds
Public health and social welfare	Art. 31 *Mandatory responsibilities:* Management, maintenance, and equipment of regional and departmental hospitals; implementation of preventive health and hygiene measures Contribution to the maintenance and management of centers for the promotion of social rehabilitation and health centers located in CRs	Art. 32 Building, management, and maintenance of health posts and centers Contribution to the maintenance and management of centers for the promotion of social rehabilitation; organization and management of assistance to the needy; support to the financing of productive projects for the poor	Art. 33 Building, management, and maintenance of rural health posts, maternities, and health houses Contribution to the maintenance and management of centers for the promotion of social rehabilitation; management of assistance to the needy; support to the financing of productive projects for the poor

Table 5.6 (continued)

Functions	Regions	Communes	Rural communities
Youth, sports, and recreation (Art. 34–36)	Art. 34 *7 mandatory responsibilities, including the following:* Authorizations for opening educational groups Provision of community, socioeducational, and sports infrastructures with regional status; control of physical and sports activities at regional level; management of staff put at its disposal	Art. 35 *6 mandatory responsibilities, including the following:* Promotion and running of sports and youth activities; socioeducational practices; support for sports and cultural associations; management of stadiums, sports centers, tracks, swimming pools, wrestling areas, and so on; organization of competitions	Art. 36 Identical to communes, adapted to the rural level
Culture (Art. 37–39)	Art. 37 *5 mandatory responsibilities, including the following:* Promotion, enhancement, and development of cultural activities Monitoring historic sites and monuments; organization of cultural days, traditional cultural events, and literary and artistic competitions; setting up orchestras and traditional singing groups, theater troupes, community centers, and libraries	Art. 38 Identical to the region, except for the cultural policies	Art.39 Identical to the communes and collection of oral traditions (tales and myths) and promotion of national and local culture
Education, promotion of national languages, and vocational training (Art. 40–42)	Art. 40 Education: 6 responsibilities, including regional school map; equipment, upkeep, and maintenance of secondary schools; recruitment and support-staff salaries; provision of scholarships, textbooks, and contribution to the management of secondary schools	Art. 41 Education: 5 responsibilities, including construction, equipment, upkeep, and maintenance of primary schools and preschool facilities; recruitment and payment of costs for support staff; provision of scholarships and school grants, textbooks, and stationery; management and administration	Art. 42 Education: 3 responsibilities, including construction, equipment, upkeep, and maintenance of primary schools and preschool facilities; provision of textbooks and stationery, management and administration

(continued next page)

225

Table 5.6 (continued)

Functions	Regions	Communes	Rural communities
	Literacy: 10 responsibilities, including literacy map and plan for eliminating illiteracy, management of literacy teachers (except salaries), educational infrastructures and equipment Promotion of national languages: almost all responsibilities Vocational training: 10 responsibilities, including an inventory of regional trades and the elaboration of a directory of vocational training	Literacy: *Idem* region adapted to the communal level Promotion of national languages: *Idem* region adapted to the communal level Vocational training: *idem* region adapted to communal level	Literacy: *Idem* region and communes Promotion of national languages: *Idem* region and communes adapted to the rural level Vocational training: *idem* communes adapted to the rural level
Planning (Art. 43–46), Art. 37 of the CCL, assistance for formulating CT development plans with state contributions: Regional Development Agency (ARD) (Art. 43)	Art. 44 Design, coordination, and negotiation with the state for contracts for economic, social, sanitary, cultural, and scientific development plans (regional plans for integrated development [PRDI])	Art. 45 Identical to the region for communal investment plans	Art. 46 Identical to the local rural development plans
Territorial development (Art. 47–49)	Art. 47 Elaboration of a regional development plan (SRAT) in line with the national plan	Art. 48 Opinion on the draft SRAT at communal level prior to approval by the central government	Art.49 Identical to the communes, adapted to the CRs
Urban planning and housing (Art. 50–53) and coordinating studies under the ARD's responsibility (Art. 53)	Art. 50 Approval of master plans for regional development and urban planning and support to communes and communities	Art. 51 Elaboration of urban-planning master plans (PDU), regional development and urban-planning master plans (SDAU), detailed urban planning for concerted development zones (ZAC), urban renewals and regrouping of lands; building permits, subdivisions, planning certificates, licenses for demolition, fencing, and felling	Art. 52 Identical to the communes

Source: Compilation from the CCL 2010.
Note: CCL = Code of Local Government; CR = rural community; CT = territorial collectivity.
a. The table excludes CA responsibilities

Box 5.1

Financing and Responsibility Assignments in the Region of Dakar

Financing Urban Transport

The Urban Transport Development Fund (*Fonds de développement des transports urbains*; FDTU) was created in 1997, and its institutions were set up by Law 2003-20 of July 20, 2003. Members of the fund include the state; the region of Dakar; the towns of Dakar, Guédiawaye, Pikine, and Rufisque; the communes of Bargny, Diamniado, and Sébikhotane; and private stakeholders. It undertakes multiyear investment programs and contributes to their implementation.

The FDTU is replenished annually by central government contributions (the largest share); the territorial collectives (CTs) (in principle, on a par with the central government for a sum of CFAF 400 million, although this has been temporarily reduced); and private stakeholders. The fund also has income from investments as well as from user charges and fees from the operation of urban infrastructure and amenities. The CTs' participation is defined proportionally based on population and the level of their operating revenues. In practice, the FDTU is not truly operational.

Waste Management

The responsibilities of the Community of Agglomerations of Dakar (CADAK), notably in the areas of household refuse collection, were taken over by the central government after the urban commune of Dakar encountered problems in this domain. The commune found itself unable to satisfactorily assume this responsibility because of its choice of arrangements for sharing the funding with the arrondissement communes (CAs) at the time they were created, and the impossibility of funding household refuse collection led to repeated strikes.

After the central government (following intervention by the state inspector general and an opinion from the Council of State) had issued a deficiency report (which pointed out service disruptions, recurrent cash-flow problems, and a buildup of debts, among other issues), it took over this responsibility from the urban community (CU). The concession contract that the CU had signed with an Italian company (which proved to be a failing firm) was terminated, and management of the service was split into two parts. The central government took over and now directly manages the personnel (1,900 employees) while transport and landfill disposal were contracted out to local private companies (one per zone), paid on a tonnage basis.

In 2005, the CADAK and the Community of Agglomerations of Rufisque (CAR) reached an intercommunal agreement on waste management.[a] The budget to manage urban solid waste for the region of Dakar was put into a Ministry of the Environment account, with the president of the CADAK-CAR agreement having the exclusive authority to release funds. Currently, this mechanism seems to be a subject of debate.

Note: a. Decree 2006-1021 of October 4, 2006, on the transfer of powers.

Box 5.2

Mandatory Expenditures for Communes (Law 96-07)

- Office expenditures, archives, basic administrative documentation
- Maintenance of territorial collective (CT) headquarters (excluding lavish improvements)
- Expenditures for registers and civil-status documents as well as payment of government officials responsible for civil registration in the arrondissement communes (CAs)
- Expenditure for the collection of local taxes
- Wages and salaries of permanent staff and remuneration of the government officials belonging to other administrations responsible for local service
- Pensions and allowances
- Maintenance of cemeteries and urban-planning plans
- Taxes and other levies on the CT's revenues
- Payment of debts due (notably expenses authorized but not settled, interest on debts, and capital repayments)
- Maintenance and cleaning of communal roads
- Provision of local public services set out in the law or regulations
- Disinfection and hygiene in compliance with regulations
- Mandatory contribution to national fire protection service (2 to 3.5 percent of ordinary revenues)
- Expenditure and participation for development expenditures listed in approved development plans
- Expenditures resulting from the transfer of central government powers under the provisions laid down in the laws on the transfer of powers (Art. 259).

Box 5.3

CTs' Responsibilities for the Primary Education Function

Responsibilities assigned to territorial collectives (CTs) in the area of primary education involve only communes and rural communities (CRs) (the regions being responsible for lower and higher secondary schools). Our various interviews (with the Ministry of Education, mayors, and school principals) enabled us to assess which responsibilities are actually discharged by the communes (or arrondissement communes, CAs) and CRs.

(continued next page)

Box 5.3 (continued)

Responsibilities for teaching staff and control over the "school map," the school program, and textbook content have not been transferred to the CTs and lie instead with the Education Inspectorate. On the other hand, recruitment of nonteaching support staff (for example, caretakers or gardeners) and the provision of textbooks and school materials are the communes' responsibility.

For the CRs, a good share of school operating expenses is paid by the School Fund, which is funded by parents—those who can afford to pay—through a minimum enrollment fee per child and optional additional contributions. This fund makes it possible to buy textbooks and school materials and remunerate support staff (mainly caretakers). If the School Fund cannot provide textbooks and school materials or pay for the maintenance of the school, the central government bears the cost of these services. Textbooks and materials can also be given as gifts by associations, including international associations.

The maintenance of the premises is rarely or not at all ensured. In principle, transfers from the Decentralization Allocation Fund (*Fonds de dotation de la decentralisation;* FDD) (see box 5.4) should finance the responsibility of day-to-day maintenance. This provision is included in the decree sent to the CTs as part of the "mandatory expenditures for the education function."

At the level of capital expenditure, the ministry confirmed to us, for example, that no CT had yet borne the entire cost of constructing a primary school. In the wealthiest urban communes, the largest commitments made were for building an extra classroom or sanitary facilities, for instance. This means that it is central government or donor funding, through programs like the Education Plan for Dakar Suburbs (*Plan d'éducation dans les banlieues de Dakar*), that makes school construction possible.

Box 5.4

Funding the Recurrent Operating Expenditure: The Road Network Program

The Autonomous Road Maintenance Fund (*Fonds d'entretien routier autonome*) was created on September 30, 2007. It is administered by representatives from the central government, the territorial collectives (CTs), and civil society and funded through the taxes on petroleum products. The Community of Agglomerations of Dakar (CADAK) is not the only entity that can claim a share of the fund, and it is thus currently evaluating the recurrent maintenance costs (net of tolls), stating its wish to adjust its maintenance expenditures in line with the total share it will receive from the fund (the sharing will be based on "objective" criteria not yet finalized—or at least not yet published) and from operating revenues.

some public services, they *should* choose to do so, which also requires them to enter these mandatory expenditures into their budgets. Mandatory expenditures are restrictively listed by law.[20]

Mandatory expenditures must be included in a CT's budget, failing which the draft budget will be refused by the state representative vested with supervisory authority. As in the communes, the CAs are required to budget for mandatory expenditures, notably those arising from projects decided upon jointly with the town, the central government, or any public body. All other expenditures are optional.

Competences Effectively Exercised through Local Expenditures

In Senegal, the local public expenditure system and the central government expenditure system follow the same rules. The local system is based on the principle of *separation of the authorizing officers from the public accountants* (expenditures are committed by the authorizing officer, controlled for conformity by the financial controller, then certified, cleared for payment, and paid). This principle and process ensure that expenditures comply with the legally required conditions of regularity and are also in line with the decisions of the local assemblies.

Nonetheless, the link between the functions and competences exercised and the expenditures as they appear in the budgets and accounts is relatively weak, which makes it impossible to accurately retrace the CTs' budgetary effort for each of the responsibilities involved. There are several reasons for this weak link, and here we will mention the five main ones.

Inflexibility of local expenditures   Local expenditures are often inflexible, either because they are directly based on the expenditure structure of the central government before the transfer of responsibilities or because management of the current budget has become a routine matter.

Focus on balanced accounts, not cost assessment   The local accounting system, by nature, is almost exclusively focused on respecting the rule of producing balanced budgets and accounts rather than on ascertaining the costs of providing public services. In those accounts based on a functional classification, many of the expenditures are not disaggregated. It is thus doubtful that the expenditures listed in the CTs' budgets will allow the full cost of the local public services to be evaluated—particularly given these three factors:

- The central government bears some of the costs of providing the transferred services, and the consolidation of CT and central costs is far from perfect. The consolidation involves compensation through the FDD for the supply of material and human resources to the CTs for the responsibilities transferred.

- Other actors intervene in local public service provision, and their contribution, like that of the central government, is inadequately recognized in the accounts or even ignored. The case of the town of Dakar illustrates this point. The Public Expenditure and Financial Accountability (PEFA) report for the town of Dakar lists the entities and institutions for which certain expenses are absent in the CT's accounts (Giovanni and Chomentowski 2009, 18 *ff.*). In the main, they involve the schools, community centers, and health centers that were brought within the communal boundaries by the laws on the transfer of powers. The underestimated amounts are probably minimal in the case of schools—which do not have their own budgets or substantial own resources—and thus most of the school-related expenditures (except for teaching staff) are included in the communal budget. This is not the case for community centers, for which the town assumes expenditures for buildings and staff but not for grants to associations—likewise for health center and hospital expenditures, for which the town bears only a part of the costs. The expenditures of the *Crédit communal* (an institution offering loans to individuals) are only partly known, as are the operating expenses incurred by the services of the municipal rates office. The remaining expenditures are assumed by the central government or other actors (associations; other CTs; and private, public, national, or international donors).

- The overlapping expenditures of the town of Dakar and the CAs are only partly reported. The CAs, which have restrictively defined responsibilities, are self-governing like all the other communes. However, they receive grants from the town for their operation (see box 5.5), and some of their current expenditures, mainly for personnel, are borne by the town (in Dakar, this

Box 5.5

Financial Relations of CADAK Member Towns, Including Dakar

The law provides that the resources of the communities may come from international donor grants, member-town contributions, government grants through the Decentralization Allocation Fund (*Fonds de dotation de la décentralisation;* FDD), the Fund for Local Government Infrastructures (*Fonds d'équipement des collectivités locales;* FECL), or any other fund as well as from gifts. Each town's contribution is determined annually by a decree of the Ministry of Decentralization and Local Government based on the ordinary revenues (business tax included) collected by the towns over the three previous years.

(continued next page)

Box 5.5 (continued)

The Community of Agglomerations of Dakar (CADAK) receives the member-towns' contributions (CFAF 250 million in 2006), including CFAF 190 million from Dakar, CFAF 15 million from Guédiawaye, and CFAF 15 million from Pikine. The CADAK's other current resources are provided exclusively by the central government, which finances the salaries (about CFAF 75,000 a month) of 1,900 refuse collection employees through the CADAK's treasury account, replenished by an independent budget line ("supplementary state actions"). The CADAK's capital spending, which does not appear in its budget, is covered by a special Treasury account. (A 1999 law establishes the special status of Dakar, authorizing payment through the consolidated investment budget.)

Aid from foreign donors is not direct but instead transits through the central government (as of the 1999 establishment of the Support Program to Communes [*Programme d'appui aux communes*; PAC] and later the Program to Strengthen Local Government Investment [*Programme de renforcement et d'équipement des collectivités locales*; PRECOL]). Funding through this channel is devoted to urban development and involves, to a large extent, intercommunity groups (which receive 38 percent of PRECOL funds). What is involved here, therefore, is the cofinancing of investment (and operations) by the Senegalese state (through the FDD, FECL, and other funds) and international donors.

In the case of the CADAK, the investment aid received through PRECOL is devoted exclusively to developing the CADAK's road infrastructure. The source of funding is shared between aid from (a) the Senegalese state (providing 10 percent plus the contribution required for clearing the rights of way for the roads program, estimated at about CFAF 1 million in 2009); and (b) international donors (the World Bank and Agence Française de Développement (AFD) providing 90 percent).

In all, the CADAK and the CAR receive, respectively, CFAF 21 billion and CFAF 5 billion from PRECOL. The CFAF 21 billion received by the CADAK includes CFAF 20 billion for investment in road networks and CFAF 1 billion for "institutional support," representing a grant to supplement operating resources, specifically the costs of strategic studies. The road network projects primarily involve the construction of expressways (including toll highways) on the territory of the three towns (the Dakar port road network; the airport zone road network; and expressways to and within Guédiawaye, to Pikine, to a forest area, and to Rufisque). For these investment projects, the CADAK is the project owner, the Public Works Executing Agency (*Agence d'exécution des travaux d'intérêt public*; AGETIP) is the delegated project owner, and the Municipal Development Agency (*Agence de développement municipal*; ADM) is the executing agency.

---

represents a little under half of the town's expenditures). The town, however, receives no precise information on these expenditures.

The arrangements for the towns' overall grants to their CAs are defined annually by a presidential decree countersigned by the prime minister.[21] The aggregate amount to be distributed is calculated as a fraction (10 percent) of average revenues over the three previous years—40 percent of which is allocated among the CAs on a lump-sum basis and in equal shares, and 60 percent of which is allocated according to population size.

Expenditure obligations The expenditure obligations stemming from the financial transfer formulas affect the structure of local expenditures.[22] The grant from the FDD to each CT is a general-purpose grant,[23] which means that the funds can be freely assigned. However, this grant has been allocated for expenditures relating to the transferred responsibilities,[24] including these functions: national education, public health and social welfare, youth and sport, regional services for planning, territorial development, urban planning and housing, and environment and natural resource management. It specifies how the central government allocated its spending among these different functions in the year before their transfer and encourages the presidents or local executives to use this as a guide, with support from the administrative authorities, in a spirit of collaboration and consultation.

In other words, although the use of the FDD grant is not a question of *mandatory* expenditures, local elected officials were asked to try to structure their expenditures to match, as closely as possible, the previous spending pattern. In fact, the decrees on expenditure allocation define how resources are to be assigned to the responsibilities for which they are intended. As a practical matter, only four functions are involved: health and education collectively represent nearly 80 percent of the funds spent by central government, and the budget lines for culture and for youth and sports account for the remaining 20 percent. In other words, the nine other assigned functions were, in all likelihood, either not performed by the central government before the transfer or were perhaps concentrated in a limited number of CTs.

The transfer amounts received by the CTs as compensation for the assigned functions (that is, around 70 percent of the FDD) remain extremely modest. For 2009, they totaled CFAF 14.6 billion, which indicates that few services can be effectively provided by the CTs.

Front-end commitments Many CTs automatically commit expenditures at the beginning of the year for the salaries of municipal employees and the charges for subscription services such as electricity, water, and telephone. Moreover, there are also invoices concerning works contracts (committed before the public procurement reform was implemented in 2008). In the case of the town of Dakar, 80 percent of expenditures fall outside the scope of the standard procedure for commitments and control of committed expenditures (Giovanni and Chomentowski 2009, 10).

Limits of local public expenditures   Finally, as the "Balancing Local Budgets and Debt" section will further describe, local public expenditures are modest, be they operating or investment expenditures.

All of these five reasons raise doubts about the effectiveness of certain transfers of responsibilities to the CTs.

Issues Regarding the Exercise of Transferred Responsibilities

Few responsibilities are exclusive: many are performed at overlapping levels of local government. Planning, for example, involves local development plans and community investment plans as well as local or regional plans for integrated development.

In the towns, responsibilities are shared more clearly. The CAs have limited but exclusive responsibilities: management of their local markets; small-scale sanitation and hygiene works; participation in household refuse collection; monitoring and routine maintenance of public lighting; desanding and maintenance of roads, squares, and green spaces; and maintenance of school, sanitation, sports, and community equipment.[25]

Yet in practice (and in the minds of the CAs' elected officials, according to the prefect of Dakar), things are not quite so clear-cut. As in all decentralized states, the local elected officials seek to increase their legitimacy and thus the scope of their powers.

The concept of mandatory expenditures linked to the transferred responsibilities is of only relative use. The levels of local spending are the same as they were before decentralization. Controls of their legality are de facto ineffective.

Many of the responsibilities laid down by law are not truly carried out and, in any event, not using CT funding (such as for municipal policing and roads). Based on our interviews, the responsibilities truly discharged at the local level seem to relate mainly to three functions: education, health, and youth and sports. The other responsibilities, although legally assigned to the CTs, are performed using the financial and human resources of the central government (or foreign donors, if need be). The decentralization of responsibilities is thus incomplete, even ineffective.

At the same time, however, the demand for a greater degree of decentralization is making itself felt through political pressure (as our interviews with regional and CA representatives indicated).

Moreover, the way in which the laws on responsibilities are written allows gray areas to persist. The precise delimitation of powers remains unclear in some of the transferred areas of responsibility—for example, in river water management. The dividing line between CA and town responsibilities is clearly problematic, as the PEFA report points out regarding electrification and the management of souks and markets (Giovanni and Chomentowski 2009, 4, 21).

Local Taxation

Excluding resources provided by the central government (in the form of grants, cost-sharing contributions, participations, and advances)—which the following section ("Intergovernmental Transfers") addresses—local resources include taxes and other levies, income from property and land, user charges and fees, and miscellaneous revenues (as shown in tables 5.7, 5.8, and 5.9). In Senegal, the concept of "own resources" for the CTs is neither defined in the legislation nor used. The communes, the CAs, and the CRs do not have the same resources in terms of either composition or amounts.

Table 5.7 Operating Revenues of the Communes (Towns) in Senegal[a]

Local taxes	User charges or fees and revenues from communal property	Investment revenues	Miscellaneous revenues
1.1. Direct taxes • Fiscal minimum tax (and the tax representing the minimum tax, TRIMF [Taxe Représentative de l'Impôt du Minimum Fiscal]) • Business tax • Tax on developed property • Tax on undeveloped property • Surcharge on undeveloped or insufficiently developed property • Licenses 1.2. Additional percentage tax • On the fiscal minimum tax and on the TRIMF • On business tax • On licenses 1.3. Direct communal taxes • Tax on the value of professional premises • Tax on household refuse collection • Street cleaning tax • Sewerage tax • Licenses payable by traders selling beverages in addition to business licenses • Tax on sewing machines used for professional purposes • Tax on horse-drawn vehicles	2.1. Revenues from communal property 2.1.1. Revenues from private property: • Rental of buildings or communal land • Deductions for housing and furnishings • Rental of souks, butcher's booths or rooms, restaurants, snack bars, and shops 2.1.2. Revenues from public property: • Fees for places in covered markets, fairs, markets, slaughterhouses, and stockyards • Road occupancy fees • Land used for burials • Cemetery concessions • Pound charges • Charge on cafe terraces, balconies, and protruding constructions • Revenues from permits for parking and occupancy of the public highway	• Gifts and bequests together with investment costs • Cost-sharing contributions • Loan funds • Proceeds from the disposal of assets, the sale or exchange of properties • Proceeds from the sale of impounded animals or equipment not reclaimed within prescribed deadline • Revenue from the duly authorized nonrecurrent additional percentage tax • Memorandum items, capital transfer, or cost-sharing contributions from central government to carry out investments scheduled by central government on communal land • Contributions from partners under budget support programs	• Sixty percent of receipts from fines imposed by criminal courts or police fines for violations and petty offenses committed within the commune's jurisdiction • Revenue from communal services • Reimbursement of staff hospitalization expenses • Fees for the issuance of administrative and civil registration documents • Fees for signature legalization • Fees for storage of coffins • Revenue from funerals and charge for erecting a cemetery monument • Charge for disinfecting and insect control • Eventual or unexpected revenues

(continued next page)

Table 5.7 (continued)

Local taxes	User charges or fees and revenues from communal property	Investment revenues	Miscellaneous revenues
1.4. Indirect taxes			
• Slaughter tax • Tax on distribution of gasoline, diesel, and all other fuels • Tax on electricity consumption • Water tax • Tax on advertising (billposting or signs) • Tax on night halls • Tax on health inspection of oysters and mussels • Tax on paid admissions • Tax on entertainment and gaming • Tax on furnished accommodation			

Source: General Tax Code (Code général des impôts) Law 1992–40, situation at the end 2010.
a. Excluding central government contributions.

Table 5.8 Revenues of the Arrondissement Communes in Senegal[a]

Local taxes	User charges or fees and revenues from property	Investment revenues	Miscellaneous revenues
1.1. Direct taxes • Fiscal minimum tax (and TRIMF) • Licenses • Business tax 1.2. Indirect taxes • Tax on distribution of gasoline, diesel, and all other fuels • Tax on electricity consumption • Tax on water consumption • Tax on paid admissions • Tax on entertainment and gaming • Tax on horse-drawn vehicles	2.1. Revenues from communal property 2.1.1. Revenues from private property: • Rental of buildings of communal land • Deductions for housing and furnishings • Rental of souks, butcher's booths or rooms, restaurants, snack bars, and shops 2.1.2. Revenues from public property: • Fees for places in covered markets, fairs, markets, slaughterhouses, and stockyards • Charge on cafe terraces, balconies, and protruding constructions • Revenues from permits for parking and occupying the public highway	• Gifts and bequests together with investment costs • Cost-sharing contributions • Proceeds from the disposal of assets, the sale or exchange or properties	• Thirty percent of receipts from fines imposed by criminal courts or police fines for violations and petty offenses committed within the commune's jurisdiction • Revenue from services provided by the CAs • Reimbursement of staff hospitalization expenses • Fees for the issuance of administrative and civil registration documents • Fees for signature legalization • Charge for disinfecting and insect control • Contingent or unexpected revenues

Source: General Tax Code (*Code général des impôts*) Law 1992–40, situation at the end 2010.
Note: TRIMF = tax representing the minimum tax (*Taxe Représentative de l'Impôt du Minimum Fiscal*)
a. Excluding central government contributions.

Table 5.9 Revenues of the Rural Communes in Senegal[a]

Local taxes	User charges or fees and revenues from property	Investment revenues	Miscellaneous revenues
1.1. Direct taxes • Fiscal minimum tax and TRIMF • Tax on developed property • Tax on undeveloped property • Business tax • Licenses 1.2. Additional percentage tax (capped at 50 additional centimes) • On the fiscal minimum tax and on the TRIMF • On business tax • On licenses 1.3. Indirect taxes • Tax on distribution of gasoline, diesel, and all other fuels • Slaughter tax	2.1. Revenues from communal property 2.1.1. Revenues from private property: • Rental of buildings of communal land • Deductions for housing and furnishings • Rental of souks, butcher's booths or rooms, restaurants, snack bars, and shops 2.1.2. Revenues from public property: • Fees for places in covered markets, fairs, markets, slaughterhouses, and stockyards • Charges on cafe terraces, balconies, and protruding constructions • Revenues from permits for parking or occupancy of the public highway • Revenues from road occupancy charges • Pound charges	• Gifts and bequests involving further investment costs • Cost-sharing contributions • Proceeds from the disposal of assets, the sale or exchange or properties	• Sixty percent of receipts from fines imposed by criminal courts or police fines for violations and petty offenses committed within the commune's jurisdiction • Fees for the issuance of administrative and civil registration documents • Fees for signature legalization

Source: General Tax Code (*Code général des impôts*) Law 1992–40, situation at the end 2010.
Note: TRIMF = tax representing the minimum tax (*Taxe Représentative de l'Impôt du Minimum Fiscal*)
a. Excluding central government contributions.

A distinction is made between ordinary (operating) resources and investment resources. These are then broken down either by type or by functional classification.

As in all unitary states, even decentralized ones, the organization of (local) taxes lies within the exclusive competence of the Senegalese state. Yet because financial transfers from the central government do not make up the major part of the CTs' resources, the CTs rely overwhelmingly on taxes. (In Dakar in 2007, 92 percent of fiscal revenues recorded in the administrative account are collected by the General Directorate of Taxation and Property [*Direction générale des impôts et des domains*; DGID].) They cannot therefore neglect this source of income. In recent years (between 2004 and 2006), the share of taxes in total communal resources has, in fact, increased by 4 percentage points.

Local taxes are listed under the General Tax Code (*Code général des impôts*; CGI).[26] Local direct and indirect charges and user fees come under the CCL.[27]

Local taxing powers are restricted to the communes and CRs. The regions, which have no fiscal resources, receive only FDD grants, receipts from administration of real estate property, proceeds from operating patrimonial assets, and user charges for services rendered.

Taxation in the communes and CRs is managed mostly by the central government. The tax rates and bases are generally set, or at least governed, by law (as, for example, the rural tax). For taxes collected through the tax register, the deconcentrated services of the DGID undertake the registration of taxpayers; the tax base office determines the tax due by each one; and the Treasury services collect it. Appeal and litigation procedures are under the jurisdiction of the state. At the beginning of each of the first two quarters of the financial year, the central government grants the CTs an advance payment equal to 25 percent of the amounts of direct local taxes collected in t-1.

Communal Resources

Direct communal taxes and additional percentage tax (piggyback tax) on direct taxes   The business tax, licenses, the combined business tax (*contribution globale unique*; CGU), property taxes, and the tax representing the minimum tax (*Taxe Représentative de l'Impôt du Minimum Fiscal*; TRIMF) constitute the main fiscal resources for the communes. The various direct communal taxes and the additional percentage tax on direct taxes are described below:

- *The fiscal minimum tax* (and the related piggyback tax)[28] is considered a per capita tax scaled to an individual's income, assets, and occupation. It is levied on any person over 13 years of age residing in Senegal, and the receipts accrue to the commune of residence. The central government is to collect it based on the tax roll on behalf of the CTs. In practice, it is not collected.

- *The tax representing the fiscal minimum* (and the piggyback tax)[29] is a flat-rate withholding tax scaled to income and payable on salaries or pensions. The central government collects it on behalf of the CTs. Collection of the tax is efficient despite the practical problems of addresses because employees are, as a rule, domiciled in the location of the establishment employing them or with the public service that pays their pensions.

- *The combined business tax* (CGU) is levied on all taxpayers whose economic activities of providing goods and services fall under the category of industrial and commercial profits. The CGU[30] is "representative," which is to say that it replaces the following: (a) the income tax based on industrial and commercial profits, (b) the fiscal minimum tax, (c) the business tax, (d) the value added tax (VAT), (e) employers' flat-rate contribution, and (f) the licensed premises tax. It is a flat-rate tax scaled on the turnover estimated by the tax authorities. The CGU is collected through the tax roll and paid in three yearly installments, accruing to the central government and the CTs. Its distribution formulas are defined each year under the Budget Law.

- *The business tax*[31] (excluding taxpayers subject to the CGU) is payable by any nonsalaried person engaged in a trade, industry, or profession in Senegal. Those excluded are notably farmers, the public sector, schools or training institutions, savings banks, and cooperatives. It is based on the rental (land registry) value of the business premises, including those liable for the tax on developed property (*Taxe foncière sur les propriétés bâties*; TFPB). Comprising a fixed charge and a proportional charge, it is collected by the central government on behalf of the CTs. This is the main local tax for urban CTs, as noted in table 5.7.

- *The taxes on developed and undeveloped property*[32] are levied annually on behalf of the CTs. Those excluded are notably buildings or land occupied as a principal residence, public property and land, and various infrastructures (such as ports, airports, and dams). The taxes are based on the land registry rental value. The tax rate for developed property is 5 percent or 7.5 percent (factories and industrial facilities); it is 5 percent for undeveloped property.

- *A surcharge on undeveloped or insufficiently developed property*[33] (if the market value of the construction is lower than the land value) is levied on behalf of the communes of the region of Dakar and the regional capitals, according to progressive tax bands (from 1 percent to 3 percent) set at the national level.

- *The licensing fee and piggyback tax*[34] are levied on behalf of the CTs. They are payable by any individual or legal establishment selling alcoholic or fermented beverages and are separate from the business tax. They are flat-rate taxes scaled to location, type of economic activity (such as bar, cafe, or restaurant), and turnover. The rates are defined by law and cannot be modulated by the communes.

- *Shared-tax transfers* correspond to the taxes collected by the central government, a share of which is returned to the communes.

- *The annual tax on motor vehicles* is payable (unless tax exempt) by owners of a vehicle registered in Senegal. The rate is progressive depending on the type of vehicle and engine rating. Payment procedures are strict (including penalties or impoundment for nonpayment), thus guaranteeing the tax yield.

- *The capital gains tax on property* is based on the difference between the purchase value (which can be reassessed) and the resale or transfer value. The rate is 15 percent.

All of these taxes are collected through the tax rolls except for the TRIMF and the CGU, for which payment is voluntary. The tax rolls are issued in two stages: the first ("primitive" roll) most often comes out in April, and the second (supplementary roll) in May. Once the notice of assessment has been sent, taxpayers have two months in which to pay. In the case of the TRIMF and CGU, the Treasury services have to locate (communalize) the base and transfer the receipts to the CT concerned.

Direct communal taxes   The most important of these taxes is currently the tax on household refuse collection. It is established by the central government services through the tax roll, along with the developed property tax (TFPB), and levied on much the same tax base in those communes that provide this service. The tax rate (6 percent for Dakar, 5 percent for the other communes) is set by law, with a ceiling for persons not liable for income tax.

The other direct levies, of minor importance, are the charges levied on the value of professional premises, the street-cleaning tax, the sewerage tax, and licenses payable by traders selling beverages in addition to the business license fee and the tax on sewing machines used for professional purposes.

Local indirect taxes   These taxes yield relatively substantial revenues (around 5 percent of the communes' total revenues in 2006) but prove difficult to manage. The highest-yielding taxes are those on electricity consumption and advertising, such as the following:

- *The tax on advertising* (billboards, posters, or illuminated signs) is an optional communal tax.
- *The tax on electricity consumption for public lighting and domestic use* is an optional tax that the communal councils may or may not choose to levy. Capped at a maximum rate of 2.5 percent, it is collected by the electricity operators (SENELEC, the national electricity company) upon payment of electricity bills and then passed on to the communes.
- *Other indirect local taxes and charges* generate either zero or much lower yields. They include the taxes on the following: slaughterhouses; distribution of gasoline, diesel, and all other fuels; water consumption (collected by the national water company [*Société Nationale des Eaux*, SNE] and repaid with apparently no problems to the CTs); night halls; inspection and meat stamping; health inspections of oysters and mussels; paid admissions, entertainment, and gaming; and furnished accommodation.
- The taxes on electricity and water consumption are shared equally between the central government and the CTs, with 50 percent for both parties.

User charges and fees   These operating revenues are listed in tables 5.7, 5.8, and 5.9 under the general heading "user charges or fees and revenues from property." It was impossible to separate out these two types of revenue for want of available information. By definition, a user charge or fee must contribute to covering the costs of service provision. It was not possible to check whether this was the case for all of the items listed under this heading. What can be said, however, is that the rental of communal property and land and the charges or fees for rights of use have strictly nothing to do with the nature of the user charges or fees as defined above.

Resources of the Arrondissement Communes

As shown by a comparison of tables 5.8 and 5.9 reporting the respective resources of the communes and CAs, the latter have access to only a limited number of resources, be they tax or nontax.[35] The CA receives a grant from the town or the central government, which is a mandatory expenditure for the town.

The arrangements for this general-purpose grant to be transferred by the towns to their CAs are determined each year by a presidential decree, countersigned by the prime minister.[36] The total amount to be distributed is calculated as a percentage (10 percent) of the town's average revenue over the previous three years—of which 40 percent is shared equally on a flat-rate basis among the CAs and 60 percent according to their population size.

Resources of Rural Communities

A rural tax is levied by the central government (generally with the assistance of the village chiefs) on behalf of the CRs—or on behalf of the CAs if the territory is not covered by CRs. The tax liability criteria are the same as those applied to the fiscal minimum tax. This flat-rate tax is collected through the tax roll; its rate is set by the departmental council and varies between CFAF 500 and CFAF 1,000 per taxpayer. At the beginning of each year, the central government advances to the CRs half of the receipts forecasted based on the nominative rolls approved for the financial year.

A quarter of the rural tax proceeds are paid into a national solidarity fund for the development of the CRs. The arrangements for sharing rural tax receipts among the CRs (and the arrondissements) are set by decree.

The CTs' Leeway in Local Taxation: Base Effects and Rate Effects

Senegalese legislation does not define the own resources for which the CTs may freely adjust the tax criteria, that is, the tax bases and tax rates. Therefore, we cannot globally assess the degree of local fiscal autonomy as defined by Dafflon and Madiès (2008).

As a first step, however, we can distinguish between (a) those taxes, levies, and user charges or fees whose proceeds are reserved exclusively for the CTs (exclusive resources), and (b) those that are shared between the central government and the CTs. Table 5.10 shows the respective lists of these resources.

As a second step, we can try to assess the CTs' degree of fiscal freedom by differentiating those resources for which they have the power to modulate the tax bases and rates. Generally speaking, Senegalese CTs have virtually no discretionary power to set the rates (rate effect) of the taxes they benefit from. At best, they have only the choice of whether to levy the tax. And even if a CT decides to levy a tax, the deconcentrated tax services (DGID) may not put this into effect if it does not have the necessary resources. In such a case, the tax is not collected.

The CTs can bring only the "base effects" into play or, in other words, use their power to increase the taxable base. There are two types of base effects:

- *An intensive base effect (or productivity effect)*. The CT can increase the yield of the fiscal machine by assigning it additional resources (5 percent of communal operating expenditure is dedicated to the services of the municipal rates office), and towns such as Dakar are recruiting employees to this end.

- *A more conventional extensive and indirect effect*. By welcoming new residents and economic activities, the CT can hope to bolster the proceeds of its taxes, charges, and fees.

Table 5.10 Exclusive Local Taxes and Shared-Tax Revenues of CTs in Senegal

Exclusive taxes	Shared-tax receipts and shared-tax transfers
• Business tax • Taxes on developed and undeveloped property • Surcharge on undeveloped or insufficiently developed property • Advertising tax (billboards, posters, or illuminated signs) • Household refuse collection tax • Other direct taxes (charges on the value of professional premises, on street cleaning, on sewerage, and on sewing machines used for professional purposes) • Other indirect taxes (on slaughterhouses; the distribution of gasoline, diesel, and all other fuels; night halls; meat inspection and stamping; health inspections of oysters and mussels; paid admissions; entertainment and gaming; and furnished accommodation) • Licenses payable by traders selling beverages, in addition to business license fees	• Shared-tax transfers • Annual tax on motor vehicles • Duties on transfer of ownership • Road tax • Capital gains tax on property Other shared-tax receipts: • Tax on water consumption (50 percent for central government, 50 percent for CTs) • Tax on electricity consumed for public lighting and domestic use (50/50) • Fiscal minimum tax • TRIMF • CGU • Rural tax (RC)

Source: General Tax Code (*Code général des impôts*) Law 1992–40, situation at the end 2010.
Note: CGU = combined business tax (*contribution générale unique*); CT = territorial collectivity; TRIMF = tax representing the minimum tax (*Taxe Représentative de l'Impôt du Minimum Fiscal*).

Various indications during our interviews suggest that the first of these base effects produces results: making additional human or material resources available has, in some cases, reinforced the productivity of the levy because it can improve tax base identification and addressing.

The second base effect seems to be more unreliable, albeit with positive results at times. One case was mentioned to us in Yene concerning the introduction of a pirogue tax concomitant to the development of the harbor facilities. Another case in point is the town of Dakar, which had taken on the responsibility for administering the advertising tax. The town decided to extend the reach of the tax and the number of liable persons to increase its yield.[37] By mobilizing 15 enumerators, it established a file of 10,000 potential taxpayers. Yet linking up the town's taxpayer files with those of the DGID has turned out to be problematic (Giovanni and Chomentowski 2009, 33).

Issues Regarding Local Taxation

The issues concerning local taxation are manifold, as is evidenced by the following inventory:

- Tax procedures, particularly the issuance of tax rolls, are always very late. The primitive rolls are received by the tax collector in May or June, and the supplementary rolls in August or September, which results in a loss of tax revenue.

- The identification of tax bases is often inaccurate and the addressing unreliable—so much so that the DGID has to grant substantial abatements (of around 10–12 percent of shadow revenues).

- Overall, tax revenues come in late and incomplete. The funds reach the CTs around June or July. Nonetheless, this is a definite improvement on previous years, when funds would arrive toward September. While awaiting funds, the communes operate using advance payments from the central government, as previously mentioned.

- The electricity tax raises hefty problems, particularly in Dakar, where the state electricity company SENELEC refuses to pass on the tax they have collected on the grounds that the CAs either fail to pay their electricity bills for public lighting or settle them very late. For its part, the town, which is responsible for public lighting, deplores the lack of maintenance on the network operated by SENELEC. A final difficulty arises from the fact that the law[38] stipulates that the tax be remitted to the CAs, whereas the town is the authority responsible for public lighting. In an attempt to solve this commercial conflict, the central government has created a budgetary envelope (the Public Lighting Fund [Fonds d'éclairage public]) and is considering making it into an independent legal entity. The fund would assume the cost of the electricity bills for public lighting and the expenses for maintaining and equipping the network.

- The predictability of revenues remains marred by uncertainty. The gap between budgeted and collected revenues is often wide. Is this due to a lack of budget transparency or to technical difficulties that are impossible to foresee ex ante? The answer is probably both (Giovanni and Chomentowski 2009).

- Low-yield taxes are not collected because the tax services or Treasury deem that the cost of collecting them is higher than their yield.

- According to the DGID, the services in charge of tax bases are too few and focus on high-yield taxes (mainly those paid by companies) rather than on "mass" taxes with a high number of taxpayers and low average yield. Communes wishing to mobilize more of their tax potential must provide local agents to bolster the central government services that assist with tax assessment and addressing (for example, the city of Dakar provides more than 10 local government agents, paid by the city, to assist central government tax collectors). Adding local forces to make up for the lack of enough central agents limits such efforts to the largest CTs.

- Registration of taxpayers is incomplete.

- Addressing errors are frequent (the DGID often attributes these errors to the town or commune services).

- The central government grants exemptions, mainly to companies, without informing or compensating the CTs concerned.

- Companies delay paying their taxes until the sum of arrears becomes large enough to obtain a full or partial amnesty.

- The communal list of tax addresses for persons liable for the TRIMF and the CGU is flawed (thus, all government officials are "located" in the commune where their payroll services are situated, regardless of the officials' actual place of residence).

- Payment of taxes is often late.

- The tax recovery rate is low, and most of the resources collected for the (large) communes ultimately come from the collection of taxes levied on large companies; thus, in Dakar, the top 30 taxpayers alone accounted for 45 percent of tax receipts for 2008.

- The CTs (communes) voice a demand for greater decentralization of the fiscal chain to make tax recovery more effective.

- Under Senegalese law, the "charges for services rendered" (or user charges) are precisely defined. This involves the sum demanded from users to cover the costs of a given public service or the start-up or maintenance costs of a public work in direct exchange for services provided by the service or for use of the work. There must therefore be a correlation between the amount of the charge and the actual cost of the service rendered, but with no requirement that the amount of the charge be the exact equivalent of the service rendered. If both conditions are met, the contribution demanded is a charge for a service rendered. Otherwise, it constitutes a tax.

- It was not possible to check whether the amounts of user charges or fees were commensurate with the services provided to the beneficiaries. Should this not be the case, there may be a disconnect between the basis for calculation and the amount paid by the user.

Intergovernmental Transfers

Senegalese law provides that any transfer of powers to a CT shall be subject to an evaluation by the central government of the net expenditure transferred and an opinion from the National Council on Local Development (*Conseil national de développement des collectivités locales*; CNDCL). It must be accompanied by "a concomitant transfer from the State of the resources and means necessary for the normal exercise of these powers."[39] The "resources necessary for the exercise of their powers are bestowed upon them either through tax transfers or through grants or through both."[40]

The central government must therefore compensate any new expenditure resulting from the statutory amendment to the rules relating to the exercise of the transferred responsibilities. This includes special grants for some CTs if "the lack of resources is likely to compromise the exercise of the public service missions."[41]

These resources are at least equivalent to the central government's expenditures for the year before the transfer. A part of these resources is directly allocated to the CTs through the FDD. Another part is allocated to deconcentrated government authorities when these put at the CTs' disposal the material and human resources (which remain under the authority of the state's local-level representative) as well as the movable and immovable property required for the discharge of their new responsibilities.[42] The CTs' use of state services is regulated by agreements.

The transfers received by the CTs are many, even though their total amount remains modest compared with other local resources. Some, such as the FDD and FECL transfers, are explicit and regular; others are occasional, while yet others are less explicit.

The Decentralization Allocation Fund (FDD)
The FDD was officially created in 1996[43] to cover the net expenditure incurred by responsibilities transferred to the CTs. The prescribed method for calculating

the fund[44] stipulates that the appropriation created by the 2007 Budget Law must be equivalent to 3.5 percent of the VAT, as long as the responsibilities involved remain unchanged. As a practical matter, this rate can be modified—not to match changes in the expenses linked to the exercise of the responsibilities but in the event that new responsibilities are transferred. Moreover, the grant thus established cannot be below a percentage of total state revenues, excluding loans and external contributions.

The two percentages used to calculate the size of the grant, as well as the way the funds are allocated, are set each year by the Budget Law, after an opinion from the CNDCL.

Calculation of the minimum grant has been modified with respect to the provisions of the 1996 law that created the FDD. The grant amount must be at least equivalent to the central government's expenditures over the year preceding the date of the transfer of responsibilities and is applicable for two years after the implementation of the Budget Law. This supposes, for example, that in 2007 and 2008, the central government transferred to the CTs the equivalent of the expenditure allocated to the responsibilities transferred in 2006.

In practice, it was through the 2006 Budget Law (for a 2007 start-up) that the procedures inherent in the FDD were put into effect. Previously, it was the Ministry of Finance that had determined the level of FDD funds in a discretionary manner, involving a lump-sum amount from the state budget. The 2003–05 Decentralization Action Plan of the Ministry of the Interior (the ministry in charge of local authorities in 2003) says, "It should be pointed out that until now the way in which the FDD envelope is determined has never really been clarified with regard to Law 96-07, just as the setting of the rates has never been the subject of a real parliamentary debate." Donors do not contribute to FDD funds. The amounts involved are shown in table 5.11.

Arrangements for allocation of the FDD[45]   Transferred responsibilities give rise to cost burdens, which are borne either by the CTs themselves or by the deconcentrated government services made available to the CTs by their supervisory authorities. In both cases, the FDD compensates the expenses incurred. The funds are distributed on a top-down basis, following a series of criteria on how the grants are to be shared.

An annual decree sets the criteria for distributing the decentralized grants, and the amounts allocated are determined by an annual interministerial decree between

- The CTs (regions, communes, CAs, and CRs), the distribution criteria for which must be defined within the Budget Law; and
- The deconcentrated government authorities working for the CTs.

Table 5.11 Trends in FDD and FECL Funding to CTs in Senegal, 1997–2009
CFAF, billions

Year	FDD (section 3.6.1[a])	FECL (section 3.6.2[b])
2009	14.93	12.5
2008	16.60	11.5
2007	13.34	10.5
2006	12.34	7.0
2005	12.67	6.0
2004	10.09	4.0
2003	9.09	8.0
2002	8.09	4.0
2001	7.29	3.8
2000	6.59	3.5
1999	5.89	3.5
1998	4.89	3.5
1997	4.89	3.5

Source: Data from the Directorate of Territorial Collectivities 2010 (DCL).
Note: CT = territorial collectivity; FDD = Decentralization Allocation Fund (*Fonds de dotation de la décentralisation*); FECL = Fund for Local Government Infrastructures (*Fonds d'équipement des collectivités locales*).
a. Law 96-07 of March 22, 1996.
b. Decree No. 12248 of October 15, 1988.

In the accounts, this distribution is based on these three criteria (as shown in figure 5.3):

- The "operating expenditure of the regions" and "the allowances of local elected officials"

- The "compensation" to the communes and CRs

- "Support for deconcentrated services," for which the CTs sign utilization agreements with the central government. This support is not used for burdensome responsibilities (such as minute taking for meetings in small CRs or delimiting cattle tracks in zones where lands have not been clearly assigned).

Decision-making process   When the grant amount has been recorded in the state budget and has been voted upon, the CNDCL proposes distribution criteria. The CNDCL convenes in January. The process for validation, commitment, and so forth then takes three months. The CTs' account is credited with the funds around May, June, or even July.

Allocation of funds   The law stipulates that funds allocated from the FDD be unearmarked. Yet the decrees governing distribution specify that the resources must be assigned to the responsibilities for which they are intended (as discussed previously within the "Assignment of Responsibilities" section).

Figure 5.3 The Decentralization Allocation Fund (FDD) in Senegal

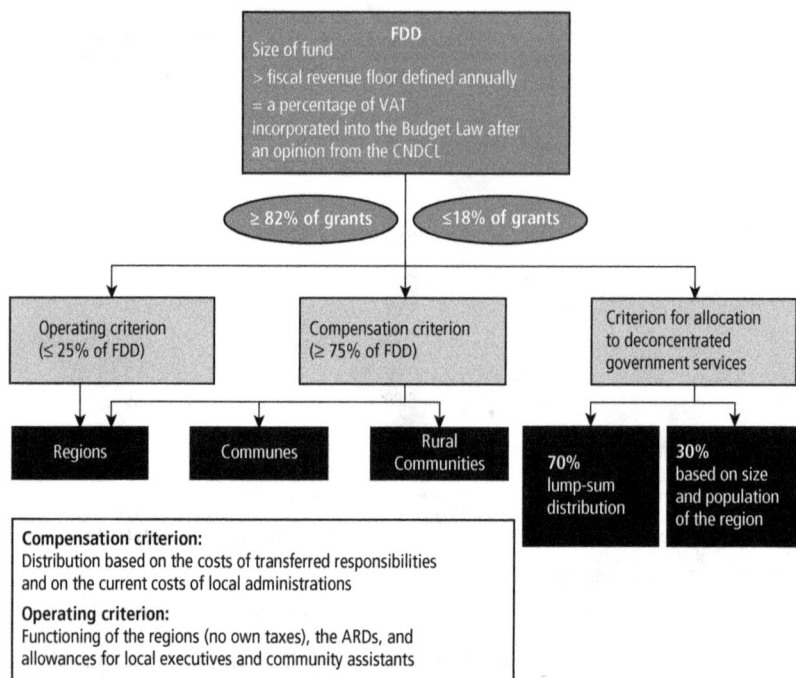

Note: ARD = Regional Development Agency (*Agence régional de développement*); CNDCL = National Council on Local Development (*Conseil national de développement des collectivités locales*); FDD = Decentralization Allocation Fund (*Fonds de dotation de la décentralisation*); VAT = value added tax.

Allocating recurrent financial transfers among the communes   According to a study by the Municipal Development Agency (*Agence de développement munici-pal*; ADM), the allocation of financial transfers (shared-tax transfers, FDD, and other operating transfers) were to the overall advantage of the small communes between 2004 and 2006 (CFAF 2,700 per capita against CFAF 960 per capita for the towns and the communes, respectively, of the region of Dakar and CFAF 1,960 per capita for the regional capitals) (ADM 2008). As a result, these trans-fers now represent a higher share of operating resources in the small communes (42 percent) than in the regional capitals (30 percent) and even more so com-pared with the towns and communes in the region of Dakar (6.7 percent).

Financial transfers have thus played an apparently equalizing role in the fiscal capacity of these different categories of local government, and this despite the absence of explicit equalizing mechanisms, notably for the FDD. An exception to this absence of an explicit equalizing mechanism is the rural tax, for which an equalization fund exists, albeit of limited effect. However, no information is available on this. The equalizing effect doubtless stems from the fact that the shared-tax transfers are redistributed based on the communes' population size. The total equalizing effect of the mechanism could be put into question, however, if the assumption is made (confirmed in many other countries) that the cost and range of local public services grows with the commune's population size.

The Local Government Investment Fund (FECL)

Functioning of the FECL   Created in 1977, this special fund account is aimed at reinforcing the CTs' investment capacity. Incorporated into the budget of the Ministry of Decentralization and Local Government and jointly managed by the Presidency of the Republic, the Ministry of Finance, the Ministry of Local Government, and the Mayors' Association, the FECL initially had the status of a cost-sharing fund functioning as a special Treasury account. It enabled grants and loans to be allocated. At the end of the 1980s (1988–89), the central government had also set up the *Crédit communal*, whose role was to act as a bank for the CTs and provide them with loans. It was housed at the *Banque de l'habitat du Senegal*, but this experience was to prove unsuccessful because the bank collapsed on account of its prohibitive rates.

Before the creation of the ADM in 1997—whose intervention has changed both the orientation and allocation of the FECL—funds from the FECL were divided between an ordinary fund and specific grants. The specific grants were allocated on a project basis, while the ordinary funds were allocated to the CTs on the basis of the following performance criteria:

- Control of payroll costs (to be less than 40 percent of the three-year average of current revenues)
- Achievement of adequate financing capacity (surplus rate above 25 percent).

This mechanism was reformed with the creation in 1997 of the ADM, whose remit was to implement the donor-funded programs to support the communes (first PAC, then PRECOL). The ADM took over the loans that had been granted by the *Crédit communal* and receives the corresponding repayments from the communes (as of 2009, this concerned only two communes). The functioning of the FECL is shown in figure 5.4.

Allocation of funds   Since the creation of the ADM and the setting up of decentralization programs, most FECL resources are used to finance the matching funds required by international donors. It provides funding for three programs (2009 figures):

- The National Local Development Plan (*Plan national de développement local*; PNDL) for the CRs, amounting to CFAF 4.2 billion

Figure 5.4 The Local Government Investment Fund (FECL) in Senegal

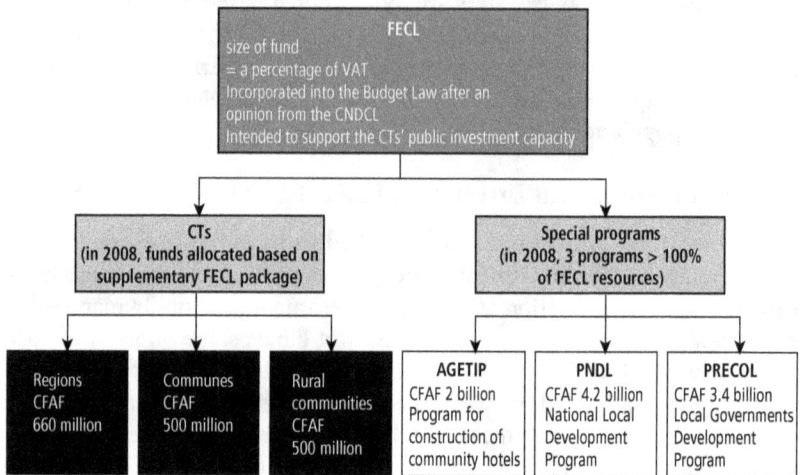

Note: AGETIP = Public Works Executing Agency (*Agence d'exécution des travaux d'intérêt public*);
CNDCL = National Council on Local Development (*Conseil national de développement des collectivités locales*);
CT = territorial collectivity; PNDL = National Local Development Plan (*Plan national de développement local*);
PRECOL = Program to Strengthen Local Government Investment (*Programme de renforcement et d'équipement des collectivités locales*); VAT = value added tax.

- Program to Strengthen Local Government Investment (*Programme de renforcement et d'équipement des collectivités locales*; PRECOL), amounting to CFAF 3.4 billion (38 of which goes to the CADAK [CFAF 21 million] and the CAR [CFAF 5 million])
- The Public Works Executing Agency (*Agence d'exécution des travaux d'intérêt public*; AGETIP), responsible for the construction of community halls, which amounts to CFAF 2 billion.

The remaining funds, which today represent a very small amount, are shared among the CTs on a lump-sum basis and at the discretion of the Minister of Decentralization and Local Government, which means that performance criteria for allocation no longer exist.

FECL resources   Before the 2006 law, and like the FDD, the amount of FECL funds was determined by the central government on a discretionary basis and voted upon under the Budget Law. Under a 2007 law,[46] the FECL benefits from an appropriation equal to 2 percent of VAT (see table 5.11).

The Consolidated Investment Budget

The consolidated investment budget was introduced on an experimental basis in 2007 with a view toward developing the CTs' capacities in the area of investment and making procedures more efficient. To accelerate the uptake of investment grants, which are provided for under the budget laws and fall within the missions of the sectoral ministries, the state's contracting authority has been transferred to the CTs. The latter thus receive the budget, which they must implement in their territories on behalf of the state. This is therefore a case of delegated contracting authority and not a transfer of powers together with an accompanying financial transfer.

The implementation of the consolidated investment budget has been tested in five regions since 2007. So far, the results are not compelling, and whether the experiment will be continued is uncertain.

Issues Regarding the Central Government's Financial Transfers to CTs

The transfers received by Senegalese CTs (through the FDD and FECL) are extremely modest—representing, on average, 20 percent of their total revenue. The decree on the distribution of FDD funds stipulates how the transferred funds are to be allocated to each CT and to each area of responsibility. In fact, for a good many CTs, only four out of the nine assigned functions receive grants (education, health, youth and sport, and culture). The other functions are not compensated by a grant as is statutorily required. Because the grants are categorized by area of responsibility, the FDD's seemingly "general" grant is somewhat a misnomer. The FDD outlines the overall scope for earmarked grants rather than giving a truly general grant.

The distribution criteria for FDD funding are not defined by the decree. They appear to be discretionary, variable over time, and therefore difficult to predict. This means that before receiving the decree, the CTs do not know how much funding they will receive or when. It should be noted that their grants can change over time, regardless of the fund's overall envelope (some CTs may receive funds some years and not others). From what some of our interlocutors told us, the personality of the CT's elected official can also marginally influence the amount of funding received, notably from the FECL.

The funds paid out of the FECL have changed considerably over time, as now only a small fraction of the FECL is not allocated to projects (PNDL, PRECOL, and AGETIP) and is shared among the CTs on a lump-sum basis. For example, the Senegalese government contributes 50 percent of PNDL project funding (40 percent by the FECL and 10 percent by the CTs involved), the rest being ensured by donors. FECL funds are thus channeled mostly into project financing—in partnership with the ADM, for example—and not into direct funding to the CTs.

This project financing approach and the criteria imposed by the ADM for obtaining FECL funds help to kick-start a virtuous budgetary momentum for the participating CTs, which in this case have to show their capacity to mobilize fiscal resources, rein in the most sensitive expenditure items (particularly payroll), and generate enough savings to ensure their long-term financial solvency.[47] But what is also needed are adequate funds that are predictable and stable over time—which was not yet guaranteed at the time this chapter was written.

The fact that transfer payments to the CTs are low and that certain assigned responsibilities receive no grant nonetheless gives the impression of an implicit "bailout" of the CTs or, in other words, a vertical imbalance of their accounts that obliges a "lender of last resort"—either the central government or external donors—to restore their balance. Indeed, some public services cannot be delivered by the CTs for want of resources (through grants or taxation) but must nonetheless be provided. In this case, it is the deconcentrated government services that take over. It appears that decentralization in Senegal relies de facto, to a large extent, on mechanisms of deconcentration and not delegation (the assignment of a specific task) or devolution (transfer of powers and corresponding resources). As deconcentrated government services are thus made available, this softens the CTs' budget constraint (which is perfectly defined in law) and brings to light the phenomenon of an indirect bailout, not through an overt financial rescue of CTs to redress their fiscal imbalance but by a series of less-visible measures.

The pendant of this lack of hard budget constraint at the local level is the variability and uncertainty (not to mention arbitrariness) that seemingly hold sway in the mechanisms for channeling national fiscal resources down to CTs—a state of affairs denounced by many of our interlocutors.

Balancing Local Budgets and Debt

Given the last-mentioned remark above, the analysis of CT finances in Senegal would be incomplete if it went no further than simply presenting expenditure and revenue. To complete the picture, the analysis should also address the budget-balancing constraints that weigh on CTs because of the rules on borrowing.

Budget Balance

Budgetary procedure is laid down in the law. A budgetary orientation debate is held before the budget is voted upon by the CT council, which must intervene by March 31 at the latest. In practice, only the large communes (for example, Dakar) manage to approve their budgets before the end of the calendar year.

The principle of "real budget balance" is enshrined in the law. Thus, the CTs are forbidden to run budget deficits. The budget balance is "real" if

- The budget entries are transparent;
- The "current section and the capital section," respectively, are balanced; and

- The financial transfer from the current revenue section to the capital section, added to the own resources of the capital section (loans and any depreciation allowances excluded), is higher than or equal to the loan principal repayment falling due within the year.[48]

"The levy on the current section for the benefit of the capital section shall represent a share of these revenues," this share being set by decree and dependent on the type of CT.[49] The law also describes the procedure for an ex officio levy.[50] Thereafter, if the approved budget is not in balance, the state's representative imposes a budget that is, by definition, in balance.

"Rolling Budgets"

The CTs are often faced de facto with expenditures that lead them to adopt the practice of "rolling budgets." A distinction should be made between this practice and the advances received from the central government. When certain expenditures have been committed but not cleared for payment because revenues have run dry, these expenditures are spread over the following financial year as expenditures committed but not cleared for payment (*dépenses engagées non encore mandatées*; DENEM). Enterprises that have delivered services but will be paid at a later date (for want of CT resources) thus ensure the CTs' cash flow. Although such strategies enable the CTs to present apparently balanced budgets, they also pass the problems on to the following budget year; in other words, the deficits roll over to the budget of year $t + 1$.

In reality, the principle of budget annuality (a legal requirement) is not respected. The complementary period instrument exists and enables the financial controller to continue recording operations relating to year t until the end of February $t+1$. Yet, in many communes and particularly in the largest towns, the accounts show arrears. In the case of the town of Dakar, Giovanni and Chomentowski (2009) confirm this situation, as does our own information obtained for the most recent fiscal years (see box 5.6).

Control and Limitation of Borrowing

The CTs are only authorized to borrow to finance their investments. Initially, loans were granted by a single banking entity, the *Crédit communal*.[51] This instrument was authorized to lend to the CTs after a positive opinion from the National Lending Committee (*Comité national des prêts*; CNP) composed of state representatives (Presidency of the Republic, the Ministry of Finance, and Ministry of Local Government). The CNP determined, on a case-by-case basis, (a) the fraction of the loan to be financed from FECL resources, thus out of budget appropriations (and at subsidized rates); and (b) the fraction to be financed by the *Crédit communal*, thus through bank financing (using an instrument akin to the loan-grant combination offered by the French *Caisse*

254 THE POLITICAL ECONOMY OF DECENTRALIZATION IN SUB-SAHARAN AFRICA

Box 5.6

The Town of Dakar and Its Arrears

The town of Dakar evaluates arrears on a DENEM (*dépenses engagées non encore mandatés*, or expenditures committed but not cleared for payment) basis. This involves expenditures committed during fiscal year *t* and approved as compliant by the financial controller in *t* but not cleared for payment and, more to the point, not disbursed in *t*, subsequently appearing in the budget of year *t* + 1.

The expenditures are thus automatically recommitted in *t* + 1, as they had already been committed in *t*. These are then cleared for payment and paid in priority at the beginning of *t* + 1, even if the budget for *t* + 1 has not yet been voted upon or approved by the prefect.

Sometimes, therefore, the DENEMs correspond to the amounts owed for services performed in *t* (for example, a delivery awaiting payment) and thus are outstanding debts, but sometimes not. They include not only real arrears but also certified commitments not cleared for payment (from an accounting viewpoint: provisions for works that have been realized but not yet paid for). For example, the DENEMs of the town of Dakar represented 8.5 percent of the budget implemented in 2005, 17.4 percent in 2006, and 19.5 percent in 2007.

---

des dépôts et consignations and its subsidiary the *Caisse d'aide à l'équipement des collectivités locales* in the years before decentralization).

Today this instrument is no longer used. All CTs' loans are channeled through the FECL and, from what we were told, these are for very small amounts. All investments are thus necessarily financed out of the CTs' operating surplus, supplemented if needed by their own investment revenues, including investment grants. The communes (the towns) can "take on debt" indirectly with the ADM within the framework of municipal contracts (since 1999). The indirect "loans" from the ADM are not recorded as loans by the beneficiary town but aggregated with other investment funding resources (autofinancing and grants). A town that has signed one of these contracts "repays" the ADM in the form of a "contribution" to ADM expenditure.

This system highlights a problem in the communal accounting system because the municipal contract funds are not recorded in the communal budgets, whereas the repayments do indeed appear as communal expenditures.

Municipal contracts within the framework of PRECOL   Municipal contracts are signed between the ADM and the commune, after completion of the urban, organizational, and financial audits. It comprises the following three components:

- Priority Investment Program (*Programme d'investissement prioritaire*; PIP)
- Municipal Adjustment Program (*Programme d'ajustement municipal*; PAM)
- Priority Maintenance Program (*Programme d'entretien prioritaire*; PEP).

To be eligible for PRECOL funding, the commune must meet the following conditions:

- Be up to date with the repayment of PAC loans and of the municipal credit accounts
- Have begun to operate the equipment realized within the PAC framework
- Have allocated at least 3 percent of its ordinary revenues to equipment maintenance
- Keep the ratio of payroll expenditure to current revenues under 40 percent.

The financial resources for the municipal contract are sourced as follows:

- Grant allocated by the ADM and concerning all PAM support measures and part of PIP
- Loans repayable over 12 years at 4.25 percent calculated on the PIP amount
- Autofinancing representing the commune's contribution to the financing of its PIP
- The commune's contribution to the ADM's functioning (1 percent of the funds allocated to the commune).

The communes do not carry out real studies on the "sustainability" of their debts because (a) the level of debt is low (for the town of Dakar, the debt burden amounts to 1–2 percent of its budget); and (b) the "sustainability" of a CT's debt depends primarily on its forecasted capacity to generate savings (chiefly its fiscal revenue forecasts) and on the recurrent costs associated with its loan-funded infrastructures. However, both the forecasted savings capacity and the recurrent costs are highly uncertain, and thus neither has been subject to in-depth simulations. Finally, because the debt is carried by the ADM, it should basically be up to this entity to ensure the current and future solvency of a town benefiting from a municipal contract. The ADM thus declares that it places great importance on the mobilization of the CTs' fiscal resources.

Finally, the 2009 draft Budget Law capped loans to the CTs at CFAF 500 million, which implied that the central government envisaged lending to the CTs within a legal framework not mentioned a priori in the CCL.

Financial Balance and Cash Flow

Should an unexpected and urgent expense arise during the year, the CTs' chief administrative and financial officer can make a transfer between budget lines for this expense, which means that other budgeted expenditures must be reduced. For the commune, it is the mayor who arbitrates the reductions.

The central government can grant cash advances to CTs able to justify that "their cash-flow situation compromises the payment of indispensable and urgent expenditures and that this situation is not due to insufficient resources or a budget imbalance."[52] In practice, these advances are very elastic. For example, they were capped at CFAF 500 million in the 2008 draft Budget Law.

The administrative accounts of the town of Dakar show in the operating section—under "Miscellaneous revenues" (line item 749, "Contingent or unexpected revenues")—state advances with a cumulative total since 2004–08 of CFAF 11.3 billion. The administrative accounts for the years concerned show no repayment to the state, but the balance of the revenue and expenditure account for 2007 indicate a repayment of CFAF 1.7 billion, giving a total cumulative net advance of CFAF 9.6 billion. This cumulative advance is higher than the amount of business taxes collected by the town in 2008.[53]

Issues Relating to Budgetary and Financial Balance

There is a real issue regarding the transparency of budget entries. This is chiefly visible in the large discrepancies between forecasts and execution in fiscal matters.

The constraint of balancing budgets underlies many gaps between forecasts and the execution of investment spending. Apart from investment operations being subject to numerous hazards, the actual rate of saving does not always enable investment operations to be financed as forecasted within the current budget year. Thus, an examination of the town of Dakar's accounts shows large arrears in payment for works contracts alone (the electricity network, for example). As a result, the town of Dakar has received advances from the central government that have so far given rise only to partial repayments.

In addition, accounting problems complicate the task of analyzing the accounts from the perspective of achieving sustainable financial equilibrium:

- State advances are currently entered into the administrative account, whereas any repayments are not (they only appear in the balances of the revenue and expenditure accounts). It would be advisable for the said advances not to be entered into the administrative account to avoid artificially boosting the amounts saved by the CT. They should instead be recorded only in the financial accounts under "nonrecurrent revenues," as should any repayments made.

- The rules for recognizing the communes' operations with the ADM reveal a problem in the communal accounts because funds received under municipal contracts are not entered as loans in the communal budgets. Instead, they are aggregated with other investment revenues such as grants or autofinancing, whereas the repayments for these "loans" do appear as communal expenditures (even if they are described as "contributions to ADM expenditure").

In conclusion, local budget constraint is "soft," which legitimizes the central government's acceptance of accounting lags, the supply of state employees or resources to the CTs, or occasional external interventions (generalized donor funding).

Revenue and Expenditure Statistics

The available statistics are few and far between and by no means exhaustive. It is difficult to find data that group all of the CTs (regions, communes, and CRs). Most of the statistics commented on in this section are from the *Guide des ratios financiers 2004, 2005, 2006* (ADM 2008). This means that the data cover the Senegalese communes but do not include either the regions or the CRs.

It should be noted that the CTs' (communes') share of gross domestic product (GDP) in Senegal is excessively low, with communal expenditure in 2006 accounting for around 1 percent of GDP[54] and 6 percent of total state revenue.

CT Expenditure

The most recent data from the ADM (2008)[55] make it possible to summarize the trend and structure of communal expenditure of the period, as presented in table 5.12.

Table 5.12 Communal Expenditure Per Capita in Senegal, 2006

	2006 expenditure	Change 2004–06 (percentage points)
Total expenditure per capita (CFAF)[a]	10,756	—
Current expenditures per inhabitant (CFAF), including (as a share of current expenditure)	8,070	—
Mayor's office (%)	14	3
Municipal Rates office (%)	5	0
Grants—participations (%)	7	−8
Commercial equipment (%)	1	0
Communal property (%)	1	0
Roads, green spaces (%)	2	0
Refuse collection (%)	5	1
Workshops, garages (%)	6	0
Water services (%)	1	0
Sanitation (%)	0	−1
Public lighting (%)	3	−3

(continued next page)

Table 5.12 (continued)

	2006 expenditure	Change 2004–06 (percentage points)
Economic intervention (%)	1	0
Education, youth, culture, sports (%)	9	0
Health, hygiene, social welfare (%)	13	0
Cemeteries, funerals (%)	0	0
Feasts, ceremonies (%)	2	−1
Other (%)	28	0
Total current expenses (%)	**100ᵇ**	—
Investment expenditures (CFAF per capita)	2,686	—

Source: ADM 2008.
Note: — = not available.
a. Total expenditure is assimilated to actual revenue.
b. Difference due to rounding.

Total spending for the Senegalese communes stood at a little over CFAF 50 billion in 2006, or about 6 percent of the state tax revenue (against 3.2 percent in 1998). By way of example, total local expenditure per capita was in the region of CFAF 10,000 in 2006. Current expenditure represents 80 percent of total spending, a third of which goes toward payroll expenditures. The predominance of actions in the areas of (a) education, youth, culture, and sports; and (b) health, hygiene, and social welfare is not clearly visible (no more than 20 percent of spending for both these areas), whereas current expenditure for institutions (the mayor's office, for example) is sizable. The debt burden is almost negligible (less than 1 percent). The increase in current expenditure remains moderate and somewhat irregular from one year to another.

Investment expenditure, however, has been much more buoyant (averaging more than 20 percent per year), even though the amounts involved remain modest (CFAF 2,700 per capita in 2006). Investment levels distinguish the towns (medium size or small), which invest considerably more than the rural communes.[56] Paradoxically, regional capitals invest less than the other communes but benefit from municipal contracts that add to their own investments.

Overall, therefore, the observed levels of local expenditure are low. And this raises doubts not only about the effectiveness of certain transfers of powers but also about fast-growing, albeit modest, investment spending, which for the moment appears to generate only low recurrent running costs.

Trend and Structure of the Communes' Revenues

The most recent financial data that are complete and provide a breakdown by commune are for the year 2006. (ADM's statistical yearbook was being updated as this chapter was written.) Table 5.13 presents the aggregate figures for 2006. More recent data showing a breakdown by local authority are not available.

Table 5.13 Trend and Structure of the Communes' Budget Revenue in Senegal, 2004 and 2006

	2004	2006
Communes' total budget revenue (CFAF, billions)	43.7	50.7
Communes' total operating revenues (CFAF, billions), including	40.4	47.3
Property taxes (%)	10	10
Fiscal minimum tax (%)	5	4
Business tax, licenses, and CGU (%)	43	46
Municipal taxes (%)	4	5
Property income (%)	8	9
Revenue from sale of goods and services (%)	1	1
Central government transfers (CFAF, billions)	8.0	10.2
Shared-tax transfers (CFAF, billions)	1.8	2.6
FDD (CFAF, billions)	3.0	4.0
Other operating transfers (CFAF, billions)	0.9	0.8
FECL (CFAF, billions)	0.6	0.8
Other grants (CFAF, billions)	1.7	2.0
Communes' revenues / state tax revenues (%)	6.00	5.80
Transfers / communes' total revenues (%)	17.90	20.21
Transfers / state tax revenues (%)	1.07	1.17

Source: ADM 2008.
Note: CGU = combined business tax (Contribution Générale Unique); FDD = Decentralization Allocation Fund (Fonds de dotation de la decentralization); FECL = Fund for Local Government Infrastructures (Fonds d'équipement des collectivités). The nomenclature in this table is that used for the communes' revenue and expenditure accounts and taken up by the ADM's statistics. Working with the available aggregate data, it is impossible to provide a breakdown using the categories shown in table 5.7.

The budget revenues of the Senegalese communes (including transfers) amounted to CFAF 50 billion in 2006, equivalent to around 6 percent of the state budget revenues. This percentage has almost doubled since 1998 but has remained stable since 2004. The CTs' tax revenues grew briskly between 2004 and 2006, as did central government transfers (notably revenue from shared-tax transfers and the FDD), with the result that the share of transferred resources relative to other resources has remained constant. In 2006, central government transfers (shared-tax transfers, FDD, FECL, and other transfers) represented 13.2 percent of this total, or about 1.1 percent of state revenues. Added to these amounts is external funding, which mainly includes ADM funding under the PAC as well as direct aid from external donors.

However, the rate of growth of these different types of resources is uneven: The business tax rose by 36 percent between 2004 and 2005 but by only 1 percent between 2005 and 2006. Shared-tax transfers increased by 38 percent over the first two-year period but by only 6 percent between 2005 and 2006.

Revenues from direct local taxation account for over four-fifths of the CTs' operating revenue. In 2006, they stood at around CFAF 11,000 per capita. Their growth was fueled, above all, by the business tax, whose receipts rose by an average 17 percent annually between 2004 and 2006. This tax is levied mainly on economic activities, with households benefiting from generous exemptions or reductions. The fiscal minimum tax remains marginal, given that it is difficult to collect—except in the large towns where the proportion of salaried workers makes it more easily deductible at source. Revenues from the other taxes (particularly property taxes) are increasing little, more slowly than the population growth rate and inflation. Because the business tax is concentrated in a small number of communes based on the location of economic activities, the level and growth of local taxes differ substantially across the CTs. The local tax yield per capita is six times higher in Dakar for the business tax, the fiscal minimum tax, and the TFPB than in the rest of the country. What's more, interregional disparities in fiscal capacity are increasing.

The proportion of the communes' other ordinary revenues (user charges and fees, income from land and property, and revenue from sale of goods and services) dropped over the period, from 15 percent in 2004 to less than 13 percent in 2006. However, this average decrease masks two very different situations: in the rural communes, mostly lying outside the region of Dakar and the regional capitals, user charges and fees and revenue from sale of goods, services, and property continue to account for nearly a quarter of ordinary revenues, whereas elsewhere this share does not exceed 10 percent.

Data on Transfers and Financial Balance

The apparent contribution of central government transfers can be summarized, in table 5.14, as ensuring the financial balance of the communes from 2004 through 2006.

Current revenue (including mainly tax revenues) grew faster than expenditure, which enabled a sharp increase in both operating cost savings (current revenue minus current expenditure including interest) and net operational savings (operational savings net interest), given the very low amounts of borrowing and thus interest payments. Operational savings therefore rose by more than 30 percent over the three-year period.

Capital expenditure increased by 20 percent over the period and accounts for between a quarter and a fifth of current revenue. On average, about one-third of this expenditure was covered by own investment resources. But this percentage dropped dramatically, from 44 percent in 2004 to 5 percent in 2006. As a result, the communes' investment effort was mostly and increasingly funded by autofinancing. The share of autofinancing in funding communal investments thus increased from 56 percent in 2004 to 77 percent in 2006. Finally, the

Table 5.14 Communes' Financial Balance in Senegal, 2004 and 2006
CFAF, millions

Revenue	2004	2006	Expenditure	2004	2006
Current revenue	40,392	47,297	Current expenditure	34,115	36,434
Carryover	3,276	1,017	Financial expenses	234	0
Actual revenues	37,116	46,280	Net saving	6,044	10,862
(Tax-sharing receipts)	1,791	2,619			
(FDD)	2,956	4,018			
(Other central government transfers)	863	825			
Capital revenue	3,721	2,805	Capital expenditure	8,490	12,217
(FECL)	630	823	Capital repayment	0	0
(Other central government transfers)	1,760	1,973			
Net saving	6,044	10,862			
			Closing balance	1,275	1,450

Source: ADM 2008.
Note: FDD = Decentralization Allocation Fund (*Fonds de dotation de la décentralisation*); FECL = Fund for Local Government Infrastructures (*Fonds d'équipement des collectivités locales*).

closing balance, although positive, is far from robust (covering around 15 days of administrative expenses).

Central government transfers, it seems, played only a relatively marginal role in these outcomes. Certainly, their increase from around CFAF 4 billion to CFAF 7 billion funded 40 percent of the increase in current expenditure, but the operating transfers represent scarcely more than 15 percent of current revenue.

On the investment side, the contribution of transfers to financing investments is also weak. It accounts for around one-third of autofinancing and ultimately not more than a quarter of communal capital spending.

With such an effort geared toward communal investment, recurrent operating costs should be visible. However, they seem either low or nonexistent. These figures raise a number of questions, first on the expenditure side:

- Are the current expenditures entered elsewhere—in other public (state) budgets or association budgets? (This is doubtful, at least on a large scale.)

- Are recurrent expenditures not implemented or, in other words, are the services related to equipment poorly or not at all delivered?

- For investments, are maintenance costs poorly or not at all assumed?

- The contribution of transfers to current expenditure seems remarkably low—admittedly with some intermittent increases but limited overall. How is this to be explained in the context of decentralization?

On the revenue side, it is quite striking that the communes' financial balance basically depends on autofinancing. What confidence can be placed in the measurement of the CTs' autofinancing? Very likely, debt entries are quite incomplete, as previously mentioned. For example, they omit the loans granted by the ADM to most of the communes.

On the expenditure side, it is not certain that local budgets record all capital spending. Under these circumstances, local investment budgets probably fail, to a large extent, to track the real investment efforts. They probably greatly underestimate the amount of future repayments that must be taken into account to ensure the financial sustainability of the Senegalese CTs.

Notes

1. Constitution of 2001, Title XI, Art. 102.
2. Law 96-06, Art. 6.
3. Law 96-06, Art. 6.
4. Law 96-06, Art. 6.
5. CCL, Art. 12.
6. CCL, Art. 13.
7. CCL, Art. 17.
8. CCL, Art. 17.
9. CCL, Art. 77.
10. CCL, Art. 79.
11. The arrondissement communes were created in 1996 by Law 96-09 of March 22.
12. CCL, Art. 192.
13. Decree 76-63 of 1973.
14. CCL, Title VI and Art. 344 ff.
15. Circular d01737 of March 1997.
16. CCL, Art. 344 and 358.
17. This point is examined in detail in the Public Expenditure and Financial Accountability (PEFA) report (Giovanni and Chomentowski 2009) on the specific case of the town of Dakar, regarding the extent of compliance between the accounting nomenclature used and the International Monetary Fund's (IMF's) Government Finance Statistics classification.
18. Law 96-06, Art. 3.
19. The responsibilities are described in detail in Title 2 of Law 96-07 of March 22, 1996, amended by the laws of April 15, 2002, and August 25, 2004, Art. 16–27.
20. Law 96-07, Art. 257–259.
21. Decree 2007-408 of March 16, 2007, laying down the modalities for distribution of the town's overall grant to the arrondissement communes.
22. For more details on the allocations and grants from the central government to subnational government units, see the "Intergovernmental Transfers" section of this chapter.

23. Law 96-07, Art. 61.
24. Circular 01738 MINT/DCL of March 21, 1997.
25. Law 96-09 of March 22, 1996.
26. Law of July 9, 1992, amended by Law 2004-12 of February 6, 2004.
27. CCL, Art. 250 *ff.*
28. CGI, Art. 201.
29. CGI, Art. 207.
30. Created by Article 74 of Law 2004-12 of February 6, 2004.
31. CGI, Art. 242.
32. CGI, Art. 215 and 218, respectively.
33. CGI, Art. 234.
34. CGI, Art. 275.
35. Law 96-09, Art. 23.
36. Decree 2007-408 of March 16, 2007, laying down the distribution mechanism for the town's overall grant to CAs.
37. Prefectoral decree of January 13, 2004.
38. Law 96-08 of February 5, 1996 (Art. 23, Ib).
39. Law 96-06, Art. 6.
40. Law 96-06, Art. 6.
41. Law 96-06, Art. 6.
42. Law 96-06, Art. 8–9.
43. Law 96-07, Art. 58.
44. Provided for under Law 2007-07 of February 12, 2007.
45. Law 2007-07 of February 12, 2007.
46. Law 2007-07 of February 12, 2007.
47. The ADM analyzes the commune's performance through financial audits. The tax revenue-to-budget ratio is used to analyze the commune's financial autonomy. The prospective financial analysis is based on the three previous years. It serves to establish the criteria that the ADM imposes on communes that have signed a municipal contract.
48. Law 96-06 of February 5, 1996, Art. 346.
49. Law 96-06 of February 5, 1996, Art. 346.
50. Law 96-06 of February 5, 1996, Art. 347.
51. The *Crédit communal* was created by Decree No. 88-1296 of September 19, 1988, on the creation and organization of communal credit, taken up again within the framework of the PAC following the 1997 creation of the ADM.
52. CCL, Art. 255.
53. Analysis by F. Audras, November 2009, internal document, AFD, Paris.
54. Senegal's GDP was CFAF 4,894 billion in 2006 (data from the *Agence nationale de la statistique et de la démographie*).
55. Post-2006 expenditures are not recorded uniformly. Therefore, they will not be used statistically in the present analysis.
56. Not to be confused with the CRs (rural communities).

References

ADM (Agence de développement municipal). 2008. *Guide des ratios financiers des communes 2004, 2005, 2006.* Dakar: ADM.

Badiane, E. 2004. "Développement urbain et dynamique des acteurs locaux: le cas de Kaolack au Senegal." Doctoral thesis, Université de Toulouse III-Le Mirail.

Dafflon, B., and T. Madiès. 2008. "Décentralisation: quelques principes issus de la théorie du fédéralisme financier." [Decentralization: A Few Principles from the Theory of Fiscal Federalism.] Notes et documents 42, Agence Française de Développement, Paris.

Giovanni, C., and V. Chomentowski. 2009 "Évaluation de la gestion des finances publiques de la ville de Dakar." Public Expenditure and Financial Accountability (PEFA) report, World Bank, Agence Française de Développement, and Public-Private Infrastructure Advisory Facility, Paris and Washington, DC. http://www.adm.sn/download .php?chemin=actupdf/&filename=RAPPORT_PEFA_DAKAR_mai_2009.pdf.

Chapter 6

Decentralization: A Comparative and Cross-Cutting Analysis of the Stakes

Thierry Madiès

This chapter compares the decentralization processes of the four Sub-Saharan countries analyzed in the previous chapters. These countries were proposed by the Agence Française de Développement and therefore are not intended to make up a representative sample. The approach taken here breaks down into two steps:

- First, we show how the analytical guide described in chapter 1 is robust enough to allow a comparison of eventual gaps between the founding constitutional and legal texts on decentralization and the on-the-ground realities in countries that are seemingly disparate from an institutional standpoint.

- Second, we will underline how, beyond these differences, this guide enables us to point up similarities that help us to gauge the relative effectiveness of the decentralization processes in the four countries. The chapter concludes with some practical lessons to be learned from the comparison.

The Analytical Guide: An Enabling Blueprint for Cross-Cutting Comparisons

To begin with, remember that the analytical guide outlined in chapter 1 that steered the four country studies is not a normative guide. It views decentralization as a dynamic process—not as a targeted point of equilibrium—whose trajectory and "starting conditions" vary from one country to another. The way this process is piloted should take into account the specific constraints facing each country. It will also depend on the political will of their public authorities.

In all events, public authorities need to have access to a dashboard enabling them to measure the extent to which the reality on the ground deviates from the texts adopted by the legislature, which are often complete (at least in

Francophone Africa, because they generally mirror what was done in France—for better or worse). The analytical guide provides this institutional dashboard. More specifically, it compares the four countries against a set of criteria that can be divided and grouped under seven headings (or blocks) as shown in table 6.1 at the end of this chapter:

1. Recent history of decentralization in the country in question

2. Institutional design for decentralization

3. Budget process and balance of accounts, along with borrowing and debt

4. Assignment of responsibilities and budget autonomy

5. Fiscal resources

6. Intergovernmental transfers

7. Statistical data available to measure the progress of decentralization over time.

At this point, it is worth recalling the justification for the criteria used in the analytical guide. Decentralization is regarded here as an institutional process rooted in a country's specific history. In this respect, what matters is first to understand the historical background by examining the reasons and political will that prompted the country to decentralize (see block 1 in table 6.1).

However, that historical understanding is not enough. The relationships forged on the ground between deconcentrated authorities and decentralized authorities should also be examined because these relationships reflect the extent to which the will (or capacity) to decentralize translates into practice. The field observations are then compared with the institutional design (see block 2 in table 6.1).

Next, to be workable from a financial perspective, decentralization must be built on an accounting and budgetary framework that permits close monitoring of the accounts of decentralized local governments and, ultimately, the construction of dashboards to help steer the decentralization process (see block 3 in table 6.1).

Yet it is impossible to implement coherent budgetary rules without first having precisely defined the responsibilities to be devolved to decentralized local governments (a somewhat political choice, to be reached by consensus). This point is crucial because significant discrepancies often exist between the responsibilities devolved by law and those devolved in practice—with effective exercise of devolved functions and budget autonomy being key factors (see block 4 in table 6.1).

Once agreement has been reached as to the responsibilities to be transferred, the question naturally arises of what resources decentralized local governments have at their disposal to discharge their new responsibilities—a question that implies they have sufficient own resources to give them an adequate degree of fiscal autonomy (see block 5 in table 6.1).

In expenditure and revenue comparisons of decentralized budgets, most developing countries—as indeed transition economies and emerging countries—show a vertical fiscal gap, meaning that local governments do not have adequate own resources to cover both standardized expenditure (for delegated functions) and own expenditure (for devolved functions). In these circumstances, central government budget transfers fill the gap (see block 6 in table 6.1). These intergovernmental transfers, however, are framed by different objectives that must be correctly identified. They may or may not be linked to the performance of local-level management. Moreover, the transfers may be stable over time and therefore predictable or, on the contrary, discretionary and consequently unpredictable. In all instances, the transfers will affect local government autonomy as well as the risk posed by decentralized governments, a risk that also depends on their borrowing capacity (see again block 3, table 6.1).

Last but not least of the problems facing the analyst, the statistical data on decentralized public finances are incomplete (see block 7 in table 6.1). Unfortunately, there is a lack of reliable and robust data on decentralized public spending covering multiyear periods. In most cases, the accounting system does not classify expenditure by function, so the progress of decentralization cannot be measured against a list of devolved responsibilities—which poses even more problems for assessing the situation "before" and "after" decentralization. At best, spending is classified by type of expenditure (personnel expenditure, purchases of goods and services, external works, financial expenses, and so forth). The situation is less precarious where own and transferred resources are concerned.

Decentralization, but Not Quite: Common Traits Despite Institutional Differences

The comparative guide in table 6.1 enables a cross-cutting analysis of our four case studies. The informed reader will have understood that the analysis proposed is inevitably relative and subject to caution because each country analyzed has its own specific historical context, political framework, and institutional design. Despite these difficulties and reservations, this section will show that, beyond their differences, the countries come up against similar problems when implementing their "decentralization" process. To our knowledge, the pilot study summarized in table 6.1 is the first attempt at cross-country analysis based on a single analytical tool, and thus it is more than simply a juxtaposition of case studies. This is one original feature of our work.

Four fundamental aspects emerge from a cross-cutting analysis using the comparative table. These aspects include historical timing of decentralization, driving forces behind the decentralization process, confusion about the very nature of decentralization, and the impact of intergovernmental transfers on budget autonomy.

Historical Timing of Decentralization

The countries studied set out on the path to decentralization in the mid-1990s (more recently for Kenya). However, some of them (like Senegal) had already implemented some elements of decentralization at a much earlier date (in Burkina Faso, even before independence). Kenya is unusual in that it chose to "recentralize" after independence. The rhythm at which decentralization has been implemented over recent years has not been continuous in any of the countries.

Driving Forces behind the Decentralization Process

The decentralization process (table 6.1, block 2) was put into place

- Under varying degrees of pressure from international donors, with decentralization being included in the principle of conditionality;

- As a result of the central government's political will (more or less affirmed, depending on the country) to improve the provision of local public services for its citizens;

- In response to the central government's attempts to reduce the pressure on its own public finances by transferring its budget constraint problems to the decentralized level;

- With the central government's stated determination to keep some power to control the decentralized authorities, although how this is achieved varies across countries;

- As an occasional political maneuver to manage aspirations to autonomy in certain regions;

- Sometimes drawing on the experiences of neighboring countries (Burkina Faso looked to Mali) or more or less following the example of the former colonial power (Burkina Faso chose a more original path than Senegal, perhaps because its reassertion of decentralization is more recent).

Confusion about the Very Nature of the Decentralization Process

A central government's wish to retain control depends on the political context and the history of each of the four countries, but in practice it leads to confusion about the very nature of decentralization.

The term "decentralization"—meaning the devolution of powers to fully autonomous local governments—is not really applicable to any of the studied countries, albeit for reasons that differ for each country, as we shall explain. We should underline, at this point, that the state of affairs in Ghana is paradoxically clear: "decentralization" refers to territorialized public authorities, encompassing not only deconcentrated central government services but also decentralized subnational governments.

More specifically, for each of the four countries in the study, we find the following:

- Overlapping responsibilities between different tiers of decentralized local government, if they exist, and also between the central government and decentralized governments (table 6.1, block 4)
- Varying concepts of budget and financial autonomy across the four countries (table 6.1, blocks 4 and 5)
- In one way or another, persistent supervision (in the broad sense) by the central government over decentralized local governments (table 6.1, block 2).

Overlapping responsibilities between different tiers of local government and between the central government and decentralized government (table 6.1, block 4)
When different levels of local and central government share the same or similar responsibilities, the question then arises regarding "who is responsible for what?" by virtue of the principle of responsibility that is supposed to guide genuine devolution of powers. This is all the more problematic because, in each of the countries, large cities have frequently taken over responsibilities that the central government has failed to perform, which only confuses matters further.

We will, however, highlight one difference between the Francophone and Anglophone countries concerning the responsibilities devolved to local government. In the Francophone countries, "packages" of functions have been assigned (in law, at least), even if these turn out to be far from effective on the ground (basic education and literacy; drinking water and sanitation; culture; youth, sports, and recreation; and sometimes, but not always, health). In Francophone Burkina Faso, for example, the Ministry of Health is slowing down the transfer of responsibilities because its negotiating power is superior to that of the Ministry of Territorial Administration and Decentralization. In Anglophone Ghana (not to mention Kenya), the situation is different: there is no clearly identified package of assigned responsibilities but rather a list of tasks often framed in terms of expected results.

Unfortunately, the scarcity of information makes it difficult for us to judge whether the quality of services provided by decentralized governments is better than when the services were provided by the central government. What we do notice, however, is that the cities (at least, each country's capital and second largest city) have taken over some responsibilities that the central government could not provide, and they fund these from their own resources, which generally speaking is a step forward for their citizens. In small rural municipalities, citizens' strong identification with their elected mayor—although local chieftaincies are sometimes present—makes the mayor accountable to them (even for some responsibilities that are not transferred to the mayor, which was particularly evident in Burkina Faso). Finally, there is the question of the technical capacities, such as project management skills, needed to provide certain services. This issue, however, applies as much to deconcentrated authorities as it does to decentralized authorities.

How the concepts of budget and financial autonomy compare across the four countries (table 6.1, blocks 4 and 5)   In Senegal and Burkina Faso, local governments have little, if any, autonomy on the taxation front, at least for the "main taxes" (tax bases and rates are set nationally). Nonetheless, we do not have the impression that this issue is really present on the agenda in either of these two countries. What is quite clearly observable, however, is that elected officials are trying by all possible means to create a margin of maneuver by introducing new taxes—which unfortunately are not very productive—and, more interestingly, by helping deconcentrated fiscal services identify the taxable bases for the taxes that fuel their own resources (or even by assisting in the tax collection).

In Ghana and Kenya, decentralized governments enjoy slightly more flexibility on the tax front than in Burkina Faso and Senegal (discretion to adjust rates and bases, albeit only to a limited extent in practice). Regarding spending, however, it is clear that their powers are perhaps more limited than those in the Francophone countries. (In Kenya, for example, there are strict guidelines on local authorities' budget spending, with specific percentages for earmarked expenditures.)

Persistent supervision by the central government, broadly speaking, over decentralized local governments (table 6.1, block 2)   In one way or another, decentralized local governments remain under the supervision (in the broad sense) of the central government:

- Local governments have limited budgetary and financial autonomy.
- In Senegal and Burkina Faso, there exists a legality control (this most often involves ex post control of local government acts, whereas for budgetary matters, the control is ex ante). In Ghana and Kenya, there are guidelines, which are sometimes strict.
- In all four countries, there is some degree of competition between the legitimacy of the elected authorities and that of the central government's representatives. In Burkina Faso, the governor's legitimacy is apparently superior to that of the president of the regional council. In Kenya, there is an ambivalent

relationship between mayors and members of parliament—national elected officials representing electoral constituencies.

- In Burkina Faso and Senegal, the deconcentrated authorities generally tend to view local elected officials as lacking the ability to discharge the functions assigned to them and in need of back-office support. The elected officials, on their side, consider the problem to be chiefly one of resources, which are too scant to allow them to recruit competent staff to cope with their new responsibilities. An appropriate assignment of functions between deconcentrated and decentralized authorities would mean that the former play a fully "supporting" role to the latter.

- In Kenya and Ghana, the participation of centrally appointed members in subnational executive and deliberative bodies is another means of exercising control over local governments. This is not the case in Burkina Faso and Senegal.

- In all four countries, central government officials hold key positions in the local authorities. In Burkina Faso and Senegal, given that there is no local civil service, the "directeurs généraux des services," who are central government officials, play an important role, especially (but not only) in small rural communes. Their expertise gives them an advantage over the mayors. In Kenya, central government officials also hold management positions and, in Ghana, the budget authorizing officer is appointed by the president (this point is still under discussion). The question of whether to create a local civil service is repeatedly raised in these countries.

- The question of the customary authority of chieftaincies and their relationship with the decentralized authorities arises in all four countries. These are two different types of legitimacy that are sometimes at odds. Even when they are not personally present in the assemblies and local executive bodies, the traditional chiefs are represented and have sound relays. This means the coordination between the mayors and traditional chiefs is necessary, especially concerning land policy, which is a highly sensitive issue.

Impact of Intergovernmental Transfers on Local Autonomy

The question of budget transfers from the central government to local governments is crucial because when transfers are substantial, they reduce the financial autonomy of local governments (table 6.1, block 6). Similarly, the local governments' budget autonomy disappears when these funds finance transferred responsibilities and specify exactly which budget items they are to be assigned to, as in Burkina Faso and to a lesser extent in Senegal.

At the same time, large transfers can affect risk in two ways:

- They can reduce decentralized government risk, in the sense that subsovereign risk is passed back to the sovereign level.

- The above effect, however, must be qualified if the central transfers to decentralized governments are unreliable (because this multiplies risks—both the sovereign risks and those linked to decentralized governments).

Their impact on decentralized government risk is thus ambiguous and will depend on how regularly the transfers are paid (and whether or not they are discretionary). These transfers have several features:

- Budget transfers represent a relatively small share of local resources in Senegal and Burkina Faso, whereas they make up a much larger share in Kenya and reach up to 80 percent in Ghana.
- In the Francophone countries, certain transfers are intended to finance packages of decentralized responsibilities. This is apparently not the case in the two Anglophone countries.
- Transfers intended to finance local government investment fail to take into account the recurrent operating expenses that strain local budgets. This is a problem in Burkina Faso because capital spending has to account for a third of forecasted spending. In Ghana, there is a tendency to classify what are actually operating expenditures as capital expenditures.
- In Kenya and Ghana, transfers are partly determined by performance indicators at the communal (municipal) level. This is not the case in Senegal and Burkina Faso, although it should be mentioned that, in Burkina Faso, performance indicators are currently coming into play for the Permanent Development Fund for Territorial Authorities (*Fonds permanent de développement des collectivités territoriales*).
- Alongside explicit transfers, there are implicit transfers. These involve local expenditures that are directly reimbursed by the central government, notably the salaries of central government officials working for local governments in all four countries. In the same vein, some transfers may be granted on a discretionary basis, which results in a lack of visibility for decentralized authorities and leads them to adopt opportunistic behavior instead of mobilizing their own resources. Additionally, of course, there is the risk that the central government will exert pressure on local elected officials.

Conclusions and Lessons To Be Learned

Anglophone countries are often presented as more "decentralized" than Francophone countries. The evidence presented in the preceding chapters shows that, in fact, this is not the case and that this perception stems from confusion about the term "decentralization." Local government budgetary and financial autonomy is highly controlled in all four countries, even though practices vary. Kenya, for instance, is a country with a low level of decentralization in the sense of the devolution of responsibilities.

The question thus arises as to whether, instead of constantly navigating between deconcentration and devolution in a context where local government resources are excessively low, it would not be better to first rationalize the deconcentration process before moving ahead with devolution. It should be borne in mind that decentralization is a process whose implementation phases depend on the individual trajectory of each country and, most likely, it cannot be rolled out in capital cities and rural municipalities simultaneously given that that within-country situations are so vastly different.

Seen from this angle, the concept of "progressiveness" developed in Burkina Faso—if applied consistently along with a road map detailing devolved roles, devolution timetables, training of local expertise, and funding—is an approach that warrants further study to identify lessons to be learned. However, what must be avoided are excessively slow devolutionary processes that lead deconcentrated levels to endlessly block the decentralization process.

A fundamental question concerns capacity building for local elected officials and local administrations because a successful transition from deconcentration to an effective devolution of powers requires improvements in this area. (International donors could contribute to capacity building at little cost.)

One important point, however, argues in favor of devolution rather than simply deconcentration. We observed that local elected officials, even though they are not officially autonomous, seek to broaden their room for maneuver because they are held accountable by their constituents (which would no doubt be less true for deconcentrated, thus nonelected, authorities).

Overall, we can identify three key challenges for successful decentralization in these countries:

- *Ensure that, in the end, deconcentrated authorities effectively assume their role of supporting decentralized authorities* (for project management, for instance). This supposes that the former do not feel they have been divested of their former powers to the benefit of the latter. The relationships between elected and deconcentrated authorities need to be complementary (which necessarily means clearly defining their respective tasks, even within devolved areas of responsibility). It is up to local governments, their elected officials, and legislative assemblies to decide on public policy and priorities, with deconcentrated authorities providing technical support and advice on project feasibility and implementation.

- *Find a means of narrowing the gap between local expenditures and revenues.* One approach would be to endow local governments with current resources (particularly through more user fees) that are as far as possible linked to the effective provision of services—and thus to a certain efficiency in exercising devolved responsibilities.
- *Encourage the population's participation in decision making and monitoring of local public policies.* This implies greater transparency and, for the general public, better access to information. (Experience shows that local newspapers and local radio can fulfill this role, provided that the importance of local dialects is not neglected.) "Social accountability" schemes are already in place in Anglophone countries as well as in a number of Francophone countries such as Benin, Cameroon, and Senegal (especially in the Fissel region). In a small rural community in Burkina Faso, we even witnessed the local executive body, at year-end, justifying to a popular assembly how they had used the receipts from the "cart tax" (a tax created by the local authority to increase its own resources).

Four Countries, Four Decentralization Processes

Burkina Faso is still in an experimental phase of its decentralization process, but the principles of progressiveness for the devolution of responsibilities and of experimentation are interesting. The approach is based on selecting a sample of local authorities, deconcentrating certain responsibilities before devolving them, and then extending this approach to other local authorities while gradually phasing in the effective devolution of selected responsibilities.

Kenya, until recently, had chosen the path of "recentralization." The new constitution, adopted in 2010 and due to enter into force in 2012, may well give fresh hope for a decentralized approach. However, the areas of conflict inherent in the text make the outcome of the implementation phase highly uncertain.

Ghana, for its part, is attempting to pursue the deconcentration and decentralization processes simultaneously (or in parallel).

Senegal drew inspiration from the French-style decentralization model, yet its effectiveness still seems weak, which raises the question: What are the objectives and implementation strategy?

Table 6.1 Guide Comparing the Status of Decentralization in the Four Reference Sub-Saharan African Countries

	Burkina Faso	Ghana	Kenya	Senegal
1. Recent History of Decentralization				
Key dates in recent years	Commitment to decentralization (re)affirmed in early 2000s (General Code of Territorial Collectivities [*Code general des collectivités territoriales*] adopted in 2004).	• 1992 Constitution (Chapter 20) and Local Government Act (462) of 1993. • Ongoing reforms since 2009, but it is still not possible to gain a clear picture of the process being undertaken.	• Timid progress toward decentralization since early 2000s after a postindependence period when central government powers were reinforced at the expense of local governments. • New constitution adopted by referendum in August 2010, modifying notably the organization of the local public sector.	Decentralization process deepened during second half of 1990s (1996 Code of Territorial Collectivities [*Code des collectivités territoriales*] and the 2001 Constitution).
Reasons prompting decentralization	• Political will (at least at one time) for greater involvement of the population in local decisions. • Experience of neighboring countries (especially Mali). • Pressure from international donors.	• Democratization process after a military regime. • Pressure from international donors. • Language barrier: no imitation of Francophone African countries. • Attempt to integrate traditional chieftaincies in the decentralization and territorialization process (after unsuccessfully trying to control them). The chieftaincies may give their opinion on members appointed by the president and have intermediaries within the District Assemblies.	• Internal political situation and negotiations with civil society and the opposition. • Experience of neighboring countries (in particular, Tanzania and Uganda). • Pressure from international donors. *Note:* The tribal issue has long been closely linked to the questions of decentralization and hinders the process.	Consolidation of national unity.

(continued next page)

275

Table 6.1 (continued)

	Burkina Faso	Ghana	Kenya	Senegal
1. Recent History of Decentralization				
Political will for decentralization	• Political support on the whole from the government, but the Ministry of Territorial Administration and Decentralization responsible for these issues carries little weight compared with the line ministries (such as the Ministry of Health). • Strong support from the local elected officials whom we met.	According to some, there is new momentum since the "decentralizers" returned to power at the end of December 2008. In reality, it is less a process of decentralization than of more deconcentration, with local grassroots participation and a determination to improve services provided to the public.	• No apparent will from central government to decentralize until recently (2010 reform); on the contrary, quite a pronounced centralizing trend. • Ambiguous central government policy with seemingly little support for genuine devolution. • Seeming lack of coherence in pursued goals (aim of improving local management but so far no willingness to transfer real power to local authorities). The Local Authority Transfer Fund (LATF) (the financial arm of the Kenya Local Government Reform Program since 1999) provides an example of giving local authorities access to more resources but with strict budget rules laid down by the Ministry of Local Government.	• Persistent gap between the decentralization laws and the situation on the ground (no real political will to implement decentralization as laid down in the legislation). • Yet decentralization has population's support because it enables greater awareness of local problems.
2. Institutional Framework of Decentralization				
Implementation of the decentralization process	• Principle of progressiveness (written into law) and a logic of experimentation (49 pilot municipalities).	A declaration of intent and legislation adopted in 2009 aimed at activating laws that have already been passed but not implemented.	Reform in progress.	Implementation of decentralization provided for by law but probably too rapid to be effective on the ground.

	• The rule of progressiveness has two dimensions: it involves functions to be decentralized over time, but it also materializes in the fact that decentralized functions are subject to deconcentration before being fully devolved to local governments.			
Number of tiers of decentralized governments and deconcentrated administrative units	• Two levels of decentralization: regions and communes (of varying status). • Three levels of deconcentration: regions, provinces, and departments.	• One decentralized level: the districts (metropolitan, municipal, and district assemblies; MMDAs). • Two deconcentrated levels that group the various deconcentrated central government departments: regions and districts.	• One single decentralized level: local authorities. • Four levels of deconcentration: provinces, districts, divisions, and locations. • In addition, there is a special entity: the constituencies (electoral districts for parliamentary elections).	• Two levels of decentralization: regions and communes (of varying status). • Three levels of deconcentration: regions, departments, and arrondissements.
Relationship between deconcentrated authorities (and more generally the central government) and decentralized local authorities	• Ambiguous relationships between deconcentrated and decentralized authorities, particularly in the regions (strong historical legitimacy of governors compared with the regional council president, who is elected by indirect universal suffrage). • The role of prefect (department) is obsolete. (The mayor now holds a comparatively stronger position.)	• What is denoted as "decentralization" actually refers to all territorialized public institutions; that is, both deconcentrated and decentralized institutions. • The district assemblies operate both as managing authorities for deconcentrated central government services and as decentralized local governments.	• Constituencies and local authorities are put into competition (either wilfully or due to the legacy of the past) to provide local public services (the same responsibilities) within a context where members of parliament have greater political legitimacy than the mayors. • Mayors are elected through indirect universal suffrage by municipal councillors, some of whom (one-fourth) are centrally appointed.	On paper, decentralization is in the sense of devolution, but in reality it is more akin to deconcentration than devolution: many assigned responsibilities are still funded and managed by deconcentrated central government services.

(continued next page)

277

Table 6.1 (continued)

Burkina Faso	Ghana	Kenya	Senegal

2. Institutional Framework of Decentralization

Burkina Faso	Ghana	Kenya	Senegal
• A *still open question*: Are deconcentrated services playing their role of supporting the decentralization process pending capacity building at the local level (the central government has "deconcentrated" expenditures before transferring them to local governments)? Or do these units hinder the decentralization process? • The secretary general of a commune is a state-appointed official.	• *Consequences*: overlapping responsibilities between deconcentrated central government services and local governments in a context where deconcentrated authorities are better endowed than decentralized authorities (more specifically, in the areas of education and health). Central government is determined to keep control of the situation. • District assemblies comprise elected members (70%) and members appointed by the President of the Republic (30%).	• The mayor is not the authorizing officer of the budget; it is the treasurer who implements the budget after approval by the Finance Committee. • The town clerk (the local authority's CEO) is a central government official. *Note:* Kenya is creating new deconcentrated entities (unlike Ghana). The number of districts has increased over recent decades. There are too many levels of deconcentration (provinces, districts, locations, sublocations) with powers and territorial boundaries that overlap those of local authorities. The new constitution appears to be heading in the right direction by simplifying matters and focusing efforts on the regional and county levels as well as clarifying the mandate devolved to "local authorities."	

Supervision	Ex post supervision of local government acts and ex ante supervision (particularly but not only) relating to budgetary control.	• Local autonomy concerning expenditure is guaranteed by law (LG Act 462 of 1993, Art. 11). • Limited autonomy in practice owing to supervision (guidelines and formal control), particularly of the administration of finances. • Ex ante budgetary control but also ex post control.	• Ex ante supervision of provincial commissioners regarding local governments' budgets. • Implicit supervision, as the authorizing officer is a central government official (and not the mayor). This is thus akin to an "appropriateness" control. • Supervision given the participation of central government officials in municipal council committees. • Controls of budget execution are routinely monitored by the Ministry of Local Government through the Kenya Local Government Reform Program and the LATF process. It is the ministry that remains ultimately responsible for the proper execution of local budgets.	Ex post supervision of local government acts and ex ante supervision (particularly but not only) relating to budgetary control.
Local civil service	• No: the secretary general is a central government official, and support staff are under contract with the local government. • Recurring debate on whether to establish a local civil service.	• No: there are central government officials in local governments (the latter use this situation to have part of their payroll funded by the central government). • Local government service planned to integrate deconcentrated officials into the decentralized services.	• No: there are central government officials in the municipalities (at least in the supervisory positions). • In the municipalities, support staff for local services exist for low-level positions.	• No: there are central government officials in local governments. • Support staff are under contract with the local government. • Recurring debate on whether to establish a local civil service.

(continued next page)

Table 6.1 (continued)

	Burkina Faso	Ghana	Kenya	Senegal
3. Decentralized Budget				
Accounting classification of revenue and expenditure	• Classification of expenditure by type but not by function (the Ouagadougou local authority is currently setting up a functional nomenclature). • Individual communal initiatives to establish a functional classification: there is therefore an emerging need.	Classification by expenditure type.	Classification by type and summary classification by function.	Classification of expenditure by type and function.
Budget balance	Adopted administrative accounts are in "actual balance" (in practice, the current account must show a 20% surplus to fund capital expenditure).	Current budget is balanced.	• Budgets must be presented in balance, taking into account the surplus or deficit and commitments brought forward from previous years and the need for working capital in the local authority. In practice, budget deficits are common because revenues tend to be artificially inflated. • This seems to call into question the budget annularity principle.	Budgets and accounts must be presented in "actual balance," and savings forecasted in the budget should at least enable debt-servicing costs to be covered for the budget period, given that the cash balance appearing in the accounts must not exceed a limited fraction of current revenues.
Treasury single account	Yes: the rule of separating the duties of authorizing officer and accounting officer.	No: local governments deposit their funds in commercial banks.	No: local governments deposit their funds in commercial banks.	Yes: the rule of separating the duties of authorizing officer and accounting officer.

Salary arrears and late payment of revenue due by the central government to local governments	Apparently not.	• Delays for central government transfers (District Assembly Common Fund; DACF). • Apparently no salary arrears for staff paid by local governments (flexibility relates to contract renewal).	Yes: salary arrears and delays in financial transfer payments.	Yes: delays in central government transfers and salary arrears.
Auditing and transparency of accounts	—	• Accounts submitted on time. • Audits are belated.	• Accounts submitted on time (LATF requirement). • Auditing is effective but belated (auditor general).	• Most local governments do not produce administrative accounts but rather a compte de *gestion* (book of entries and outlays), which is provided by the treasurers at the end of the fiscal year. • Accounts submitted late. • Auditing leaves much to be desired for lack of resources.
Borrowing capacity	None for the time being.	Low borrowing ceilings.	• High levels of municipal indebtedness. • Measures implemented by the central government designed to reduce local government outstanding debt.	Capacity much in question.

4. Assignment of Responsibilities and Budget Autonomy

Devolution process	Progressive process, responsibility by responsibility and over time (deconcentration, then devolution).	The devolution and deconcentration processes appear to be parallel rather than complementary.	• n.a.: no transfer of "packages" of responsibilities. • Discretionary: local authorities take the initiative and then negotiate with the relevant ministry.	No progressive process.

(continued next page)

Table 6.1 (continued)

	Burkina Faso	Ghana	Kenya	Senegal
4. Assignment of Responsibilities and Budget Autonomy				
Effectiveness and funding of devolved responsibilities	• Broad transfer of responsibilities provided for by law but limited in practice (primarily limited to basic education and literacy, health, supply of drinking water, and sanitation). • Resistance from certain ministries. • Funding is guaranteed and increasing but insufficient (not concomitant).	• Situation unclear. • Education and health remain the responsibility of the ministries and their deconcentrated services.	Assigned responsibilities have been reduced over time except when local authorities have taken them over.	• Responsibilities that are actually transferred are relatively limited: education, health, and youth and sport. • Guaranteed funding by the Decentralization Allocation Fund (*Fonds de dotation de la décentralisation;* FDD): discretionary until 2006.
Budget autonomy	• In theory, none (the transfer of responsibilities describes in great detail the tasks that local governments must provide). • Marginal adjustments possible, but they are minor for lack of adequate own financial resources. They include school supplies and support staff (but using own resources).	• Yes, for expenditure that can be financed by own revenues. • The central government replaces local governments for the responsibilities that they do not assume.	In theory, very little, given that precise percentages of central government transfers must be earmarked for certain types of expenditure when drawing up the budget.	• Limited in practice (the transfer of responsibilities describes in great detail the services that local governments must provide). • Marginal adjustments possible for school supplies and support staff, for example (but using own resources).
Exclusive or shared responsibilities	The list of assigned responsibilities provided for by law is meant to refer to exclusive responsibilities. In practice, however, the analysis of local service production shows that responsibilities are shared, with the central government being predominant.	One level of local government. Responsibilities shared with the central government.	One level of subnational government, hence exclusive responsibilities. There is, on the other hand, a problem of coordination with the constituencies as well as the deconcentrated authorities.	No exclusive responsibilities, hence the problems of coordination.

5. Fiscal Resources

Main own resources (share of local resources, excluding borrowing)	Own resources comprise some minor taxes and user fees and charges, but the amounts are totally inadequate for devolved responsibilities or those within the local government's discretion.	• Developed land not taxed (undeveloped land falls within the jurisdiction of the traditional chieftaincies). • Business taxes. • Market stall fees, licenses.	Varies greatly across local authorities: largest fraction of local revenue comes from property rates, single business permits, market fees, and, residually, the contribution in lieu of rates (CILOR)—the tax the central government pays for municipal land and buildings that it occupies (a tax with poor payment rates).	Main own resources: • Motor vehicle tax • Graduated flat-rate tax (TRIMF) • Tax on developed and undeveloped land • Tax on real estate gain • Business taxes • Licenses.
Shared or exclusive taxes	The six main local direct taxes are shared among the communes and regions (assigned according to the derivation principle).	Exclusive taxes.	Exclusive taxes only for municipalities.	Only the communes receive tax revenue (not the regions).
Financial autonomy	• No autonomy in defining tax bases or setting tax rates. • The only leeway: creating new taxes and levies and mobilizing communal staff to improve identification of tax bases and collection rates.	• Setting tax rates but under supervision prescribed by law. • Rate setting is debated in the MMDAs.	• Little autonomy but some flexibility in setting bases and rates for certain taxes. • Apparently low in practice.	• In practice, no autonomy in defining tax bases or setting tax rates. • The only leeway: creating new taxes and levies and mobilizing local authority staff to improve identification of tax bases and collection rates.
"Territoriality" of taxes and incentives	Business tax is levied where companies are registered, making it a "deterritorialized" tax and exacerbating inequalities that advantage Ouagadougou and Bobo-Dioulasso.	n.a.	The single business tax is levied in the place where companies are registered.	TRIMF presents a fiscal domiciliation problem (employees pay this tax in the commune where they are employed).

(continued next page)

Table 6.1 (continued)

	Burkina Faso	Ghana	Kenya	Senegal
5. Fiscal Resources				
Mobilization of tax bases and collection rates	• Poor mobilization of tax bases because taxpayers are not identified. • Tax collection by central government tax office officials and Treasury officials. • No significant delays in issuing and sending out tax rolls. • Collection rate (compared with issued rolls) seems high, but it is difficult for the communes surveyed to know whether issued rolls are complete relative to local economic activities.	• Tax collection raises problems. The tax collectors are private agents paid according to their performance.	• Tax collection by local authority officials. • Very low collection rate. • Poor knowledge of tax bases.	• Poor mobilization of tax bases because taxpayers are not identified. • Tax collection by Treasury officials. • Delays sending out tax rolls. • Poor collection rate, or even zero for low-yield taxes where the cost of collection would exceed the amount collected.
User fees and charges	Not used enough.	Few user fees and charges.	Approximately 20% of total local authority revenues.	Relatively numerous (fees for pound and for places in markets, fairs, and so on).
6. Intergovernmental Transfers				
Defining the objectives (such as funding of transferred responsibilities, equalization)	• General operating block grants. • General purpose investment grants. • Permanent Development Fund for Territorial Collectivities (*Fonds permanent de développement des collectivités locales*; FPDCT). • Transfers earmarked for funding assigned responsibilities (through the Ministry of Territorial Administration and Decentralization). • No equalization objectives.	• Objectives undear. In principle, the District Assemblies Common Fund (DACF) should fund development expenditure but may deviate from this in practice. • No equalization objective for resources but (marginal) acknowledgment of "financial needs."	• LATF: general grants for investment and current expenditure. • CDF (Constituency Development Fund): investment grant. • RMLF (Road Maintenance Levy Fund): for roads. • No equalization objectives.	• Decentralization Allocation Fund (*Fonds de dotation de la décentralisation*; FDD): covering the net cost of responsibilities assigned to local governments. • *Fonds d'équipement des collectivités locales* (FECL) to enhance local government investment capacity. • The FDD appears, in practice, to have an equalizing effect.

Type of transfers (revenue sharing, conditionality and earmarking of transfers, and so on) and incentives (performance-based transfers)	• General operating and investment grants are, in principle, not earmarked. However, because responsibilities in the deconcentration phase are under vertical control of the ministries, actual freedom of use is limited. • Line ministry grants are all earmarked, as are the discretionary grants (for example, provincial officials, decentralization support structures, and investment grants). • Between 2007 and 2010, transferred shared revenue was earmarked (10% tax on petroleum products). • No performance indicators except for grants paid by the new FPDTC (created in 2007).	• DACF and DDF (District Development Facility) are earmarked for development expenditure. • Needs (for DACF) and performance (for DDF) are taken into consideration.	• Revenue-sharing (LATF): 5% of personal and corporate income taxes. • CDF: 2.5% of government ordinary revenue. • Both the LATF and the CDF are earmarked. • Performance indicators exist in theory for the LATF but are not effective in practice.	• FDD: discretionary earmarking provided for by law, but earmarking of resources prescribed by implementing decrees. • FECL: fund earmarked for investment. • No incentive aspect or performance-based indicators.
Adapting transfers to meet desired objectives	The stated aim is to increase unearmarked general grants. Communes will then define their priorities in accordance with minimum levels set by the central government. (Problem: minimum levels that are too demanding exhaust available resources and thus reduce the decision-making autonomy of local governments.)	• Problems of coherence between the two funds (DACF and DDF). • No operating grants. • A sometimes broad conception of "development expenditure" eligible for funds.	Capital expenditure has increased because of the LATF and the CDF, but operating grants are low.	The whole transfer system is ill-adapted.

(continued next page)

Table 6.1 (continued)

	Burkina Faso	Ghana	Kenya	Senegal
6. Budget Transfers				
Implicit transfers	Salaries of central government officials made available for communes.	Salaries of central government officials made available for the MMDAs.	Salaries of central government officials made available for local authorities.	Salaries of central government officials made available for communes.
7. Statistical Data				

Ratio between own resources and transfers	• The most recent statistical information obtained data from 2006. The ratio cannot therefore be calculated.
	• Small proportion of fiscal transfers.
		• Own resources: 20%.
		• Transfers: 80%.
		• World Bank study on districts' own resources: 15–20% (but wide disparities, reaching more than 40% in some districts).
			• Budget transfers account for a relatively high proportion, with wide disparities among local governments (60% for own resources and 40% for transfers).
			• According to a study on the five largest local governments:
			  ○ Own resources: 38%.
			  ○ Transfers: 62%.[a]
				• Own resources: 80%.
				• Transfers: 20%.

Note: CEO = chief executive officer; — = not available; n.a. = not applicable.
a. Transfer data include 2007–08 averages for the five largest local governments, with a considerable difference between Nairobi, where 71 percent of the budget was funded by central government transfers, and Kisumu, where this proportion was only 49 percent.

Chapter 7

Comments and Concrete Ways Forward

The results of this research on the political economy of decentralization in the four selected Sub-Saharan countries were presented on May 21, 2010, at the Agence Française de Développement (AFD) headquarters in Paris. The day of discussion brought together the AFD's key partners on the topic and researchers from different institutions working on decentralization in Africa as well as the World Bank. Two speakers provided an outsider's view of the work compiled in this volume. The publishers wished to include their comments in this book. We thank Frédéric Audras and Gérard Chambas for making this possible.

Comments: *Gérard Chambas*

In Sub-Saharan Africa, decentralization often dates back many years, and today it has become more deeply rooted and widespread in practically all of the countries. Most often, it is a key option for authorities looking not only to overcome the shortcomings of central governments but also to reinforce national unity and facilitate the participation of their populations.

However, although decentralization policies are currently in progress, few analytical studies both encompass decentralization as whole and focus specifically on Sub-Saharan African countries, even though country studies and studies on specific topics do exist.[1]

This shortfall of analyses contrasts with the importance of the stakes, which include two crucial aspects: strengthening national cohesion in the states concerned and promoting an acceptable level of central government effectiveness in the provision of public goods (education, health, local infrastructure, and institutions).

For this reason, it is particularly opportune that the AFD's research department has supported a study that takes into account multiple aspects of decentralization in Sub-Saharan Africa.

Method Adopted

The singularity of the analytical method adopted by the team of experts mobilized by the AFD is that it addresses, using a joint and multidisciplinary approach, the institutional aspects of decentralization as well as local government fiscal and financial choices.

A crucial preliminary step in this approach was to design an analytical guide for decentralization in Sub-Saharan Africa. Among the key elements of this guide, the authors sought specifically to highlight five major aspects.

(1) Institutional Characteristics

This aspect aims, on the one hand, to identify the reasons behind the decision to decentralize and, on the other hand, to assess the level of political will driving decentralization. An analytical survey is also carried out, from the viewpoint of institutional economy, of the arrangements for the decentralization process (the degree of progressiveness; institutional choices, particularly the number of government tiers in the decentralized and deconcentrated architecture; the nature of the relationships between deconcentrated authorities and decentralized governments; the form of local government supervision; and the eventual existence of a local civil service).

(2) The Budget Process and Balance of Accounts

The analysis involves the implementation of the single treasury principle, accounting classification methods, the application of budget balancing criteria, the existence of salary arrears, late payment of revenues due from the central government to local governments, and finally the methods used to ensure the transparency of accounts.

(3) The Assignment of Responsibilities and Budget Autonomy

This part of the analytical guide aims to investigate the arrangements for the transfer of responsibilities to local governments and to assess their level of budget autonomy. The guide also includes an analysis of the area of exclusive or shared responsibilities.

(4) Local Government Resources

This is a large section in the analytical guide, serving to distinguish between fiscal resources, budget transfers, and borrowing capacity:

- *Fiscal and nonfiscal resources.* The analysis includes the main local own resources (fiscal revenues and nonfiscal revenues [user fees and charges]), the degree of local government financial autonomy, the territoriality rules applied to local taxation, and the situation regarding the collection of local resources.

- *Budget transfers.* Having identified the objectives of central government budget transfers to local governments (earmarking for operating or investment

expenditure, funding areas of responsibility assigned by the central government, and equalization funding), the mechanisms for these transfers are also
studied—including, among other aspects, their nature as incentives. The
authors also evaluate implicit transfers, notably the provision of staff by the
central government.

- *Local government borrowing capacity.* Generally speaking, this capacity is
assessed as low or uncertain. In the specific case of Kenya, overindebted local
governments risk contributing to a general public debt crisis (reminiscent of
the Argentinean crisis with the provinces' debt burden).

(5) Local Financial Autonomy
This autonomy is evaluated using the ratio between local own resources and
central government transfers.

Results Achieved
The resulting analytical guide was applied as uniformly as possible to a diverse
sample of four countries (Burkina Faso, Ghana, Kenya, and Senegal). This is a
valuable advantage, because so far the studies available are generally carried out
using different methods, often making comparisons difficult if not quite simply
impossible.

The diversity of the four sample countries derives from their respective levels
of development, their institutional traditions (particularly administrative), and
their decentralization policies.

The results obtained using this analytical guide furnish possible answers to
some often-neglected questions, which are nonetheless key if one wishes to be
in position to meaningfully intervene in decentralization programs. Below, we
consider four of these questions.

(1) The Motivation and Rationale for Decentralization
Choosing to decentralize appears first and foremost to be a political choice
to strengthen national cohesion. It may be an opportunity to encourage the
participation of populations and to involve traditional authorities through a
variety of arrangements.

However, the goal of improving the efficiency of public goods provision,
widely foregrounded in the scientific literature on decentralization, does
not clearly emerge in the country studies, whereas it is an essential issue for
development, as highlighted by Chambas, Brun, and Rota Graziosi (2010b).

(2) Political Will
The political will to promote decentralization varies widely among countries
(Jacob 1998). The impetus quite frequently comes from donors, which may of
course run counter to enabling national ownership of the process.

(3) Institutional Framework

Institutional frameworks vary considerably but, based on the available country studies, it seems impossible to clearly identify any one system as being preferable to another. In certain countries (Ghana and Senegal), the deconcentrated government structures are in strong competition with decentralized local governments, which are financially less well endowed. Central government supervision is surprisingly strong in Ghana and Kenya, contrary to common opinion. Finally, institutional arrangements, particularly in Ghana, give a large place to the participation of traditional authorities in local government administration (unlike in Burkina Faso or Senegal).

(4) Budget Processes, Balance of Accounts, and Mobilization of Resources

The findings of the analytical guide reveal a broad array of systems and processes. The impact of differing administrative traditions, notably between the Anglophone and Francophone countries, helps to explain why the single unified treasury principle applies to Burkina Faso and Senegal but not to Ghana or Kenya.

As for local governments' own resources, these seem to be particularly low for the whole sample. The retrocession of fiscal revenues by the central government is often irregular, as are transfers. In this regard, the team commissioned by the AFD thus reaches the same conclusion as Chambas, Brun, and Rota Graziosi (2010b).

Outlook

The results of the analysis serve to identify and guide appropriate avenues of research with a view to drawing up operational guidelines to promote decentralization in a useful way. Applying the same method to the situation in new countries may reveal other issues that are impossible to apprehend on the basis of the four countries selected.

One initial category for study would be to identify criteria for assessing the effectiveness of decentralization. This could include criteria relating to participation of the population and the degree of democratization as well as the capacity to mobilize financial resources and the quality of local public goods provision. More generally, consideration could be given to the quality of local governance, which should be brought up to the standards of central state governance. Finally, local government efficiency should be assessed using performance indicators—one major difficulty being to distinguish which results are attributable to the central government and which are attributable to local governments because their spheres of action often overlap.

Once these analyses have been carried out, we could then attempt to answer many crucial questions:

• Is one of the keys to successful decentralization to join forces with traditional authorities?

- What are the most effective principles for institutional design, and how should the interaction between decentralized and deconcentrated structures be organized?
- How can resources be efficiently mobilized for the benefit of local governments (local own resources, fiscal retrocessions, central government transfers, loans, and so on)?
- What role should donors play, and how can their involvement incentivize greater local government efficiency?
- How can equalization targets between local governments be achieved, and how can decentralization become a successful instrument for reducing inequality and poverty?
- What can be done to improve the quality of local governance?
- How should local governments' areas of responsibility be defined and limited?

To sum up, the study conducted at the request of the AFD provides an analytical framework that should prompt further research intended to meaningfully promote decentralization in African countries. From a strictly economic standpoint, the challenge is considerable because it involves reestablishing or reinforcing an acceptable standard of state effectiveness in the provision of public goods, which is one of the crucial prerequisites for development.

Actionable Avenues: *Frédéric Audras*

This book is remarkable in several respects. It provides tools, information, and original ways of looking at the decentralization process in the four Sub-Saharan countries included in the ambit of the study. It gives donors and development stakeholders food for thought from a methodological, operational, institutional, and political viewpoint (in the sense of interpreting the interplay of the actors involved in decentralization).

But additionally this work questions and challenges donor practices. This was certainly not one of the initial objectives of the study's sponsors, but it is clearly one of the results: Our way of looking at these four countries has tended to change after reading this book. The lines of convergence and divergence between the countries are not those we were expecting, which raises questions about our support mechanisms and funding. The great merit of this work—and the great merit of its authors—is to have observed and analyzed situations through a different prism than that of the development stakeholders.

From a methodological standpoint, the work is built around an institutional and budgetary analytical guide that is of a universal nature or, in other words, it can embrace diverse geographies and, in particular, French or Anglo-Saxon style models of decentralization. On reading the book, it is satisfying to note that this guide is highly effective.

The institutional approach thus integrates multiple criteria such as economic (the "production of local services"), social (the "protection of minorities"), and historic dimensions, analyzing how the concept of decentralization has developed over time: Does the process involve deconcentration, delegation, or genuine devolution? Applying this approach to the four sample countries reveals just how important a role history plays in the construction of governance systems.

For the four countries under consideration, the implementation of a decentralization process seems more about responding to donor expectations than to the common desire of national and local political actors. The donors perceive decentralization as a policy that promotes better (national and local) governance and, for the populations concerned, access to public services that are of higher quality and more evenly distributed nationwide. However, within these four countries, the effective implementation of a decentralization policy seems to come up against obstacles of a historical and cultural nature. Ideas about national unity and the creation of a strong state (postdecolonization) thus sit uneasily with cooperation between a central government and local political actors if they do not belong to the same political groups or affiliation.

Moreover, central ministries (in particular, the interior and finance ministries) are not, on the whole, convinced of the effectiveness of decentralization. As a result, unwieldy legal and financial mechanisms are kept in place to control the activities of local governments, even when legislation has theoretically granted them considerable leeway for action. These factors slow down the setting up of local public services and facilities, leading populations to doubt the effectiveness of transferring powers to decentralized local governments.

This observation, which the authors develop during the country analyses, is likely to shift the direction of donor strategies. Decentralization support programs could, for example, incorporate training for local elected officials and capacity building for national and local administrations, based on a progressive logic of "deconcentration then devolution"—that is, training ministry employees who will then become local government officials. This approach would strengthen the actors' sense of ownership, in full respect of the historical and cultural setting, and eventually create the conditions for improved effectiveness in the transfer of powers to decentralized subnational governments. As is already the case in many Sub-Saharan African countries, it would help to coordinate and harmonize support from donors and development stakeholders (including nongovernmental organizations) with cooperation between towns in the North and the South.

Using the example of the four countries, the authors' financial and budgetary approach to decentralization has the advantage of clarifying the definitions of the indicators that measure a local government's autonomy. In chapter 1, Bernard Dafflon defines the notions of financial autonomy (concerning local government resources)[2] and budget autonomy (concerning expenditures). This distinction is fundamental. Certainly, these two definitions are of valuable help in understanding decentralized local government budgets, and the measurement of how effectively responsibilities are discharged relies on these two definitions.

Again, the book reveals contrasting situations in the four countries studied. Although legislative and regulatory mechanisms have been adopted that set out the fiscal and financial framework for decentralization (areas of assigned responsibilities, financial resources allocated, and so forth), decentralized local governments' real capacity to act turns out to be limited in practice. This is the case in Burkina Faso, Kenya, Senegal, and, to a lesser degree, Ghana.

The low level of financial autonomy observed may evidently be explained by the inadequacy of financial transfers from the central government, the absence of true decision-making capacity regarding local taxation, and the weak local revenue-raising capacity (such as taxes, fees, and charges for use of public facilities). Low financial autonomy points to a lack of budget autonomy for decentralized local governments: the central government fails to provide them with the additional authority needed to mobilize resources but passes on to them the political responsibility for the inadequacy of their means of action. Moreover, the lack of budget autonomy is exacerbated by the relative unpredictability of revenue collection (transfers and local taxes collected by the tax offices) as well as by the fact that some central government financial transfers are earmarked or tied to the exercise of certain responsibilities (in Kenya, for example).[3]

These findings are not new. To circumvent such difficulties, central governments, with donor support, have often introduced specific mechanisms to provide decentralized local governments with financial resources.

This is the case in Senegal, for instance, with the creation of the Agency for Municipal Development (*Agence de développement municipal*; ADM) in 1997, which implements (through an executive agency) municipal support programs (PAC then PRECOL).[4] The ADM receives the bulk of the Investment Fund for Territorial Collectivities (*Fonds d'équipement des collectivités locales*; FECL) resources and benefits from subsidized loans from donors. This funding is used to carry out investment programs on communal territory, with the communes repaying to the ADM the equivalent of the on-lent amounts. This financial package thus allows the communes, which have no access to external resources (there is no local government financing market), to have the benefit of the infrastructures and facilities vital for meeting their populations' needs (implementation of municipal contracts). However, because the commune is not the project owner, the communal budget does not track either revenues or expenditures for this type of investment project. The value of these investments and the way they are funded (indirect borrowing through the ADM) do not appear on the commune's balance sheet, whereas the debt repayment *is* shown in the budget.

Although this type of arrangement may prove effective in mobilizing external resources, it does not help to strengthen the budget autonomy of decentralized local governments because it is based on a project funding rationale (implementation through an entity other than the decentralized government) rather than on a budget funding rationale (implementation by the decentralized government).

More broadly, the crux of these difficulties lies in the capacity to mobilize own resources or, in other words, in the growth of central government fiscal revenues (part of which feeds into the transfers to local governments) and decentralized fiscal revenues (local taxes). These two levels are inextricably linked because local and national tax collection is carried out by central government tax services. In the context of public finances in developing countries, in particular Sub-Saharan Africa, it is hard to imagine precedence being given to improving local rather than national tax collection rates.[5] This means that the question of financial autonomy and correlated budget autonomy of decentralized governments seems to hinge, above all, on their ability to come up with and propose to the central government novel ways of mobilizing new resources. The research headed by Chambas (2010b) has, for instance, analyzed the solutions developed by several countries (in particular, Benin, Cameroon, and Côte d'Ivoire). The results are nevertheless disappointing: the pragmatic approach of some local governments (such as Dakar and Ouagadougou), which finance agents to help the fiscal services collect local taxes, appears to be the most effective even if its impact has been diluted over time (for lack of staff motivation over the long run).

This dual approach to decentralization—institutional and fiscal—developed by this book's authors and "tested" on four countries is synthesized in a comparative analytical guide. This approach could be extended by developing an operational tool[6] based on a spreadsheet that immediately identifies (in graphic form) a country's characteristics in terms of the financial and budget autonomy granted to decentralized local governments. With the authors' encouragement, an experimental version of this tool has been designed and remains open to any improvement. Here, we will take a look at how it was constructed.

1. Financial autonomy is measured against six criteria[7] assessed in the analytical guide:

   • Level of decentralized governments' own resources

- Exclusivity of taxes collected
- Decision-making authority of decentralized government concerning taxes (decisions on tax bases or rates)
- Capacity to mobilize tax bases
- Quality of local tax collection
- Effective capacity to resort to borrowing.[8]

2. Budget autonomy is also measured against six criteria, all taken from the analytical guide:
   - Discretion over the assignment of central government financial transfers
   - Effectiveness of such transfers to fund the responsibilities devolved to decentralized governments
   - Budgetary freedom to assume assigned responsibilities
   - Quality of the budgetary and accounting framework
   - Quality of the budget balancing guidelines set for local governments through national regulations
   - Level of arrears owed to local governments by the central government (such as the wage bill for central government officials and central government financial transfers).

3. For each country, each criterion is "rated"[9] from 1 to 5 by applying the observations and comments in the comparative matrix developed in chapter 6.

4. The tool plots the results on "dashboard"-style graphs.

In this approach, the comparative analysis of autonomy in each of the four countries studied produces figures 7.1, 7.2, and 7.3, broken down as follows: Figure 7.1 illustrates the comparative financial autonomy in the four countries. Figure 7.2 attempts to measure budget autonomy in local government spending choices. Figure 7.3 places the estimated results in a portfolio-style cross-analysis comparing the two measures of autonomy: financial and budget.

Financial Autonomy

The graph shown as figure 7.1 displays the comparative financial autonomy in the four countries, pointing to Ghana's position as being more advanced because it appears to have both local tax resources (over which local governments have some margin of maneuver, albeit under supervision) and significant own resources (up to more than 40 percent of total revenue in some districts). However, the capacity to collect these resources remains weak.

Figure 7.1 Financial Autonomy: Assessment and Comparison of the Four Reference
Countries in Sub-Saharan Africa

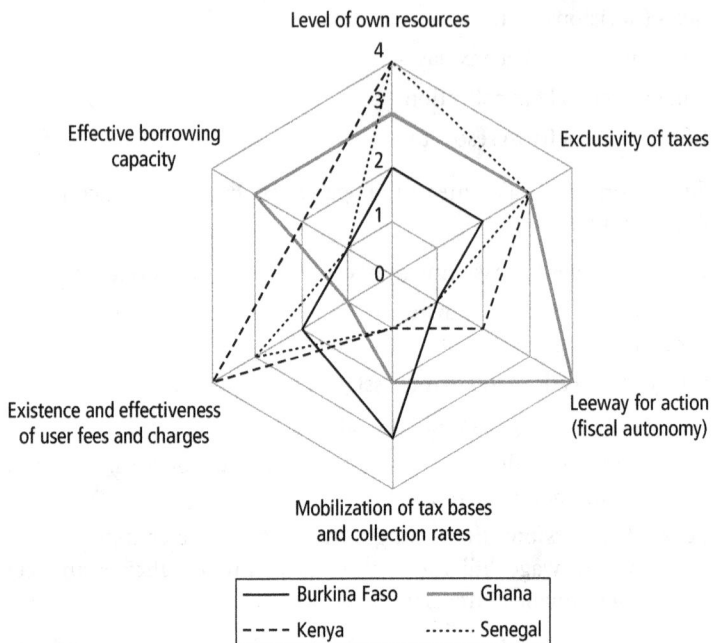

In Kenya, the capacities of decentralized governments to mobilize own
resources appear more constrained, even though they seem to have greater
leeway to introduce fees and charges for use of public facilities (which represent
about 20 percent of total local government revenues) and to resort to borrowing
(this aspect should be relativized in view of the current high debt levels of local
administrations).

The decentralized governments in the two West African countries (Burkina
Faso and Senegal) display low fiscal autonomy—which clearly stems from
inadequate systems for identifying tax bases—and, as in Senegal, the low yields
of some taxes (the collection costs apparently exceeding collected amounts).

Budget Autonomy

The results concerning the degree of budget autonomy (figure 7.2) are appreciably
different. Decentralized governments in Burkina Faso and Senegal, unlike the
two other countries, appear to have budgetary tools enabling them to integrate
political choices voted upon by elected officials. In practice, however, the quality
of these tools seems to be limited de facto by low levels of own resources and

Figure 7.2 Budget Autonomy: Assessment and Comparison of the Four Reference Countries in Sub-Saharan Africa

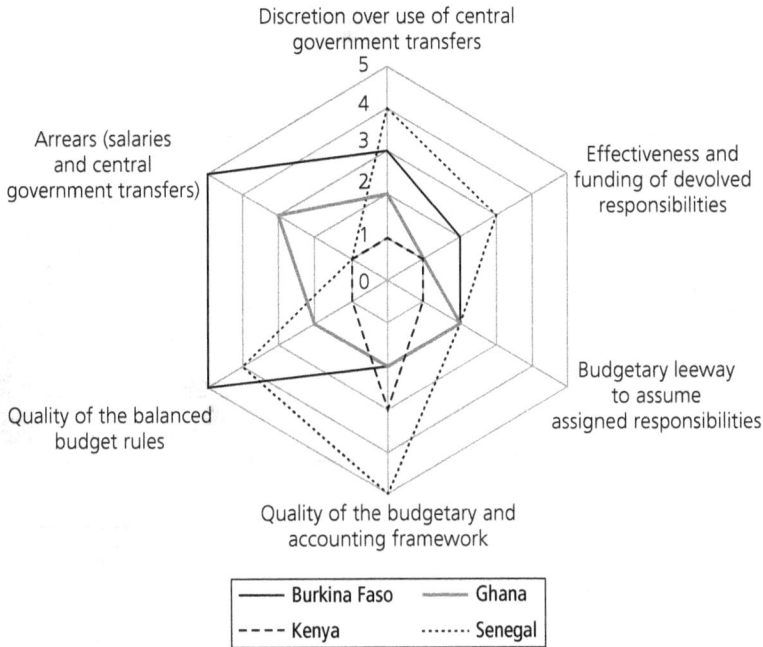

central government transfers. As a result, decentralized governments in both countries try to finance to a minimal degree the responsibilities that were devolved to them.

In parallel, the budget autonomy of decentralized governments in Ghana seems, at first glance, to be weaker and based on more basic budget and accounting tools. Nevertheless, these local governments appear to have more flexibility in financing assigned responsibilities thanks to their greater revenue-raising capacities. Finally, the decentralized governments in Kenya seem restricted regarding their real budgetary power, even though the quality of the budget and accounting framework has recently improved thanks to incentive-based procedures implemented by the LATF (Local Authorities Transfer Fund).

A Cross-Analysis of Both Forms of Autonomy

More generally, this comparative analytical approach can be enhanced by attempting to plot each country within a two-dimensional matrix (financial and budget autonomy) whose values aggregate the 1-to-5 ratings of the

Figure 7.3 Financial and Budget Autonomy in Four Sub-Saharan African Countries: A Cross-Perspective

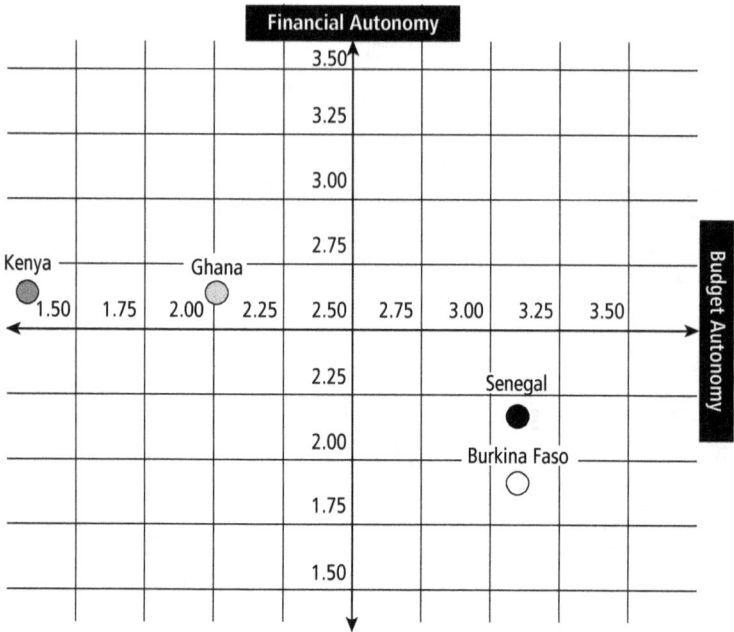

different criteria shown previously in figures 7.1 and 7.2. This gives the matrix represented in figure 7.3.

In addition to the results shown in this matrix, which clearly highlight the strong segmentation between two groups of countries, this type of representation has the advantage of identifying priority areas in which to deploy support and capacity building for decentralized governments. These priority areas may be represented by zone (illustrated by a major objective) as figure 7.4 shows.

At this stage, these elements are of relative use because the criteria need to be more detailed and should probably integrate the context of each country to a greater degree. Yet the objective here is to broaden the perspective pioneered by the authors of this book, building a multicriteria analytical tool that allows the donors and development stakeholders who set up and fund decentralization support programs to better target the needs of each country and to better coordinate their actions.

Figure 7.4 Financial and Budget Autonomy in Four Sub-Saharan African Countries: Priority Areas for Support and Capacity Building

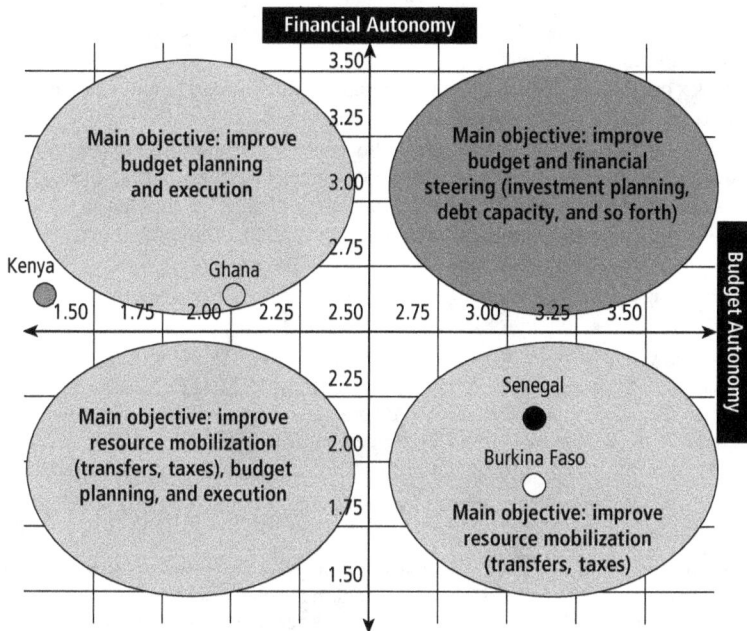

Decentralization certainly does not boil down to a matter of indicators and criteria, but these nevertheless remain instruments for measuring development aid effectiveness.

Notes

1. This notably includes the study devoted to own local revenue that was presented during the same workshop and conducted at the request of the French Ministry of Foreign and European Affairs (Chambas, Brun, and Rota Graziosi 2010a).
2. Fiscal autonomy is a subcomponent of financial autonomy.
3. This is the case with Kenya's Road Maintenance Levy Fund, for example, which is a transfer earmarked for financing road maintenance.
4. The Support Program to Communes (*Programme d'appui aux communes*; PAC) and the Program to Strengthen Local Government Investment (*Programme de renforcement et d'équipement des collectivités locales*; PRECOL) are programs to strengthen local authorities and develop municipal infrastructure.

5. This is perfectly understandable: likewise in developed countries faced with high debt ratios, there is a move toward "nationalization" of local taxes, whose growth momentum is greater than that of central government taxes.
6. Intended for operational teams that are developing local government support, advisory, and funding projects.
7. The six criteria are derived from the methodology designed to allow a comparative approach for the four countries.
8. Measuring financial and budget autonomy is a tricky issue as this implies an attempt to quantify (and, indirectly to qualify) the degree of decentralization. Moreover, the method used to measure financial autonomy is still far from consensual and definitively decided upon. On this subject, see Dafflon and Madiès (2008, chapter 5), which also gives bibliographical references on work in progress.
9. This rating from 1 to 5 is an attempt to quantify this chapter's comments.

References

Chambas, G., J.-F. Brun, and G. Rota Graziosi. 2010a. "Mobiliser des ressources locales pour les collectivités décentralisées en Afrique subsaharienne." Working paper, Centre d'Études et de Recherches sur le Développement International (CERDI), CNRS University of Auvergne and the French Ministry of Foreign and European Affairs, Paris.

———. 2010b. *Mobiliser des ressources locales en Afrique subsaharienne.* Paris: Éditions Economica.

Dafflon, B., and T. Madiès. 2008. "Décentralisation: quelques principes issus de la théorie du fédéralisme financier." ["Decentralization: A Few Principles from the Theory of Fiscal Federalism."] Notes and documents 42, Agence Française de Développement, Paris.

Jacob, J.-P. 1998. "La décentralisation comme distance. Réflexions sur la mise en place des collectivités territoriales en milieu rural ouest-africain." *Politique Africaine* 71 (October): 133–47. http://www.politique-africaine.com/numeros/pdf/071133.pdf.

Index

Boxes, figures, notes, and tables are indicated by *b, f, n,* and *t,* respectively.

A

accounting classification,
    see Classification
AFD (Agence Française de
    Développement), 2, 287
Africa, Sub-Saharan. *See* decentralization
    in Sub-Saharan Africa
Agence Française de Développement
    (AFD), 2, 287
Ahwoi, Kwamena, 110, 112–113
analytical guide to decentralization, 3,
    9–43, 288–290
    in absence of quantitative data, 10
    assignment of responsibilities
        between tiers of government,
        24–29, 28*t*
    budgets, decentralized, 18–24, 19*f,*
        22–24*t*
    comparative cross-cutting analysis
        allowed by, 10, 265–267
    contextualization, importance of,
        9–10, 17–18
    definitions, 17, 31*b*
    institutional economy study of
        legislation, 9, 11–18
    intergovernmental transfers, 32*t,*
        36–39, 37*t,* 38*t*
    phases of, 9

political economy field studies and,
    10–11. *See also* Burkina Faso;
    Ghana; Kenya; Senegal
relationships shaping/distorting
    institutional design, 11–15, 12*f*
revenue structures and systems,
    30–36, 31*b,* 32*t*
statistical data, 39–42, 41*t*
theoretical norm not required for, 9
uses of, 290–291, 294–295
Anglophone *versus* Francophone
    countries, 269, 272–273, 274,
    290
assignment of responsibilities between
    tiers of government, 288
    in the decentralized budget, 21
    analytical guide to, 24–29, 28*t*
    in Burkina Faso, 65–76, 66–72*f*
    comparative cross-cutting analysis,
        269–270, 281–282*t*
    decision-making autonomy *versus*
        budget decentralization, 29
    functional classification, 25
    functional decentralization matrix,
        22–24*t,* 25, 26
    in Ghana, 132–137, 133*b,* 134–135*t*
    institutional mapping, 26–28, 28*t*
    in Kenya, 177–181, 178–181*t*

statistical data (*continued*)
    for Senegal, 257–259t, 257–262, 261t
    type, classification by, 28t, 41–42, 41t
Sub-Saharan Africa. *See* decentralization
    in Sub-Saharan Africa
Switzerland
    fiscal federalism, second-generation
        theories in, 6n3
    functional classification in, 25
    government units, interrelationships
        of, 13

T

Taugourdeau, Emmanuelle, xxii–xxiii,
    2, 207
tax
    exclusive, 31
    shared, 31
tax terms, definitions of, 21b
taxation, local. *See* revenue structures and
    systems
temporal variation in intergovernmental
    systems, 15
territory, institutional mapping of, 26
A Theory of Justice (Rawls, 1971),
    105n40

transfers. *See* intergovernmental transfers
transportation in Senegal
    road maintenance network, 228b
    urban transport responsibilities, 227b

U

*Union Economique et Monétaire Ouest
    Africaine* (UEMOA or West
    African Economic and
    Monetary Union), 52t, 103n26
urban transport responsibilities in Dakar,
    Senegal, 227b

V

Vaillancourt, François, xxiii, 2, 107, 161

W

waste management responsibilities in
    Dakar, Senegal, 227b
Weingast, B. R., 43n2
West African Economic and Monetary
    Union (*Union Economique et
    Monétaire Ouest Africaine* or
    UEMOA), 52t, 103n26
Wiseman, J., 6n3, 43n1
World Bank, 6n1, 143, 287

ECO-AUDIT
Environmental Benefits Statement

The World Bank is committed to preserving endangered forests and natural resources. The Office of the Publisher has chosen to print *The Political Economy of Decentralization in Sub-Saharan Africa* on recycled paper with 50 percent post-consumer waste, in accordance with the recommended standards for paper usage set by the Green Press Initiative, a non-profit program supporting publishers in using fiber that is not sourced from endangered forests. For more information, visit www.greenpressinitiative.org.

Saved:
- 9 trees
- 4 million British thermal units of total energy
- 895 pounds of net greenhouse gases (CO_2 equivalent)
- 4,034 gallons of waste water
- 256 pounds of solid waste

green press
INITIATIVE

www.ingramcontent.com/pod-product-compliance
Lightning Source LLC
Chambersburg PA
CBHW070716280326
41926CB00087B/2287